GÜNTHER VOGT

MINIATURE AND PANORAMA

VOGT LANDSCAPE ARCHITECTS PROJECTS 2000–12

WITH ESSAYS BY

OLAFUR ELIASSON
HAMISH FULTON
ROMAN SIGNER
OLAF UNVERZART
CHRISTIAN VOGT

LARS MÜLLER PUBLISHERS

MINIATURE AND PANORAMA

Christian Vogt

Photographic documentation of realised work is more than a presentation of what can be found. The choice of format, whether small image or panorama, and of colour palette, whether colour or black and white, reflects Christian Vogt's reaction to the built garden. The fresh eye of the photographer shows whether the garden is more than the author of its design had planned. The choice between miniature and panorama is a decision no longer made by the garden's designer. Commitment to and distance from the site show the designer a perception of his work through the lens of a possible generality.

MINIATURE AND PANORAMA

The geographer works through a survey scope, the botanist through a lens and the biologist through a microscope. They all share the same starting point, in that proximity to and distance from the analysed object is first conveyed via different scientific methods of analysis. Results of the geographer's research flow into maps, the botanist's into texts and drawings, and the biologist's into formulas. The shift of scale becomes clear in the approach to the documentation of the scientific findings. A landscape is beneath one's feet, a plant in the hand. Experiencing landscape is first and foremost visual. We walk or drive through landscape and in this way become a part of the object we are researching. Forest, meadow, field and river create a conglomerate that we call landscape. The only border seems to be the horizon. Concentrating on detail activates several senses. In the course of close examination, we see, smell and taste a complex entity of landscape.

The landscape of modernity is composed of separate and distinct events: the linden on the top of the hill, the path that nestles against the face of a rock, groves of trees and bushes between the fields. Our day-to-day experience is marked by functional landscapes and roadway landscapes, from which site-specific qualities have been eliminated. We are searching for identity, but without being able to describe exactly what we mean.

The form of a city is related to its surrounding landscape – on a river, among mountains, on a bank, by the sea, in the desert, surrounded by forests – Paris, Rome, Volterra, Hong Kong, Las Vegas, Berlin. The parks, squares, courtyards, cemeteries and streets that supply connections within these cities are the places in the city where urban forms of urban nature are cultivated. The built city creates a horizon, a scale for the places that form nature within a city.

The garden is a chosen place within the urban landscape; gardens today are located mainly at the edges of cities. Like the pioneers staking their claims, these garden zones expand our cities. What drives the gardener to leave the urban biotope and head for new shores? At the city's edge, we see both the landscape and the city. This perspective raises the question of the garden's origins. Is it a clearing in the forest, an oasis in the desert, a grove in a bucolic landscape, or a farmer's field? All these interpretations together represent treatments of the landscape. Existing vegetation is removed and replaced by the gardener's idealised plants. The garden differs significantly from the original genus, the agrarian square, in that it replaces economic with aesthetic premises. A new component of the garden is expressed by the design of the enclosed garden, in which the garden becomes a critical commentary on the cultural landscape. This includes a broad spectrum of possibilities where original vegetation spreads out alongside excessive design objectives.

The dramatic change in levels of reference is what shapes today's poetic fascination with the garden. In a garden, the recognition of the whole always precedes the recognition of the single parts. The scaled references are oriented toward a concrete site: the proximate neighbourhood. The garden is constructed by someone and the many small parts of the garden reflect the builder's character and personality. The gardener needs machines, just like the farmer. However, while the farmer's machines grow ever larger, the opposite is the case with the gardener. Miniaturisation, making sure the tools and the traces they leave behind can vanish, is important to the gardener, whose most important protagonists are the plants themselves. Upon discovering the world, everything seems available, immediately. But, in fact, the world of plants had already shrunk before globalisation. Landscape architecture unites a very heterogeneous group of disciplines: natural sciences, social sciences and design. When searching for nature in the city, the focus falls on different phenomena that oscillate between the miniature and the panoramic. The large field of landscape architecture is influenced in its daily practise by a number of different contributing factors. For that reason, the fragmentary presentation here of works by friends illustrates natural contributing factors alongside the office's documented projects.

Christian Vogt's work is not a pictorial documentation of realised projects, but rather a photographic commentary of undisguised views.

Olaf Unverzart's photographic research highlights the production of plants as landscape architecture's raw material. This production has long been globalised and is only conceivable via mass production.

Hamish Fulton documents his artistic work, which consists of hikes through landscapes all over the world. It is about not intervening in the landscape, and none of the natural elements will enter the space of a gallery. His work is about interpreting on a sensual-perceptual level, or is simply a journal for those who did not participate in the hike.

Olafur Eliasson photographs a journey together through the Masoala Rain Forest in Zurich as an artwork searching for natural space within an artificial landscape.

Roman Signer's interventions question the static perception of nature and increase its dynamism.

Lars Müller translates Marshall McLuhan's theory "the medium is the message" with incomparable passion into his concept of "building books".

The great breadth of the subjects, ranging from the hunt for plants to the description of *terroir* and the interior view of the developmental process, cannot be dealt with fully here. The selection is a reader's guide to built and projected works presented in this book. We live in a world that we need to rediscover. After the borders have been defined and researched, we have to relearn to understand our close surroundings.

Many of the projects featured in the first edition have now become reality. Photographs of the completed buildings expand the documentation of these projects in this edition. Also new are small design tasks created within the framework and context of specific projects. *gv*

103.
135
24

LANDSCAPE

looking seeing
downpours
sunshine cloud-cover

streets   paths   mountains   hills
valleys   ravines near and far

pastures   fields rampant   bright
cities   villages light and weather

brook and river and lake and fields
fields   pastures   rolling hills

land and water   light and weather
          clouds gaps   smoke

forests   sky   earth   border

   sublime
   immeasurable

   cragged

BROADENING THE VIEW

In the forest, if you turn over a moss-covered stone, you will see soil, worms and insects. Geological and biological processes in the forest are dependent on a complex composition and decomposition of mineral and organic substances. Unlike stone, moss stores water, leaves and needles. Small animals use it to process the substrate for the seeds that will replenish the forest with vegetation. The forest's climate helps moss to grow. This happens in places where other forest herbage does not compete. Stones and tree trunks are habitats reserved for biological specialists like moss and lichen. Their growth also marks their end, as they prepare the soil for other vegetation. The form moss covering follows the contours of its host, whether boulder or tree trunk, which is succeeded by the contours of the newly developing forest.

In the city, there is no subterranean world under the stone. The two sides of the stone are identical in mass, colour and grain. City stone by its nature represents solidity. Moss can be found everywhere in cities, in the narrow cracks in pavement and on the large expanse of flat roofs. The moss of the city acts as storage and filter. The humidity of the night air is stored, the dust of the day filtered. Growth and decay of the moss is related to climate. Evaporation takes care of cooling during the day. The moss bed accumulates heavy metals and dust. The change from day to night creates a time horizon – a poetic dialogue between nature and culture.

What kind of nature do we expect to find when taking a walk in the city?
Is it an original, untouched, wild nature?
Or another nature, that of a cultivated or exploited landscape?

Or a third kind of nature, the garden, the constructed utopia? May we hope for an escalation of naturalness when we re-approach nature?

The history of how the garden is perceived teaches us that the concept of nature has always been closely linked to political developments and social change. The English garden illustrated for the first time the difference between garden varieties. Contrary to the geometric-ornamental French style that had previously dominated garden design, the English garden's almost invisible design created a language that visualised ideas and utopias for a new society. The differences are clearly seen and felt on all levels. Contemporary presentations are still used today; in them the French type of garden was illustrated by plans of the layout, and the English-style garden was shown in "views". The English garden attempted to create a relationship between the free horizon and the individual outlook using perspective. The garden as communicative element allowed the viewer to devote the eye to an infinite nature, without submitting to the pressure of nature's sublime. This utopian approach was especially obvious in the eighteenth century, when the mountain became the symbol of the sublime. Miniaturised mountain landscapes illustrated the paradox of how mountains were made to look like unlimited nature, yet still measurable. Views of open landscape were replaced by the stress ratio of depth and width, by the opposition of time and space, which formed an historical depth and created the space of history. Depth of perspective no longer had the horizon or untouched landscape as its goal, but rather an architecture that recalled paragons of history. Built ruins, architecture in the Palladian style, and imitation Chinese pagodas ennobled the garden owner as the legitimate successor to an historical heritage, and also served as political and social references. While the ruins symbolised time and the ephemeral nature of civilisations, the Palladian architecture legitimised a new European state form, the city-state. The pagodas represented education and an interest in foreign cultures, but also a new perspective resulting from colonial activities.

Distance has been dissolved in the landscape of modern times. The physical relationship, the direct relationship to landscape, has been dissolved by the accelerated movement brought on by the car and airplane. We have lost the goal of our journey on the motorway of abstraction. Perceiving landscape now takes place on the boulevard of the global. Dreams are about meandering pathways through a landscape, without hindrances. The post-modern demands that we pay attention to a nature whose language we no longer understand. "A foreigner is only a foreigner in a foreign land." (Karl Valentin) *gv*

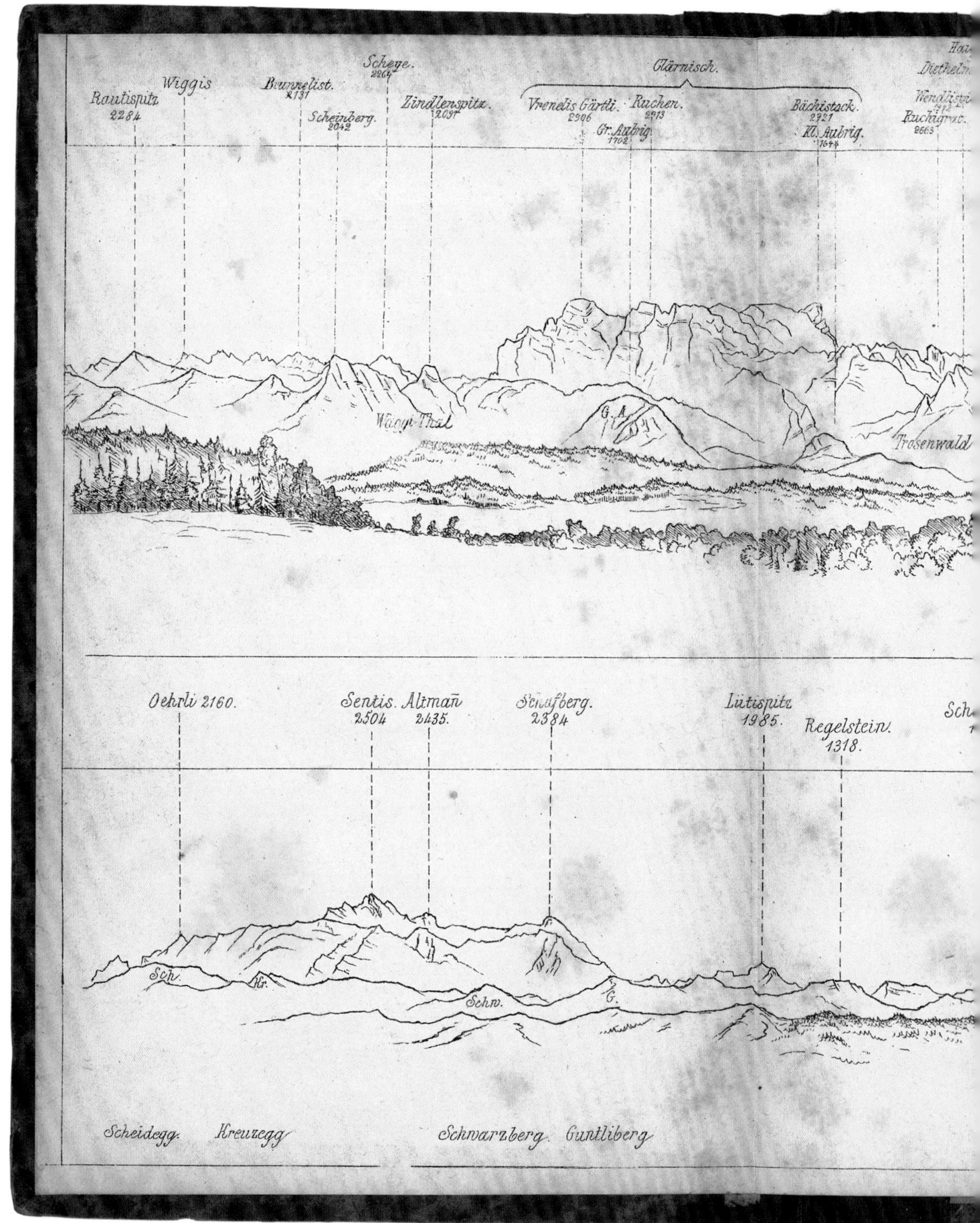

Mountain panorama as seen from the Belvedere on Zürichberg. Xaver Imfeld, 1877.

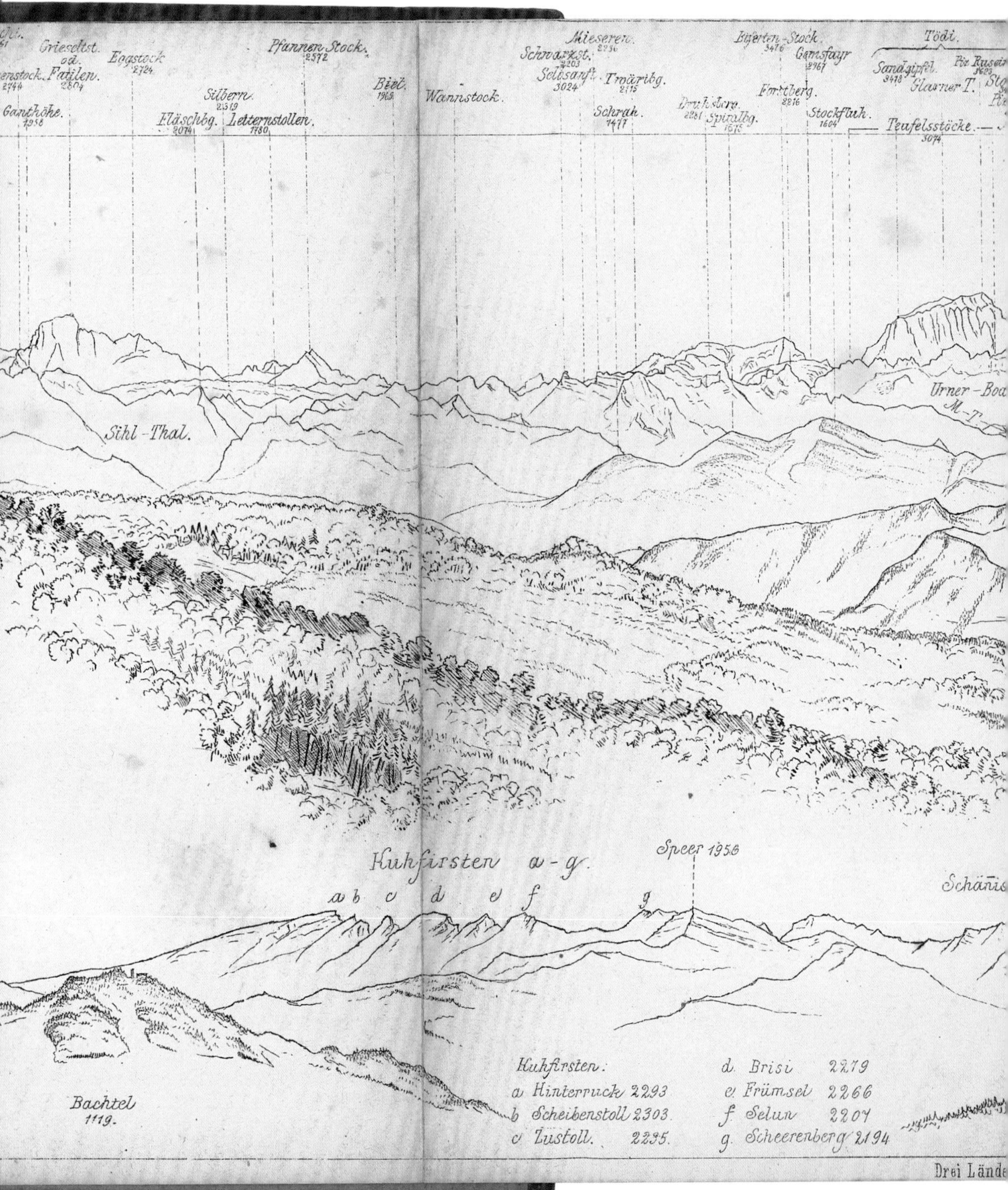

Grieseltst.
od.
Fatilen.
2804
Eggstock
2724
Pfannen-Stock.
2572
Silbern.
2319
Fläschbg.
2074
Letternstollen.
1780
Ganthöhe.
1938
Biet.
1965
Wannstock.
Mieseren.
Schwarzst.
2203
Seltsanft.
3024
Schrah.
1477
Bifertén-Stock.
3476
Gemsfayr
2967
Stockfluh.
1604
Tödi.
Glarner T.
Teufelsstöcke.
3074
Sihl-Thal.
Urner-Bod
Kuhfirsten a-g.
a b c d e f g
Speer 1956
Schänis
Bachtel
1119.
Kuhfirsten:
a Hinterruck 2293
b Scheibenstoll 2303.
c Zustoll. 2235.
d. Brisi 2279
e. Frümsel 2266
f. Selun 2207
g. Scheerenberg 2194
Drei Länd

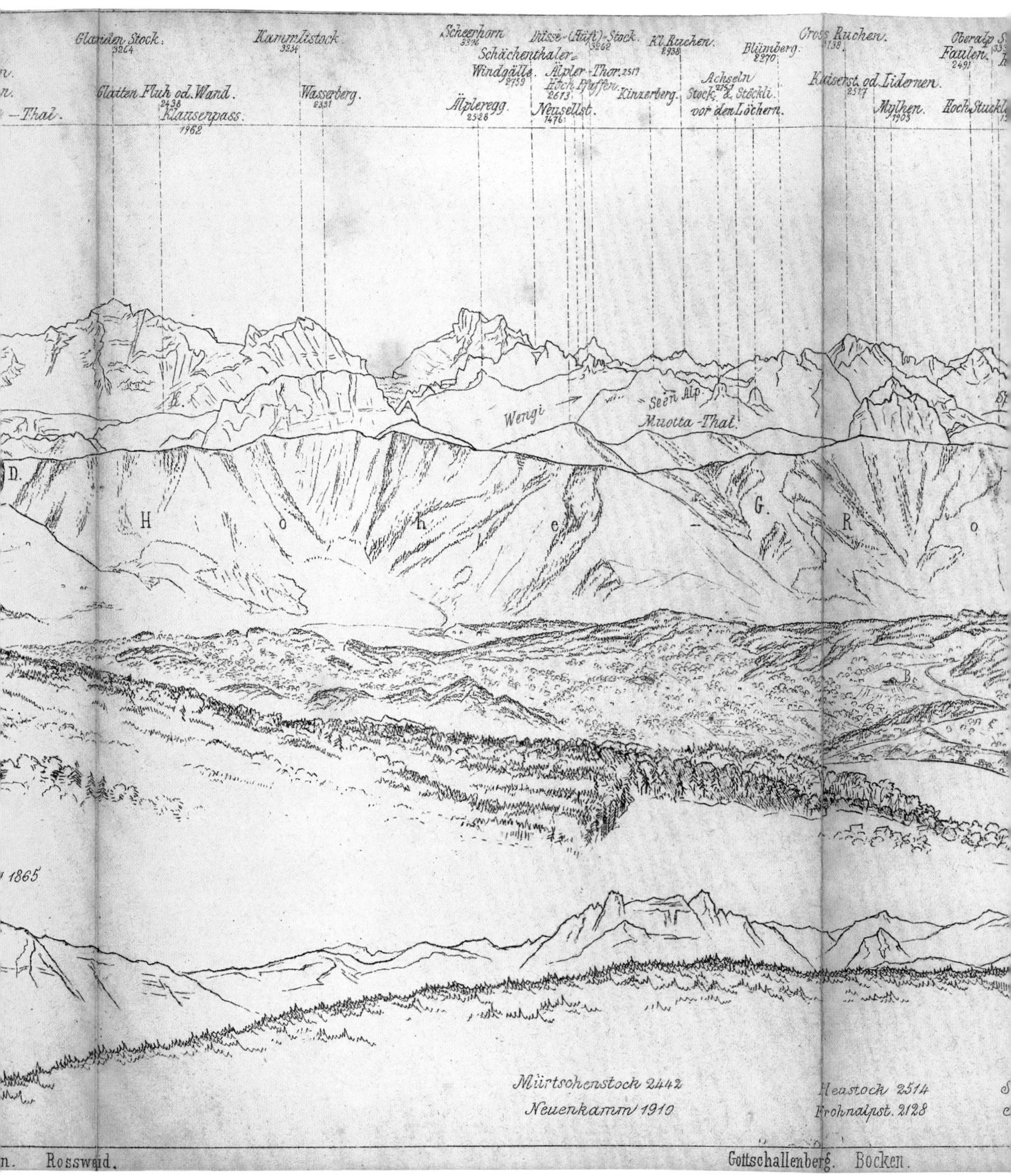
Glariden Stock.
3264
Kammlistock.
3234
Scheerhorn
3296
Düsse-(Hüfi)-Stock.
3262
Kl. Ruchen.
2938
Blümberg.
2270
Gross Ruchen.
3138
Oberalp
Faulen.
2491
Glatten Fluh od. Wand.
2438
Klausenpass.
1962
Wasserberg.
2331
Schächenthaler-
Windgälle.
2759
Älpler-Thor. 2517
Hoch Pfaffen.
2613
Kinzerberg.
Achseln
Stock.
2751
& Stöckli.
vor den Löchern.
Kaiserst. od. Lidernen.
2517
—Thal.
Älpleregg.
2528
Neusellst.
1476
Mythen.
1903
Hoch Stuckli
Wengi
Seen Alp
Muotta-Thal.
D.
H o h e — G. R o
B.
1865
Mürtschenstock 2442
Neuenkamm 1910
Heastock 2514
Frohnalpst. 2128
n. Rossweid.
Gottschallenberg. Bocken.

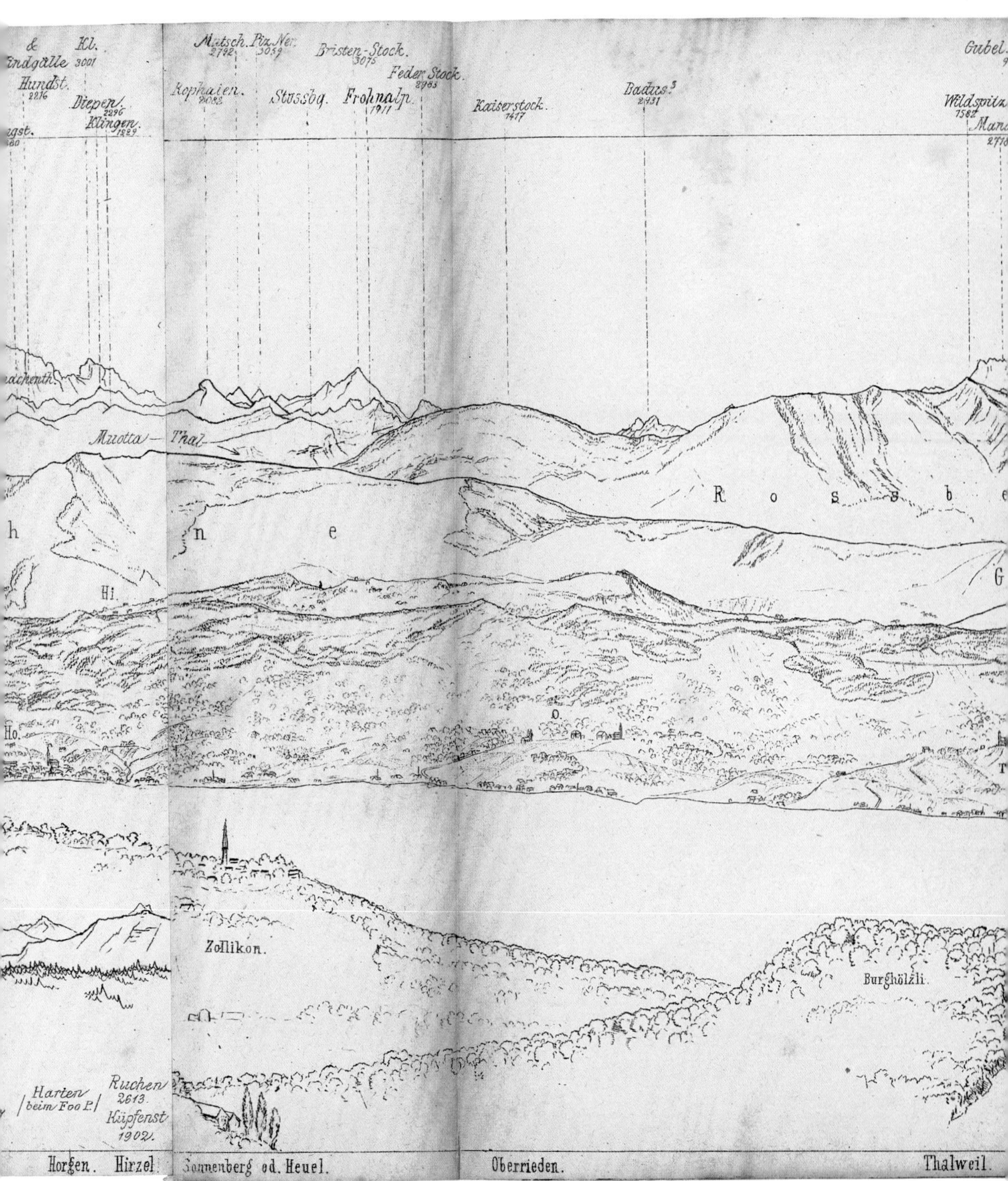
Kl.
3001
Hundst.
2216
Diepen
2296
Klingen
1829
Mutsch.
2792
Piz Ner
3059
Bristen-Stock.
3075
Feder Stock
2965
Kophaien.
2083
Stossbg.
Frohnalp.
1911
Kaiserstock.
1417
Badus.
2931
Gubel.
Wildspitz
1582
Muotta-Thal
R o s s b e
Hi.
Ho.
Zollikon.
Burghölzli.
Harten
beim Foo P.
Ruchen
2613.
Kipfenst
1902.
Horgen.
Hirzel
Sonnenberg od. Heuel.
Oberrieden.
Thalweil.

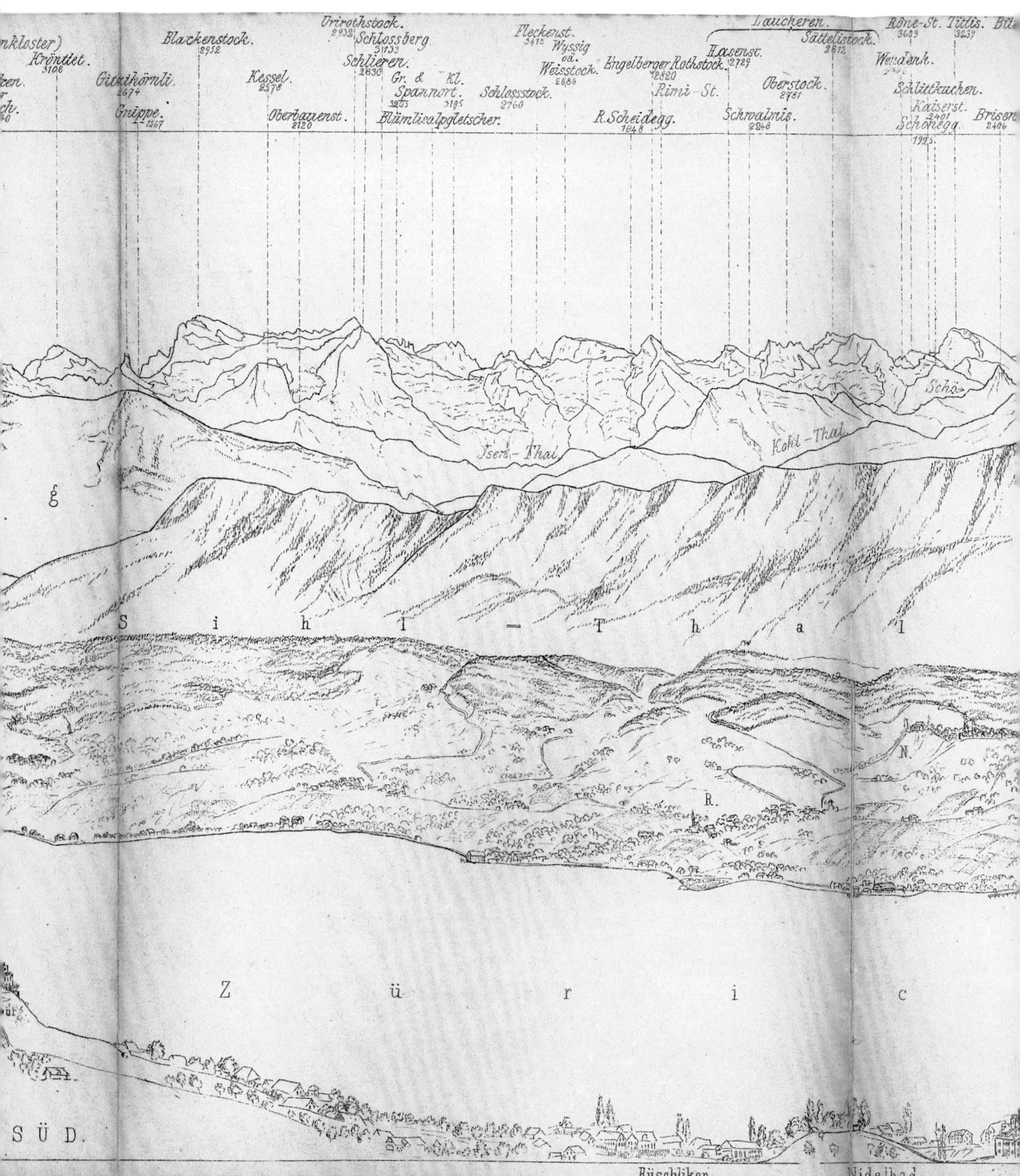
Kröntlet. 3108
Gitschihörnli. 2674
Gnippe. 1267
Blackenstock. 2952
Kessel. 2578
Oberbauenst. 2120
Urirothstock. 2932
Schlossberg. 3133
Schlieren. 2830
Gr. & Kl. Spannort. 3205 3185
Blümlisalpgletscher.
Schlossstock. 2760
Fleckenst. 3412
Wyssig od. Weisstock. 2886
Engelberger Rothstock. 2820
Rimi-St.
R. Scheidegg. 1648
Hasenst. 2729
Laucheren.
Sättelistock. 2812
Oberstock. 2781
Schwalmis. 2248
Röne-St. 3603
Titlis. 3239
Wendenh.
Schlittkuchen.
Kaiserst. 2401
Schönegg. 1925
Brisen 2406
Isen-Thal
Kohl-Thal
S i h l – T h a l
R.
N.
Z ü r i c
S Ü D.
Rüschlikon.
Nidelbad.

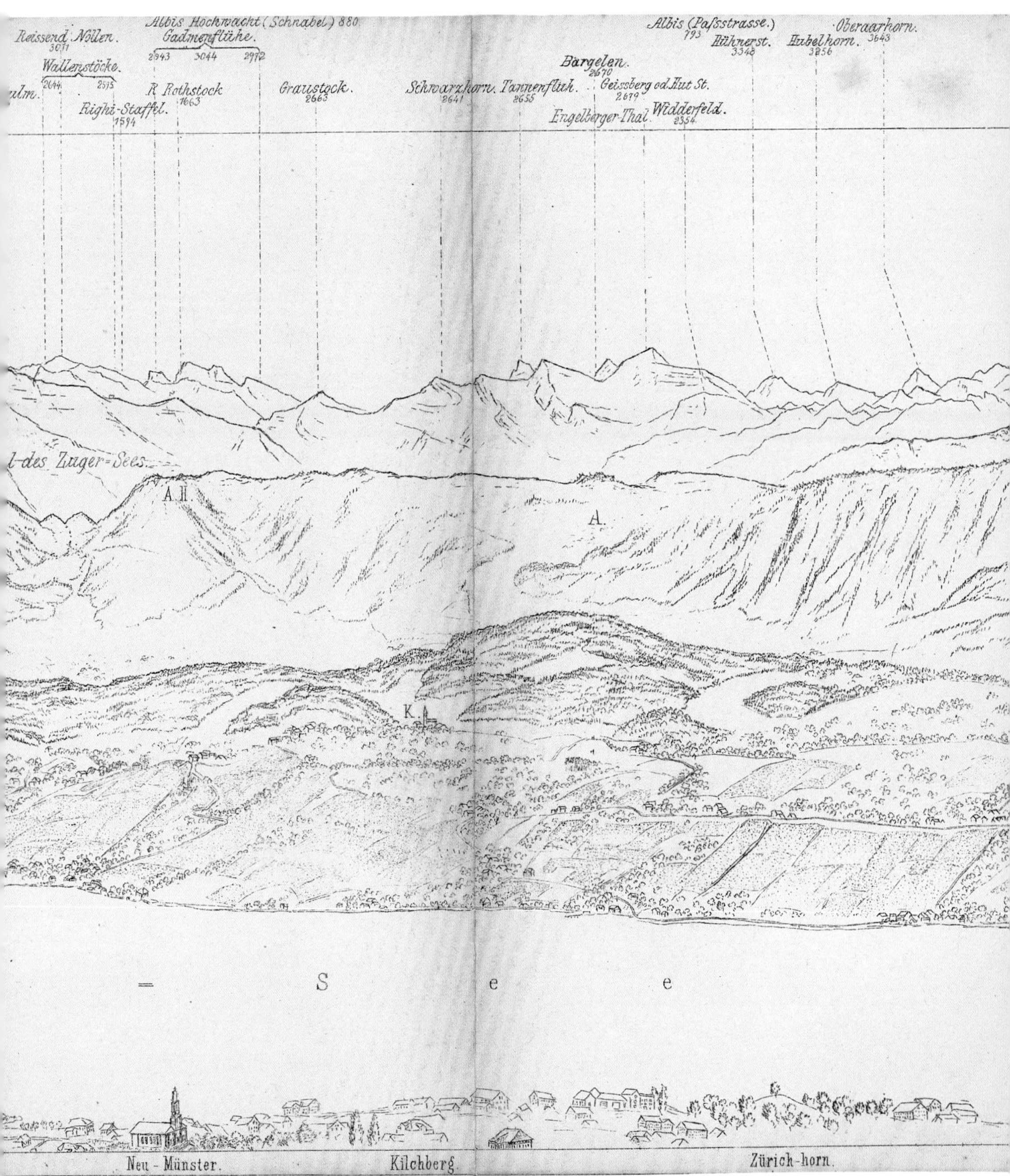
Albis Hochwacht (Schnabel) 880
Reissend Nöllen. 3011
Gadmenflühe. 2943 3044 2972
Wallenstöcke. 2644 2515
…ulm.
R Rothstock 1663
Righi-Staffel. 1594
Graustock. 2663
Schwarzhorn. 2641
Tannenfluh. 2655
Bärgelen. 2670
Geissberg od. Hut St. 2619
Engelberger-Thal.
Widderfeld. 2354
Albis (Paſsstrasse.) 793
Hühnerst. 3348
Hubelhorn. 3256
Oberaarhorn. 3643
…l des Zuger-Sees.
A.H.
A.
K.
S e e
Neu-Münster.
Kilchberg.
Zürich-horn.

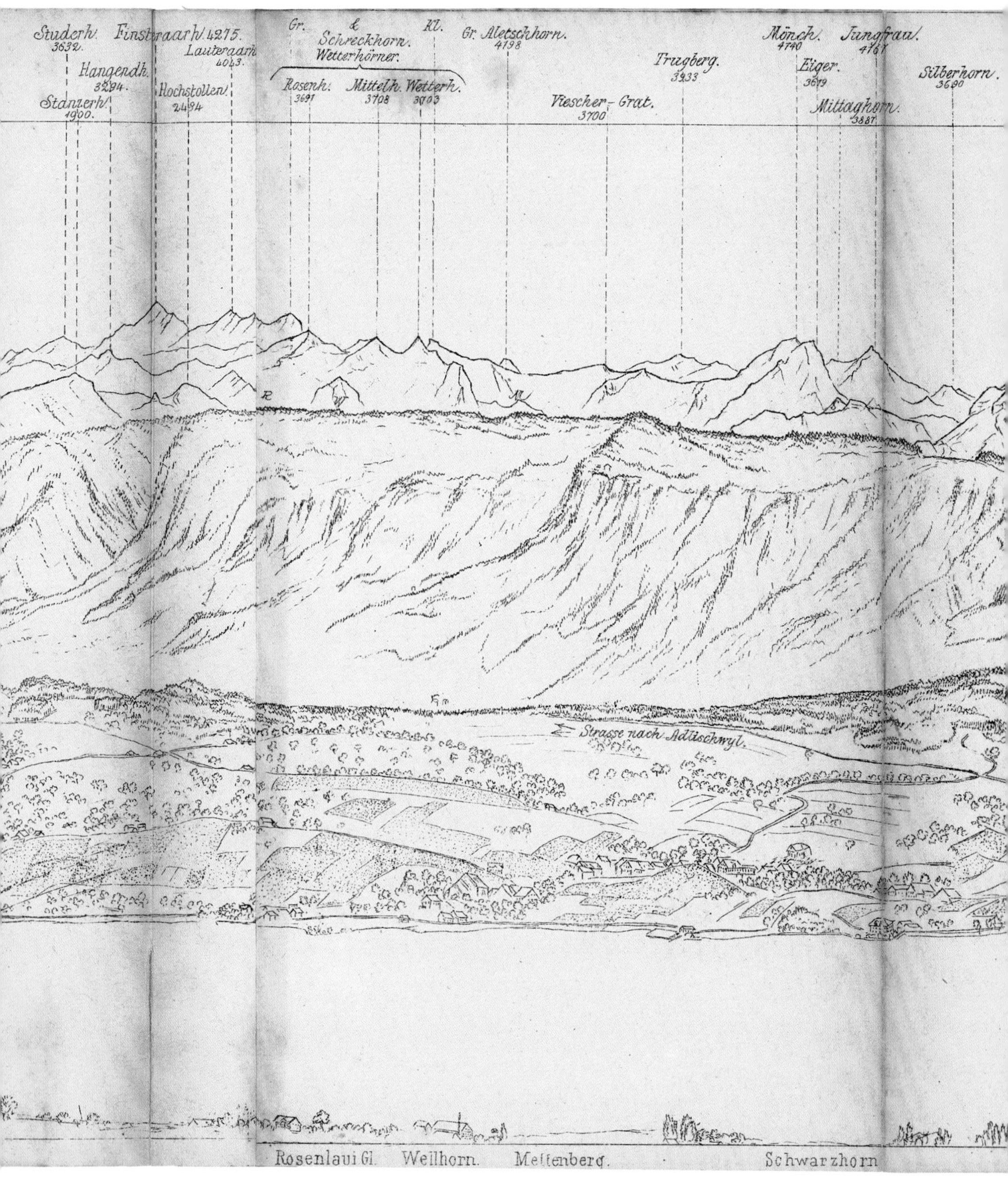
Studerh. 3632.
Finsteraarh. 4275.
Lauteraarh. 4043.
Hangendh. 3294.
Stanzerh. 1900.
Hochstollen. 2494.
Gr. & Kl. Schreckhorn. Wetterhörner.
Rosenh. 3691
Mittelh. 3708
Wetterh. 3703
Gr. Aletschhorn. 4198
Viescher-Grat. 3700
Trugberg. 3933
Mönch. 4740
Jungfrau. 4167
Eiger. 3619
Mittaghorn. 3887.
Silberhorn. 3690
Strasse nach Adliswyl.
Rosenlaui Gl.
Wellhorn.
Mettenberg.
Schwarzhorn

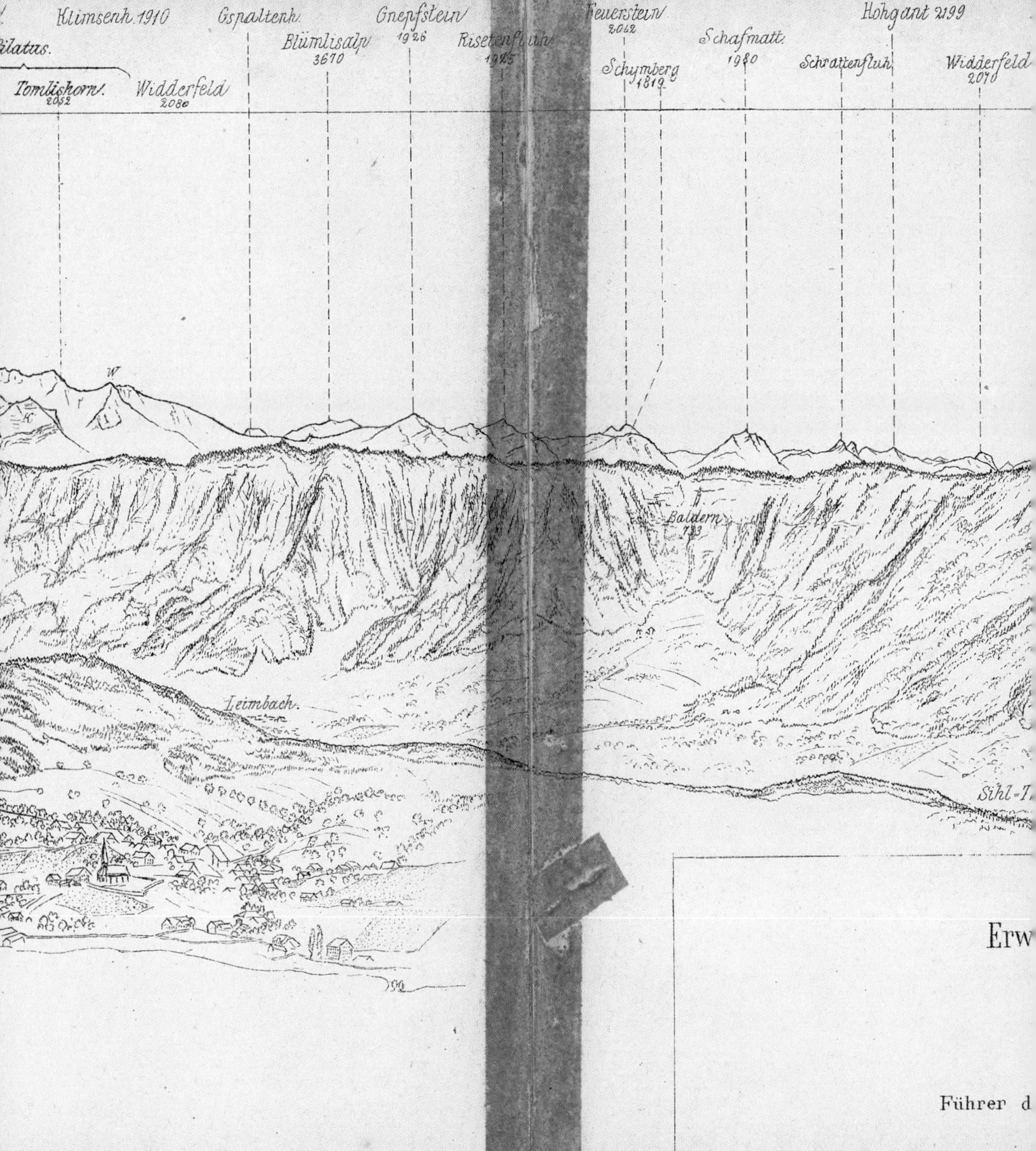

Wollishofen.

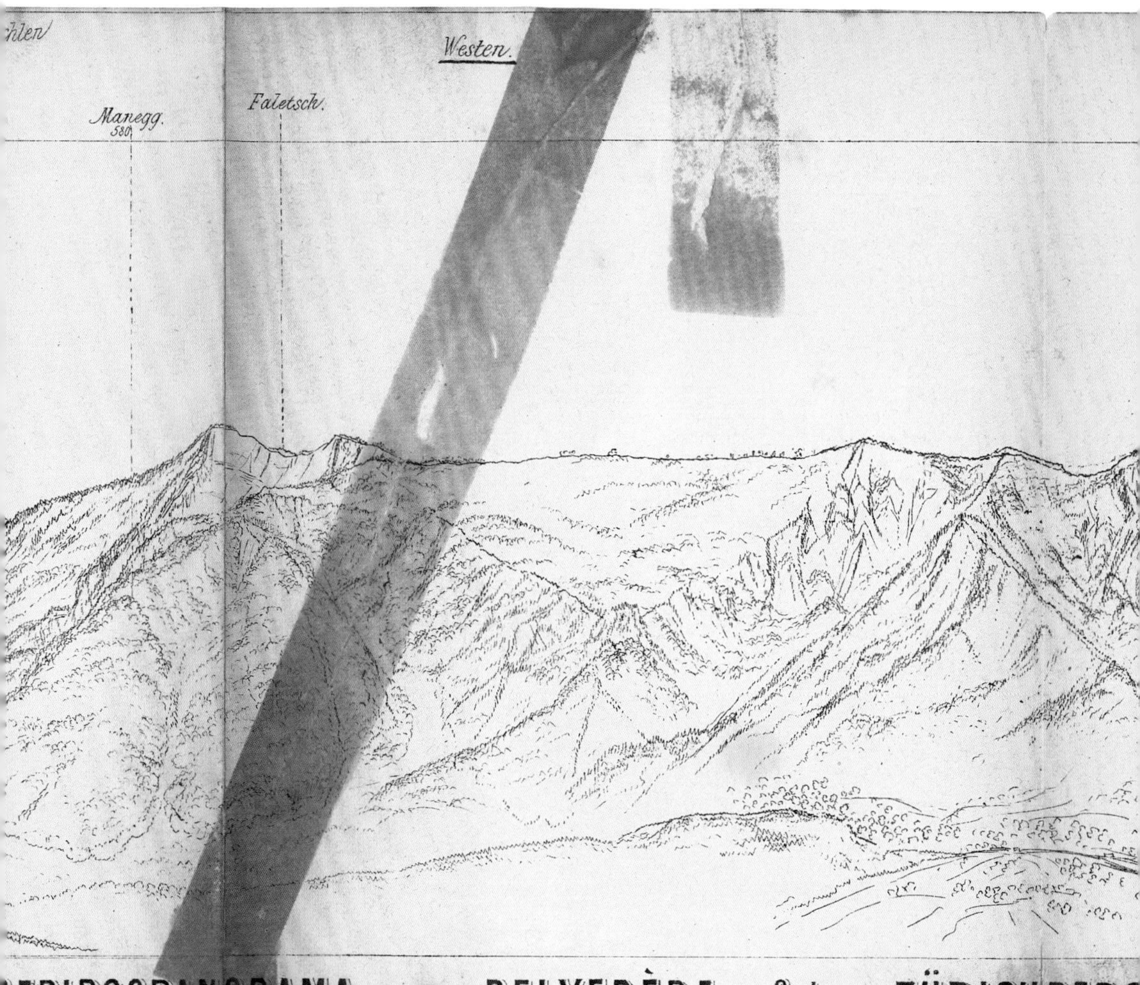
Westen.
Faletsch.
Manegg.
580
GEBIRGSPANORAMA vom BELVEDÈRE auf dem ZÜRICHBERG
rte Ausgabe des Zürichbergpanorama's oberhalb der Karolinenburg von Prof. Dr. Alb
von X. JMFELD, eidg. Jngenieur-Topograph.
Zürich, Verlag v. Caesar Schmidt.
Jn demselben Verlage sind erschienen: Gross Karte vom Zürichsee, 2 Fr. 50 Ct.
Berlepsch Reisebuch für die Schweiz. 8 Fr. 75 Ct. „ Eisenbahnkarte der Schweiz, 3 Frs.
Zürich & s. Umgebung mit Panorama & Plan 2.50. Wenng Reisekarte der Schweiz, 1.50 aufgez
an der Stadt Zürich & ihrer Umgebung Fr. 1. Verkehrskarte der Schweiz & Süddeutschlands, 1 Fr.

Uetliberg.
873

Cartography and the art of building relief maps
There is a long tradition of cartography and the art of building relief maps in Switzerland. Xaver Imfeld (1853–1909) and Eduard Imhof (1895–1986), two of the most important figures in this field, have both left significant works in this discipline. Imfeld was employed at the Eidgenössisches Topographisches Bureau and became a pioneer in the planning of mountain railways for tourists. Imhof was a professor for many years, as well as founder of the Institute of Cartography at the Swiss Federal Institute of Technology Zurich (ETH); he remains an influential figure in Swiss mapping history. Imhof taught himself how to model plaster relief maps. His two most important mountain models, Bietschhorn and Windgälle, were created for the Swiss National Exhibition in 1939.

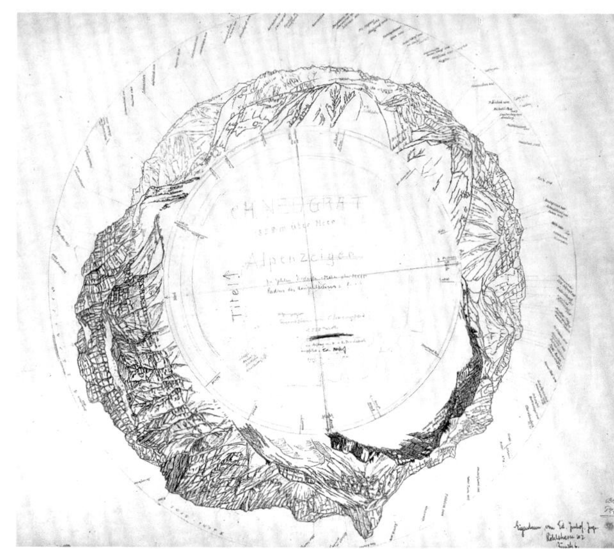
Chneugrat, 360° view of the mountains above Braunwald, Glarus. E. Imhof, 1919.

Matterhorn, 1:5000. Xaver Imfeld, 1896.

Mürtschenstock, 1:10000. Eduard Imhof, 1920–22.

Mürtschenstock, 1:10000. Eduard Imhof, 1920–22.

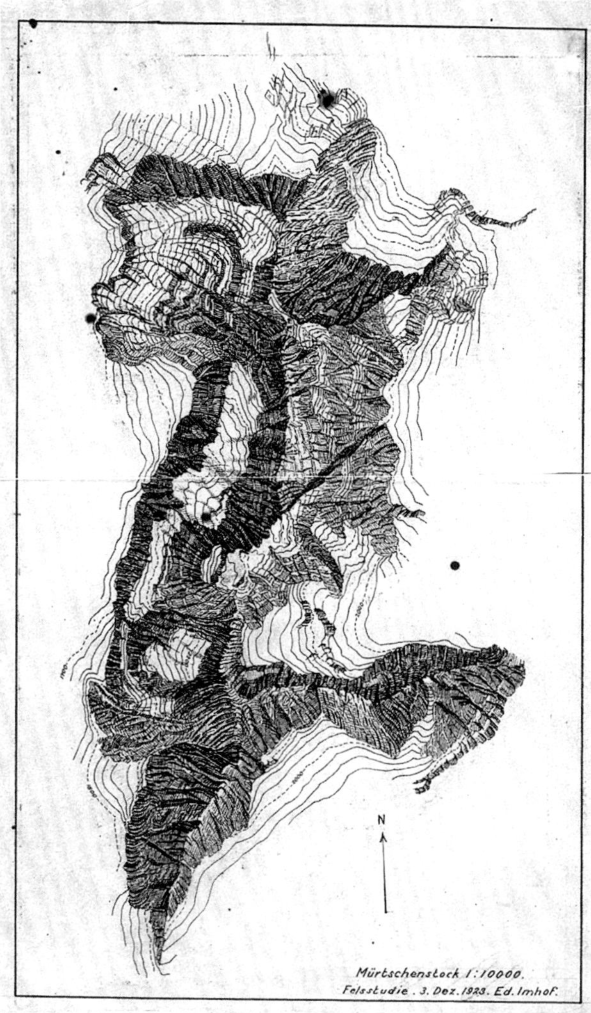

Mürtschenstock, rock study, ink on glassine. Eduard Imhof, 1923.

Eduard Imhof modelling the Windgällen relief, 1938.

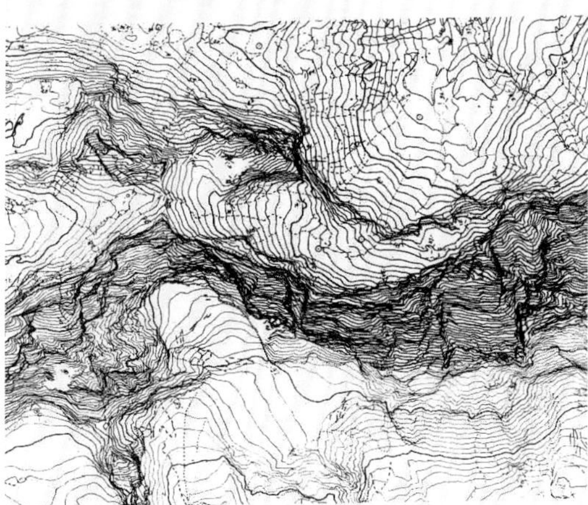

Isohypses and a pair of stereo photographs of Windgälle, essential for modelling the relief. Eduard Imhof.

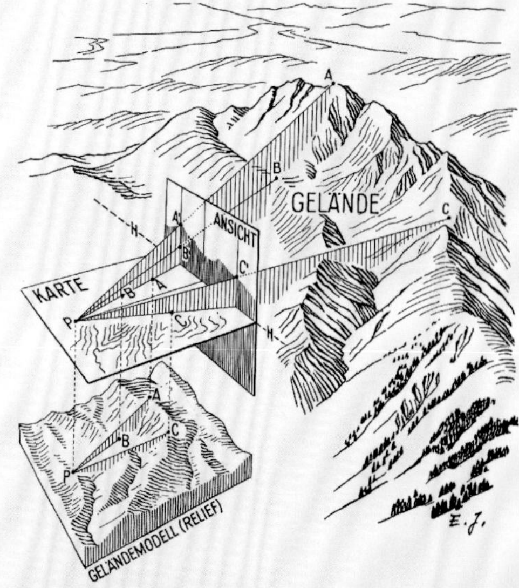

Synopsis of topographic view, map and model. Eduard Imhof, 1950.

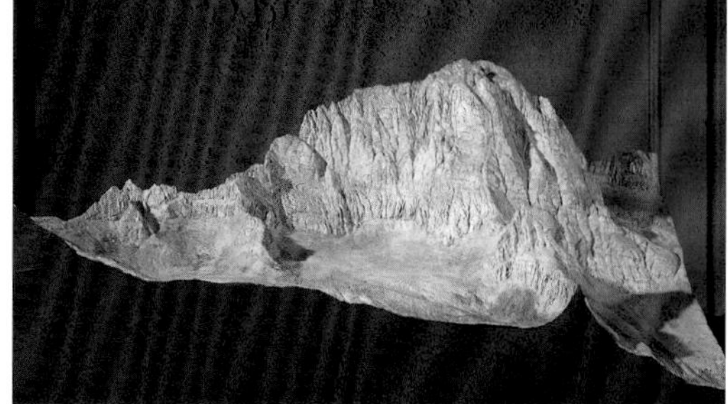

Grosse Windgälle, 1:2000. Eduard Imhof, 1937–39.

ALLIANZ ARENA, MUNICH

MIMESIS
2001–05

Client: Allianz Arena München Stadion GmbH, Alpine Bau Deutschland GmbH, FC Bayern München, TSV München 1860
Architecture: Herzog & de Meuron, Basel
Area: 160,000 m^2

The Fröttmaninger Heide.

At Munich's northern edge, where the city changes to countryside, stands the Allianz Arena, Munich's new football stadium. Until a hundred years ago, the site was a contiguous area of moorland about 150 square metres in size. Today it is primarily distinguished by a dense road network and motorway ring. All that remains of the former town centre of Fröttmaning is the church at the foot of Fröttmaninger Berg, an old rubbish heap now returned to its natural state, atop which stands a windmill called the Foenix.

Grassland is one of the most species-rich ecosystems of Central Europe. Originally created by people who used it as pastureland for sheep and goats, it later became an important habitat for many endangered plant and animal species. Since the second half of the twentieth century, various conservation projects have been undertaken to preserve and expand the grasslands in the area north of Munich. In the process, the Fröttmaninger Heide (Fröttmaning Heath), which lies to the west of the stadium, was designated a protected area.

This site-specific situation is the basis for the design of the new football stadium's surroundings. It is behind the decision to incorporate Europe's largest car park directly into the landscape and plant it with the vegetation typical of the area. The design's principal element is an esplanade, consisting of the portion of the car park that lies between the square at the entrance to the underground and the southern car park for buses, including the area immediately surrounding the stadium itself. The esplanade covers an area of 35,000 square metres and its construction involves the planting of a large amount of greenery on the car park's roof. The selection of plants is patterned after the species found in the neighbouring Fröttmaninger Heide – a mosaic of different types of vegetation. Because of its status as a public park, the composition of the vegetation was determined during the planning process. Some of the seeds were taken from the Fröttmaninger Heide, and the 620,000 plants all come from native stocks. The sowing and planting followed a graphic pattern. After an initial establishment phase, the vegetation is intended to become self-sustaining without the need for intensive additional care. In the less developed areas, it consists of only low plant cover, while bushes are also planted in the more thickly covered areas. Beyond the esplanade, in the area's border zones, small, scattered groves of trees are planted.

Visitors can access the cambered platform from the underground station, from the southern car park for buses, and via six stairways from the parking levels. The platform is covered with rolling paths that intersect diagonally, which do much to unblock the stream of spectators when the stadium is in use. Because they intersect, the ends of the diagonal paths remain hidden, and they afford close-up and distant views of the surrounding landscape. The colour of the asphalt pavement matches that of the plant substratum and suggests a uniform covering. When no game is scheduled, the esplanade serves as a public park and recreational area and a supra-regional connecting link in the network of pedestrian and bicycle paths.

Heathlands
Designing the grounds for the new football stadium at this location meant constructing a landscape. In an interplay with Fröttmaninger Berg and the windmill on its mount, the stadium leads to a prominent gate situation, whereas the landscaped parking lot and the roof esplanade of the multi-storey car park are interpreted as a part of the Munich gravel stratum. The city's park does not serve as a model. Located at the edge of the city, the heathland habitat is derived from the adjacent landscape. Only the roads are reminiscent of classic English landscape parks. The form and scale of the development correspond to the site's various functions, which range from managing large masses of people when the stadium is in operation to providing a local place of rest and relaxation at other times. The structural architecture and landscape architecture are interdependent. The architectural body will become a part of the cityscape and is a crossover between the natural and the artificial. In combination with the topographical staging, it refers to the external heathlands, which display the continuity of a cultured landscape rather than a natural one.

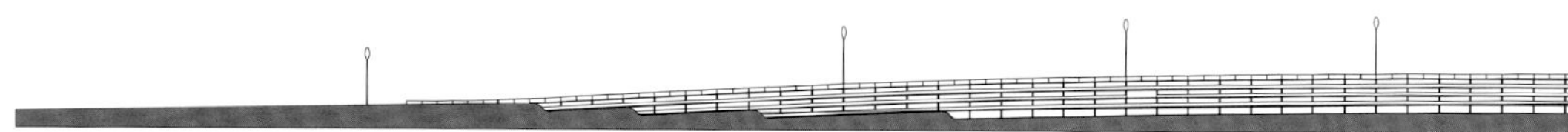

View from the east.

0 50 100 200

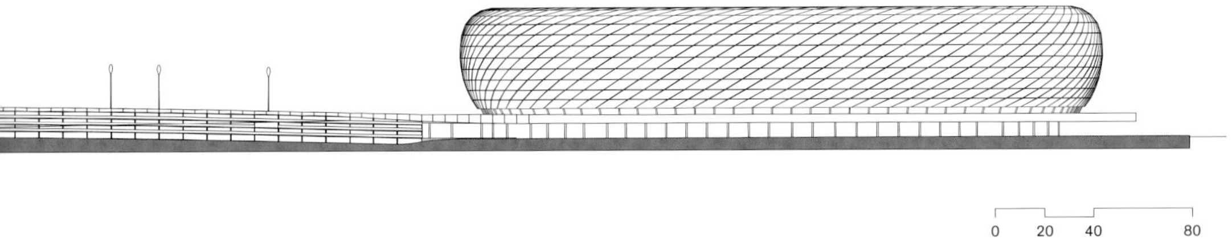

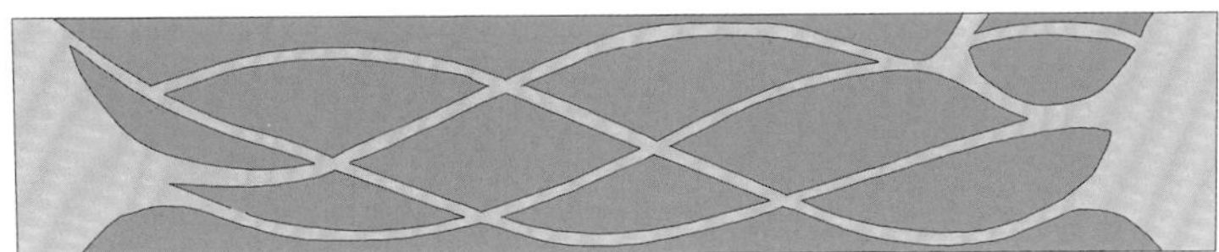

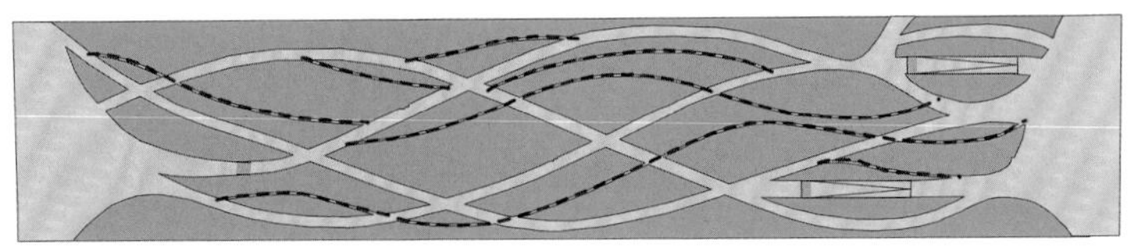

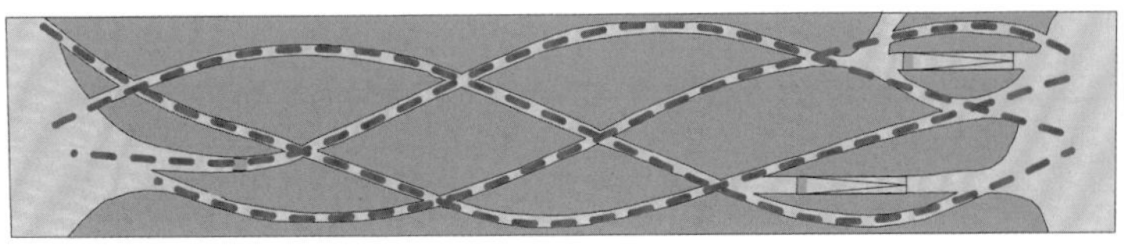

Studies for the paths.

Allianz Arena

P2
P2

P2
P1

P2

Allianz Arena

Allianz

EAST VILLAGE, LONDON
WAITING FOR A CITY
2008–12 (and more)

Client: Lend Lease
Team: Fletcher Priest Architects, Arup, Biodiversity by Design, Speirs and Major Associates, David Bonnett Associates, Tim O'Hare Associates, Waterwise Solutions, BMT Fluid Mechanics, Gardiner & Theobald, RPS Planning / Quod Planning
Area: 150,000 m^2 of open spaces

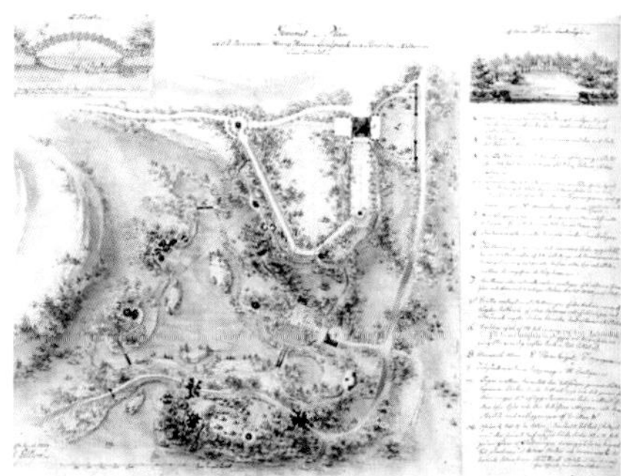

Fredrik Magnus Piper (1779) "General Plan of Henry Hoare's Park at Stourton, Lit A".

Former Railyards, Stratford, 1914, Old Ordnance.

English waterways and railways network.

East Village within the Lea River Valley, Geological map of London.

The Stratford City development was initially conceived in 2002 as a development and urban regeneration project on the former Stratford Rail Lands, which are north of Stratford town centre in East London.

When London was awarded the 2012 Olympic and Paralympic Games, the East Village was assimilated into the Stratford City master plan. The requirement to host the 2012 Games meant that the development time frame, initially fifteen to twenty years, had to be accelerated to provide accommodation for the 17,000 competitors and team members.

While there was considerable pressure to deliver the Village for 2012, the primary focus of the design team was the development of a Post-2012 Legacy Community that would contain residential, retail, office and educational facilities.

The East Village lies between the river Lea to the west and the existing residential area of Leyton to the east. The natural characteristics and urban context of these locations have been used as landscape references to inform the design of open spaces including the streetscape.

The surrounding topography, native planting and water courses inform the character of the public spaces, squares and streetscape environments creating a place of distinction. In addition to the strong connections to the surrounding context a central aspiration of the design was to develop a landscape that refers to the English tradition of landscape gardens as well as being an engineered landscape that manages the water sustainably. Close collaboration between the landscape architects, ecologists and engineers was required to develop a landscape that would not only create a sense of place but also minimise irrigation and hard surfacing, recycle run-off water, create topographical variation, possess a diversity of structures and habitats, and make extensive use of native and naturalised vegetation throughout the scheme and wetland environments. What started as a technical challenge for the team became a source of inspiration for the design of the public realm and informed a number of the design strategies used throughout the Village.

The scheme aims to create a poetic infrastructural landscape.

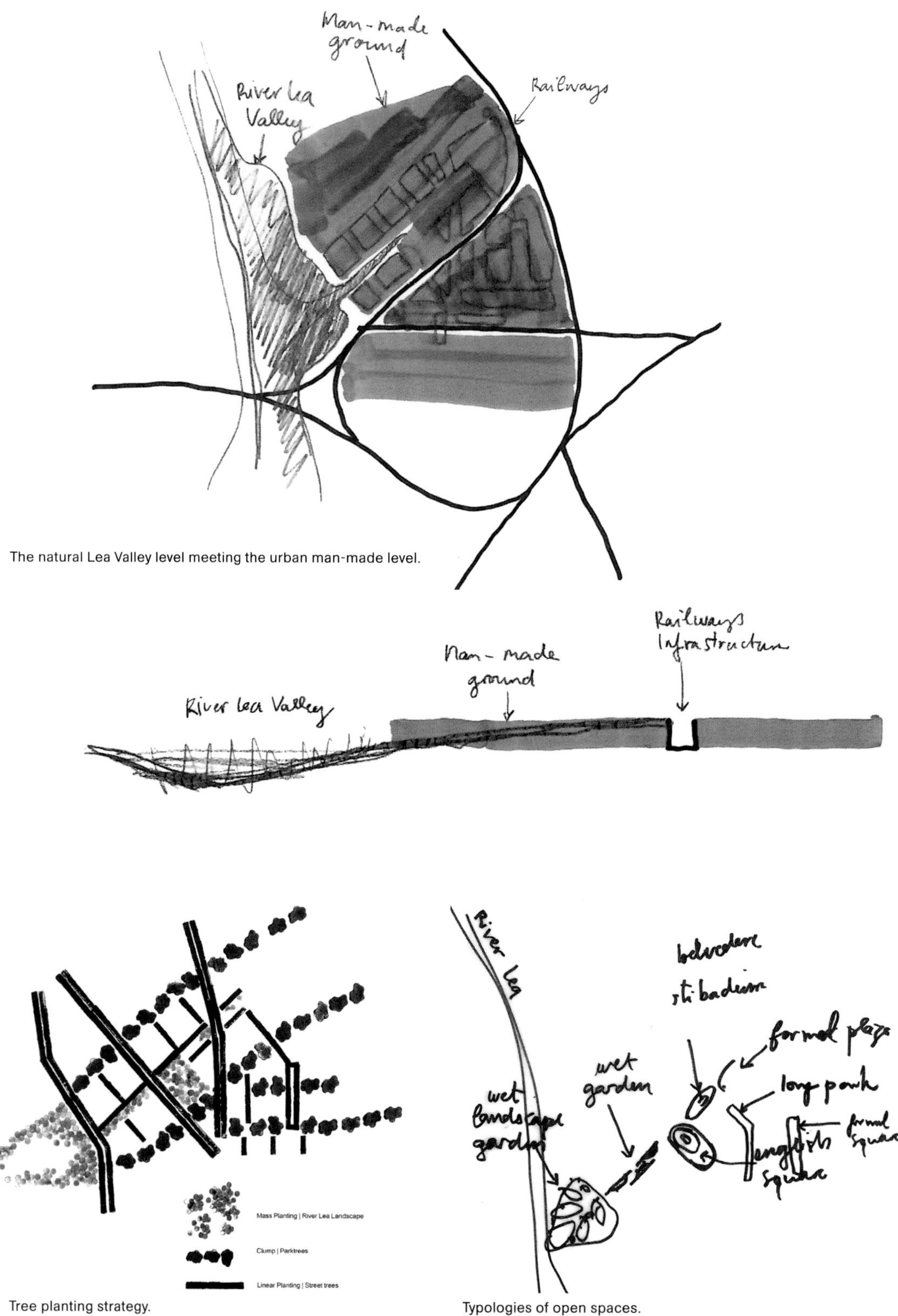

The natural Lea Valley level meeting the urban man-made level.

Tree planting strategy.

Typologies of open spaces.

Viewing axis tests.

Modelling the desire lines.

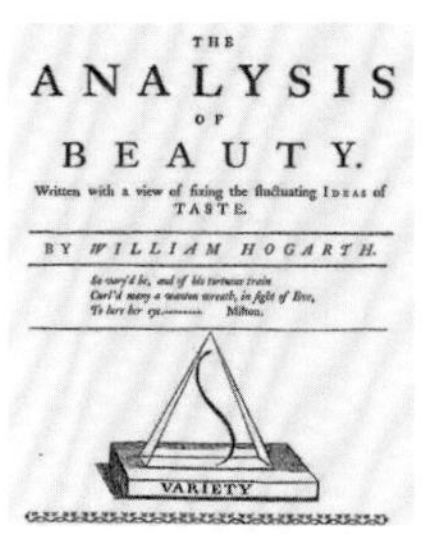

THE
ANALYSIS
OF
BEAUTY.
Written with a view of fixing the fluctuating IDEAS of TASTE.

BY WILLIAM HOGARTH.

Milton.

VARIETY

"The Analysis of Beauty"
by William Hogarth.

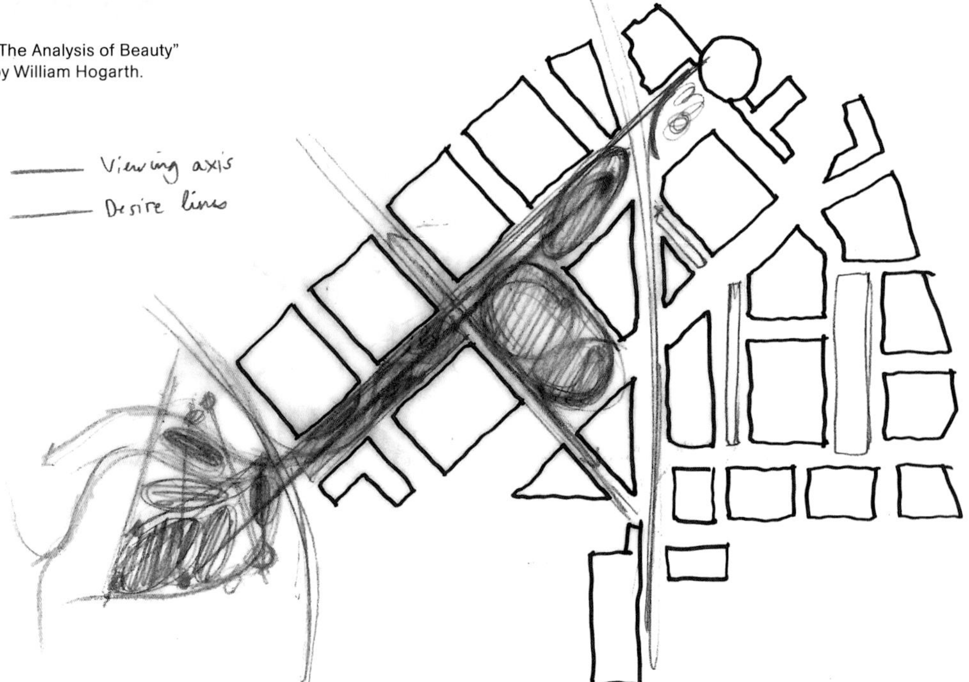

Viewing axis and desire lines across the main open spaces.

A, The Belvedere and its stibadium / Athletes Village landscape plan.

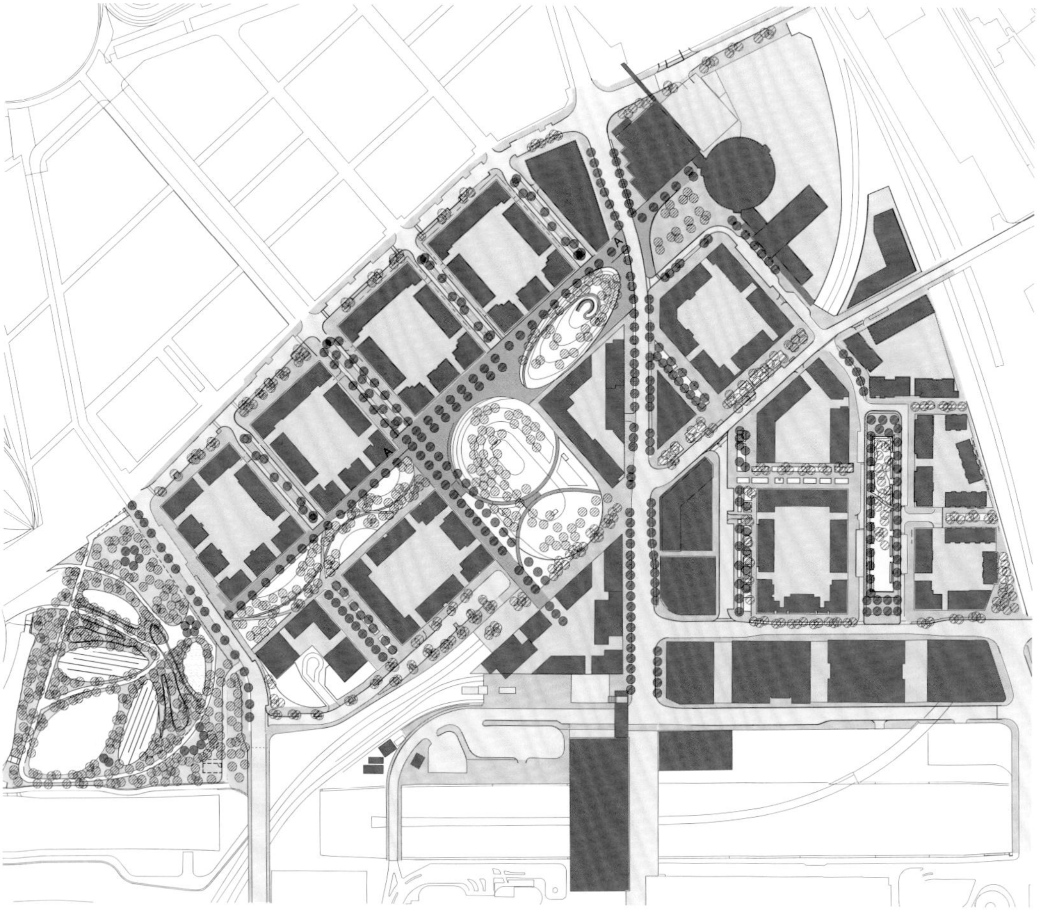

The new East London district contains 15 hectares of open spaces and streetscape.

Portlands (former Stratford Gardens).

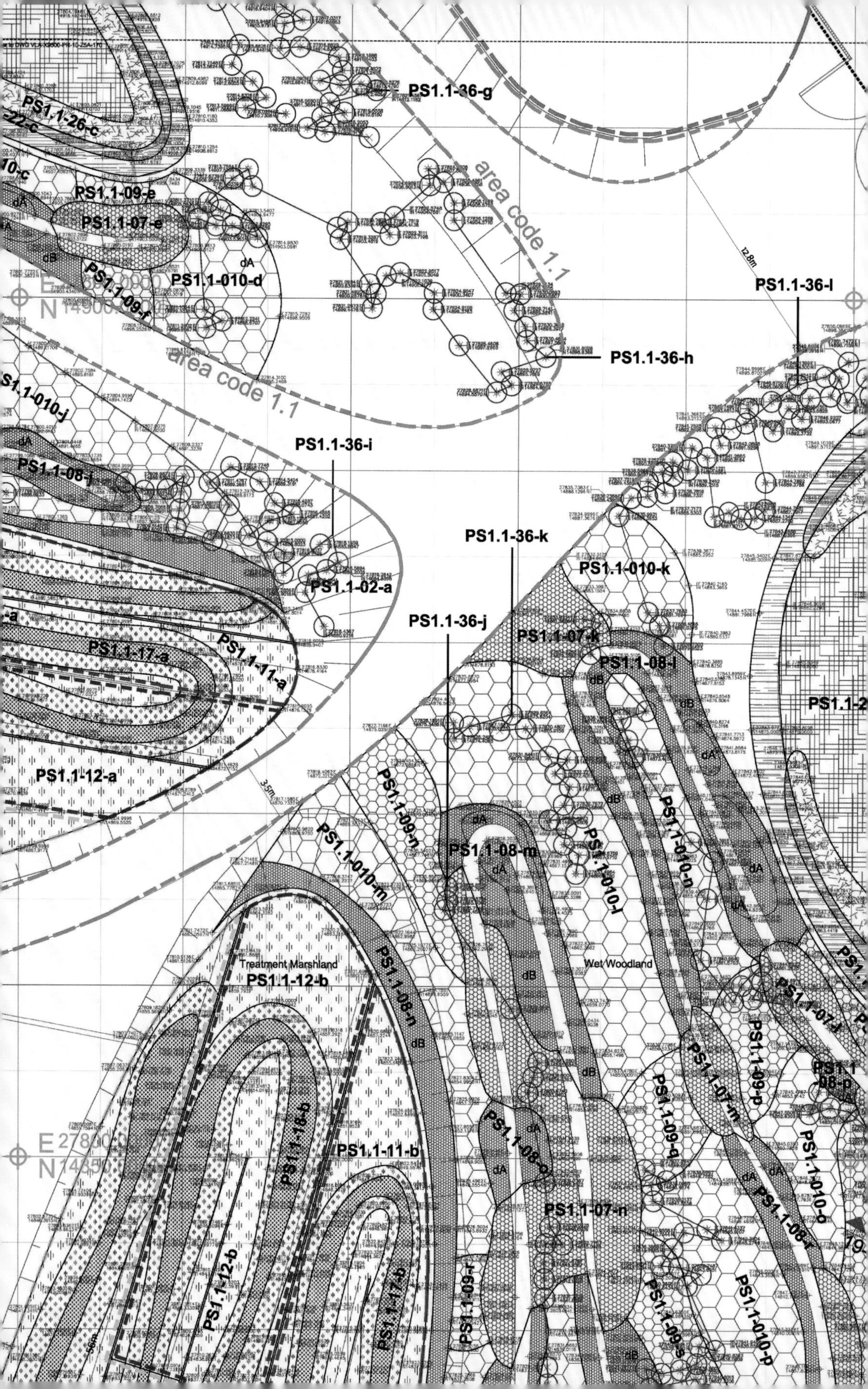

PS1.1-36-g
PS1.1-26-c
PS1.1-09-e
PS1.1-07-e
dA
dB
PS1.1-010-d
PS1.1-09-f
area code 1.1
area code 1.1
PS1.1-36-h
12.8m
PS1.1-36-l
PS1.1-36-i
PS1.1-08-j
PS1.1-02-a
PS1.1-36-k
PS1.1-010-k
PS1.1-36-j
PS1.1-07-k
PS1.1-08-l
PS1.1-17-a
PS1.1-11-a
PS1.1-12-a
3.5m
PS1.1-09-n
PS1.1-010-m
PS1.1-08-m
PS1.1-010-l
PS1.1-010-n
Treatment Marshland
PS1.1-12-b
PS1.1-08-n
Wet Woodland
PS1.1-07-l
PS1.1-09-p
PS1.1-07-m
PS1.1-09-q
PS1.1-08-p
PS1.1-18-b
PS1.1-11-b
PS1.1-08-o
PS1.1-07-n
PS1.1-010-o
PS1.1-08-r
PS1.1-12-b
PS1.1-17-b
PS1.1-09-r
PS1.1-09-s
PS1.1-010-p

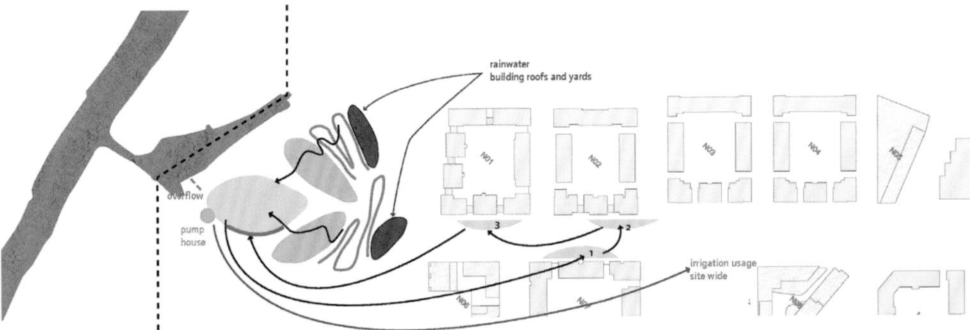

Run-off collection and filtering system
While the eastern part of the district retains most of the run-off on site in underground gravel pits, the western area drains run-off (including all developments' roof rainwater) towards semi-urban semi-natural looking ponds which are connected to the wetlands where it is then filtered through a series of stilling ponds, treatment marshlands and polishing ponds. At the end of the system is a pumping house, designed as a folly, that pumps the clean water back to the district to irrigate planting.

Section through the polishing pond of the wetlands (last phase of the filtering process) and through the treatment marshland of the wetlands (2nd phase of the filtering process).

Channelsea embankment
- Channelsea embankment meadow
- Channelsea embankment reinforced turf matting
- Channelsea embankment pre-established coir pallets

Flowering lawn Picnic area
- Bulb full sun
- Bulb shadow

Dry woodland

Wet woodland
- Sun/part sun and marginal
- Part sun/shade and marginal
- Sun/part sun and top of the bank
- Part sun/shade and top of the bank

Shrubs
- Dense thorny scrub
- Wet woodland
- Dry woodland
- Channelsea embankment shrub

Treatment marsh
- Top of the bank
- Channel marginal
- Emergent section

Marginal/Ledge planting
- Least inundation stilling ponds
- Moderate inundation stilling ponds
- Most inundation stilling ponds
- Least inundation polishing ponds
- Moderate inundation polishing ponds
- Most inundation polishing ponds

Floating leaved aquatic
- Floating leaved aquatic stilling ponds
- Floating leaved aquatic Polishing ponds

Submerged aquatic plants
- Submerged aquatic plants stilling ponds
- Submerged aquatic plants polishing ponds

Vegetated rafts
- Pre-planted vegetated rafts stilling ponds
- Pre-planted vegetated rafts polishing ponds

Ground flora planting plan excerpt
Although natural and spontaneous looking, the wetlands have been very precisely planned in terms of movement, topography, water levels and speeds, and planting. The extremely diverse palettes of ground flora, shrubs and trees have been meticulously controlled in order to generate the different habitats which will naturally filter the polluted rainwater.

NOVARTIS TRAINING CENTRE

PREFIGURED IMAGE
2004–16

Client: Novartis Pharma AG, Basel
Architecture: Peter Zumthor Architekten, Haldenstein
Area: 93,000 m^2

J. M. W. Turner, Blue Rigi, painted during a trip to Lake Zug, 1842.

View of the west bank, Lake Zug.

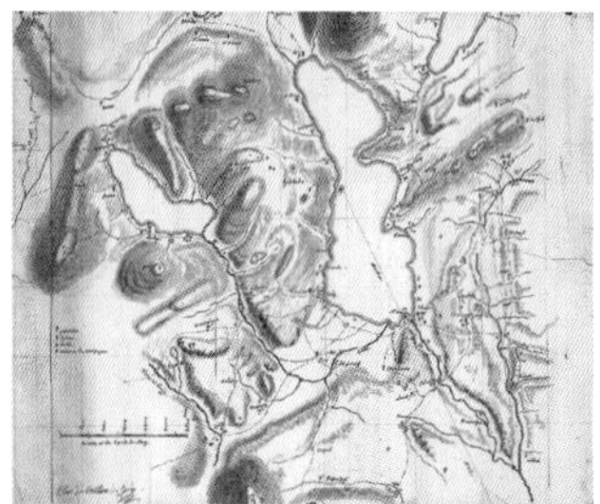

Pfyffer map of the Zug region, 18th century.

"Geological Investigation of the Alluvial Valley of the Lower Mississippi River", H. Fisk, 1944.

As the Enlightenment dawned in the mid-eighteenth century, the Alps were seen in a new light and became a desirable destination for scientists, artists and tourists. Travel journals by Beckford, Goethe, Byron and Ruskin made Switzerland the most visited country in Europe, besides Italy, from the late eighteenth century onwards.

More than anyone else, the English were very enthusiastic about the Alps, especially Switzerland. Having already been more strongly affected by urbanisation and industrialisation than any other European country, they discovered authentic nature on their Grand Tours through Switzerland. The fact that the landscape had actually been altered by centuries of cultivation did not diminish their fervour, since it very closely resembled the ideal English landscape garden and its Arcadian foundations in poetry and landscape painting. At home, one could take a piece of land and turn it into a sublime, landscaped garden "based on nature", and by adding "follies" for the educated visitor, it could seem as if one were inside a historical painting; in the eyes of travelling Englishmen, Switzerland itself was like an enormous landscape garden. Tourist destinations included dramatic mountain locales as well as the gentle Alpine foothills and lakes, whose atmospheric light so impressed William Turner that he captured it in his paintings.

The enthusiasm of tourists for the Alpine landscape inspired the Swiss themselves to discover their own landscape and to erect estates with imposing gardens outside of the city. Along the western bank of Lake Zug arose a "necklace of pearls" – landed estates integrated into the densely atmospheric moraine landscape between Lake Zug and Lake Lucerne, whose designs took advantage of the quick succession of steep hills, narrow valleys, woods and meadows. The still-visible result was a melding of the scenic cultivated landscape and the picturesque ideals of the landscaped English garden.

The Aabach estate, built in the 1930s, is one of the more recent additions to this "necklace of pearls". Here, distinctive features of the landscape were adapted into deliberate mise en scènes of landscaped spaces and optical perspectives, although construction made lasting changes to the geomorphology of the site.

The new design is based on the idea of restoring and overlapping the banks of the lake and the surrounding moraine landscape of the existing park. A long stretch of moraine is the backbone of the layout. A crest cut into the landscape in the 1930s will be rebuilt according to the original topography, turning the ridge into a characteristic element that will eventually be grouped around the central areas of the training centre. A new theme in the design is the strength of Lake Zug and the Aabach, which strongly influence the appearance of the landscape. A system of flat drains covers the plane at the foot of the moraine ridge, like an imprint of flowing water, made out of many overlapping layers of time, reminiscent of the stream that has left behind its sediment as it changed course many times over the centuries. The banks of the lake, which are now fortified, will form a flat, expansive delta.

Most of the old trees in the park – classic, dramatic vegetation and special, sometimes mighty and solitary trees – will remain. Extensive new plantings will restore the compositional principle behind the park, which links individual spaces via sightlines.

In contrast to this composition, new areas will be laid out to resemble various types of native groves. Wooded landscapes, left to their natural devices, range from the soft-wood meadow close to the lake to the elevated beech forests along the cliffs, accentuated by typical environments of meadows and wild plants.

"Floating" on wooden supports, the buildings have their own place in the context of the park landscape without interrupting the free flow of topography and vegetation. Part of the architectural concept is the immediacy of the landscape: views from each building offer various impressions of the multifaceted landscape. On walks, the attentive visitor will realise that it is a combination of culture and nature that alters the choreography, form and material of the path, the series of spaces, the atmospheric, changing vegetation, and the interplay between staging and natural dynamics. To the less attentive, the area offers a varied stroll through a section of Swiss landscape, a prefigured image.

Photographic Stroll
An existing park from the early 1930s, which is still caught up in nineteenth-century design principles. Since it was created over a period of several decades, and has had various owners, it has grown into a structure with very diverse characteristics. The new design contrasts the historical with a new type of park. Their common foundation forms the geomorphic concision of the existing elements: hill, valley, delta.

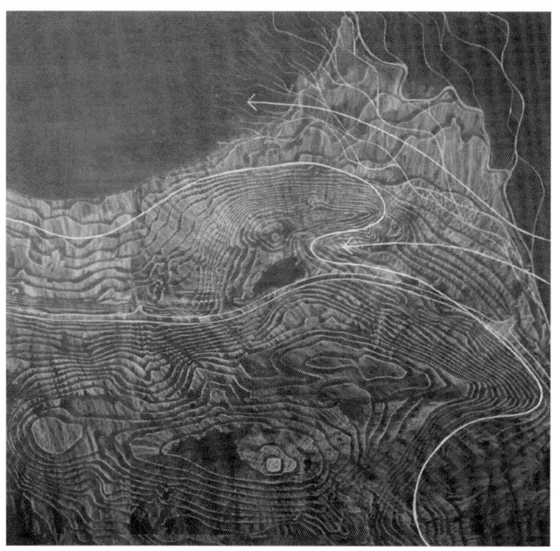

Concept sketch: Hill Valley Delta.

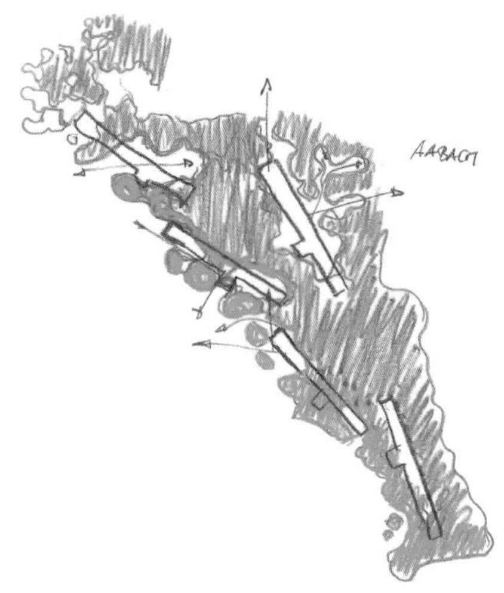

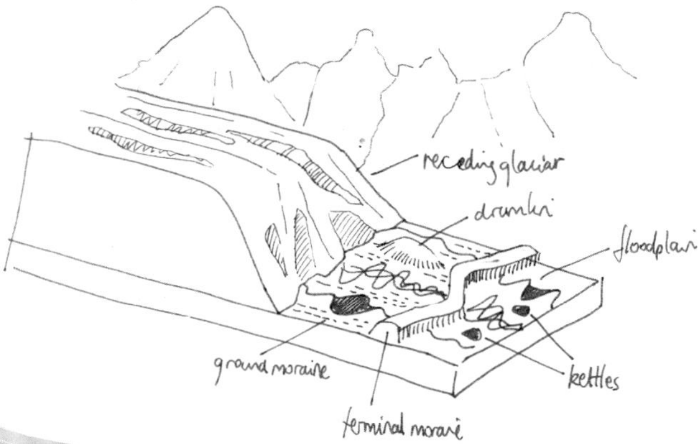

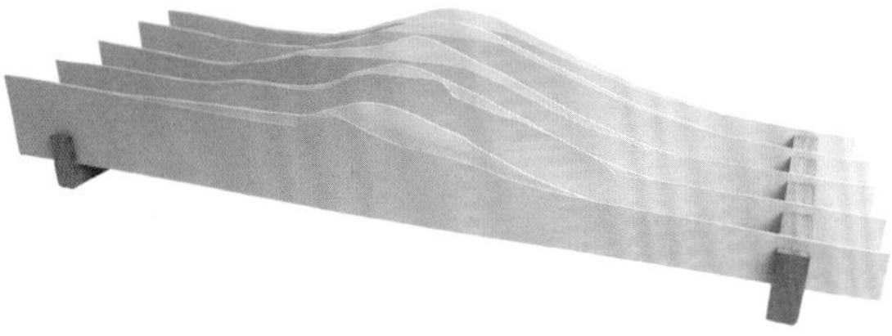

Design Process
Aspects of geology, topology, geomorphology, the choreography of paths and the vegetation are investigated using sketches, cutaways and cutaway models. A study of vegetation was undertaken in the form of a herbarium which contrasts the existing park-like vegetation in relation to a more natural type, creating a micro-topographical realisation in the form of sectional drawings.

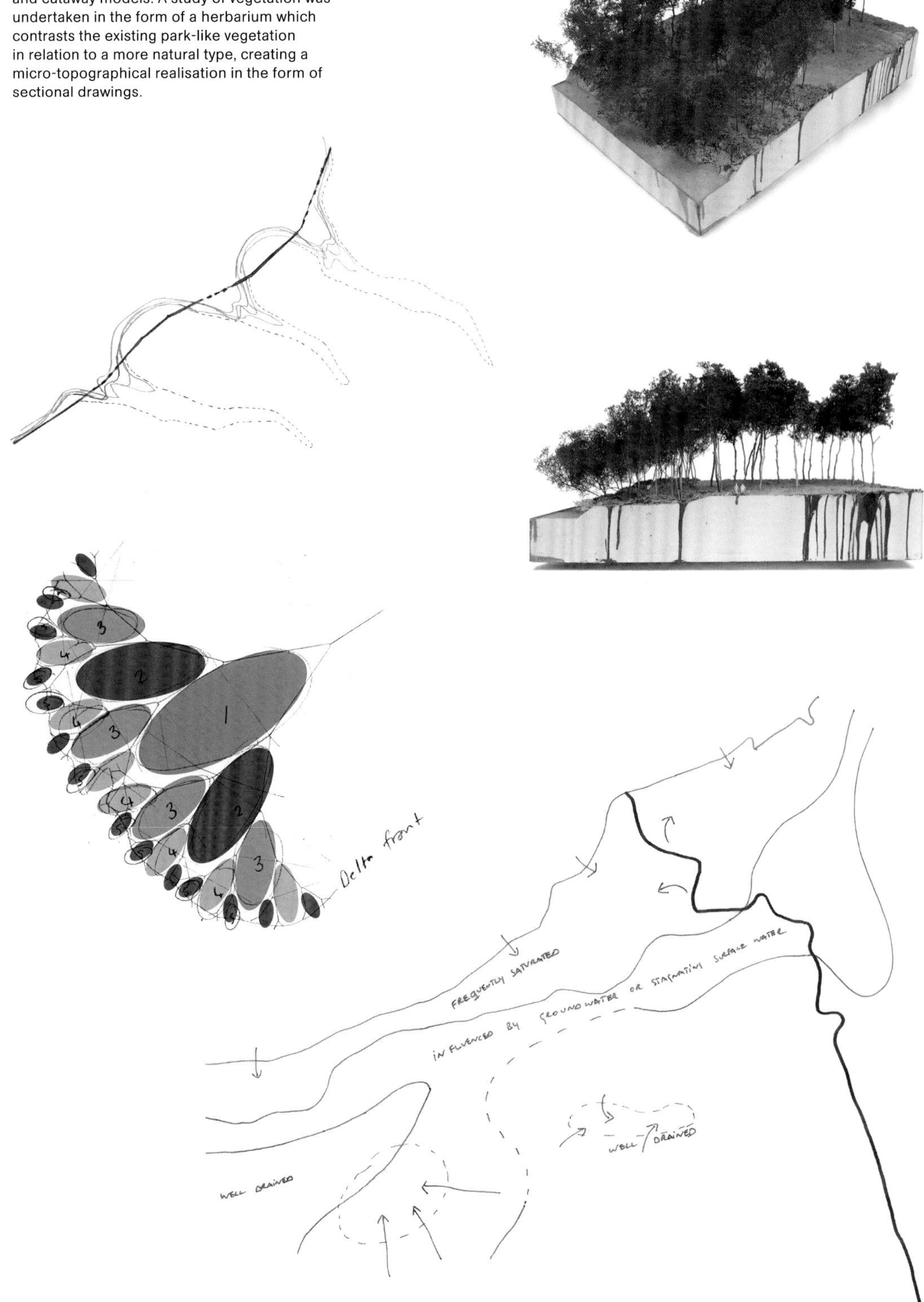

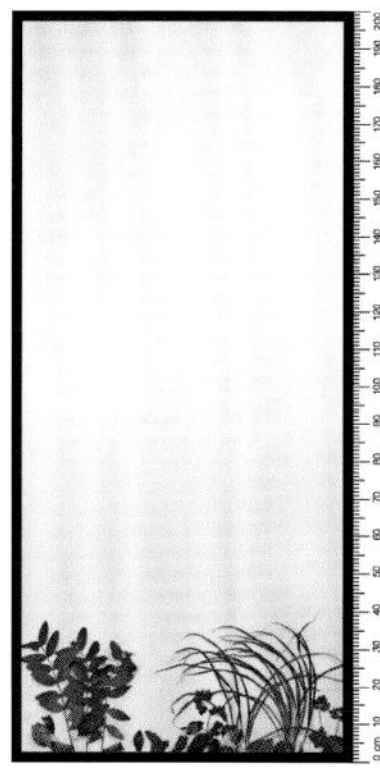

Woodland perennials herbarium.

Woodland perennials in the beech forest.

Woodland perennials and ferns herbarium.

Woodland perennials and ferns in the hornbeam-beech forest.

Iris meadow herbarium.

Iris meadow within the alder forest.

Tall grasses and perennials herbarium.

Central meadow with tall grasses and perennials.

Broadleafed perennials herbarium.

Planted delta with broadleafed perennials.

Aqueous perennials herbarium.

Lakeshore with aqueous perennials.

A
B
0
25
50
100

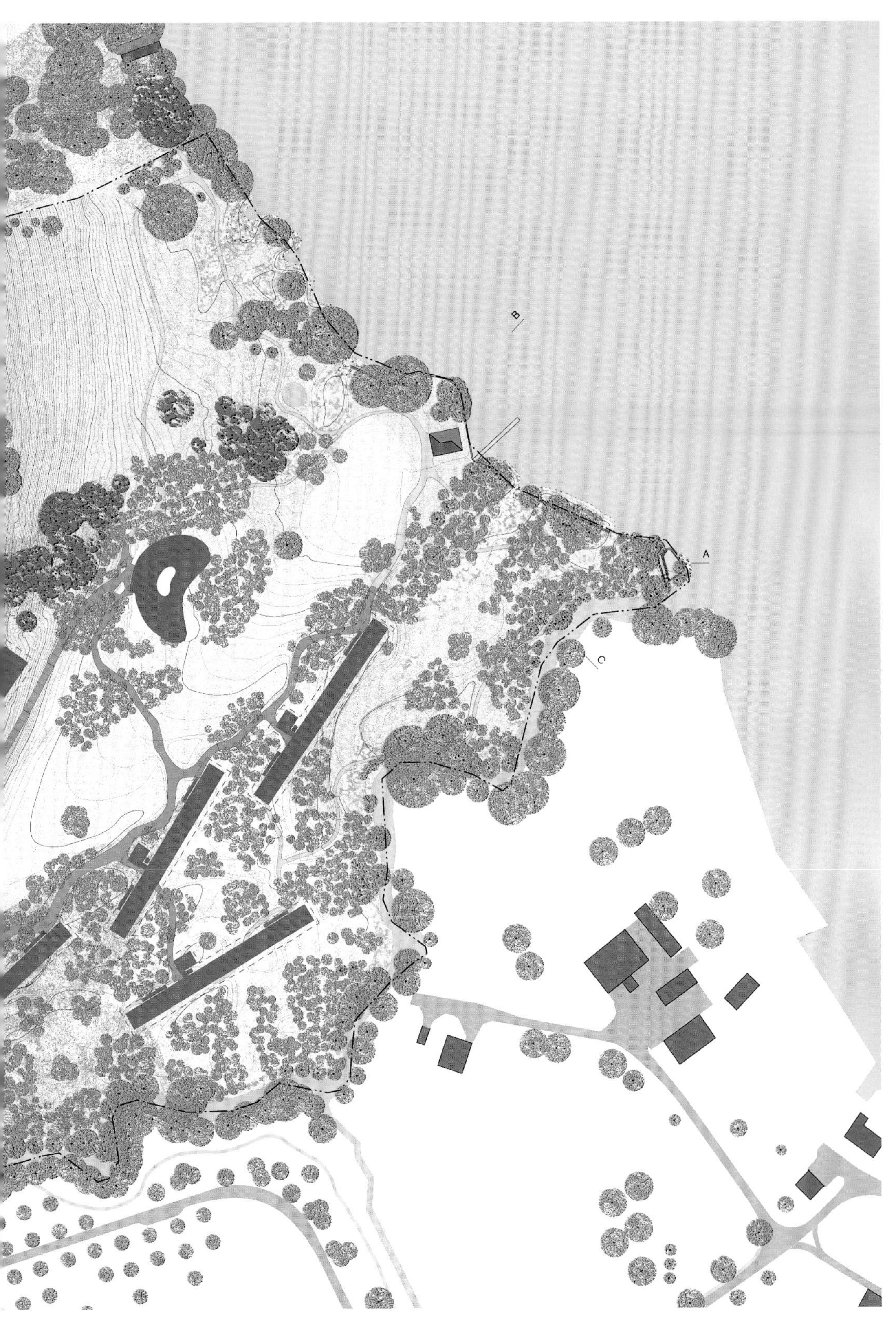
B
A
C

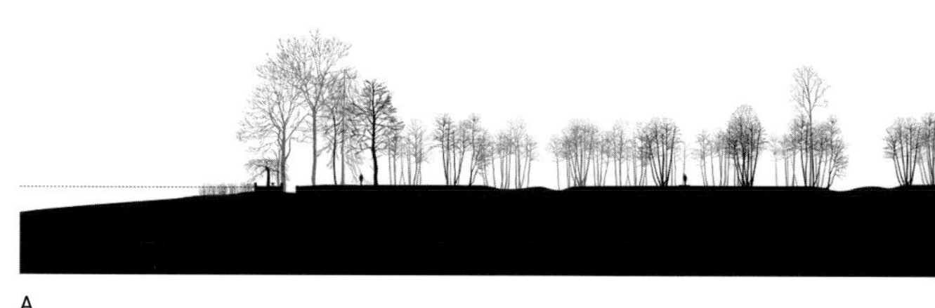

A

B

C

0 25 50

WALKS PAPER

Hamish Fulton

Hamish Fulton's artistic work documents hikes made all over the world. The landscapes he hikes in are also his studio or workshop. Yet he makes no intervention in the landscapes, nor does he collect any natural samples that find their way into a gallery or museum. The visual result of his work presents his reflections on what he experienced on the hikes. Photographs, drawings and texts on vastly different scales are the media through which he communicates the experiences of these hikes to non-participants. Driven by more than mere wanderlust, he seeks the humanisation of nature, a reappropriation of landscapes that we have already conquered, but without exploiting them this time, so that we are inspired to continue to question our relationship with nature.

HAMISH FULTON

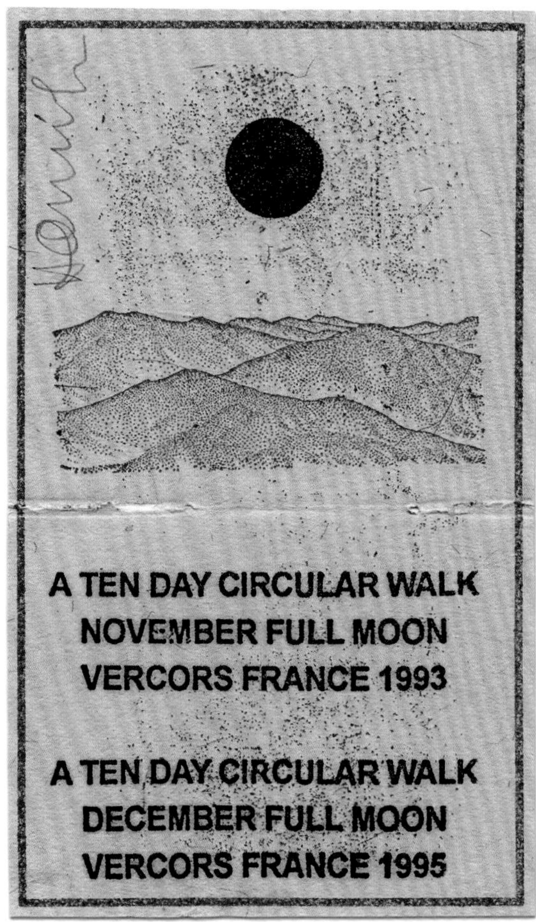

WALKS

PAPER

A TEN DAY COAST TO COAST WALK
ACROSS THE KII PENINSULA ON ROADS AND PATHS
TRAVELLING BY WAY OF THREE HILLS
KOYASAN OMINE ODAIGAHARA
AND THE MIYA GAWA GORGE
JAPAN OCTOBER 1995

17 WALKS THROUGH 11 DAYS
ON THE SAME ROUTE
STARTING AND ENDING
AT THE SAME PLACE

ALL WITHIN THE CITY LIMITS
OF SANTA FE NEW MEXICO
13-23 MAY 2003

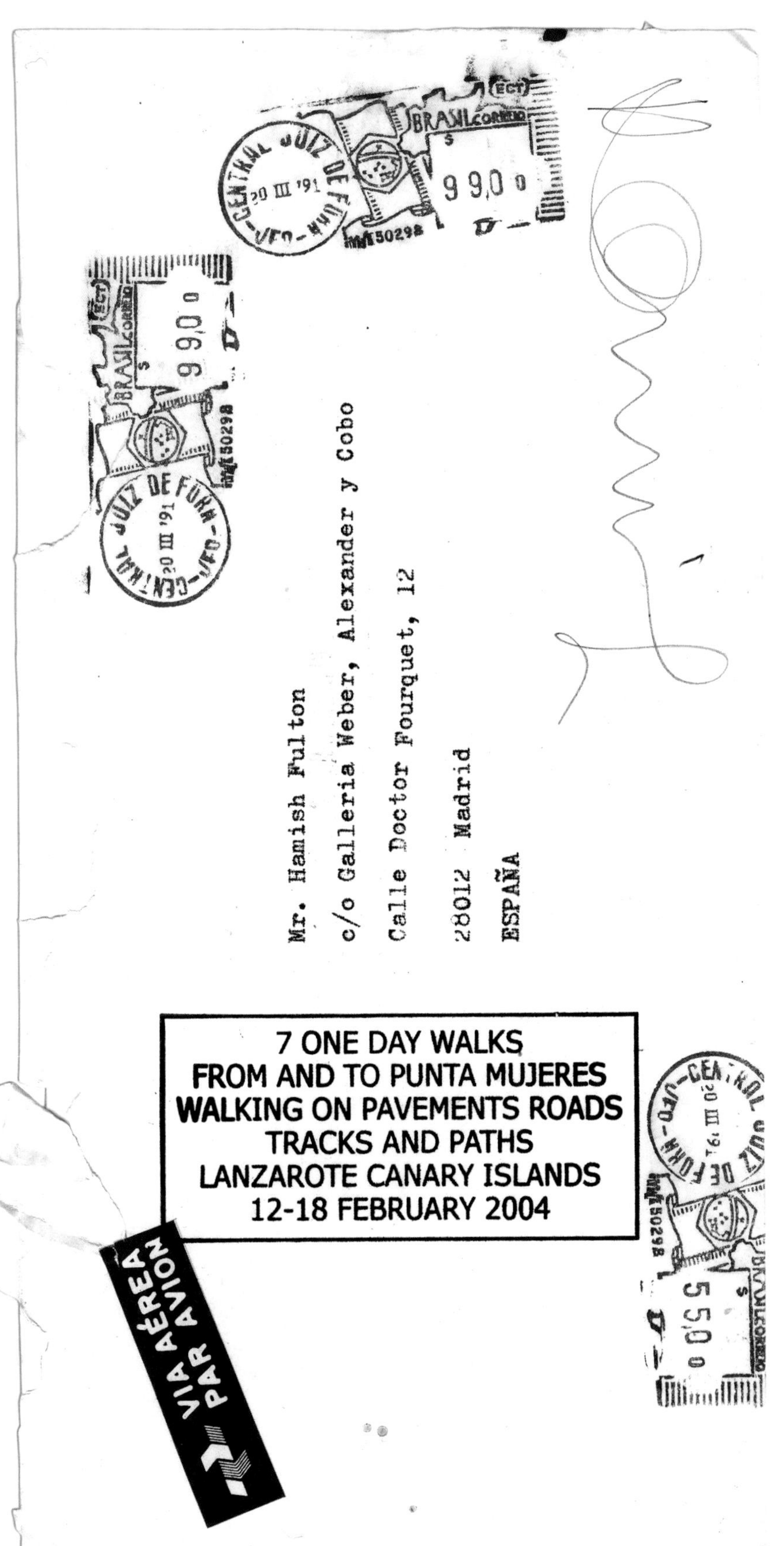

7 ONE DAY WALKS
FROM AND TO PUNTA MUJERES
WALKING ON PAVEMENTS ROADS
TRACKS AND PATHS
LANZAROTE CANARY ISLANDS
12-18 FEBRUARY 2004

EL PASO TX 799 B1
PM
25 FEB
2002
USA 80
2001
Mount McKinley, Alaska
A GUIDED MOUNTAINEERING EXPEDITION
TO THE SUMMIT OF DENALI AT 20,320 FT
VIA THE WEST BUTTRESS ROUTE
ALASKA MAY/JUNE 2004

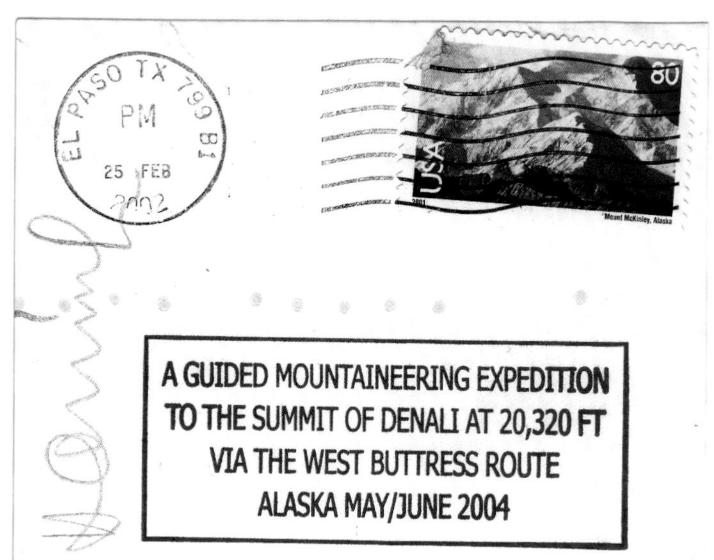

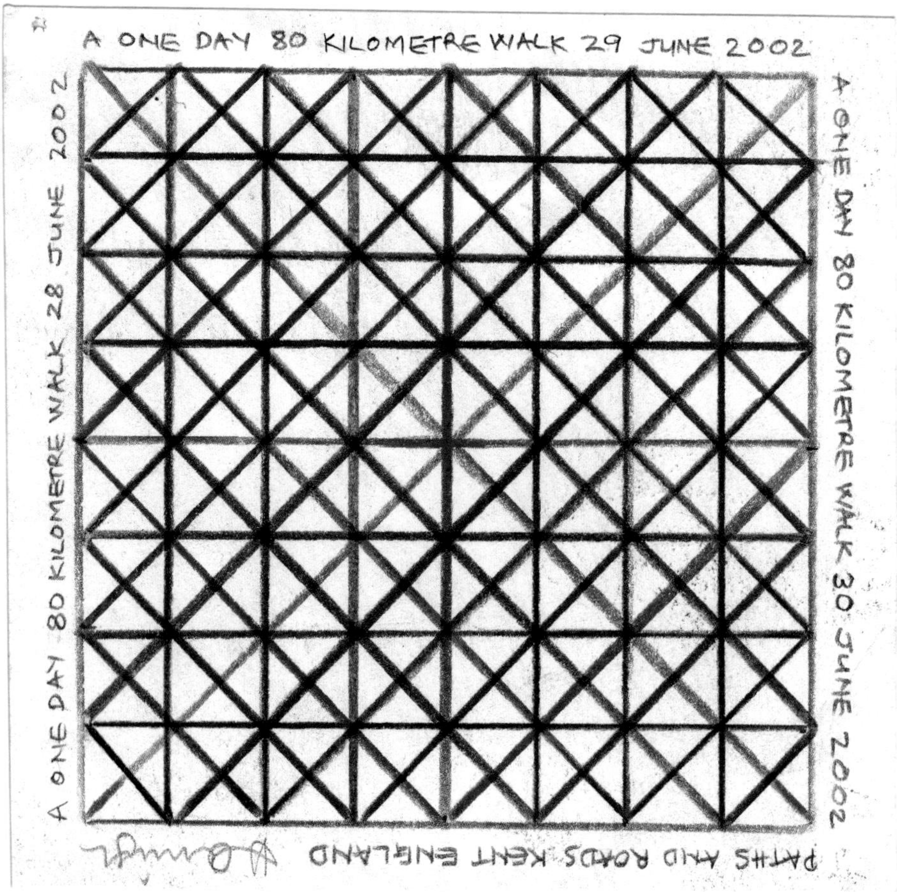
A ONE DAY 80 KILOMETRE WALK 29 JUNE 2002
A ONE DAY 80 KILOMETRE WALK 28 JUNE 2002
A ONE DAY 80 KILOMETRE WALK 30 JUNE 2002
PATHS AND ROADS KENT ENGLAND

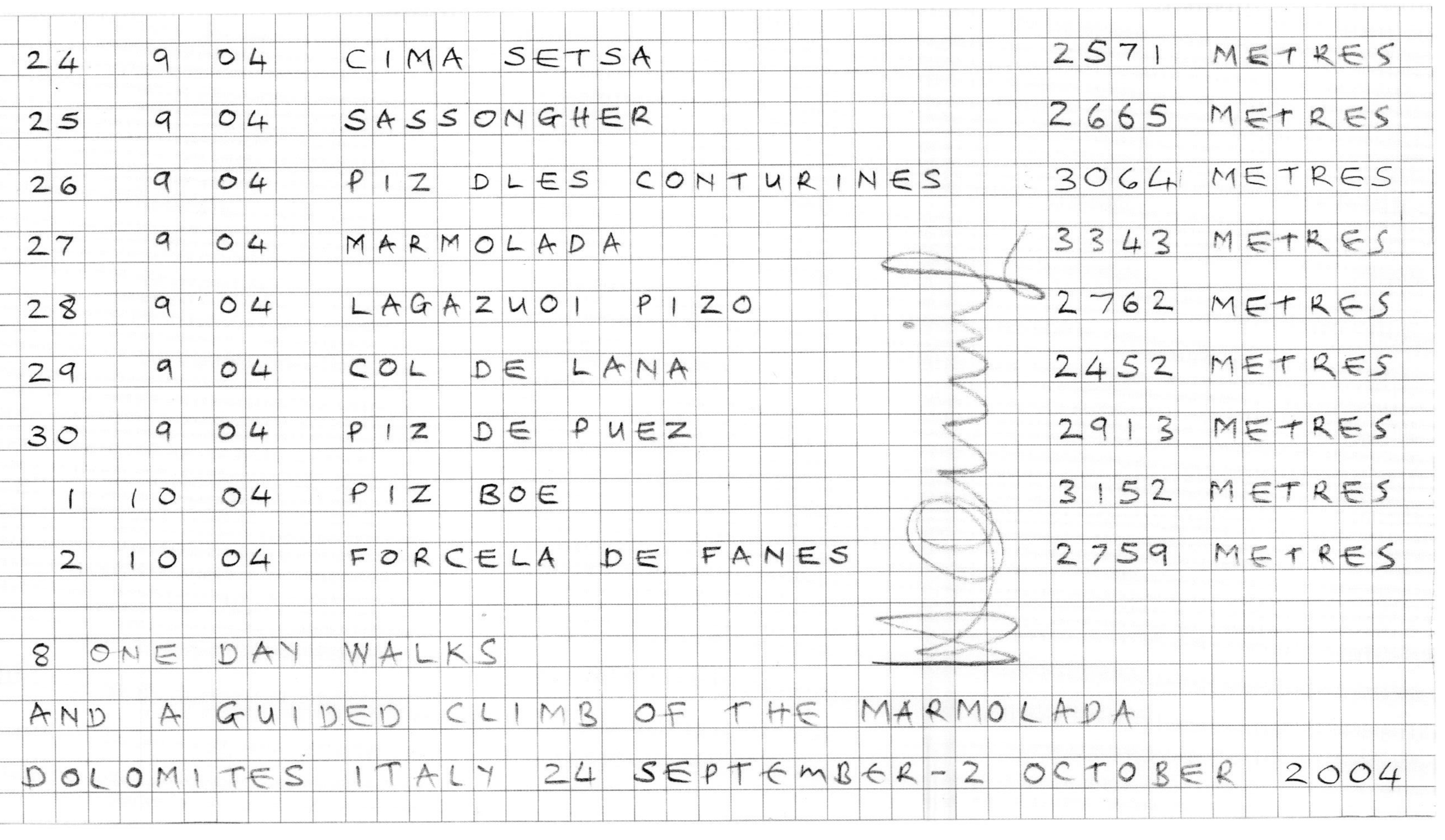

24	9	04	CIMA SETSA	2571	METRES
25	9	04	SASSONGHER	2665	METRES
26	9	04	PIZ DLES CONTURINES	3064	METRES
27	9	04	MARMOLADA	3343	METRES
28	9	04	LAGAZUOI PIZO	2762	METRES
29	9	04	COL DE LANA	2452	METRES
30	9	04	PIZ DE PUEZ	2913	METRES
1	10	04	PIZ BOE	3152	METRES
2	10	04	FORCELA DE FANES	2759	METRES

8 ONE DAY WALKS

AND A GUIDED CLIMB OF THE MARMOLADA

DOLOMITES ITALY 24 SEPTEMBER - 2 OCTOBER 2004

A BICYCLE JOURNEY FROM CANTERBURY ENGLAND TO DELEMONT SWITZERLAND JULY 1970

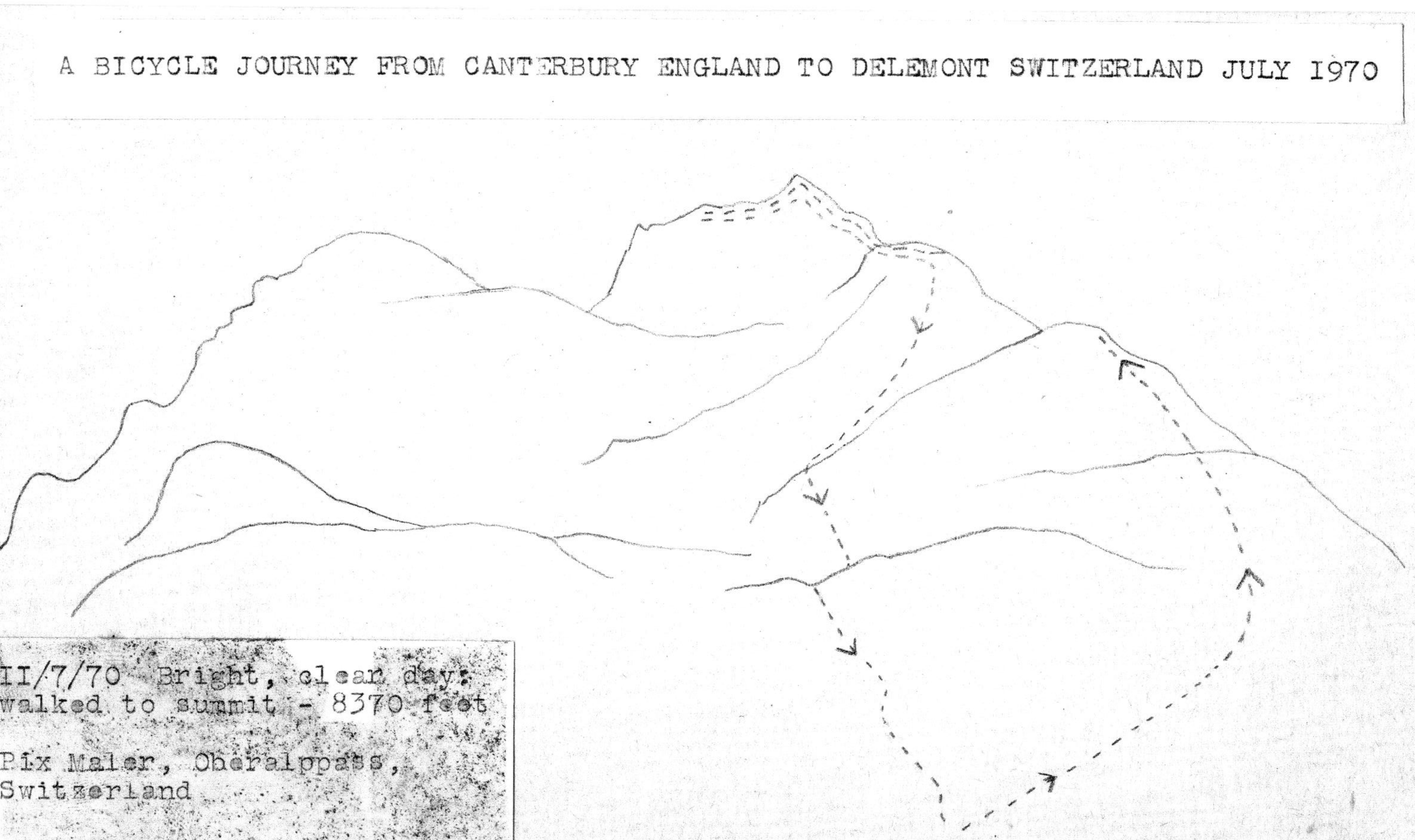

11/7/70 Bright, clear day:
walked to summit - 8370 feet

Pix Maler, Oberalppass,
Switzerland

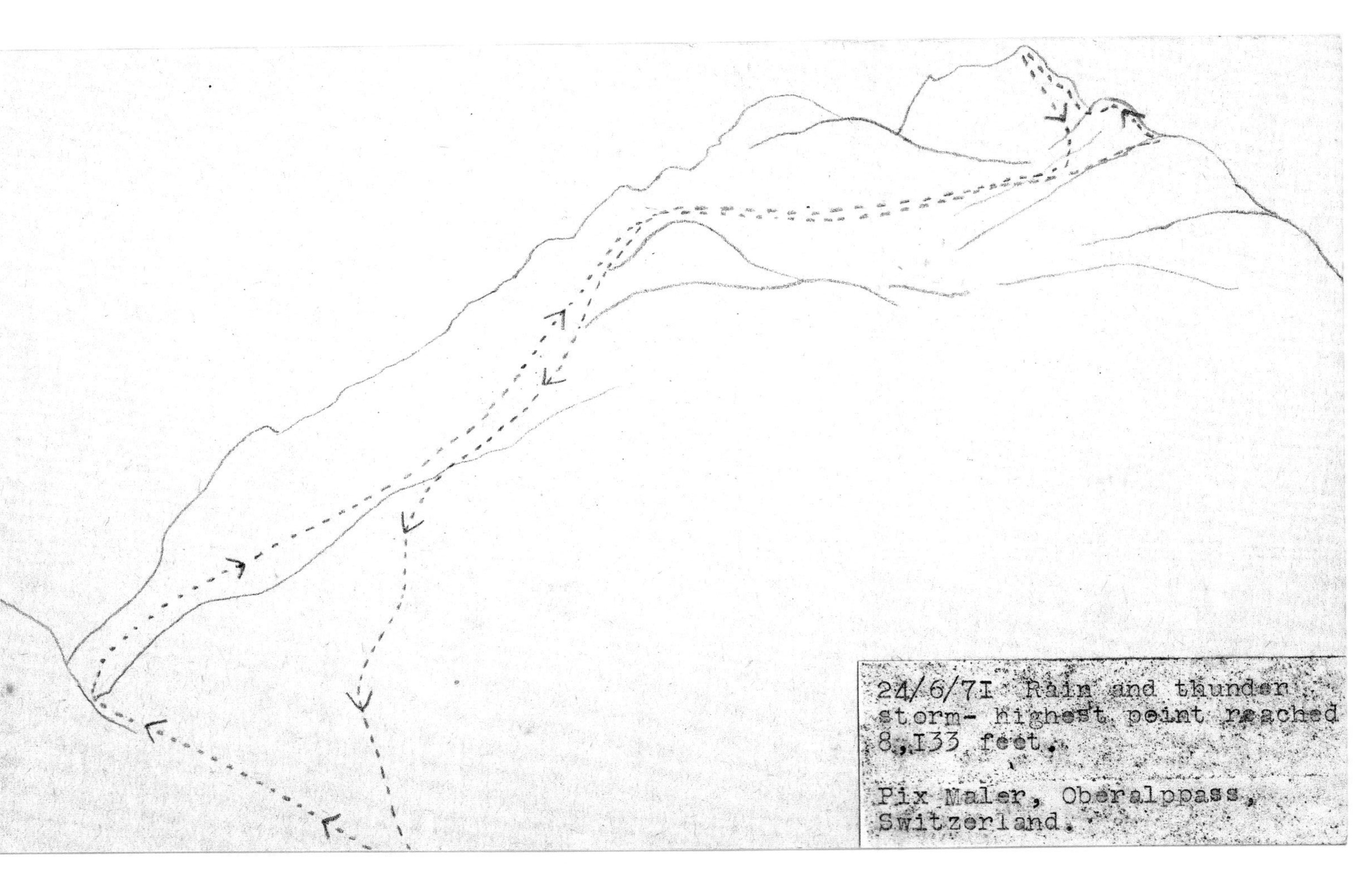
24/6/71 Rain and thunder storm- highest point reached 8,133 feet.
Pix Maler, Oberalppass, Switzerland.

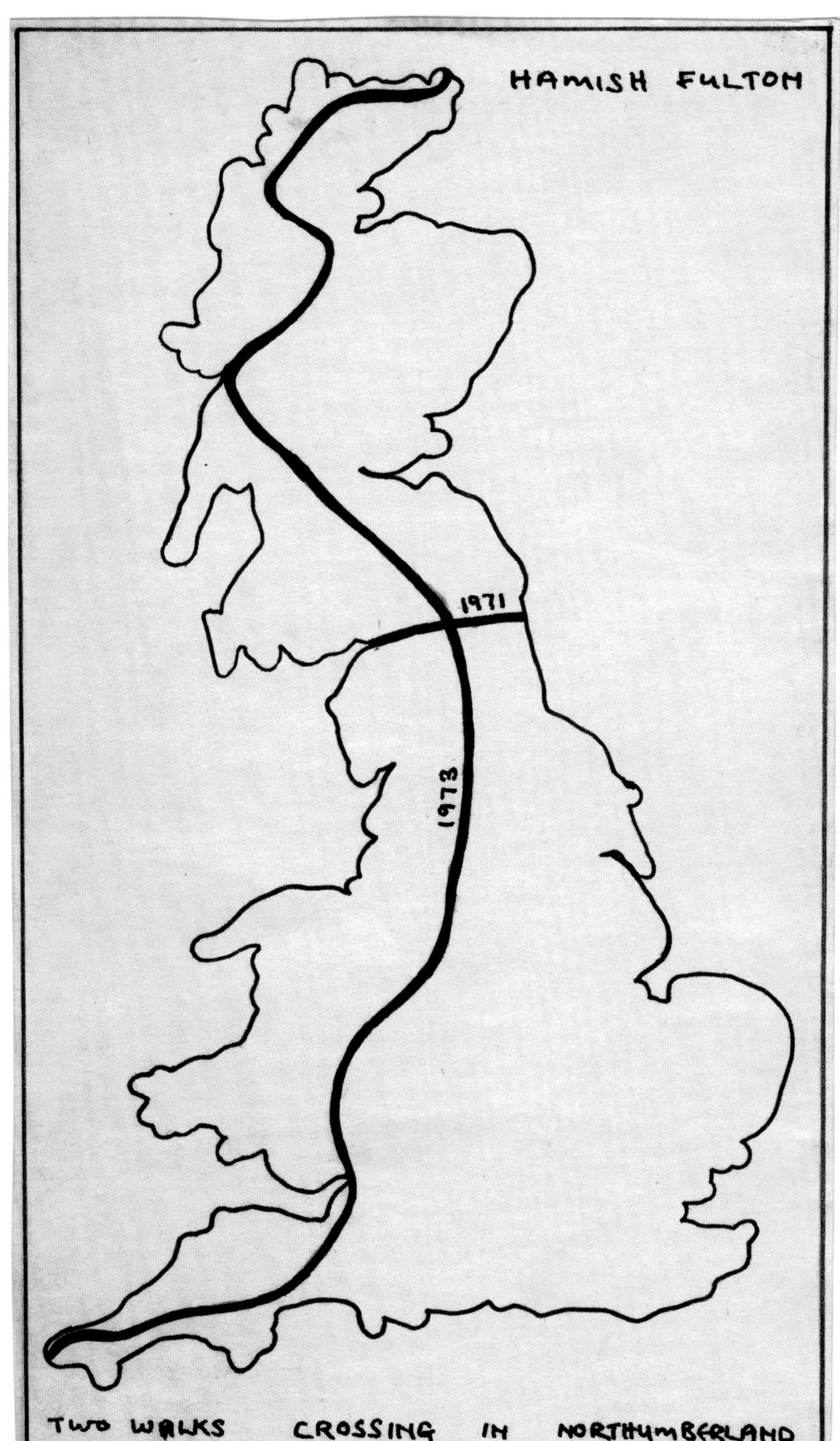
HAMISH FULTON
1971
1973
TWO WALKS CROSSING IN NORTHUMBERLAND

SEVEN ONE DAY WALKS ON COUNTRY ROADS
38 MILES EACH DAY BY THE SAME ROUTE
KENT ENGLAND 25-31 JANUARY 1997.
ON COMPLETION OF THE SEVENTH WALK
ONE IMAGINARY CIRCUIT WAS MADE FROM MEMORY

WALKING 40 MILES EACH DAY ON COUNTRY ROADS
MONDAY TO SUNDAY BY THE SAME ROUTE
THE FIRST SEVEN DAYS OF THE TWELFTH MONTH
KENT ENGLAND 1997

ROAD

ROAD

SEVEN ONE DAY WALKS ON COUNTRY ROADS AND PATHS
OUT AND BACK 44 MILES EACH DAY
MONDAY TO SUNDAY BY THE SAME ROUTE
ENDING ON THE SOLSTICE
KENT ENGLAND 15-21 JUNE 1998

SEVEN ONE DAY WALKS ON COUNTRY ROADS
38 MILES EACH DAY BY THE SAME ROUTE
KENT ENGLAND 8-14 FEBRUARY 1996.
ON COMPLETION OF THE SEVENTH WALK
ONE IMAGINARY CIRCUIT WAS MADE FROM MEMORY

CLOUD 雲
EARTH 地
FLAME 灯
RIVER 川
SNAKE 蛇
OCEAN 海
ROADS 道
A 21 DAY COAST TO COAST WALKING JOURNEY
ON ROADS AND PATHS
STARTING ON THE FIRST DAY OF MAY
FROM THE MOUTH OF THE KAMENO RIVER IN WAKAYAMA
ENDING AT THE MOUTH OF THE MIYA RIVER IN ISE
TRAVELLING BY WAY OF SHIONOMISAKI KUMANOHONGU
SHAKAGATAKE OMINE MIWASAN MOUNT HIEI MIUNE YAMA
KII PENINSULA JAPAN 1996

हिमआलय

HIMA ALAYA

ABODE OF SNOW

A GUIDED
AND SHERPA ASSISTED
CLIMB
TO THE SUMMIT PLATEAU
OF CHO OYU
AT 8175 METRES
VIA THE CLASSIC ROUTE
WITHOUT
SUPPLEMENTARY OXYGEN
TIBET
AUTUMN 2000

PARK

idling resting centres   strolling
benches armchairs portals borders

axes   dreaming   edges   voices
        water mirror pond

green carpet grass carpet
free time and open space

fountains paths webs grottoes
ruins temples
        melancholy mourning
tree and trees   shrubs hedges

shimmer stillness quietude happiness

light and shadow
        you and me

SHADOWS OF THE CITY

Central Europe is the home of the beech forest. Without human cultivation, Central Europe would still be one great, sprawling forest. The canopy forest of beeches is, as the name suggests, a forest genus. It consists of similarly sized trees, which grow at regular intervals and call to mind paragons of architecture. The soil layer is covered almost year round with warm, red-brown foliage. Only in early spring do a few perennials like the anemone make use of the light, warmth and rain to push new shoots up through the thick crown roof. This phase ends before the new beech leaves open. The beech tree's roots are always close to the surface and, in the case of older trees, some are even located above the earth. Standing alone, the flat-rooted trees would be vulnerable to high winds, but the shared crown roof stabilises the entire forest against the threat of wind.

"The order of human things progresses forward, first there were forests, then huts, then villages, later cities and finally, academia." (Giambattista Vico, *The New Science*). This theory is only sustainable from the European perspective. From a desert culture perspective, the focus is the exact opposite: the centre of culture is an oasis, a place defined by the presence of water. Only an estranged nature looks for adventure beyond nature and the cultural tradition. The transforming landscape needs new topoi for modern fairytales. Wildness, once unique to the forest, now lurks in the city. For city dwellers, places exist that are truly dangerous. We have learned to read the signs of this new danger, of criminality. The forest instead has become a place of entertainment; it is the pastoral garden.

The history of landscape architecture in modernist urban planning is multifaceted. Its increasing importance is undisputed. From the *Volkspark* in the city to the idea of the garden city and the large-scale designs in Chandigarh and Brasilia, the relationship between city and landscape is always a central issue. If the concern at first was mainly social, such as the accessibility of public, open space to a broad spectrum of the populace or the concept of cooperative ownership, later the focus was directed more at issues surrounding infrastructure, especially the mass construction of roadway networks for individual traffic or public transport. The transformation of the city, the reconversion of centrally located, industrial wasteland areas, creates valuable, often large, outdoor spaces within the city. This makes a new way of dealing with urban nature possible.

Early English gardens were often developed around existing trees. Existing forests were cleared, or clearings were made in the dense forest, which then were filled with ruins or garden sculptures. On industrial wasteland sites, the work has to be done in the exact opposite way. Here, the ruins, as the history of the site, already exist. Nature is what needs to be reintroduced. What form this will take is the question of the moment. Re-creating wilderness, or designing space according to purely aesthetic premises, is hardly suited to the demands of the site. We may know of some previous examples of such transformation processes, but they are not appropriate for urban space.

This is where the Mediterranean landscape comes in. Its original forests were completely cleared to use the wood for construction, shipbuilding or energy. The soil eroded because it was no longer protected by the forests. Water balance in these areas changed massively. After a long time, new vegetation developed on the poor, dry soil, a sparse park-like forest alternating with bush vegetation, which the tourist now considers attractive and atmospheric. Urban nature needs to become evident again and take a broader view into account. Elementary experiences with nature such as sun, wind and rain have to be a part of this new form of urban nature. Ideas are also needed for the spaces left over after planning different architecture or urban planning areas or for the changed functional demands on existing open space. These new requirements are diverse and the solutions complex because they have to be developed on top of the existing, battered nature. The problem is that we can no longer approach nature in a dialectical manner, by formulating a contrast to it. Nature has to be reinvigorated if we are to understand it at all within the urban structure. *gv*

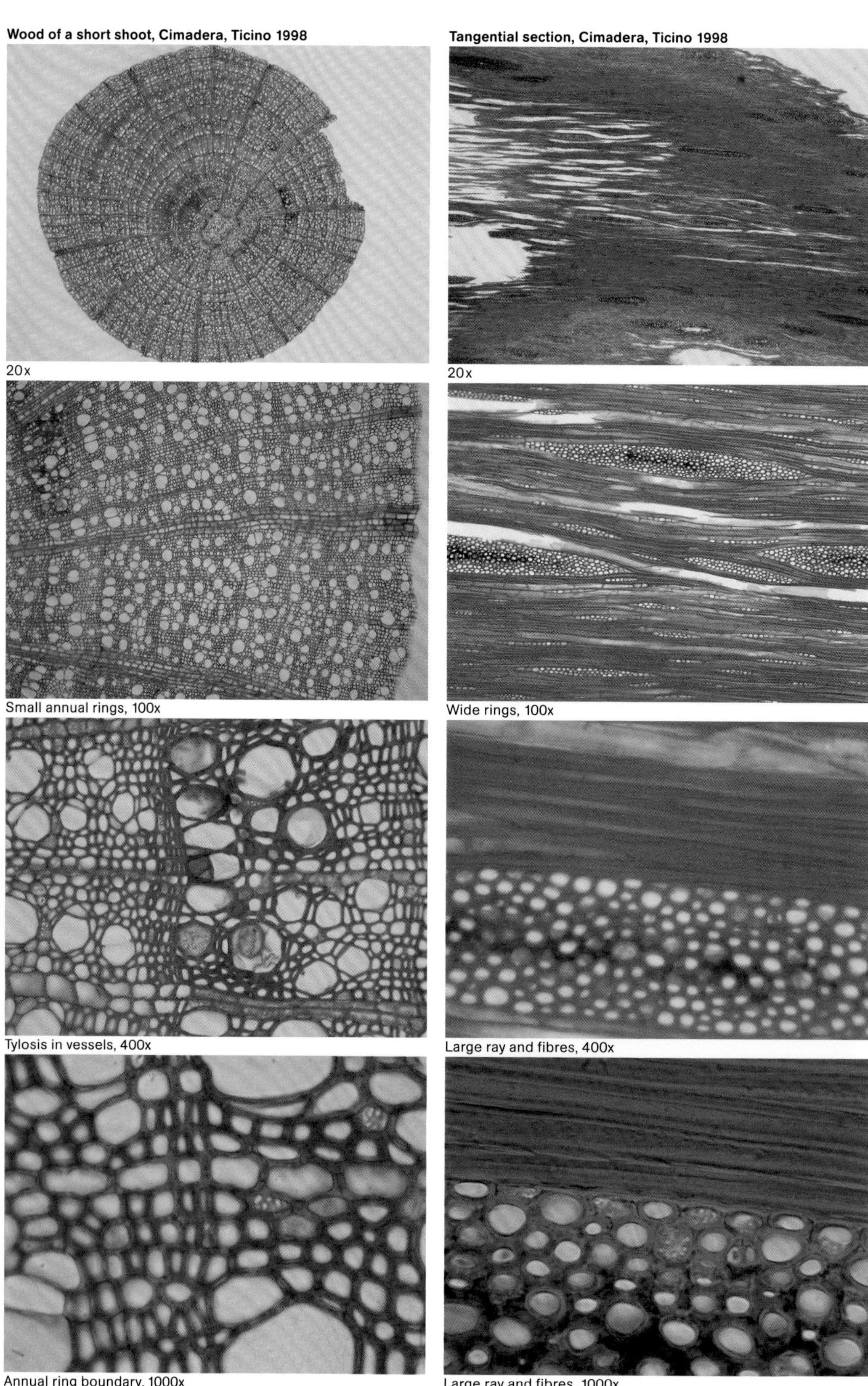

Wood of a short shoot, Cimadera, Ticino 1998

20x

Small annual rings, 100x

Tylosis in vessels, 400x

Annual ring boundary, 1000x

Tangential section, Cimadera, Ticino 1998

20x

Wide rings, 100x

Large ray and fibres, 400x

Large ray and fibres, 1000x

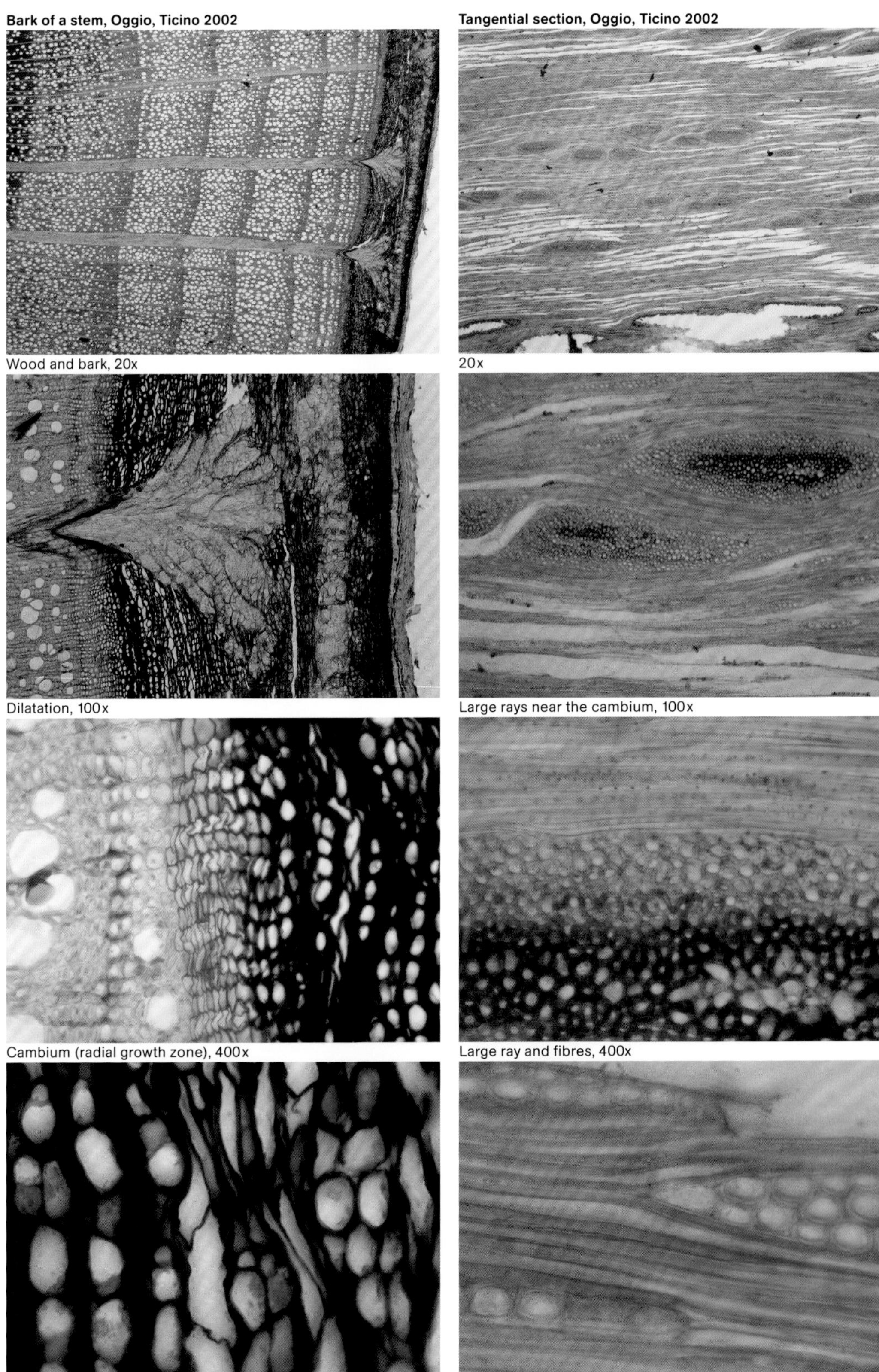

Bark of a stem, Oggio, Ticino 2002

Wood and bark, 20x

Dilatation, 100x

Cambium (radial growth zone), 400x

Uni- and multiseriate rays and fibres, 1000x

Tangential section, Oggio, Ticino 2002

20x

Large rays near the cambium, 100x

Large ray and fibres, 400x

Uni- and multiseriate rays and fibres, 1000x

Radial section, Oggio, Ticino 2002

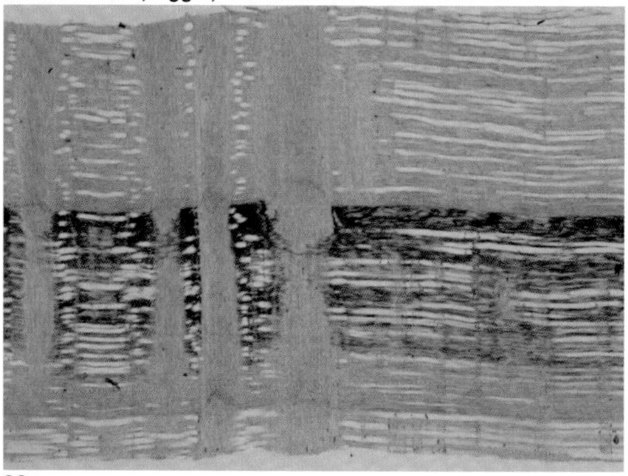

20x

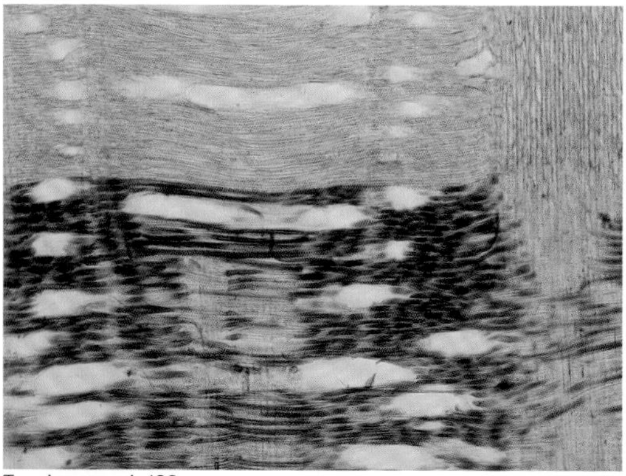

Tension wood, 100xx

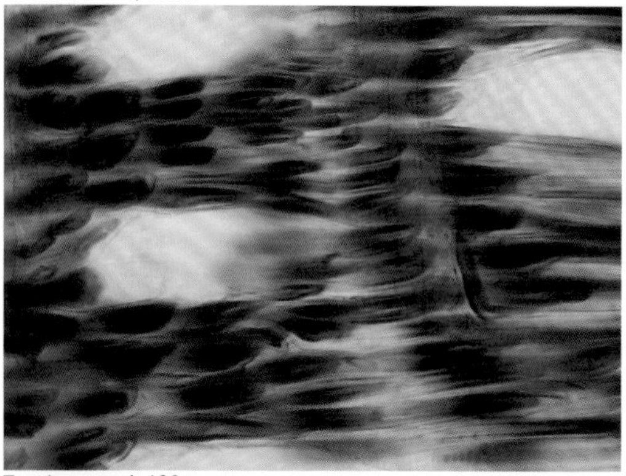

Tension wood, 400x

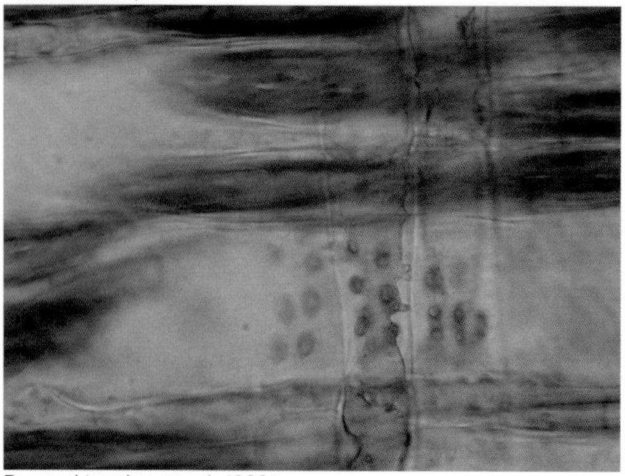

Ray and tension wood, 1000x

Root, Tiersteinberg, Fricktal 2004

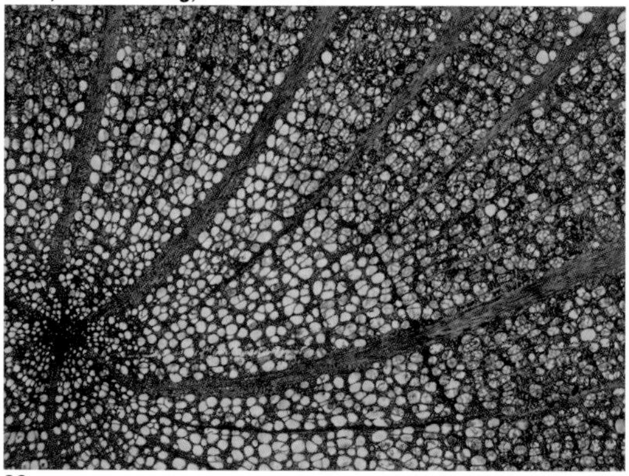

20x

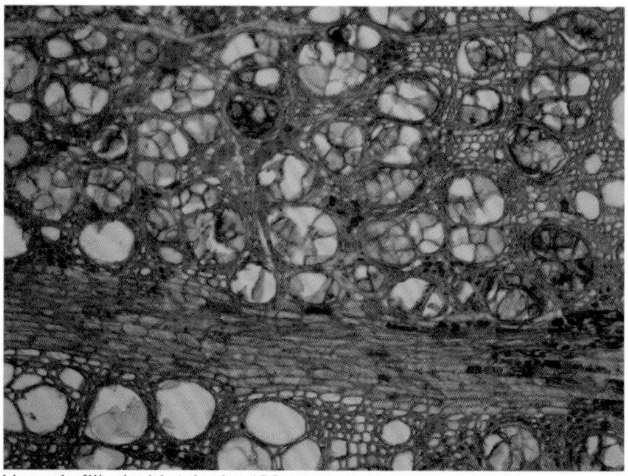

Vessels filled with tylosis, 100x

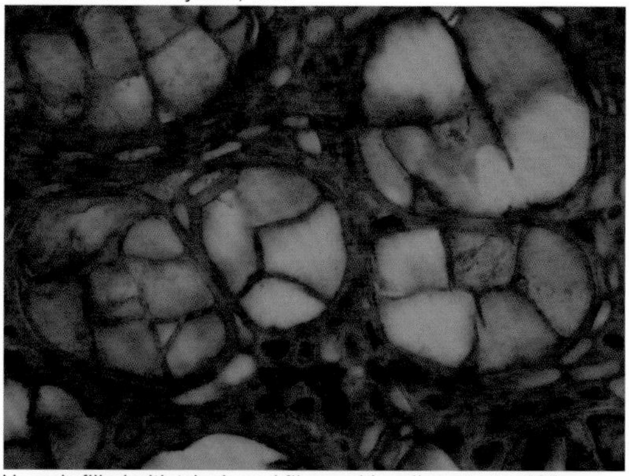

Vessels filled with tylosis and fibres with cell contents, 400x

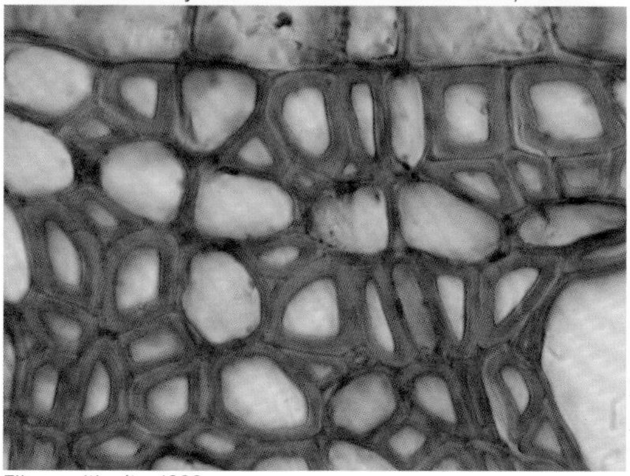

Fibres with pits, 1000x

Root, Tiersteinberg, Fricktal 2004

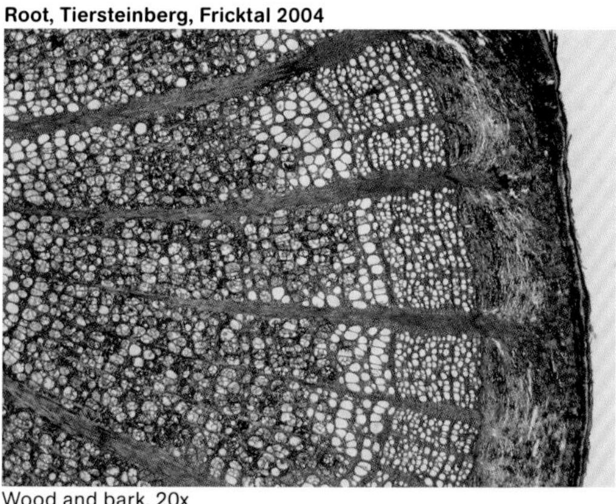
Wood and bark, 20x

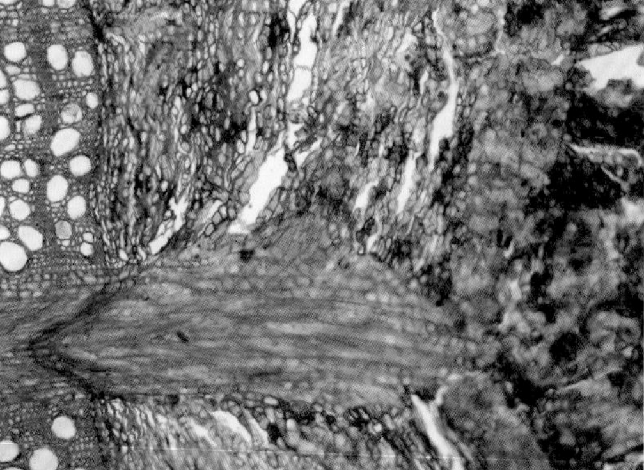
Bark with ray dilatation, 100x

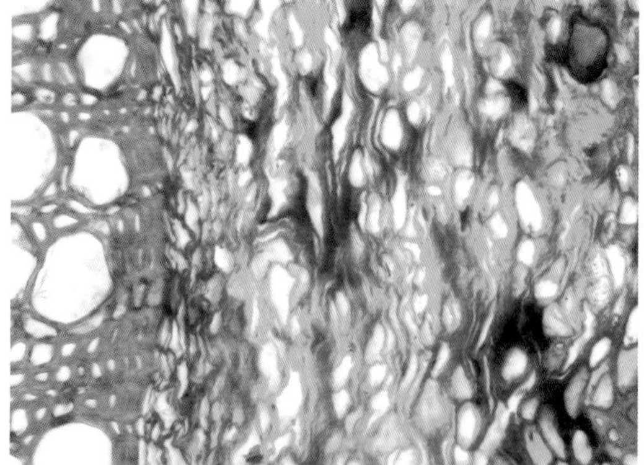
Transition from wood to bark, 400x

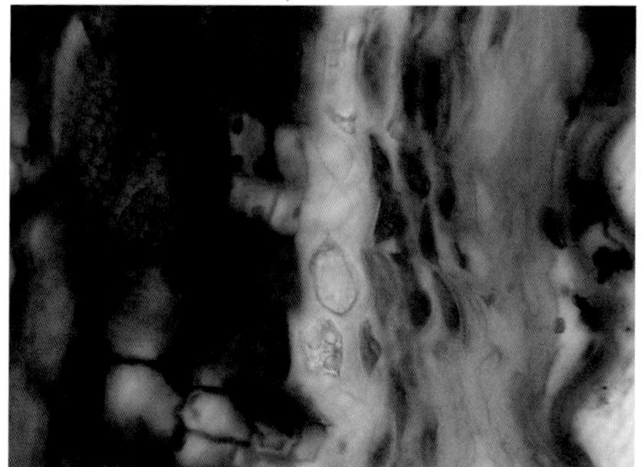
Cork cambium and cork, 1000x

Radial section, wood of a stem, Klosters 2004

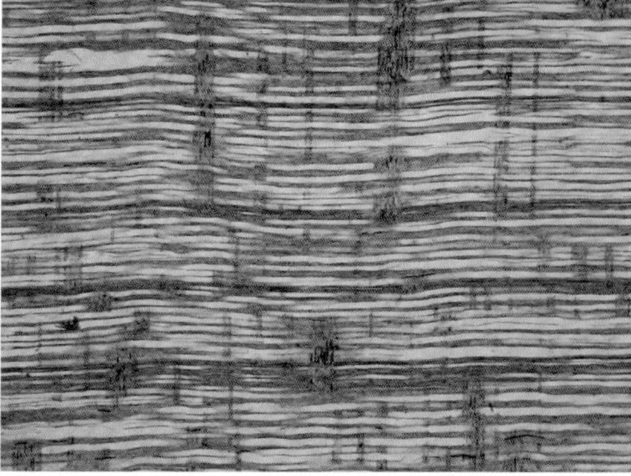
20x

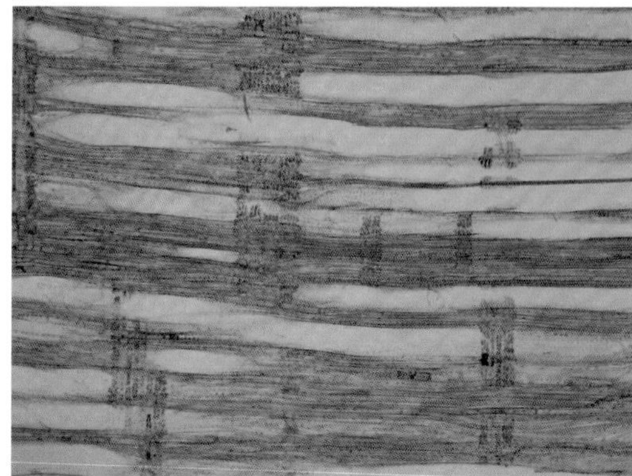
Fibres and rays 100x

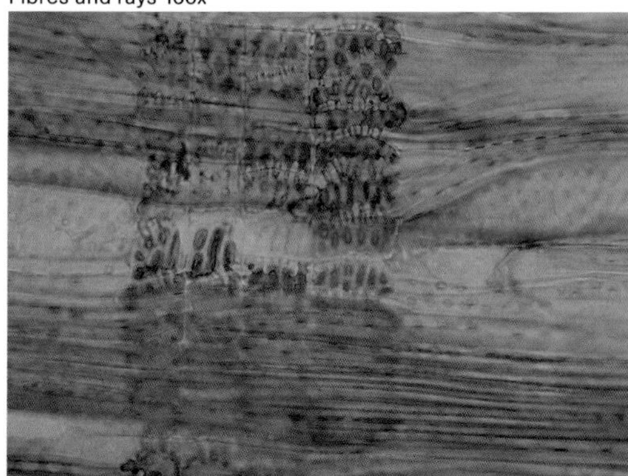
Pits in ray cells, 400x

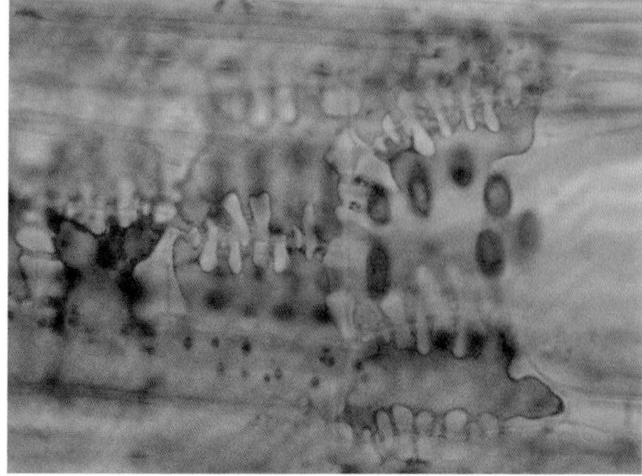
Cell walls and pits in rays, 1000x

HEADQUARTERS OF HELVETIA PATRIA VERSICHERUNGEN, SAINT GALL
MOUNTAINS OF FLOWERS
2001–04

Client: Helvetia Patria Versicherungen, Saint Gall
Architecture: Herzog & de Meuron, Basel
Herbaceous planting: in collaboration with Pit Altwegg
Area: 23,000 m²

View of the surrounding villa gardens on Girtannersberg.

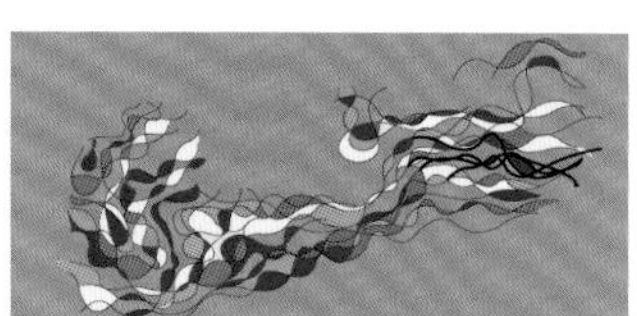

Herbaceous planting, sketch.

The park at the University of Saint Gall.

The head office of Helvetia Patria Versicherungen is located on the Girtannersberg, north-east of Saint Gall's historical old town. The site is immediately adjacent to, on one side, the exposed concrete buildings from the 1960s of the University of Saint Gall and, on the other, a villa district. The existing cruciform building was expanded by adding three slender extensions to its wings. The dark steel construction with full-height windows adjoins directly to the existing concrete parapet wall. The glass of the windows varies in transparency, and the windows appear to have been rotated along one of their four axes at random. These panes reflect the surroundings in a shattered image. The visible world dissolves into a wealth of colours and forms as if seen through a kaleidoscope. This shattered reflection in the windows of the new buildings refracts and multiplies the baroque lushness of the garden.

The point of departure for the reconception of the design of the grounds was the existing features of the site, above all its gently modelled topography. A large area was planted with perennials, both flowering and leafy, to form a coherent ground layer of diverse structure. A total of 193 species and cultivars were planted on an area of 5,000 square metres in accordance with a predetermined system. Only domesticated perennials were used, no wild ones. Only robust species that can tolerate competition were selected. The exterior consists of colourful planes of rigorously composed diversity. It is an utterly overpowering variety of plants that bloom at different times. They were all carefully harmonised and grouped in bands of colour that show off the site in ever-changing ways throughout the year. There are five groups of perennials in the southern part of the garden and four in the north. Each is composed of accent plants and main perennials, of perennials planted over large areas and infill plants that are found in all the bands. Within each group, the perennials were co-ordinated based on colour and when they flower.

The first highlight comes in spring with the bulbs, such as crocuses, narcissi and snowdrops, which are distributed in groups throughout the garden. During the summer months and into autumn, the site is characterised by the forms and colours of the flowers and the structures of the leaves. Asters and black cohosh bloom until late autumn. Small, slow-growing woody plants like hydrangeas, snowy mespilus, box trees and dwarf lilacs form linear structures that follow the contours of the terrain. These bands of shrubs, along with trees in isolation or in groups, reinforce the perception of the typography, particularly in the winter months. Grass paths were planted along these woody bands for maintenance purposes. The existing beeches and oaks, in combination with flowering trees planted in groups, articulate the space of the garden and reinforce its identity. One especially distinguished place is in front of the company restaurant. Pools of water placed in the gravel-covered area and filigree snowy mespilus as extra heavy standard trees, with their snow-white flowers in the spring and their brilliantly red leaves in autumn, lend a special atmosphere to the courtyard. Pools have been integrated into the plants at the northern addition and in front of the southern façades of the southern and eastern additions. A meandering, curved path along the islands of plants makes the site accessible. The paths are illuminated at night.

The character of the exterior grounds oscillates between private and public: the many small plants make it seem like a garden, while the path and the slightly elevated topography with the groups of trees suggest a park. What is in fact a private garden is crossed daily by large numbers of students and passers-by, as if it were a public park. It thus complements the existing park of the university and creates an impressive frame around the office buildings. The transition to the university grounds and the adjacent meadow in the east is integrated into the overall conception of the design and improves the Girtannersberg as a whole.

Herbaceous Planting
The herbaceous planting follows a strict composition. The planted area is divided into different bands, each with one main colour. Each band consists of a different mixture of perennials that are harmonised in their blooming times and colouring. A total of 193 species and cultivars were planted in this designed system on a surface area of 5,000 square metres.

A

0 5 10 20

Diagram: yellow-green with white accents

100 m² (length 25 m, width 4 m)

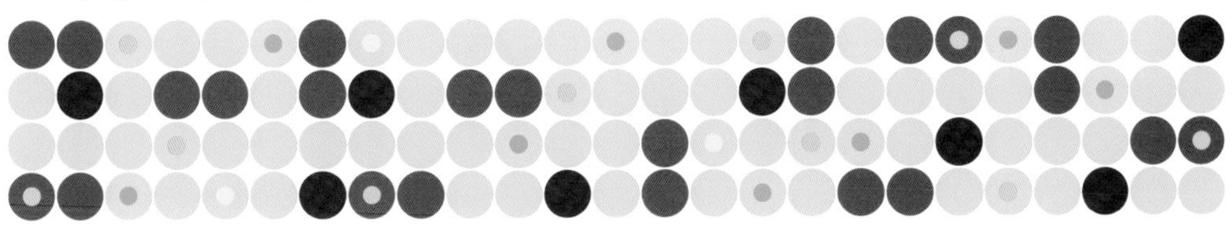

Accent Plants
Darmera peltata
Hosta 'Aphrodite'
Clematis x jouiniana 'Praecox'
Helianthus microcephalus
Deschampsia cespitosa
Carex pendula

Main Perennials
Phygelius capensis 'Yellow Trumpet'
Polystichum aculeatum
Euphorbia cyparissias x virgata 'Betten'
Astilbe Japonica Gruppe 'Deutschland'
Achnatherum calamagrostis

Ground Cover
Asperula tinctoria
Hosta lancifolia 'Stepankova'
Hosta tardina 'Halycon'
Hosta nigrescens 'Krossa Regal'
Euphorbia amygdaloides var. robbiae
Euphorbia cyparissias x virgata 'Betten'
Cardamine trifolia

Bedding Plants
Paeonia mlokosewitschii
Paeonia lactiflora 'Postillon'
Helleborus viridis
Polygonatum commutatum

Bulbs
Scilla sibirica 'Alba'
Anemone blanda 'White Star'
Crocus hybr. 'Mme. Corevan'
Narcissus poeticus
Narcissus pseudonarcissus 'Ice Follies'

Infill Plants
Dentaria pinnata
Corydalis cheilantifolia

Perennial graph: yellow-green with white accent

Blooms, colour view

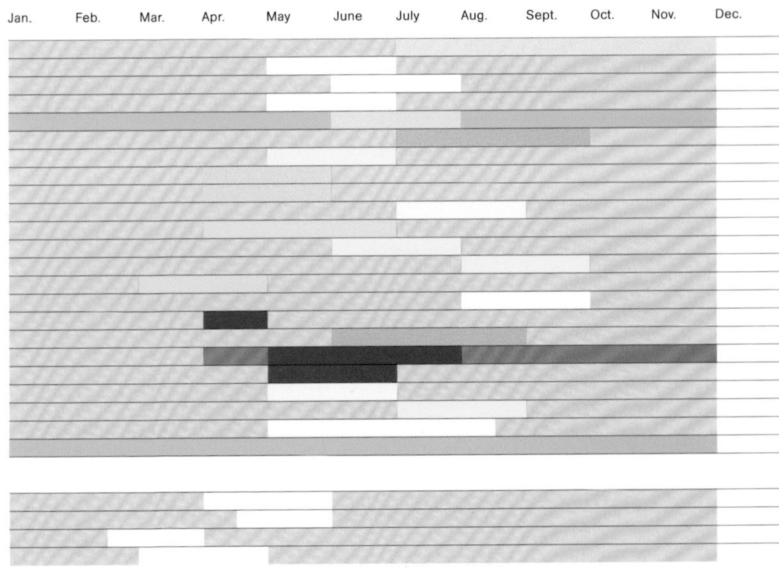

Perennials
Achnatherum calamagrostis
Asperula taurina
Astilbe Japonica Gruppe 'Deutschland'
Cardamine trifolia
Carex pendula
Clematis x jouiniana 'Praecox'
Corydalis cheilanthifolia
Darmera peltata
Dentaria pinnata
Deschampsia cespitosa
Euphorbia amygdaloides var. robbiae
Euphorbia cyparissias x virgata 'Betten'
Helianthus microcephalus
Helleborus viridis
Hosta 'Aphrodite'
Hosta lanciflora 'Stepankova'
Hosta nigrescens 'Krossa Regal'
Hosta tardina 'Halycon'
Paeonia lactiflora 'Otto Froebel'
Paeonia mlokosewitschii
Phygelius capensis 'Yellow Trumpet'
Polygonatum commutatum
Polystichum aculeatum

Bulbs
Anemone blanda 'White Star'
Narcissus poeticus
Narcissus pseudonarcissus 'Ice Follies'
Scilla sibirca 'Alba'

Diagram: blue-orange-yellow with white accents

100 m² (length 25 m, width 4 m)

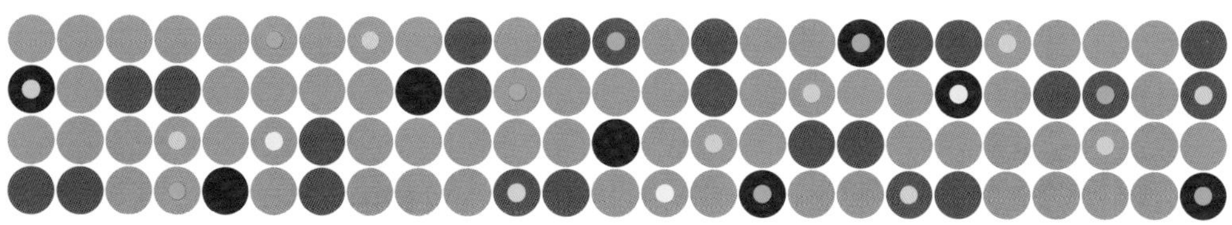

Accent Plants
Campanula latifolia var. macrantha
Euphorbia griffithii 'Fireglow'
Hemerocallis Hybride 'Franz Hals'
Aconitum carmichaelii 'Arendsii'
Clematis heracleifolia 'Wyevale'
Molinia arundinacea 'Windspiel'

Main Perennials
Helenium 'Moerheim Beauty'
Phygelius capensis 'Coccineus'
Aster ericoides 'Little Carlow'
Aster pyrenaeus 'Lutetia'
Aster amellus 'Sternkugel'
Anemone hybr. 'Honorine Jobert'

Ground Cover
Asperula taurina
Buglossoides purpureocaeruleum
Geranium himalayense 'Gravetye'
Geranium ibericum 'Rosemoor'
Omphalodes verna
Lilium umbellatum 'Erectum'

Bedding Plants
Paeonia lactiflora 'Coral Charm'
Paeonia lactiflora 'Postillon'
Helleborus viridis
Paeonia lactiflora 'Chocolat Soldier'

Bulbs
Arum italicum
Arum maculatum
Crocus chrysanthus
Crocus tommasinianus
Crocosmia 'Mars'
Crocosmia x crocosmiiflora
Crocosmia masoniorum 'Lucifer'

Infill Plants
Corydalis cheilantifolia
Dentaria pinnata
Peltraria alliacea

Perennial graph: blue-orange-yellow with white accent

Blooms, colour view

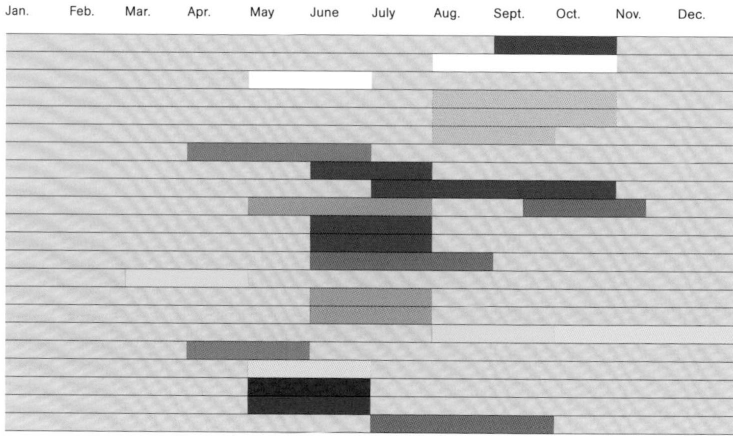

Perennials
Aconitum carmichaelii 'Arendsii'
Anemone hybr. 'Honorine Jobert'
Asperula taurina
Aster amellus 'Sternkugel'
Aster ericoides 'Little Carlow'
Aster pyrenaeus 'Lutetia'
Buglossoides purpureocaeruleum
Campanula latifolia var. macrantha
Clematis heracleifolia 'Wyevale'
Euphorbia griffithii 'Fireglow'
Geranium himalayense 'Gravetye'
Geranium ibericum 'Rosemoore'
Helenium 'Moerheim Beauty'
Helleborus viridis
Hemerocallis Hybride 'Franz Hals'
Lilium umbellatum 'Erectum'
Molinia arundinacea 'Windspiel'
Omphalodes verna
Paeonia 'Coral Charm'
Paeonia lactiflora 'Chocolat Soldier'
Paeonia lactiflora 'Otto Froebel'
Phygelius capensis 'Coccineus'

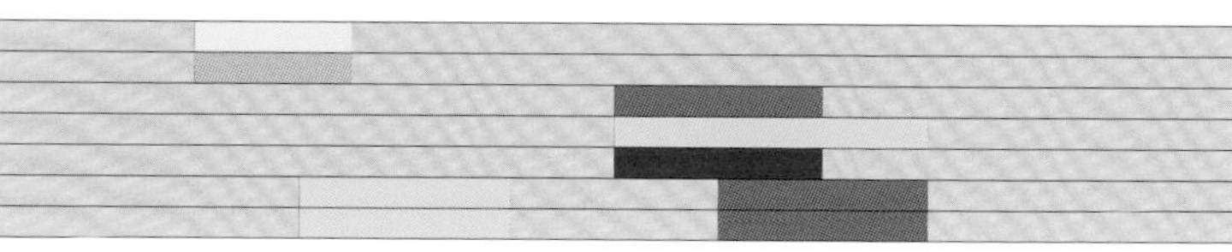

Bulbs
Crocus chrysanthus
Crocus tommasinianus
Crocosmia 'Mars'
Crocosmia x crocosmiiflora
Crocosmia masoniorum 'Lucifer'
Arum italicum
Arum maculatum

Diagram: blue-yellow with white accents

100 m^2 (length 25 m, width 4 m)

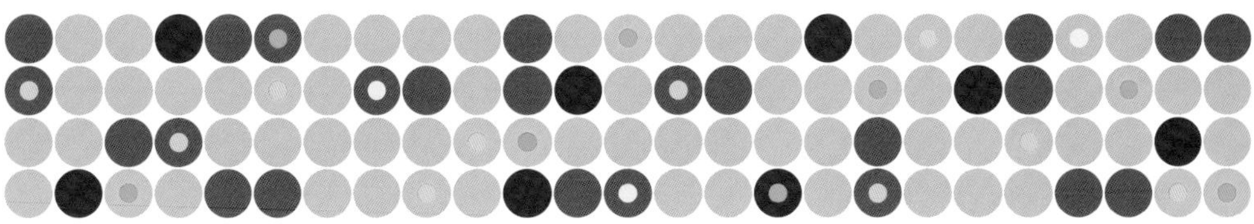

Accent Plants
Clematis heracleifolia 'Wyevale'
Helianthus microcephalus
Molinia altissima 'Transparent'
Aconitum carmichaelii 'Arendsii'

Main Perennials
Solidago virgaurea
Coreopsis verticillata 'Moonbeam'
Buphthalum salicifolium
Aster pyrenaeus 'Lutetia'
Aster ericoides 'Little Carlow'
Scutellaria altissima
Veronicastrum virginicum 'Alba'

Ground Cover
Epimedium perralderianum 'Fronleiten'
Cynoglossum nervosum
Euphorbia amygdaloides var. robbiae
Asperula taurina
Omphalodes verna
Alchemilla mollis
Amsonia orientalis

Bedding Plants
Paeonia lactiflora 'Angelika Kaufmann'
Paeonia lactiflora 'Red Charm'
Helleborus viridis
Paeonia lactiflora 'Ruth Clay'
Paeonia mlokosewitschii
Lunaria rediviva

Bulbs
Crocus chrysanthus
Crocus sieberii 'Fire Fly'
Crocus speciosus
Eranthis hyemalis
Anemone blanda 'Blue Shade'

Infill Plants
Corydalis lutea

Perennial graph: blue-yellow with white accent

Blooms, colour view

Jan. Feb. Mar. Apr. May June July Aug. Sept. Oct. Nov. Dec.

Perennials
Aconitum carmichaelii 'Arendsii'
Alchemilla mollis
Amsonia orientalis
Asperula taurina
Aster ericoides 'Little Carlow'
Aster pyrenaeus 'Lutetia'
Buphthalum salicifolium
Clematis heracleifolia 'Wyevale'
Coreopsis verticillata 'Moonbeam'
Corydalis lutea
Cynoglossum nervosum
Epimedium perralderianum 'Fronleiten'
Euphorbia amygdaloides var. robbiae
Helianthus microcephalus
Helleborus viridis
Lunaria rediviva
Molinia altissima 'Transparent'
Omphalodes verna
Paeonia lactiflora 'Angelika Kaufmann'
Paeonia lactiflora 'Red Charm'
Paeonia lactiflora 'Ruth Clay'
Paeonia mlokosewitschii
Scutellaria altissima
Solidago virgaurea
Veronicastrum virginicum 'Alba'

Bulbs
Anemone blanda 'Blue Shade'
Crocos speciosus
Crocus chrysanthus
Crocus sieberii 'Fire Fly'
Eranthis hyemalis

HOME OF FIFA, ZURICH
THE GAME OF CONTINENTS
2003–06

Client: International Football Association Fifa (Fédération Internationale de Football Association), Zurich
Architecture: Tilla Theus und Partner, Zurich
Tree sculptures: Bertjan Douma, Toni Eberle
Area: 40,000 m²

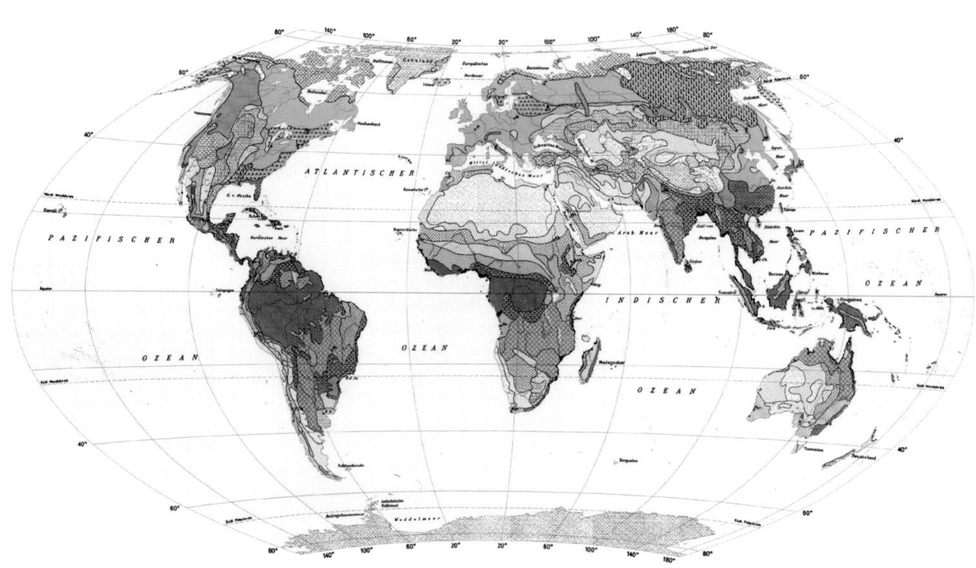

World Vegetation Zones

- Tropical rain forest
- Mangrove
- Tropical mountain forest
- Tropical semideciduous rain forest and monsoon rain forest
- Temperate rain forest
- Mountain coniferous forest
- Evergreen boreal coniferous forest
- Laurel forest and subtropical rain forest
- Sclerophyllous vegetation
- Coniferous dry woodlands and xeromorphe vegetation
- Thorn tree and succulent forest
- Tropical dry forest and campos cerrados
- Summer-green deciduous forest
- Summer-green deciduous forest with conifers
- Summer-green tree steppe
- Summer-green conifer forest
- Thorn shrubs and succulent formations
- Moist savannah
- Dry savannah
- Thorn savannah
- Black earth and temporary steppe
- Subpolar heathland and deciduous shrubs
- Dry steppe and hartpolster formations
- Paramo heathland and moist puna
- Mountain vegetation above tree level
- Tundra
- Subantarctic heathland
- Semiarid desert
- Dry desert
- Cold desert

The international football association, Fifa, is establishing its headquarters in Zürichberg, on the outskirts of Zurich. This will finally centralise all of its departments on one site. Besides the general organisational and administrative tasks taken on by a staff of 300, events with international appeal will take place here in the future. It will also determine the host countries for the World Cup and locations for important football games that will be attended by important dignitaries, VIPs and the media. In addition to the office building, there will also be a training centre with the necessary sports facilities for trainers and referees.

The diverse representational and organisational functions demanded of the site require a varied landscape concept. A park-like environment is planned, which will integrate all the functions and also create an appropriate setting for the international football association. The park is integrated into the landscape surrounding the building and offers public and private places for meetings between two people or more, as well as more secluded places in the park.

The existing chestnut lined avenue will be integrated into the concept and become a prestigious entrance to the building. The street leads to a large staircase in front of the main entrance, where individual guests or groups can be suitably received. To the east of the building, the functionally clear, structured sport and movement area leads into the corresponding four training areas and their infrastructure. The large open playing fields here convey a feeling of expanse and make a strong contrast to the park landscape.

The main element of the concept is a park-like landscape to the south and west of the building, with alternating areas of dense forest vegetation, open clearings, and lawns. This landscape is accessible by means of a meandering pathway that winds through the different forms of vegetation and offers varying views of the park and surrounding environment. The selection of vegetation is a response to the spatial context. Embedded between Zürichberg, Adlisberg and the zoo, with its Masoala Rain Forest Hall, the park landscape creates a bridge between indigenous and exotic vegetation, but also reflects the activities of Fifa as an international governing body and organiser of worldwide sport events on five continents.

The vegetation concept is continued in the landscaped, but closed, courtyard. It resembles a moist, mossy clearing in a North American cloud forest, and offers the employees a year-round attractive view.

A Special Place for Everyone
The diverse park landscape offers widely varied public and private spaces – on the edge of the footpath, enhanced by a view of the park and surrounding environment, or hidden by a group of trees. The deliberate design and its arrangement in selected places in the park create specific ambiences in the different areas. The number and form of the benches and chairs, and the directions they face, creates an immediate effect on their functional character, ranging from secluded refuge areas to social meeting places.

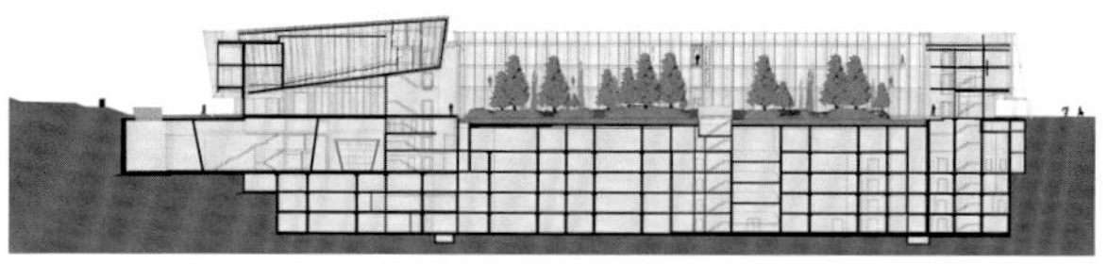

A

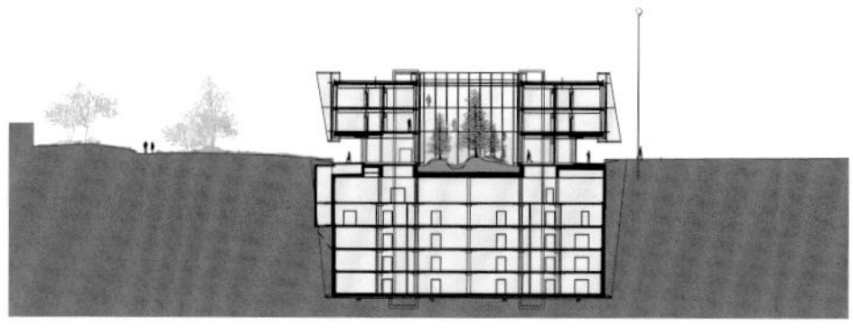

B

0 10 20 40

Course of the Year

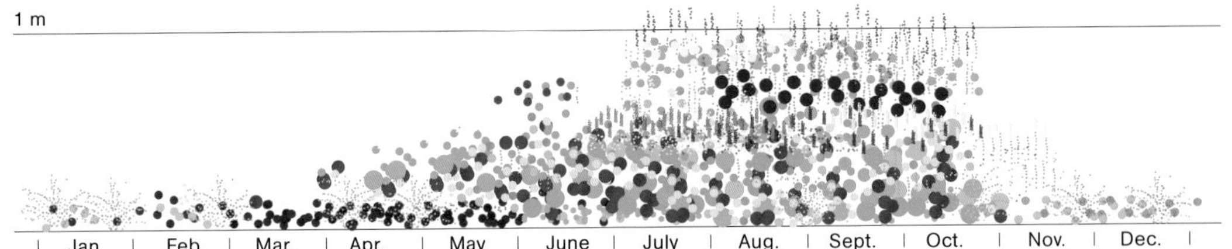

Africa: Savannah
The landscape is distinguished by wide-open spaces and low-growing vegetation. Large solitaire trees and small groups of trees with broad, umbrella-like overhanging crowns create islands of shade. Brightly coloured perennials with varying leaf forms along the periphery display the rich variety of African vegetation.

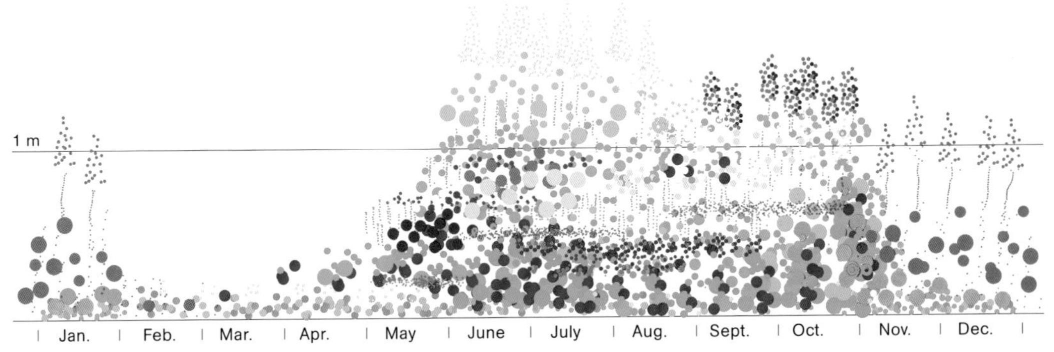

Asia: Flowering Grove
Sparse, terraced groves create a diverse landscape with alternating clearings and shady areas. An umbrella of large trees with delicate, light-coloured leaves spans loosely arranged groups of small trees with white, pink and violet blossoms. Large-leafed perennials with delicate blossoms pick up on the soft tones of the flowering trees. In autumn, the intense red of the Japanese oak trees provides a colourful accent.

Course of the Year

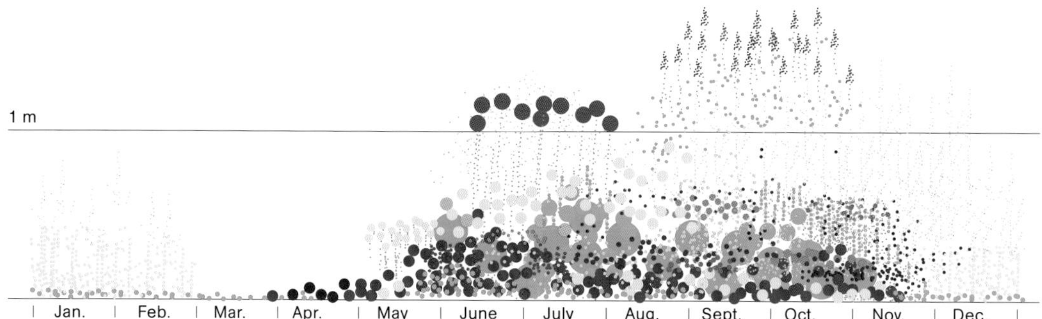

Australia: Bushland
Sturdy groups of trees with bushy undergrowth stand in a landscape of tall grass. Grey-silver leaves evoke eucalyptus forests. Mainly blue- and violet-blooming perennials and spring-flowering plants emphasise the landscape's colourful theme. The tall grass conveys the image of the bush landscape far into winter.

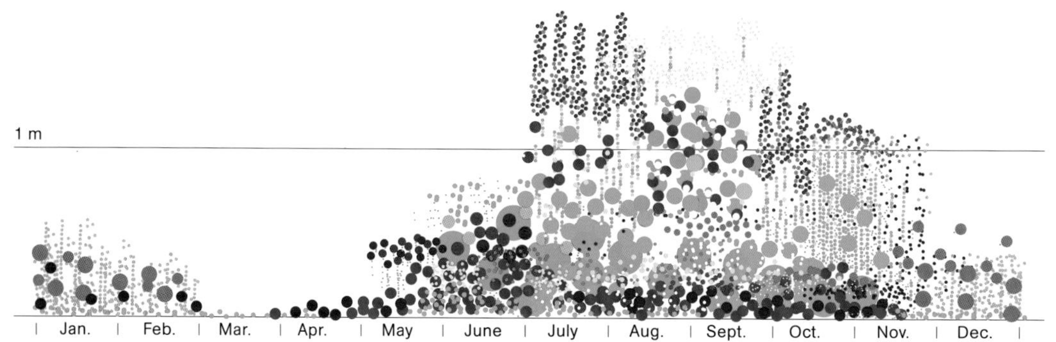

Europe: Indigenous Forest Edge
The vertically staggered forest edge, consisting of shrubs and small trees, extends the adjoining forest into the Fifa grounds. Removing the existing visual border integrates the area into the landscape. The indigenous deciduous and conifer blossoms, fruit and foliage showcase the colour and diversity of European forests. Alternating blossoming carpets of perennials encroach into the adjoining forest and emphasise the interweaving between different areas.

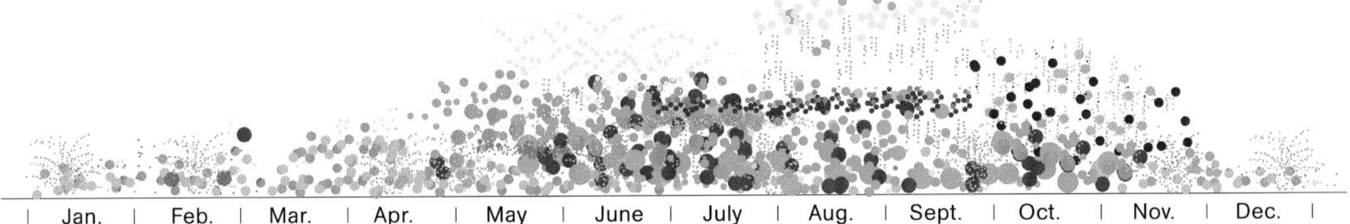

North America: Cloud Forest
Swamp cypress trees looming upward with their delicate foliage create an open grove of conifer trees. Using solitaire trees of different ages illustrates the dynamic of the vegetation. The cement sculptures of dead trees integrated into the design refer to an image of an earlier landscape and are a reminder of the former imposing height of the forest trees. The ground's strong relief is covered by dense, evergreen fern and moss. The red of the foliage is a bright colourful accent in autumn, and when the autumn leaves fall, they create a red carpet on the earth. The meandering path of dark brown lava gravel is lined with large blocks of lava.

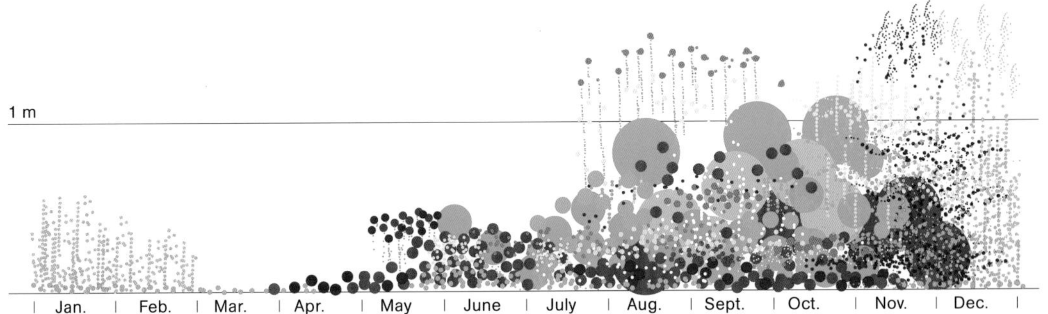

South America: Mountain Forest
This raw landscape is characterised by individual or small groups of bizarrely shaped deciduous and conifer woods. On the ground, the alternation of flat grasses and small bushes, as well as large-leaved perennials and their blossoms and fruit, emphasises the diverse character of the landscape, which encompasses the robust and the exotic.

Tree Sculptures
There are eight sculptures in the shapes of dead trees in the inner courtyard. They loom upward, like deadwood covered by lava, reaching four to seven metres above the moss and fern carpet. They are constructed from armature steel and steel netting, covered with several layers of shotcrete. The surface is treated, finely modelled and stained. The bases of the trees have an average diameter of 150 cm, and the tops are 50 to 100 cm in diameter. Each sculpture weighs up to 13.5 tonnes.

ELISABETHENANLAGE, BASEL
CHRONICLE OF THE TREES
2001–07

Client: Baudepartement des Kantons Basel-Stadt
Architecture: Christ & Gantenbein, Basel
Art: Erik Steinbrecher
Area: 20,000 m^2

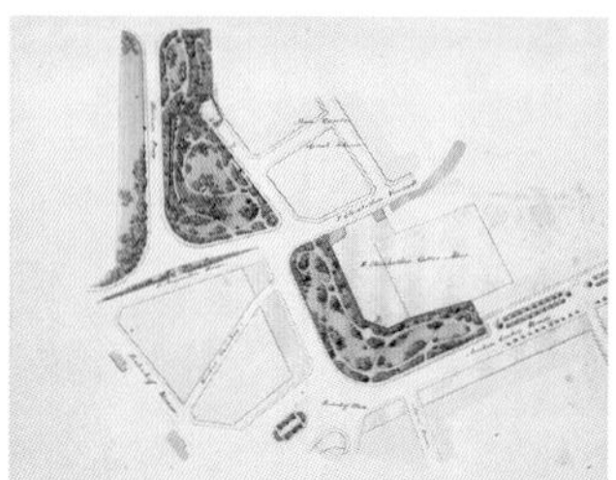

Partial map of Basel, Carl Effner, May 1860.

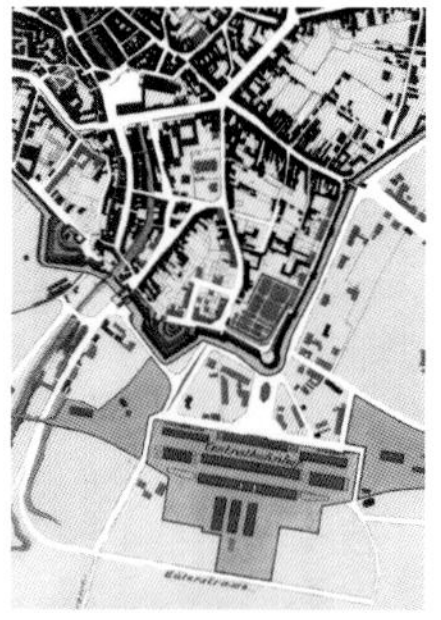

Urban development plan of Basel (1852–62). Stadelmann, 1883.

The system of green spaces in the city of Basel.

Aerial view of Basel, Louis Jules Arnout, colour lithograph, 1865/68.

The Elisabethenanlage emerged over a centuries-long process of constant design and structural changes. This area, which was not originally part of the city, was once planted with grapevines. After 1815 it was the site of a cemetery, known as the Elisabethengottesacker. That fact is still evident today, not only from the surviving maps and drawings, but also from the many valuable trees on the site. When the municipal moat was filled in and the city's fortifications were demolished in 1860, extensive green spaces resulted: a landscape garden with a system of paths that dated back to the former cemetery and an axially geometric garden with a lawn parterre and a music pavilion opposite the De Wette schoolhouse. Profound changes were also wrought by the central train station that was opened at the same time in the immediate area of the Elisabethenanlage, where the Swiss and French railway stations are located today. The outer sections of the park were repeatedly trimmed to make room for streets, trams and pedestrian walkways, gradually reducing the original green space.

In the minds of residents of Basel and guests from elsewhere, the Elisabethenanlage no longer has an independent identity, even though it certainly deserves one, given its prominent location at the train station. In its present state, it is something of a hybrid of park and public square. The ratio of paths to grassy areas is not well balanced. Although the fragments and their own formal idiom are still recognisable, they have been obscured by the accumulation of historical layers and the arbitrary interconnections between them. The competition for a project for the Elisabethenanlage, announced in 2001, was intended to find a remedy and make the site more valuable and significant as a city park.

The valuable existing trees, some of which are protected by law form the central element of this green space. It is a diverse collection of rare species from the northern hemisphere, scattered on the site. This arboretum is being improved and reinforced by new plantings. The plan is to span the park with a sparse roof, a network of diverse leaf textures, using nuances of colour to produce a hall-like space. The texture of the soil is brought out by clearing the shrubbery. The topographical structure is exposed and traced with a slightly modelled lawn that acts as a continuous floor for the park. The existing bulbs are spread across the entire lawn, producing a luxuriant, if brief, spring event.

Four architectural elements already mark important places within the Elisabethenanlage. The redesign is intended to integrate them more strongly. The Strassburger Denkmal (Strasbourg memorial) is still the fulcrum between the park and the square in front of the main train station. The axially geometric garden and its music pavilion are enlivened by the modelling of the lawn parterre. The former Abdankungskapelle (funeral chapel) is being converted to a café-bar and connected to the park via the square in front of it. A new fountain is planned there.

The system of paths is being rethought, with the current excess of paths being reduced to a sensible number. Critical factors in this planning were, on the one hand, a desire to connect the main paths through the park and, on the other, an effort to make the park a more pleasant place to spend time in. The form of the paths is based on the style of the landscape garden, which is characterised by flowing transitions and widening of paths to form plaza-like areas in special locations.

The lighting planned for the park is based on a regular distribution of points of light across the entire are. Suspended lamps, attached to a network of steel cables at the height of the treetops, provide light throughout the park and provide a sense of security in this urban space. The lights are set at two different intensities, so that the main paths are particularly well lit, while the grassy areas are less bright.

The garden within the garden: specified locations will have two plant exhibitions as artistic, object-like interventions by Erik Steinbrecher. Two fenced-in areas will have luxuriantly planted gardens in which unusual species of maples and oaks will be presented in condensed form.

Existing Trees
New Plantings

Acer buergerianum
Acer campestre
Acer capillipes
Acer cappadocicum
Acer davidii
Acer ginnala
Acer monspessulanum
Acer opalus
Acer palmatum
Acer platanoides
Acer pseudoplat. 'Rotterdam'
Acer pseudoplatanus
Acer rufinerve
Acer saccharinum
Acer saccharum 'Schneckii'
Aesculus carnea
Aesculus flava
Aesculus hippo. 'Baumannii'
Aesculus hippocastanum
Aesculus pavia
Ailanthus altissima
Alnus cordata
Celtis australis
Celtis occidentalis
Cornus florida
Cornus nutallii
Corylus colurna
Davidia involucrata
Fagus orientalis
Fagus sylvatica 'Riversii'
Fraxinus americana
Fraxinus angustifolia
Fraxinus pennsylvanica
Gleditsia triacanthos
Gleditsia triacanthos
Gymnocladus dioicus
Ilex aquifolium
Maackia amurensis
Magnolia kobus
Ostrya carpinifolia
Ostrya carpinifolia
Paulownia tomentosa
Phellodendron amurense
Platanus acerifolia
Prunus avium
Prunus sargentii
Quercus cerris
Quercus coccinea
Quercus frainetto
Quercus pubescens
Quercus rubra
Quercus x bebbiana
Taxus baccata
Sophora japonica
Styrax obassia
Tilia cordata
Tilia henryana
Tilia mongolica
Tilia tomentosa
Tilia tomentosa 'Petiolaris'
Ulmus minor
Zelkova serrata

A

B

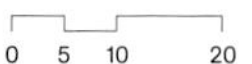

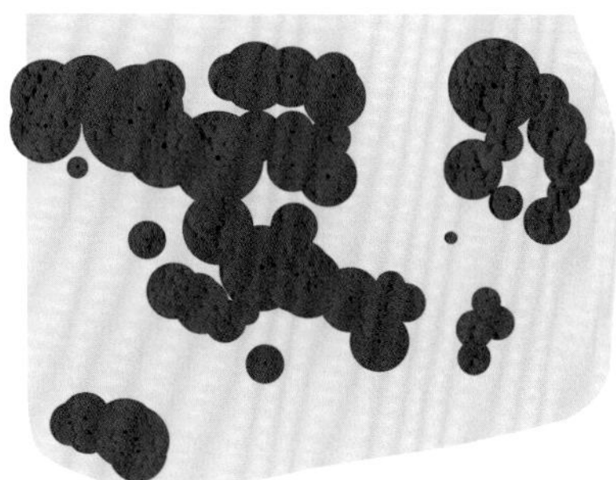
Tree population

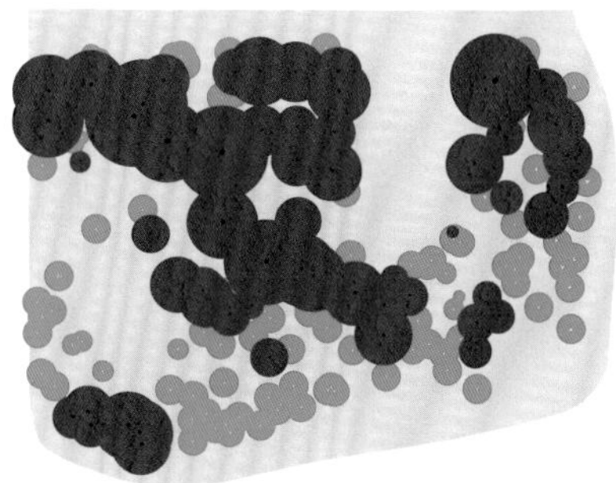
New tree population

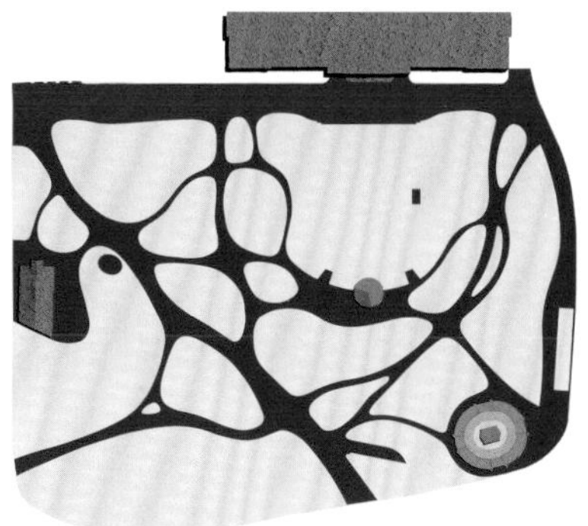
Pathways

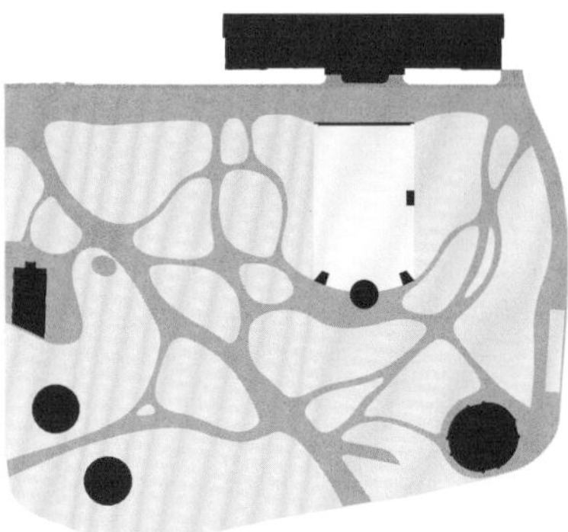
Fixtures

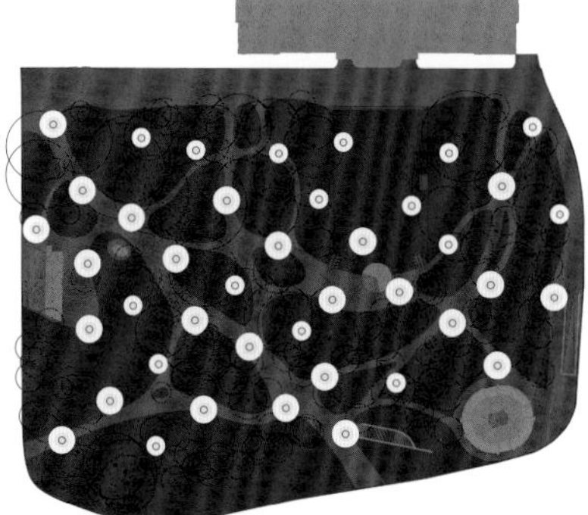
Lighting

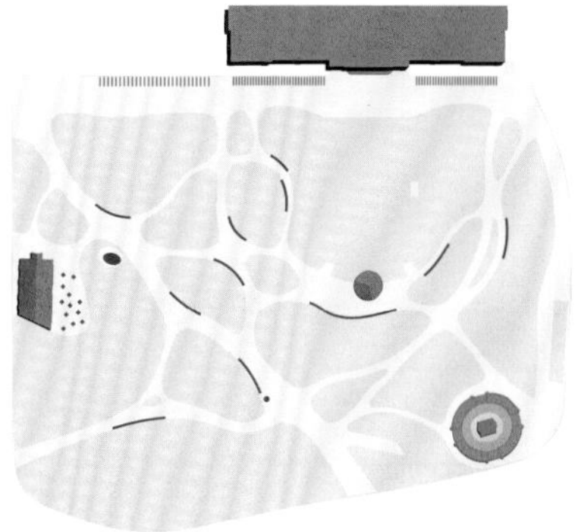
Furnishings

JUSTIZZENTRUM AACHEN
ESTABLISHED EXPANSE –
ACCESSIBLE RESTRICTION
2001–07

Client: Bau- und Liegenschaftsbetrieb NRW
Architecture: Weinmiller Architekten, Berlin
Area: 33,500 m^2

The former correctional facility.

A new Justizzentrum (Hall of Justice) is being constructed on the grounds of the former correctional facility in Aachen. Housing the state, district, administrative, labour and social welfare courts, as well as the Aachen public prosecutor's office, it will bring together six judicial authorities under the roof of a single complex for the first time in North Rhine-Westphalia. In addition to various standard and high-security courtrooms, the centre also features centralised facilities such as conference rooms, a library, an archive and a cafeteria, which will be shared by all the authorities. There will also be a public park surrounding the buildings.

Within the framework of the new construction, some of the old buildings will be demolished. The only old buildings to be preserved will be the state and district courthouses and the old facility's renovated gatehouse. The objective of the new site is not only to bring the judicial authorities together and reap the resulting advantages with respect to internal processes. Along with the construction of the new Justizzentrum Aachen, the entire area will also be redeveloped and enhanced.

The juxtaposition of clearly delimited courtyards and an open park landscape represents the guiding parameter for the design of the Justizzentrum Aachen's surroundings. It constitutes a field of tension, which encompasses the building complex and the administration of justice therein, which oscillates between sealed off space and space open to the public at all times.

Five private courtyards are being constructed, some of them inaccessible, which vary greatly in function and position. They range from the open entrance court to introverted courtyards that can be seen but not entered. The unifying design element of the courtyards is the phenomenon of water in its various forms, as standing groundwater, the watering of plants, and the revealing of the infiltration process.

By contrast, topography and vegetation are the formative and therefore the central elements of the park. Lawn sculptures echo the forms of the buildings and create clear borders. The animated topography creates a series of disparate spaces with different qualities and defines a varied exterior space. As in the English landscape garden, individual trees and groups of trees are scattered and distributed in various densities. Picturesque groves "zone" the park atmospherically and establish lines of sight that direct the visitor's gaze, affording atmospheric views inward and outward. Different species of trees are planted, and their varied appearance lends focus to individual settings and constantly evokes new moods as the seasons change. A dense row of trees along the edge of the area acts as a filter to close off the park against the neighbouring private lots and screens the private gardens from view.

The visitor explores the park along a network of meandering paths. Like waterways, these paths chart their own course through the landscape, sometimes cutting deeply into the terrain and sometimes flowing across it superficially. This flowing modulation takes up the courtyards' focus on water and incorporates that focus into the larger context by linking the design of the courtyards with that of the park.

Design Concept
Inspired by the old building's structure and the site, the idea for the design of the courtyard and park was developed using sketches and models.

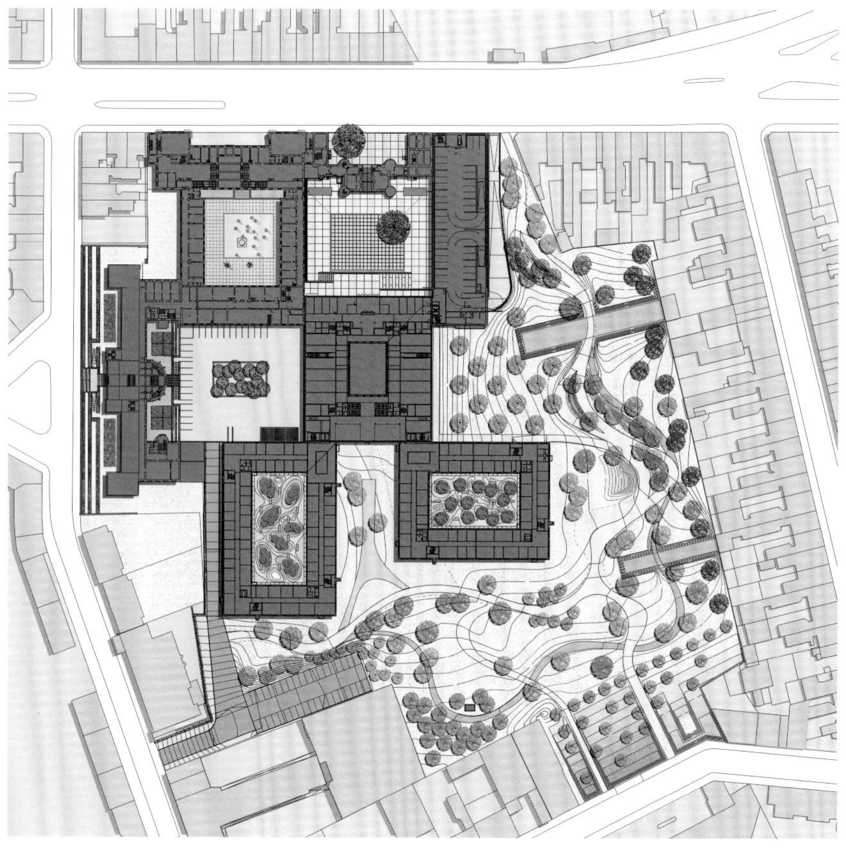

Mosaik-Belag
Sockel

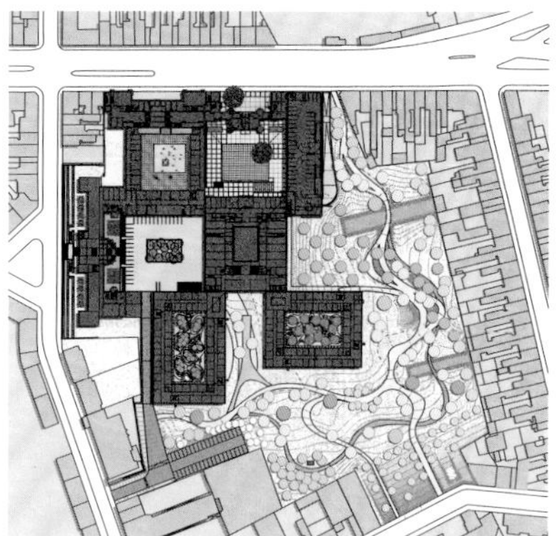

Spring

Summer

Tree grove

Tree filter

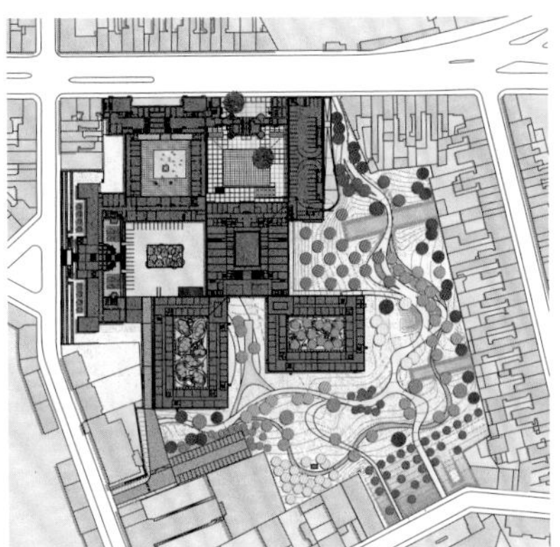

Autumn

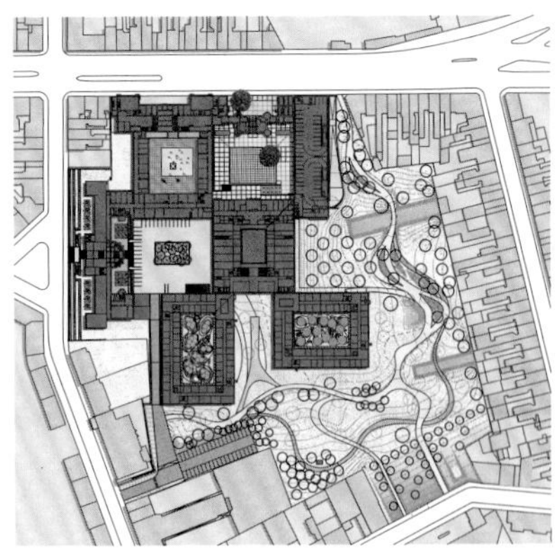

Winter

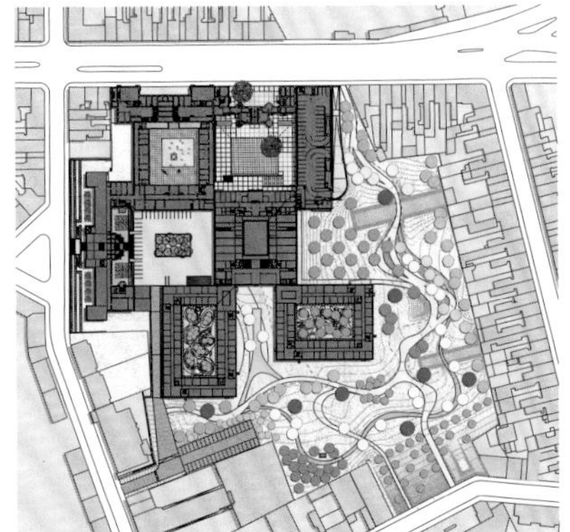

Solitaire trees

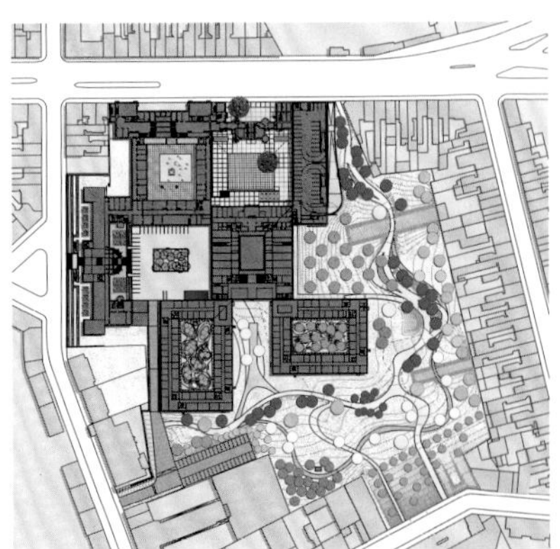

Trees lining the pathways

NOVARTIS CAMPUS PARK, BASEL
TO THE RHINE
2006–08, 2010–16

Client: Novartis Pharma AG, Basel
Master plan: Vittorio Magnago Lampugnani, Studio di Architettura, Milan
Area: 63,000 m^2

Stones deposited by storm water, Klöntal.

Novartis Park is part of the Novartis St. Johann industrial park at the border triangle in Basel. It is being converted from a production site into a research and administration centre. Besides being the company headquarters, the campus should also serve as a functional and attractive place to work and meet. Office buildings designed by different architects are now in either the construction or the planning phase.

The park will be defined on three sides by new buildings. The fourth side opens to the Rhine with cantilevered terrace steps. There is a multilevel underground garage beneath the park. Other than the banks of the Rhine, there are no cultural or natural typologies near enough to the grounds to help form the basis of a design concept. The Rhine is an essential element for this site and thus a persuasive candidate, as the only point of reference, for the source of the design concept.

Yet geological maps of the Basel area expose a hidden landscape. Beneath the urban structure, one can recognise the topography of the Upper Rhine Valley, which was formed by glaciers and sedimentary deposits, as witness to prehistoric times. Here we see the distinctive characteristics of a landscape created by glacial and water erosion: the levels and basins smoothed and scoured by glacial ice; glacial basins and gorges hollowed out by meltwater, and glacial fields and moraines created by flat meltwater deposits, as well as glacial erratics – huge boulders left behind by glacial flow. The same processes that have gone on for thousands of years still continue today, and forming and re-forming the Upper Rhine Valley and its landscape. The processes can be traced along the course of the river to its source in the Alps.

Sectional views of the valley's depression near Basel show a successive sequence of distinct, low-terraced ledges, the oldest level situated farthest from the river-bed. As an analogue to this mature geological structure, the natural vegetation follows a corresponding chronological system. The glacial valley formation is ideal for humidity-loving alluvial vegetation. Protected from strong currents and floods, these plants settled here gradually and established themselves towards the woods at the edge of the valley. They still bear witness to the glacial history of this landscape. It is the same for the massive erratics found even now in the forests around Basel, stuck between the trunks of oak and beech trees.

The design for Novartis Park traces this "hidden landscape" as a composition of the Upper Rhine Valley's geomorphic and vegetative phenomena. As in the naturally created surrounding landscape, these natural phenomena are sequentially reconstructed on a small scale and merged by means of design into an atmospheric park landscape. The park is to be understood as a slice through the landscape of the Upper Rhine Valley. It is structured in three sections.

The park area, situated farthest from the river's shore, is designed as a forest of indigenous woody plants where huge glacial erratics have remained as the oldest evidence of glacial activity. The system of paths this creates looks as if it was formed by an avalanche; it cuts a trail that leads towards the river and is lined by boulders. Large expanses of lawns form the middle section of the park, which is planted with diverse, mainly exotic, solitaire woody plants. Here, the main path branches off in two directions that cut deep into the grounds and through dense vegetation. In the third area, the lower land terraces facing the Rhine extend outward and offer open surfaces of water and plants. The vegetation surfaces leading from the alluvial, shingle beaches are comprised of tall marsh vegetation and are largely free of trees.

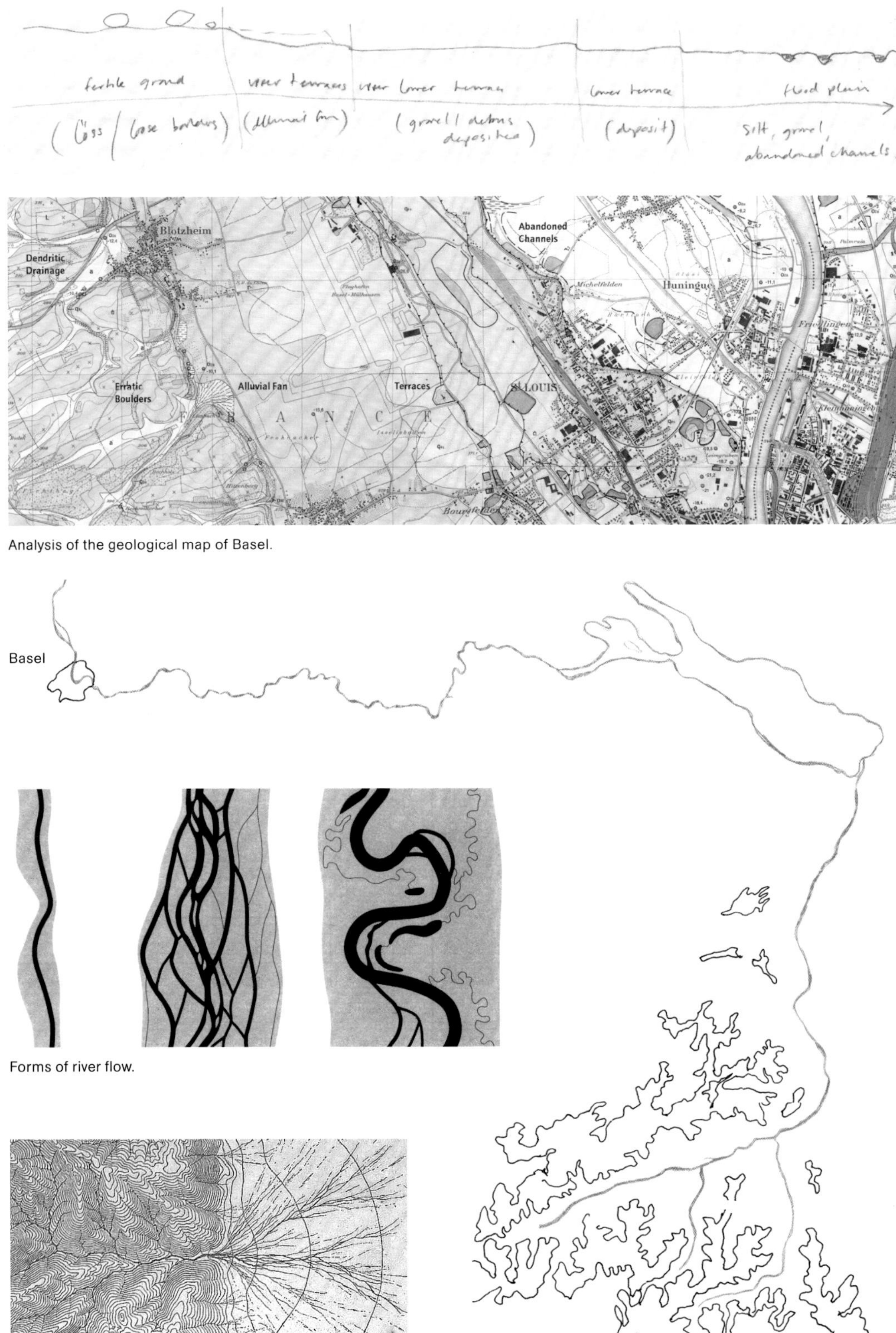

Analysis of the geological map of Basel.

Forms of river flow.

Dendritic drainage.

The course of the river Rhine.

Design Process
Based on scientific maps and diagrams, the concept for the park's design was developed using sketches, collages and models, as well as photos and renderings.

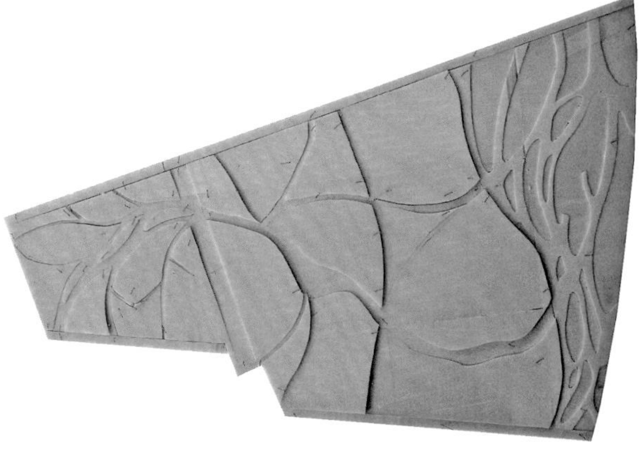

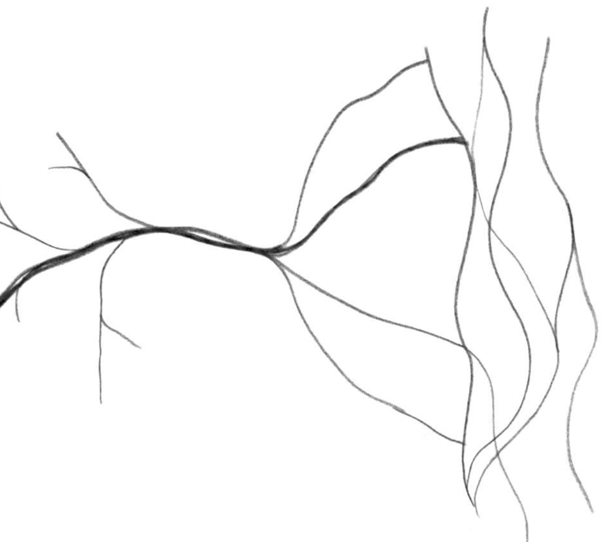

Topography studies.

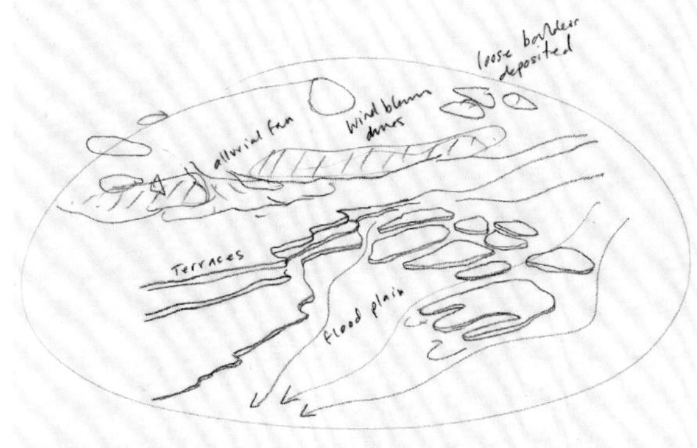

Analysis of the river-bed.

Study of river-bed forms.

Studies for the forest area.

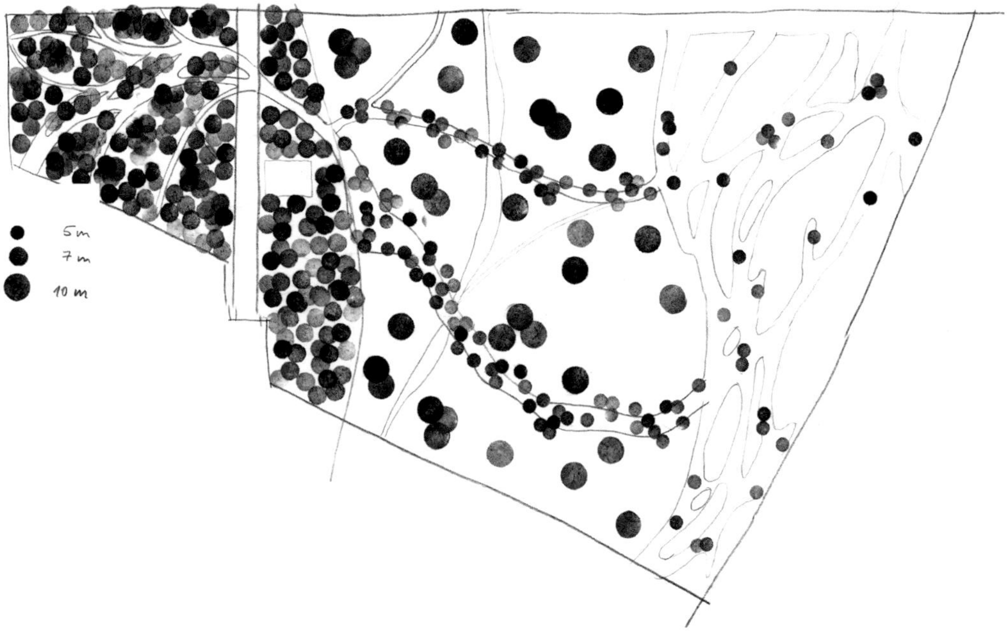

5m
7m
10 m

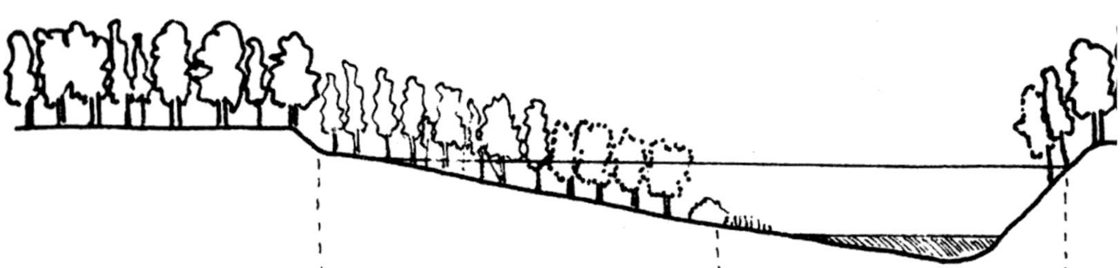

Forest area
Floodplain
River-bed

Density and allocation of trees.

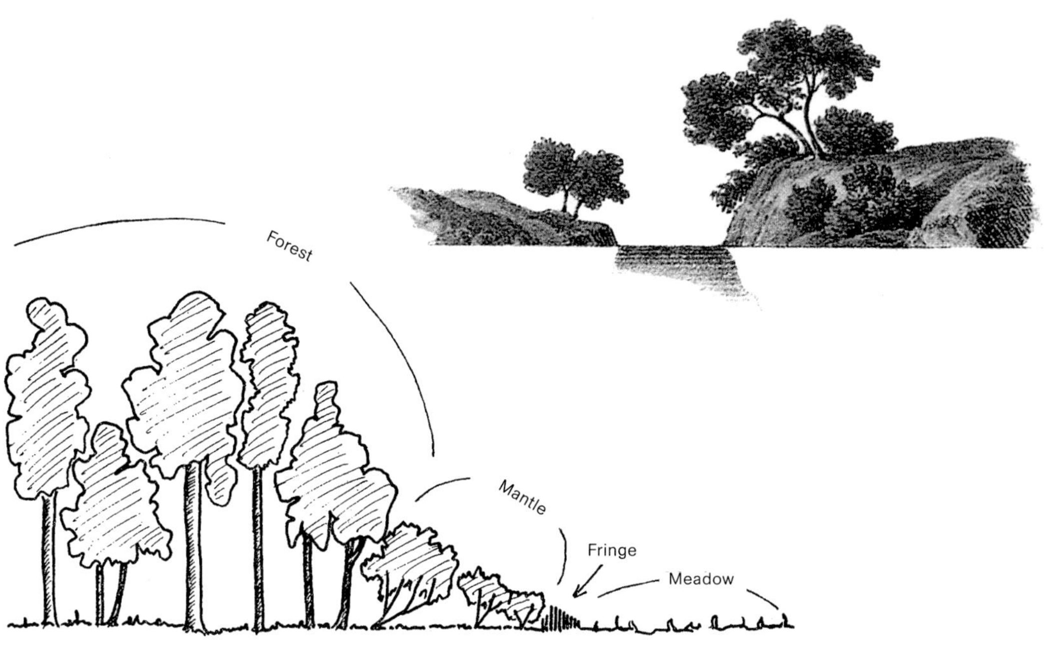

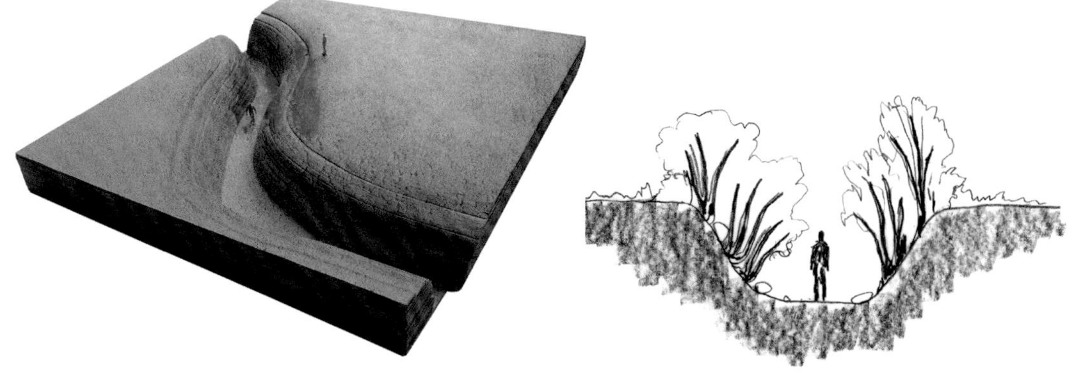

Analysis and studies for channels.

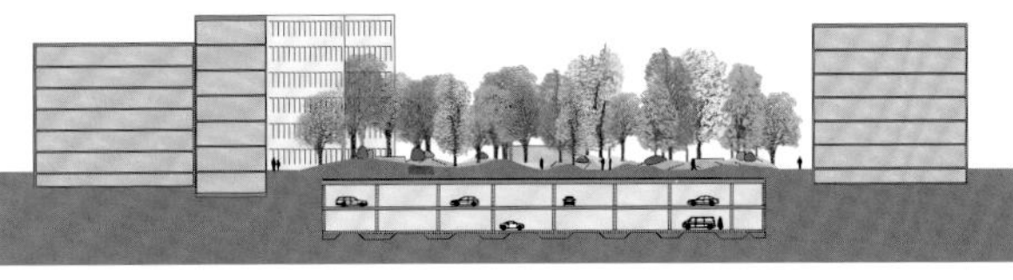

A

B

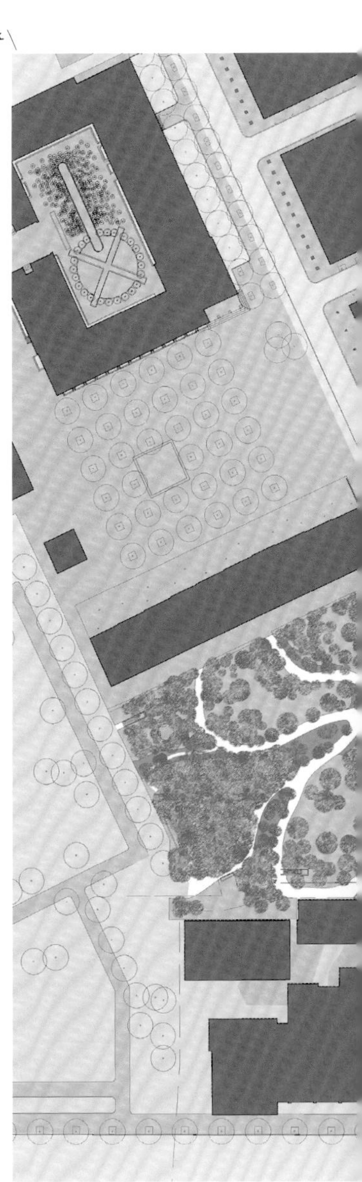

B

0 25 50 100

Landscape Model
Constructing a landscape model means conducting a dialogue with a specific local manifestation of nature. The task of discovering and revealing the substrate of a landscape is much more than the natural sciences can convey. Picking up the scent of whatever is in the wind. The model is the preliminary stage of a new reality.

Geomorphic Agents
The chronological and spatial sedimentation process of the Rhine delta forms the reference for the walls in Novartis Park. On the concrete roof of the underground parking garage something resembling a geomorphological inversion of the erosion process is revealed.

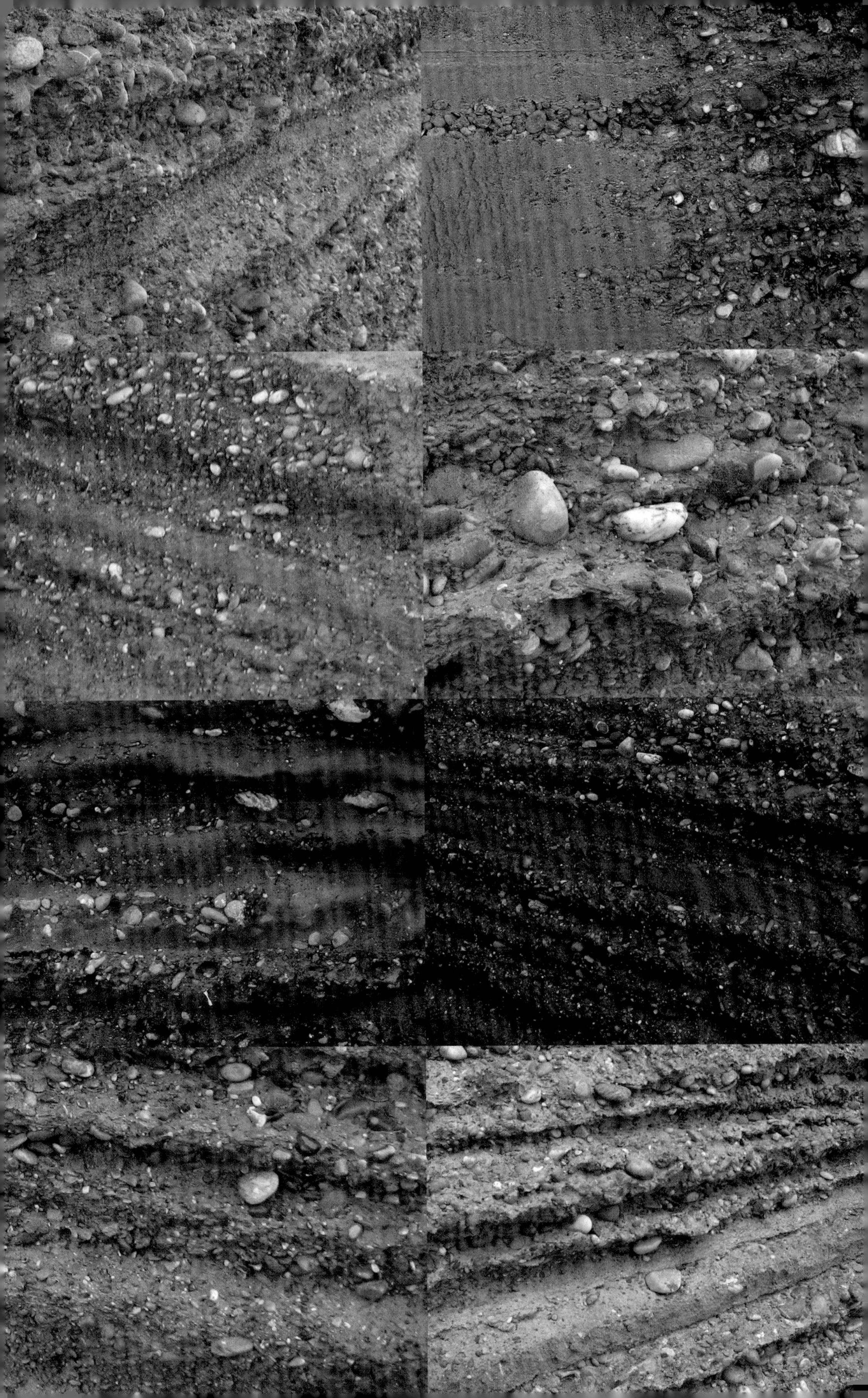

LOHSEPARK, HAMBURG
FROM WATER TO WATER
2010–18

Client: HafenCity Hamburg GmbH
Area: 47,000 m²

View of the harbour and the new HafenCity.

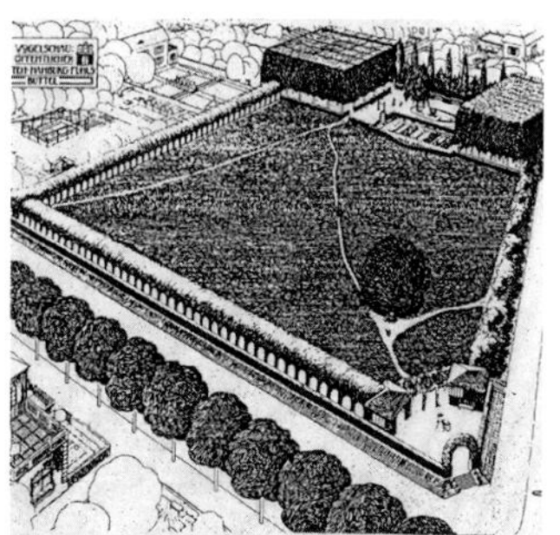

Volkspark Fuhlsbüttel, Hamburg
Leberecht Migge, ca. 1913.

Transforming the old harbour and warehouses of Hamburg into a new district with diverse architecture and a high experiential value is one of the most important urban projects currently underway in Hamburg. Here, the city is redefining itself, formulating an image for itself, and asking how we want to regard our cities in the future. The Lohsepark is the largest park in HafenCity; besides the river, it is the main element in the structure of open spaces of this new quarter of the city.

If visitors in the middle of the Lohsepark turn around in a 360-degree circle, they will experience one of the most outstanding qualities of this park: the long axis of the open space ends toward the water. The open planes of water at both ends interrupt the urban fabric of façades and bring light and air into the park. If a visitor approaches the park from the city, he experiences an entirely different aspect: the park's remarkable organisation in levels are clearly visible from the street, above the terraces covered in trees.

There are three clearly defined levels: the city, the park and the historical level. The biggest part of the open space, the park level is slightly sunken, lying about 1.5 metres below the surrounding city with its streets and promenades. This creates a clearly delineated park, without having to move large masses of soil around. The historical area is like an inlay in the surface of the park, precisely outlined by yet another change in height. Consisting of the old forecourt and a distinct seam in the park – the platforms of the old Hanover train station – the historical area lies about a metre below the level of the park. Here, more areas will be added later as part of a memorial to the Romany people deported during the National Socialist era.

In the park the distinct topography of the embankments create subspaces – some open, others closed off – allowing for temporary private usages and co-determining the directions of the paths. Although the main path leads quickly and directly through the park, side paths meander freely among the elements and the zones of the park. They join together the terraces and historical areas, uniting eastern and western promenades with each other.

In the park one will find typical native and non-native species of trees, such as oak (Quercus robur, Q. coccinea), linden (Tilia tomentosa, T. platyphyllos, T. europaea), hornbeam (Carpinus betulus), alder (Alnus glutinosa), apple (Malus domestica), cherry (Prunus avium), Japanese pagoda tree (Sophora japonica), and the katsura tree (Cercidiphyllum japonicum). Multi-trunk trees, species that grow in painterly shapes, unusual blossoms, or autumn colours lend the park a sense of structure and character.
In addition, a traditional element of the landscape park maintains the image of the "folly" in the neoclassical park: columns of oaks mark special places for people looking to take a rest, fluted hornbeams form a thick forest where children can climb and play, or a "fenced-in wilderness" with wild and whimsical plant forms provides a framework for a biotope with a rich variety of species for those interested in nature. Along the terraces and promenade, rows of honey locusts (Gleditsia triacanthos) form the boundary to the edge of the city.

At the south end of the park lies the harbour university square, an urban space and connection to the river promenade. Between the central square and the river promenade are stairs and ramps linking the various levels. In-between the sets of stairs on either side, terraced seating creates an attractive place to sit at the edge of the water. Covered in flat, dark brick, the structure makes use of typical local building material. Seen in-between the exposed concrete wharf walls, it clearly marks the beginning of the Lohsepark.

Generous spaces with a clear formal vocabulary, using details and materials characteristic of the town, lend the ensemble surrounding the Lohsepark a unique atmosphere of its own. It moves from the calm radiating from the areas along the water to urban life; from palpable history to the experiences of the present and a design that looks to the future.

The Lohsepark is part of the city's green, open space. It is the green centre of the HafenCity, as well as the continuing narrative of the ramparts that were the first ring around the old and new districts of the city. As a public park that is part of a new expansion of the city, however, it also represents a contemporary confrontation with the most important park in the city of Hamburg, and a central element in the history of public parks in Europe: the city park in Winterhude, designed by Fritz Schumacher.

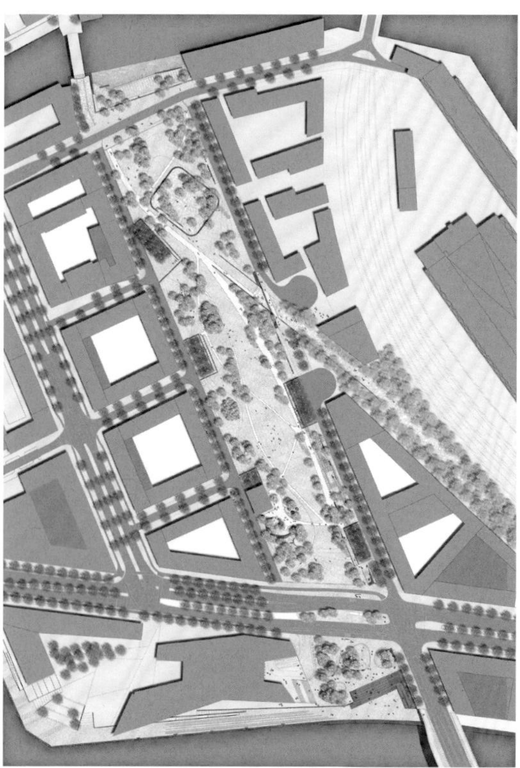

0 25 50 100

Design Concept

The old train station, the new edges of the city and the water form the local horizon of the Lohsepark. Accentuating and terracing these various elements creates the framework for a new level, the park.

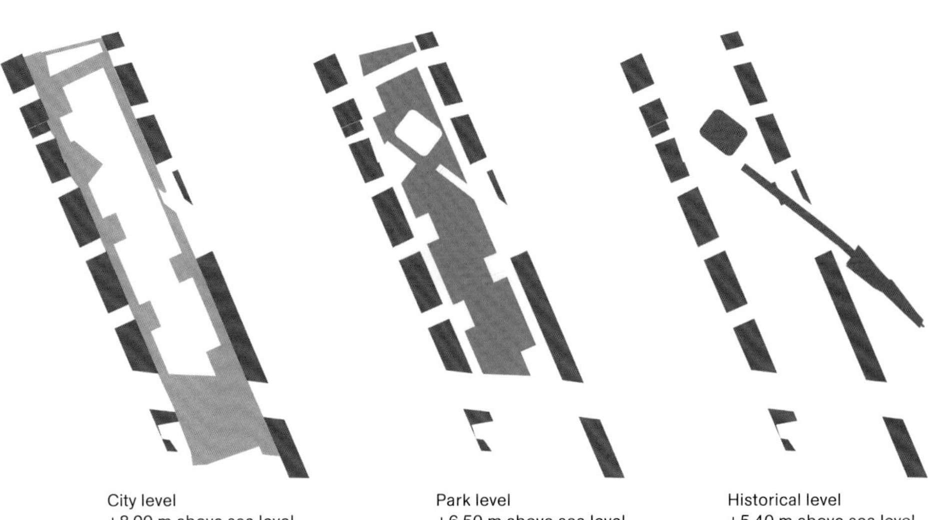

City level
+8.00 m above sea level

Park level
+6.50 m above sea level

Historical level
+5.40 m above sea level

The interior of the Lohsepark is characterised by species typical of parks. Trees from the city are part of the pattern.

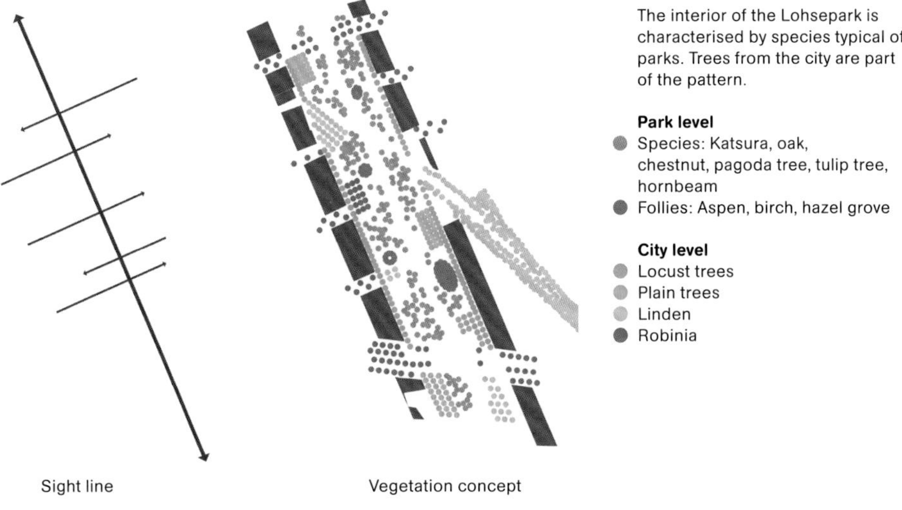

Sight line

Vegetation concept

1:1 models
Staircases are a recurring motif at the harbour in Hamburg. Studies of form and material are based on existing structures and are expressed in allusions to brick, the traditional construction material.

SQUARE

hard ground   hard edges
market theatre sound

surfaces runnels blocks slabs
sit squat chat noise

setting structures
   purpose and beginning exchange
emptiness position place

fulcrums solitudes
   shadowfall and space

feast and feasting   urban life
looking seeing
      walking waiting

TERROIR

We have not lost our knowledge of nature; it has just settled into new niches. The *cultiver le jardin* can be found today in private wine cellars. The exact appropriateness of a specific place, with all its hidden qualities of soil quality or exposure, the *terroir*, is comparable to an almost impossible translation of the sense of taste into geological terms. There is also knowledge about different grape cultivars and the forecasting of weather conditions for a certain year. All these parameters are needed to localise a specific place and time within the globalised world, by simply enjoying a sip of wine. The desire to verify origin, to ascertain this place as precisely as possible, is also common to other natural stimulants like coffee and chocolate. The identity and recognisability of a natural product promises added value for the epicure, confirming his or her connoisseurship. At the same time, it conceals a usually unrealisable desire for large scale involvement in this scientific knowledge, for a château with a vineyard, or a cultivated piece of the landscape – and also the idea of the local, being rooted in a place, utopia made reality.

The potential of urban landscape is the city's heterogeneity, a multiplication of the local. Nature can be found in the city in many different forms. The development of this diversity is only possible in the heterogeneous structure. For this reason, nature within the city is more diverse than nature in the surrounding landscape. This has to do literally with the substrate of the location. Multiply fractured, the forms of city vegetation tell the story of its history. Heterogeneity needs authenticity of location, history and use. Yet the glut of the city, the rapid and constant changing images and events, the references taken from first- or second-hand experience hinder the perception of simple relationships to nature in everyday life. At the same time, we react sceptically to change. The unusualness of the present, of progress, suddenly seems no longer positive, but threatening. The ground beneath our feet wavers; the familiar environment looms gigantic. Cities, traffic and endeavours become immense and immeasurable. The alternative, the small garden located in an abandoned industrial area, represents human scale, the seemingly controllable. It can be pointed out here that the large is at least accessible and therefore more controllable than the small, which gets swallowed up by the mass. Mistrust is also applied to political discourse. Large-scale urban planning projects are only possible if disguised as an event. Globalisation is now a bad word, interpreted as something in contrast to the private and manageable. The open society principle no longer poses a risk. We criticise the consequences of unrestricted mobility without considering the reasons behind this development. The visible and the invisible, small and large, are phenomena that can be experienced by the senses in day-to-day life. Yet whether or not the ground beneath our feet is poisoned escapes our knowledge. To answer this question, we have to rely on microscopic analysis, on the world of atoms and molecules. The image we have of our environment is, however, influenced by aesthetic predecessors. These determine our perception of nature as good and beautiful.

In the modern age, the age of the machine, the town square was predestined for the staging of public life. It served as a projection space within the urban structure, which was based on a society's mutual treasure of experience that became the history of a city. The age of motion machines – cars, trains, airplanes – has been succeeded by the age of the machines of effect. In view of the World Wide Web, the question of the function of remaining public spaces has gained importance. The difference between private and public is emphasised. The telephone booth at the edge of the square is a staged private space within public space; it has been replaced by the mobile telephone that can be used anywhere and everywhere. Inevitable eavesdropping on private conversations makes me a participant, willingly or not, in a private realm otherwise foreign to me. Private space, one's own four walls, has been made permeable. Telephone, television and computer are specific components of our private world, making the concept of a protected, shielded space virtually obsolete. Day-to-day life is flooded with digitally generated images that are without reference. Public space that poses as an ideal world is a utopia, a place that does not exist. The square, park and garden that appear as broken varieties of paradise are heterotopias, in other words, small worlds in which many different worlds can be at home and in a constant state of friction.

gv

Jura

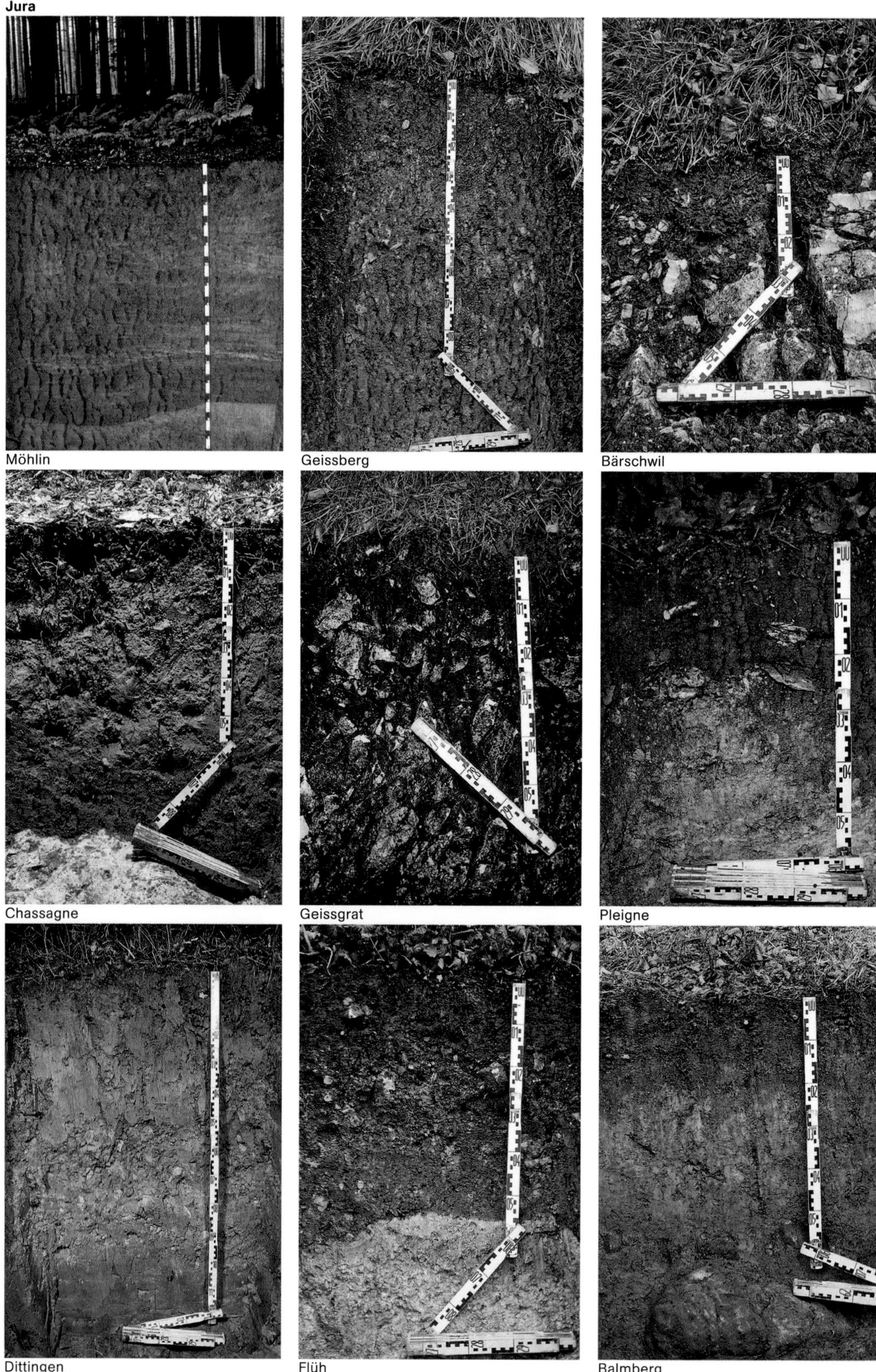

Möhlin Geissberg Bärschwil

Chassagne Geissgrat Pleigne

Dittingen Flüh Balmberg

Schitterwald

Swiss Midlands

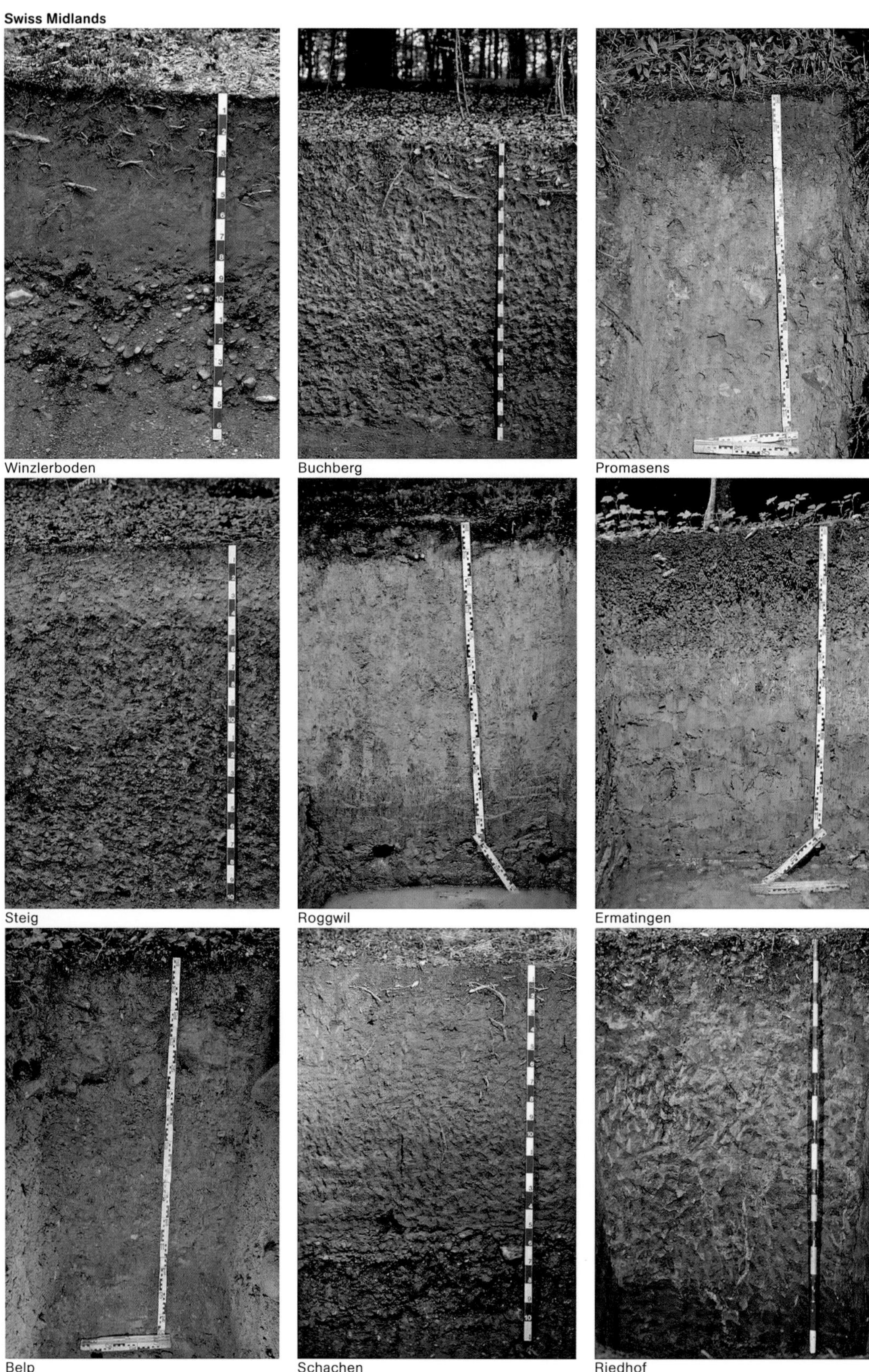

Winzlerboden | Buchberg | Promasens

Steig | Roggwil | Ermatingen

Belp | Schachen | Riedhof

Foothills of the Alps

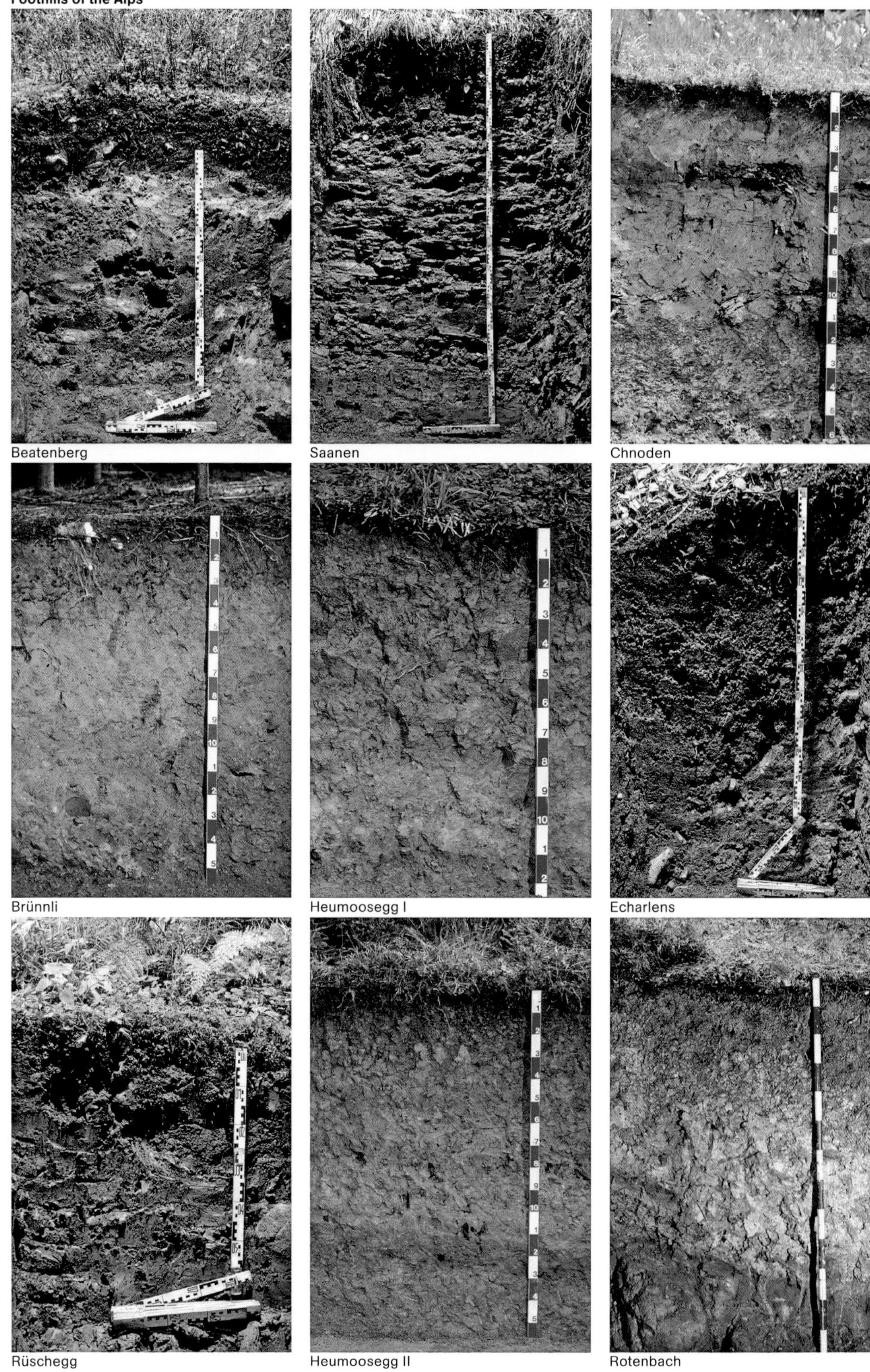

Beatenberg

Saanen

Chnoden

Brünnli

Heumoosegg I

Echarlens

Rüschegg

Heumoosegg II

Rotenbach

The Alps

Heitibüel

Obersaxen

Fläsch

Stalden

Maladers

Visp

Tujetsch

Pontresina

Ramosch

Southern Side of the Alps

Sagno

Poschiavo, Costascia da Suasar

Rodas

Intragana

Poschiavo, Balbalera

Chironico

Cima Pianca

Cademario

Copera

TRAFOPLATZ, BADEN
REDISCOVERING THE LANDSCAPE
1999–2006, 2011–14

Client: Stadt Baden, Planung und Bau
Urbanistic master plan: Diener & Diener Architekten, Basel
Architecture: Burkard Meyer, Baden and Ken Architekten, Baden
Area: 7,402 m²

In the nineteenth century, designing a public square meant centring a body within a spatial shell. A monument occupied the centre of a square and defined the space around it by moving radially outwards from the centre. The equestrian statue placed on a pedestal becomes a sacred dimension of space. The modern age, by contrast, constitutes space by delimiting it. The edges of the space create a centre without ever occupying it.

Aerial view of Baden with a view of Trafoplatz.

The culture of Japanese bonsai trees as an excerpt from the landscape.

Exotic Plant.
Constantin Brancusi,
(1876–1957).

A five-minute walk from the railway station takes you out of the urban density and into a neighbourhood previously closed to the public. The former factory grounds of the electrical engineering firm Brown Boveri & Cie (BBC), later Asea Brown Boveri (ABB), has been gradually transformed into a new neighbourhood in Baden. In accordance with urban planning guidelines, the area continues to be defined by large, autonomous volumes of buildings and retains a succession of narrow and broad exterior spaces. Mixed use – residential, services, culture and education – is being introduced. The study commissioned in 1999 did not specify a future typology for design of the transformer building's vacant lot.

The urban structure of north Baden determines the concept for this new exterior space. Its building density suggests an inner-city site, while the sightlines point to nearby natural spaces. This discovery of the landscape is the guiding idea behind this concept. Parts of the cultural landscape are introduced into the architectonic framework as objects and exhibited on stone pedestals like precise details of the landscape. In terms of space, the project for Trafoplatz is based on traditional designs for public squares and refines the idea of those designs with an eye to this specific location. Whereas in the nineteenth century, the centre was occupied by an equestrian statue on a pedestal, the modern age constitutes space by delimiting it. This design proposes an autonomous form, dominated by vegetation, between the buildings on Trafoplatz. In some ways it adopts architectural edges, while in other ways it breaks free of them. The result is a succession of spaces of different directions and sizes, offering a variety of prospects and functional connections. The square should not be grasped as a whole; in order to experience it, one must walk around it.

The use of trees typical of the region – oaks, beeches and birches – combined with a underplanting of moss, points towards the nearby forest on the hills outside the city. The trees, positioned freely and planted with appropriate density, create a filter vis-à-vis the immediate surroundings. This results in a public yet intimate space next to the busy Bruggerstrasse.

Pedestals of imitation stone connect the plants on display with the earth, but also distinguish them from it, while also making it possible to plant trees on the underground car park by providing the structure with the necessary height. The containers for the plants are made of concrete mixed with local stone and poured on site. Pounding the hardened surface with a mallet produced an imitation stone with a surface texture reminiscent of a boulder. Local stone was also used in the paving. The edges of the square, which are subject to particularly intensive use by vehicles making deliveries, were paved with asphalt rolled with natural stone gravel. The central part of the square is surfaced with a coarser permeable gravel covering. The water that collects on the surface seeps down through a subterranean layer of gravel that acts as a filter.

The vegetation creates a solid framework for a space that is then filled with public life. The centre of the square becomes a vessel designed to accommodate a multitude of activities. The square is available for special events such as open-air cinema shows, weekly markets or municipal celebrations. Movable chairs allow individuals to choose their own places to sit. The café at the main entrance to the transformer building also offers outdoor seating.

Moss
Moss is characterised by a high ability to regenerate and a broad habitat range. The chosen species that have been applied here are oriented toward the regional climate. The moss species best suited to the habitat's conditions prevails. This explains the dappled appearance, because certain mosses prevail in shady conditions and others in sunny areas. Different materials are suitable for moss plantings, such as tufa, slabs or mineral-rich substrates.

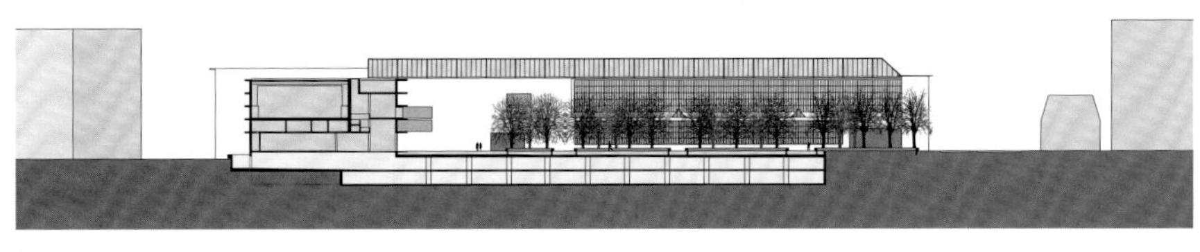

A

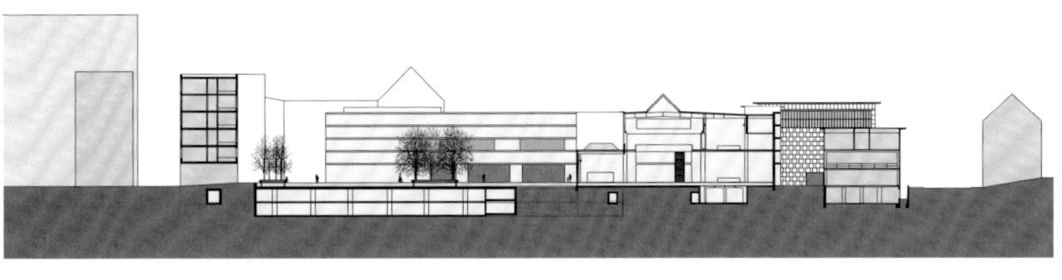

B

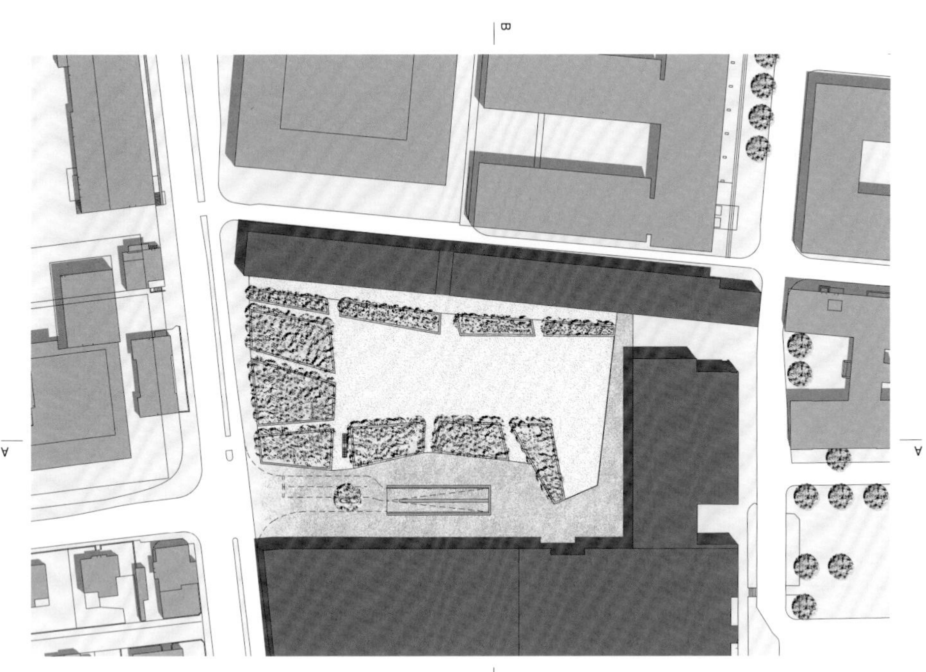

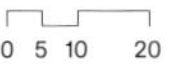

Use

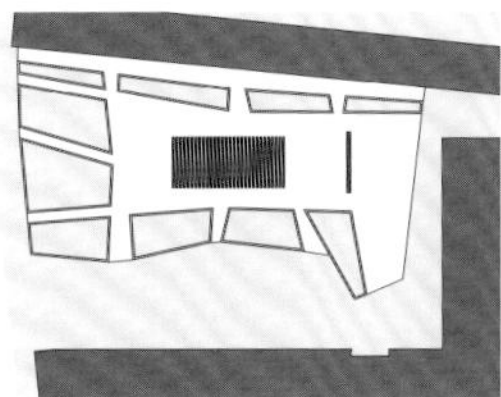

Open-air cinema

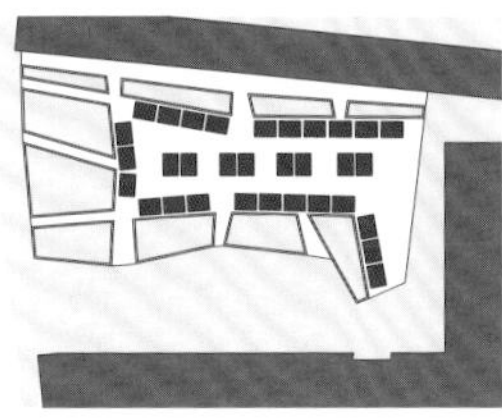

Market

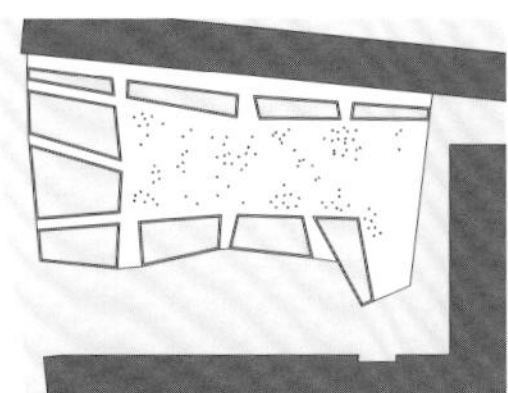

Movable chairs

Planting

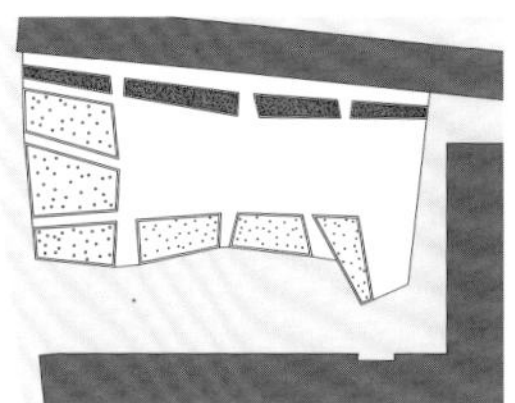

Birch

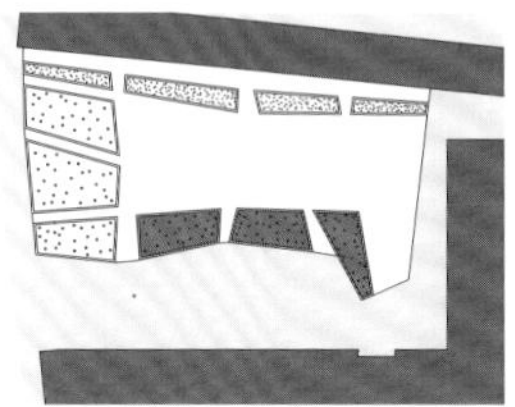

Beech

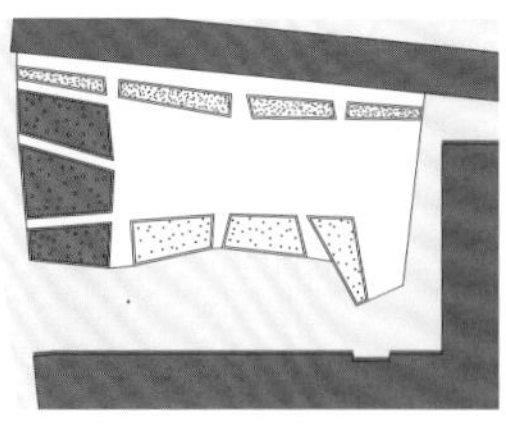

Oak

BAHNHOFSPLATZ LANDQUART
RED EARTH
2005–06

Client: Gemeinde Igis,
Gemeindeverwaltung Igis-Landquart
Area: 3,000 m²

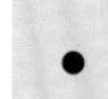

Brick production
in Landquart.

Bahnhofsplatz before reconstruction.

City streets and squares were in the past a stage setting for everyday life, where the people could develop their individuality. They have lost some of their importance in the age of the Internet and television, causing one to question what role a traditional, urban public square in front of a railway station, such as the one in Landquart, plays in this day and age. Yet it remains an issue of public space. The square is a place of comings and goings; it is traversed on a daily basis or visited regularly, though only for a short amount of time. The train station square also assumes the prestigious task of communicating the first impression of a community. It is a business card and an identity-shaping feature for the populace.

The unifying design element for the new Bahnhofsplatz is the red, rammed-earth paving. It spreads out like a carpet in front of the train station to receive the arrivals in Landquart. The hardwearing, newly developed paving material is derived from the tried and true, rammed-earth floors typical of ancient Rome. It is exceptionally resilient and proven to be robust. The special feature of this paving is the brick substrate from the local brick works that has been added to the paving material. This admixture gives the paving a reddish-brown tone and a lively surface structure, and makes the Bahnhofsplatz a unique site.

The square is framed at the side by two gardens. One is slightly elevated and consists of a group of ornamental cherry trees. There is a herbaceous garden on the opposite side, situated between two strong, existing copper beech trees. Both gardens join the square, creating two different spaces, each with its own atmosphere and quality.

The cherry grove is made up of a group of densely planted, small-crowned, cherry trees with ornamental flowers in spring and intense, colourful foliage in autumn. It is planted slightly staggered in a large trough on the extension toward Bahnhofstrasse. The trough provides the necessary structural height and makes it possible to locate the underground car park below. The cherry grove area is accessible to the public. It also has places to sit on all four of its sides, which are closed off by natural stone blocks on the long sides and steps on the two ends.

Activities on the square can also be observed from the other side. The herbaceous garden is situated between the two existing copper beeches and has a long bench running the length of its periphery, facing the open square. The bench stretches over the entire forty-metre length of the garden. In the garden between the two majestic trees, lush perennials have been densely planted, and these seasonally renew their flowering. A meandering path winds through the garden and is framed by a copper beech hedge – in honour of the pre-existing trees.

Three pole luminaires provide the lighting for the square. Floor luminaires supply additional accents to the space. In-ground luminaires beneath the copper beeches are an effective lighting concept to set off the powerful trees.

Rammed-earth Floor

In the ancient world, rammed-earth floors were the most common type of flooring. The hard-wearing, newly developed pavement material used for Landquart Bahnhofsplatz is derived from this age-old technique. The precise concentration and colour of the admixture was developed through a series of tests.

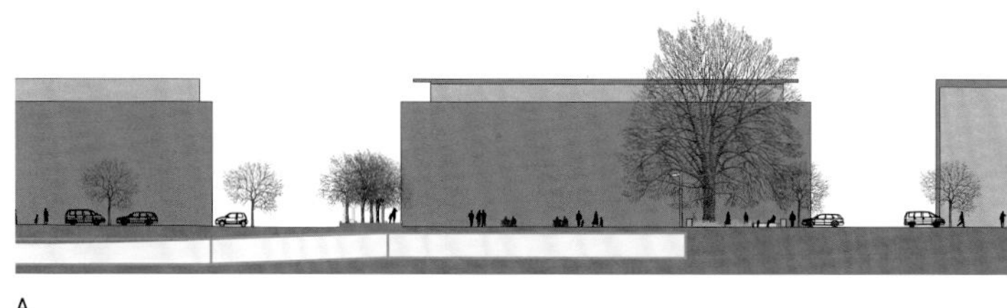
A

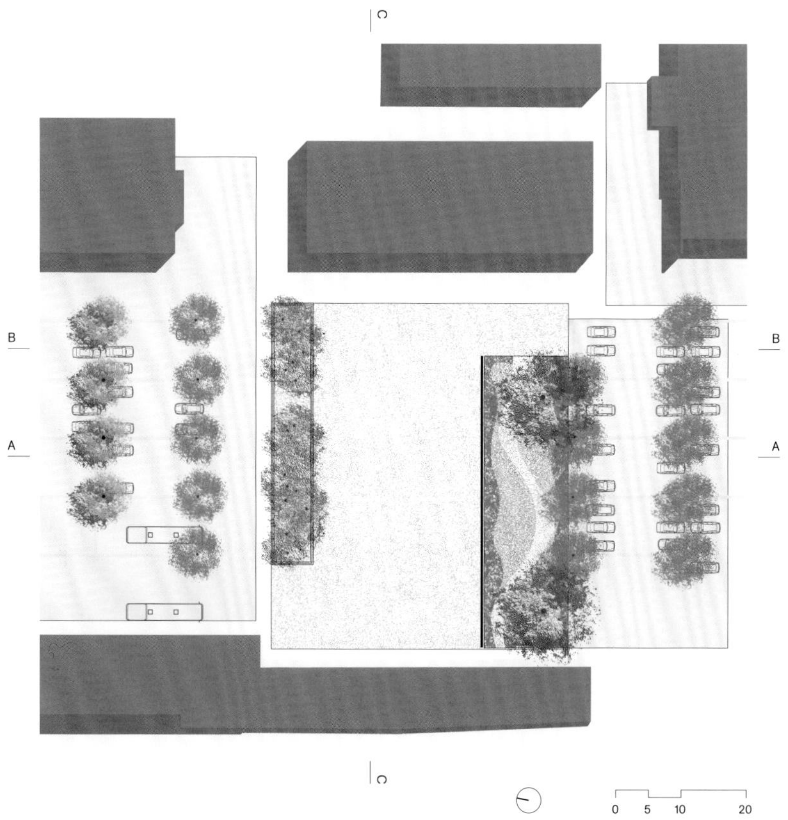
C
B
A
B
A
C
0
5
10
20

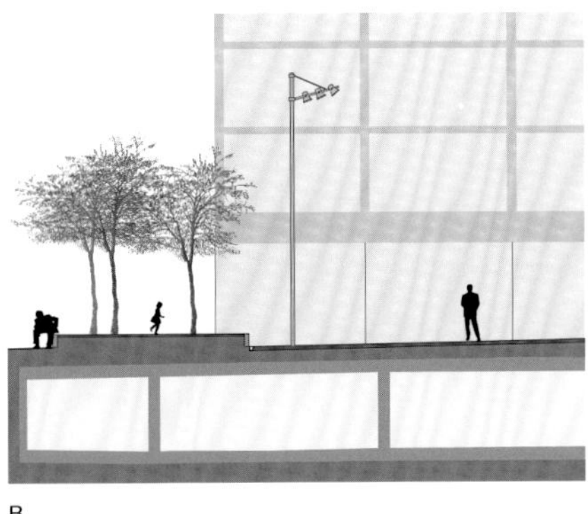

B

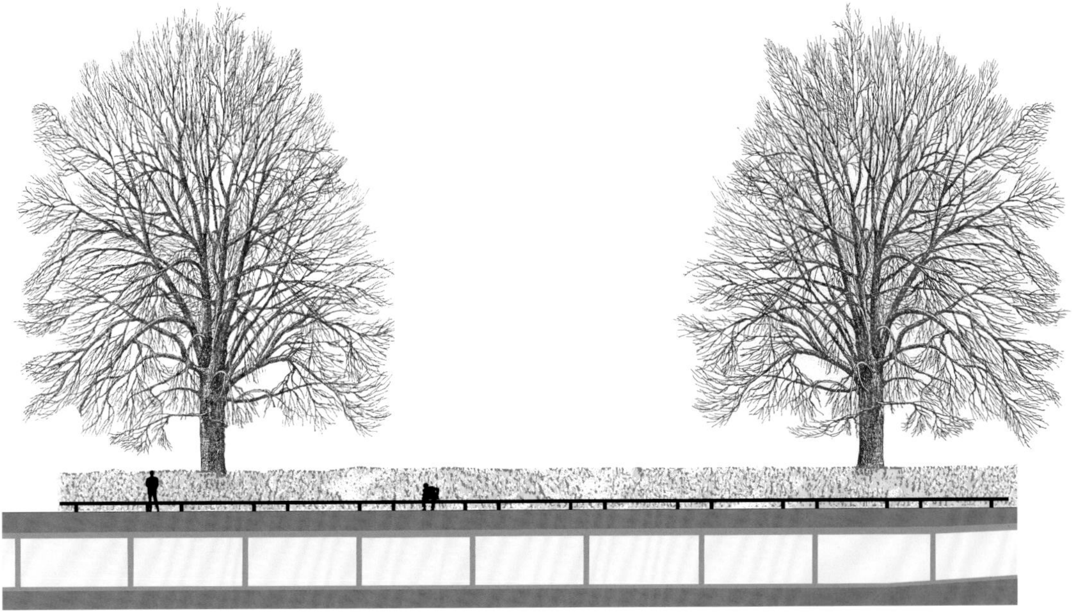

C

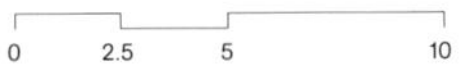

0 2.5 5 10

88

BREGENZ FESTSPIELHAUS FORECOURT

PLATZ DER WIENER SYMPHONIKER
2005–06

Client: Amt der Landeshauptstadt Bregenz, Hochbau
Architecture: Dietrich Untertrifaller Architekten, Bregenz
Area: 21,000 m²

The lakefront of Lake Constance near Bregenz.

Use before the renovation.

The Platz der Wiener Symphoniker is known internationally as the forecourt of the Bregenz Festspielhaus. Every summer for four weeks, during the festival, first-class opera and operetta performances and orchestral concerts take place, sometimes outdoors. The square in front of the festival house calls for a fitting context that will function well for the large streams of visitors during the summer festival and for the residents of Bregenz throughout the year.

The Platz der Wiener Symphoniker is situated between the city of Bregenz and Lake Constance. It is integrated into a park-like green belt between the railway tracks and the lake. The city joins the square at the side away from the lakefront. Designing a municipal square at this site would be far too metropolitan and would be inappropriate for the environment. The site rather calls for a park-like situation that incorporates the adjacent parcels of land into the surroundings, as a continuation of the existing park structures. Lake Constance's alluvial landscape serves as a basis for the plant concept. The choice of plant species refers to the local, natural environment. Woody plants from areas close to the shore are planted like a grove, forming a green spatial border like a parenthesis around the square. The grove-like planting is also a lively volume that provides a marked contrast to the festival house.

Familiar, indigenous species as well as integrated existing trees are gathered into tree groups reminiscent of an arboretum, with formations of other species such as alder, poplar, cherry and pine. In all, 373 indigenous tree species were planted. What first appears to be a homogeneous planting diversifies at the change of seasons. The differences between the various woody plants are clearly displayed during autumn colours, when the leaves fall, and during spring budding. A cherry garden placed at the intersection of the festival house's architectural axis divides the external space into east – west or main and side entrance.

There is also variation in the composition or placement of the trees, which ranges from more or less dense groups to solitaire trees. The vegetation concept and tree placement allow different spaces to develop, creating an atmospheric zoning of the grounds that is suitable for both the heavily frequented park during the festival and its everyday use.

While the vegetation concept resembles a park, the continuous paving creates a unified area and allows it to become a true square. The paving spreads out from the park's pathways, surrounds the festival house and extends down to the lakefront. Lake Constance's shingle beaches serve as a reference for the paving material. It is made of split-mastix asphalt to which varying sizes and colours of double-process chipping and pebbles have been added; their colour and diversity emerge after sandblasting of the paving surface.

During the festival, the surface of the square is lit by non-glare pole luminaires. At other times, subtle lighting directed downward provides enough light for the pedestrian area as well as views into the distance. The light reacts to the movement of approaching people and becomes brighter. A minimal level of lighting is guaranteed at all times. In additional to outdoor seats supplied by area restaurants, more chairs will be provided which visitors can arrange as they please.

The design concept creates a high degree of transparency and functions well without signs or floor markings. Emphasising the main paths that follow the lake's promenade or lead to the train station and Bregenz's city centre and the crossing of Lake Constance's cycle path makes the grounds easy to navigate for pedestrians and cyclists alike.

The Square's Paving
The shingle beaches of Lake Constance serve as the natural model for the choice of paving. The mastix paving consists of double-process chipping and pebbles of a 0 to 32 mm grading, bonded by a mastix sealing compound. Adding larger pebbles creates a larger variation of surface structure. Sandblasting frees the pebbles from the brown mastix, allowing the colour of the stones to appear.

MIGU

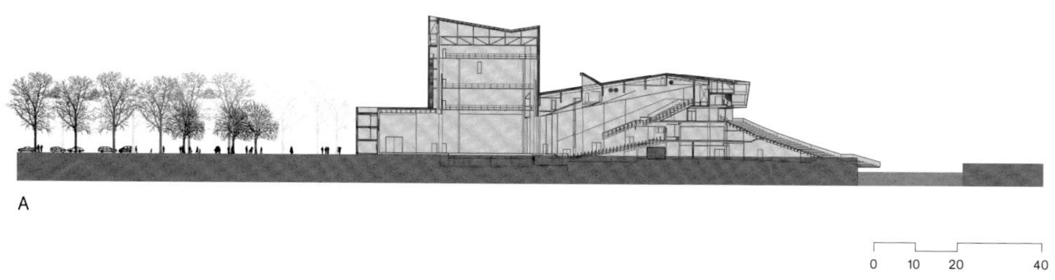

A

A

0 25 50 100

BAHNHOFSPLATZ MUNICH-GIESING
SPACE-TIME
2003–09

Client: Landeshauptstadt München
Architecture: Brigitte Kochta, Berlin
Area: Square: 9,235 m^2, Green belt: 5,625 m^2

Sequoia tree.

The train station square for Munich's Giesing district is mainly a transfer point and a traffic junction for different public and private means of transportation. Suburban rail lines, subways, buses, and trams, as well as taxis and private traffic, all merge here. As a public space, it is also an important local venue for functions that must be outdoors or for which an outdoor setting is desirable. It is an urban neighbourhood square, and thus accessible to diverse people with various goals and needs. To apply this precept, the design concept is planned as a continuous, barrier-free space; a square without sharp edges or marked borders.

The determining elements of this open space are the airy, mostly high-trimmed trees with pinnate leaves, which form a transparent tree canopy that varies with the seasons. As an element of urban planning, the new open space restores the lost scale of the site, while the elongated trunks and high crowns preserve its character and generous proportions. The space consists of ten different species of trees, all of a commanding size. The dimension, colour and texture of the bark make the individual trunks seem like pieces in an exhibition. Such simple, natural phenomena only become apparent if one passes though the site on a daily basis.

The ten tall tree species form an urban space with their crowns and trunks, which display the changes in the seasons. In spring, the late-budding trees allow the first warm rays of sun to shine through to the square unimpeded. In summer, the tree crowns cast airy, cooling shade, and in the autumn, their canopies display varied hues of yellow and gold.

Each tree is an attractive specimen in its own right, due to its own specific characteristics. For example, the Robinia pseudoacacia (locust tree or false acacia) is unique for its black bark and the seductively sweet perfume of its white raceme. There is also the Metasequoia glyptostroboides, or dawn redwood, with red-fox-coloured bark and bright yellow autumn foliage. The Fraxinus americana, or white ash, has foliage ranging from yellow and orange to purple.

Each tree changes in its own way over the course of the seasons, creating different moods and an ever-new visual allure for the square.

The seamless paving, made from water-bonded pavement, gives the open space an additional urban quality. It forms a continuous surface between Schwanenseestrasse and the green belt, and is reserved for non-motorised traffic.

Fraxinus americana/White ash
The commanding white ash rules over the high alluvial lands of North American rivers. The crown shimmers red when in blossom, then buds late in the year. Its intense autumn foliage of yellow, orange and purple makes it more appealing than the indigenous ash. The underside of the leaf is a silvery white. Because the stalk of the leaf is winged, it flutters in the wind, creating a pretty, light-hearted play of colour.

Ginkgo biloba/Maidenhair tree, Ginkgo
Ginkgo means "silver apricot" in Japanese. The fruit itself, however, smells terrible. The pit can be eaten: boiled or roasted, it is sold in Asia like our chestnut. The ginkgo leaf has a fascinating shape – as if made out of conifer needles. The tree is considered a living fossil because, as the sole example of its genus, it has survived on earth for 270 million years. The Japanese consider the tree holy and so use its delicate, light-coloured wood to make shrines and temples. Similarly, the implements used in Japanese tea ceremonies are carved out of ginkgo wood.

Gleditsia triacanthos 'Inermis'/ Gleditsia, Honey locust tree
This tree is appreciated for its airy canopy of leaves. The long brown shoots are interesting. Their seeds can be roasted and used to make gleditsia coffee, as well as in a variety of other North American Indian recipes. The long, pointed needles are prominent in the wild species; they are situated directly on the trunk in groups of threes. The tree looks armed and dangerous. The "unarmed" Inermis form is usually chosen for street trees.

Juglans nigra/Black walnut
The fruit of the black walnut is similar to the European indigenous walnut. But it is truly black, has deep ridges and its shell is so hard that the splinters were once used to deburr metal, as in sandblasting, or as a filler in dynamite. This North American tree is not easy to please and loves the best soil of warm, protected ravines.

Larix decidua/European larch
The larch is a tree that truly needs full sun. It is the only indigenous deciduous conifer tree, meaning it sheds its needles in winter. Before they fall, the needles turn a sunny yellow-green to deep yellow, bathing the autumnal larch forests in a fascinating light so suggestive that larches were once highly esteemed as the dwellings of only virtuous forest spirits. Larches live a very long time. At 500 to over 1000 years of age, gnarled and covered in lichen, they settle on airy hanging ledges or cling to the cliffs in scraggly mountain areas. Their wood is so durable and rich in resin that acids are stored in barrels made from larch wood. Water troughs and even the Wallis Suonen, the centuries-old, artificial water canal, are made of larch wood.

Metasequoia glyptostroboides/Dawn redwood
The dawn redwood was thought to be extinct until a Japanese botanist rediscovered it in the 1940s in the Chinese province of Sichuan. It has since established itself as a living fossil in European parks. Its architectural construction, red-fox-coloured bark and bi-pinnate foliage give it a delicate and exotic appearance. Before Metasequoia drops its needles in autumn, they turn a spectacular yellow. Its stoic frame and powerful trunk is particularly evident in winter.

Pinus nigra var. austriaca/Austrian black pine
The black pine is distinguishable from the Scots pine by its long, dark needles and unified grey trunk. Its wood is harder and creaks less, and the tree can tolerate more dryness and heat than the Scots pine. The wood of both trees is light in colour and widely used in furniture and cabinet-making.

Pinus silvestris/Scots pine
The long needle rosettes give the Scots pine a soft appearance. Its high adaptability enables it to survive in inhospitable, dry or cold regions. The Scots pine can thus be found on dunes, mountains and moors. Its ability to subsist on very little has made it the world's most common pine species, and it has spread from Greenland to New Zealand. Its resin is the source of the characteristic resiny, tangy perfume we associate with pine forests.

Robinia pseudoacacia/Locust, False acacia
The Parisian court gardener Jean Robin introduced the locust tree from North America in 1601. The locust has been a familiar feature of the urban landscape ever since. It can draw sustenance from even meagre, dry locations by gathering and storing nitrate in its root tubers. The black bark and picturesque shape explain why the tree is a favourite among gardeners. The locust's buds do not open until late spring. Its white raceme fills the air with a sweet perfume, and the delicate pinnate leaves are in constant movement. Its hard, durable wood was prized by the North American Indians, who used it as a material for constructing bows and arrows. The tree turns silver-grey in the wind or breeze.

Sophora japonica/Japanese pagoda, Chinese scholar tree
In late summer, the Japanese pagoda's clusters of flowers are an eye-catcher. The Chinese know how to extract medicinal properties from its blossoms, but the tree is generally considered toxic. Its medicinal properties should thus be left to sages – the Greek word for which is the source of its name. The loose foliage and painterly ramifications give an allée planted with Japanese pagodas a light-hearted quality from spring until autumn. In winter, its idiosyncratic, stodgy figure comes to the fore.

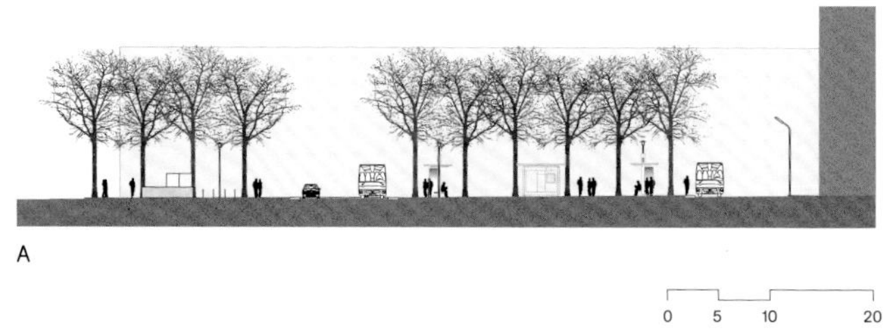

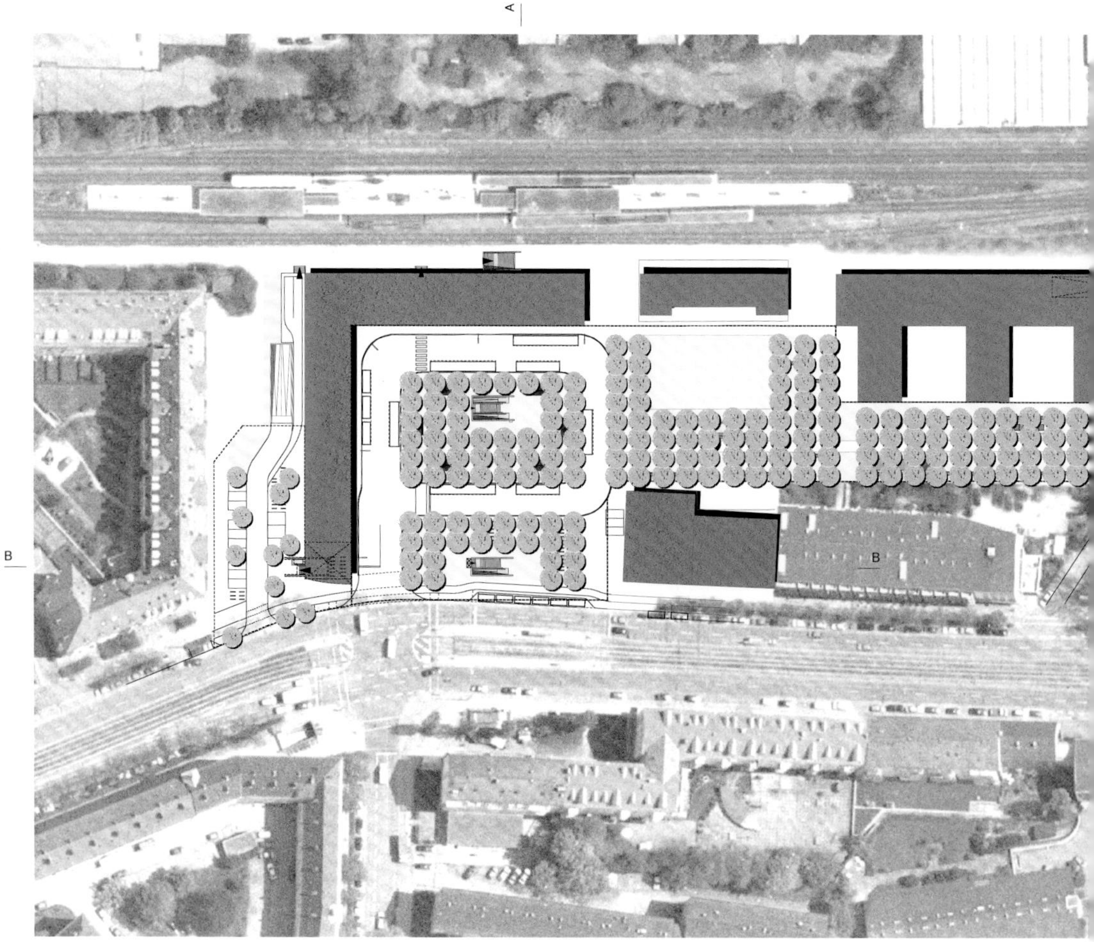

A

B

B

A

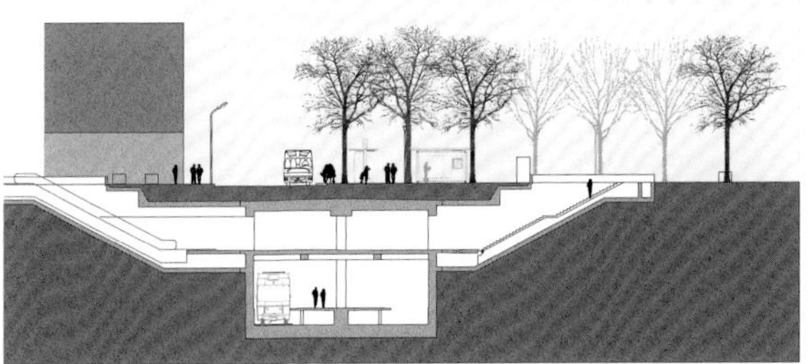

B

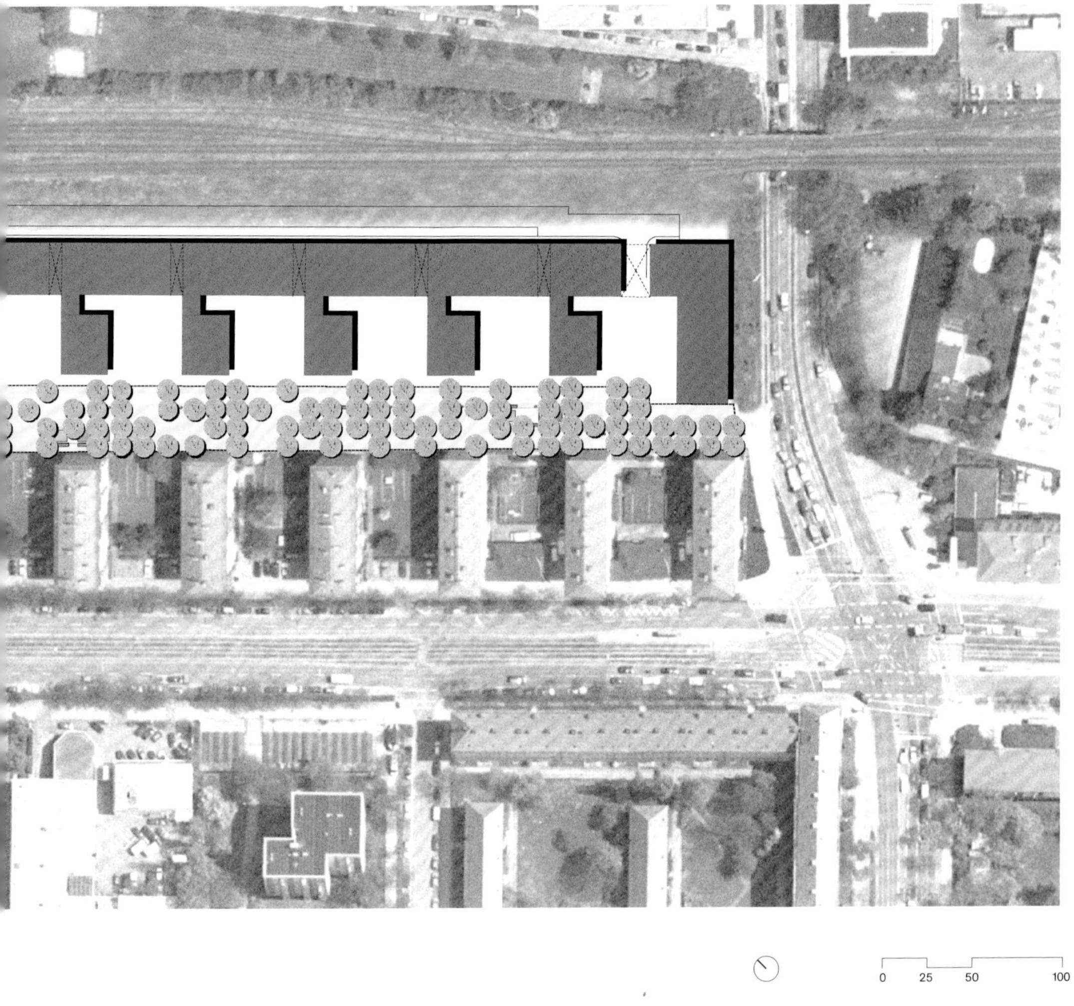

0 25 50 100

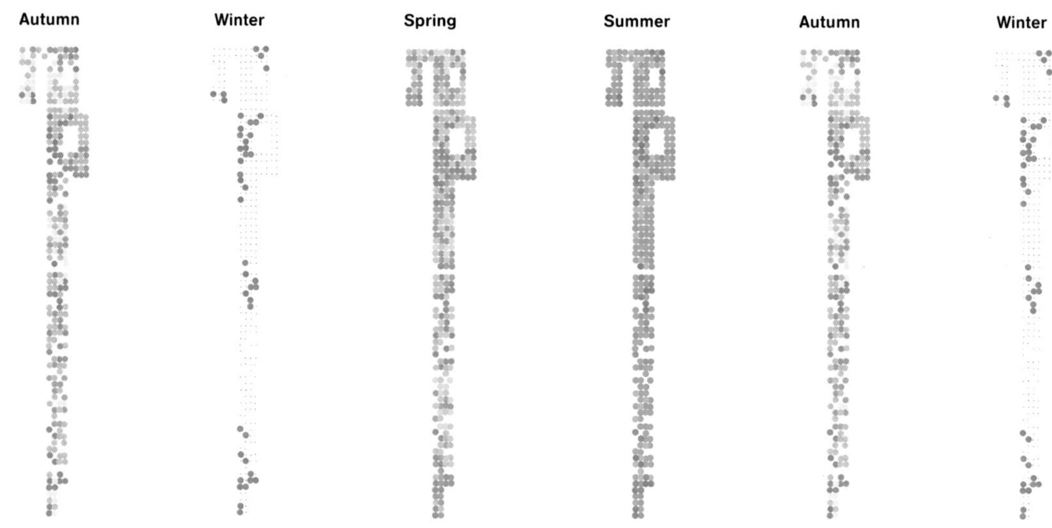
Autumn
Winter
Spring
Summer
Autumn
Winter

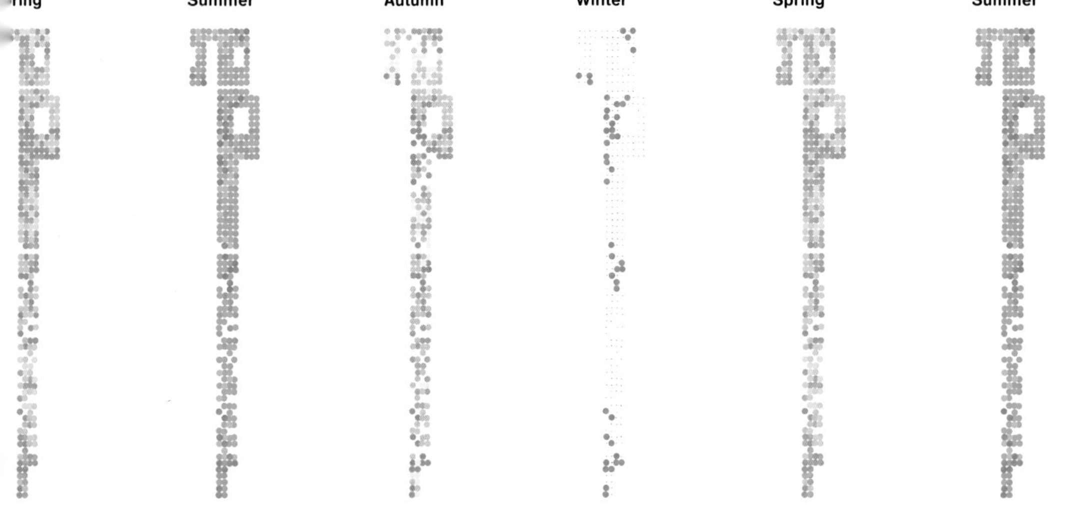
ring
Summer
Autumn
Winter
Spring
Summer

MÜNSTERPLATZ, CONSTANCE
RETURN TO THE CITY
2003–06

Client: Stadt Konstanz
Area: 6,000 m^2

The natural stone paving taken from Münsterplatz.

Constance was once the largest Roman Catholic Church diocese north of the Alps, making it an important place on the map from early times. The city is situated on Lake Constance, where the Rhine flows into the lake. Over the years the city merged with its Swiss neighbour city Kreuzlingen, so much so that the national border passes right through the buildings in places. Constance was spared much of the destruction of the Second World War, so the old town is still well preserved. Unserer Lieben Frau cathedral is testimony to Constance's significant historical role and is still an important feature of the city today. It is the tallest building in the old town and presents a prominent silhouette. The significance of this, both historically and in terms of town planning, had to be considered when developing the design proposal for Münsterplatz. The design intervention was restricted to reconstructing the square's authenticity and creating the appropriate, spatial scope for the cathedral. Modern requirements and functionality had to be considered during the planning phase. The design does not utilise many elements and materials. Only local resources were used in its construction.

The most important material used was the paving, a composite of natural stone paving and split rock, which was used to pave the entire surface of the square. It was a very economical material to use because it is easily and widely available along the eroded limestone banks of the Rhine. There was also a skilled local workforce available to collect the stones and process and lay them.

Paving the entire square with this historical local material has had a significantly calming effect on the square today. To unify the surface, the original morainal or grey wacke paving stone was removed, repaired with similar material and then laid down again.

In order to give an even stronger sense of containment to the square, the existing steps on the west side were preserved. A stairway with lateral supporting walls clarified the height difference between the garden and street to the east, and the level with the trees. Both the steps and the wall's façade are made of sandstone.

The cloister garden is emphasised by two connected U-shaped hedges of yews. The outer hedge is trimmed low and precise and defines the space. The inner hedge varies in height and thickness, creating different spatial qualities inside the garden. A long bench finishes the inner hedge and provides a place to sit and rest. At the cloister, a group of cherry trees form the entrance to the hedge garden, and as a motif recall the Barbara Chapel formerly located there. The grass is planted in spring and autumn at regular intervals with bulbs. The entrance to the Barbara Chapel's intact crypt can be opened for maintenance work and closed with a simple cover.

Natural Stone Paving
The natural stone paving used for Münsterplatz is morainal or grey wacke paving stone, made from split rock from the Rhine River's bed.

A

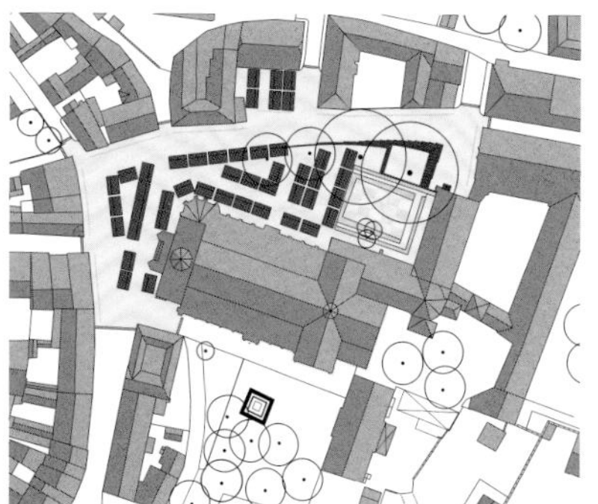

Use as market.

Lighting concept.

0 10 20 40

B

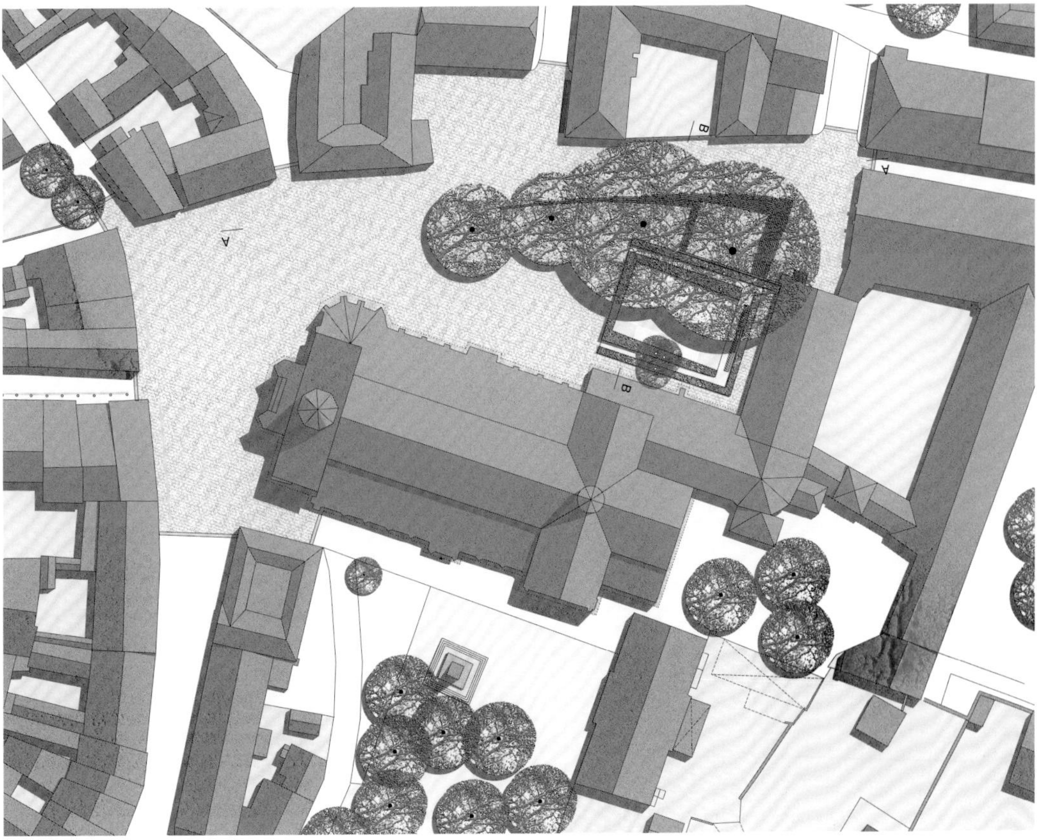

0 5 10 20

SIA HOCHHAUS, ZURICH
ABOUT A BUILDING
2006–08

Client: SIA Haus AG, Zurich
Architecture: Romero & Schaefle Architekten, Zurich
Area: 1,400 m²

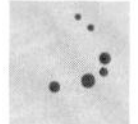

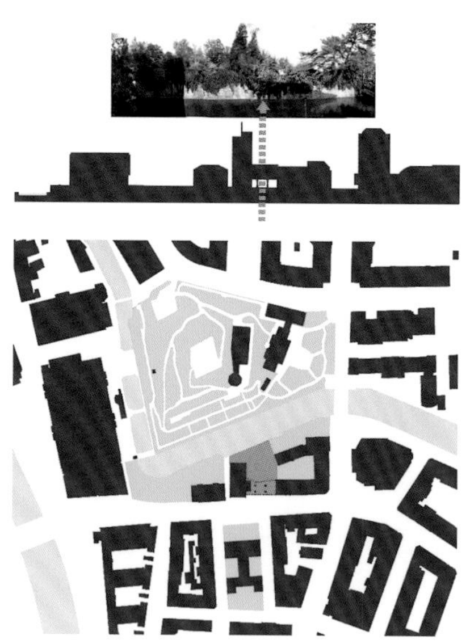

Before the remodelling of the SIA building began, passers-by would have seen a high-rise façade, but now there is an open view through the pillars supporting the building. For those who take time for a detour, the view becomes a passageway into a small public courtyard garden. In the background, the hill of the Alter Botanische Garten (old botanical garden), resembling a wall of lush greenery, limits the perspective. The courtyard lies in-between this backdrop and the street, and can be thought of as a kind of public balcony. With the high-rise behind it, and the greenery of the botanical gardens in view, the courtyard is separated by a railing from the point where the Schanzengraben is cut off; its low-lying water level is only visible when one gets closer to the railings.

The balcony seems to be covered with a dotted grey carpet. What makes the carpet special is the unusual appearance of something that is quite normal: the pavement is made of the most common construction material in the city: asphalt. However, in the dark asphalt of the courtyard the regular pattern of a large, bright circle can be seen. In this urban setting, this resembles nothing so much as a tattoo in the asphalt, but they are actually light spots created by sandblasting the surface. The dimensions of the circle are familiar, as it is modelled after the manhole covers in the streets. Despite this citation, though, the courtyard is anything but an extension of the street. The unusual pavement covers the entire surface and creates a space that is protected yet open to the public, giving a poetic side to this kind of street pavement, which otherwise seems rather hard.

Five amorphous concrete elements set in the open air provide structure to the surface without destroying the optical sightlines. The practical need for tall plant containers and the allusion to a boulder in a green space on the other side of the street determine form and material: resembling larger-than-life-size stones in a river, the planters offer space for water, soil and plants. The first element is in a fountain design, whose still, watery surface reflects the sky. If the easily moved element is made to swing, it creates, for a brief time, a pattern of waves, in which the surrounding images seem to blend. Four other elements, some mobile, others fixed, divide the space into planes. The plants are rare species of maple, and are based on the plants from the original restaurant garden that stood here before the remodelling. At the same time, it is an acknowledgement of the collection in the nearby botanical garden. As the seasons change the spectrum of various species becomes obvious: in winter the scaly or lined bark and diverse trunks determine the picture. Blossoms and the different shapes of leaves provide multifaceted views in spring and summer. In the fall, the brilliant autumn colours of the various species of maple give the courtyard a colourful accent, before the leaves fall.

What has been created is a peaceful yet constantly changing exterior that reacts to the large façade of the high-rise with a concept for generous space, combining its creative individuality with the architecture to form a harmonious whole.

An urban garden in the most immediate sense of the word – instead of the usual, lush green covering, the materials and design elements of the city were used to make a place where the public aspect of the street meets the intimacy of the garden.

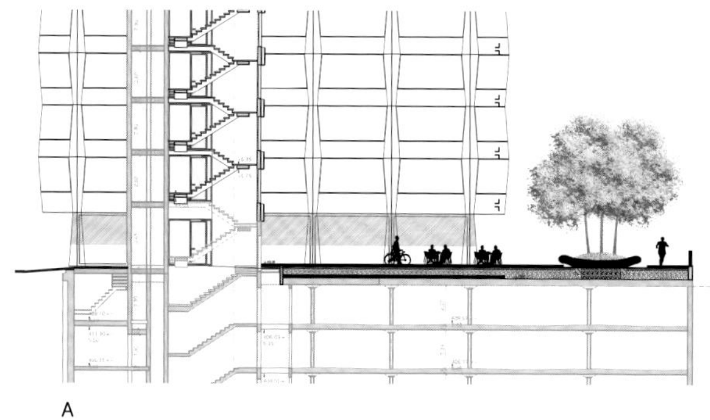
A

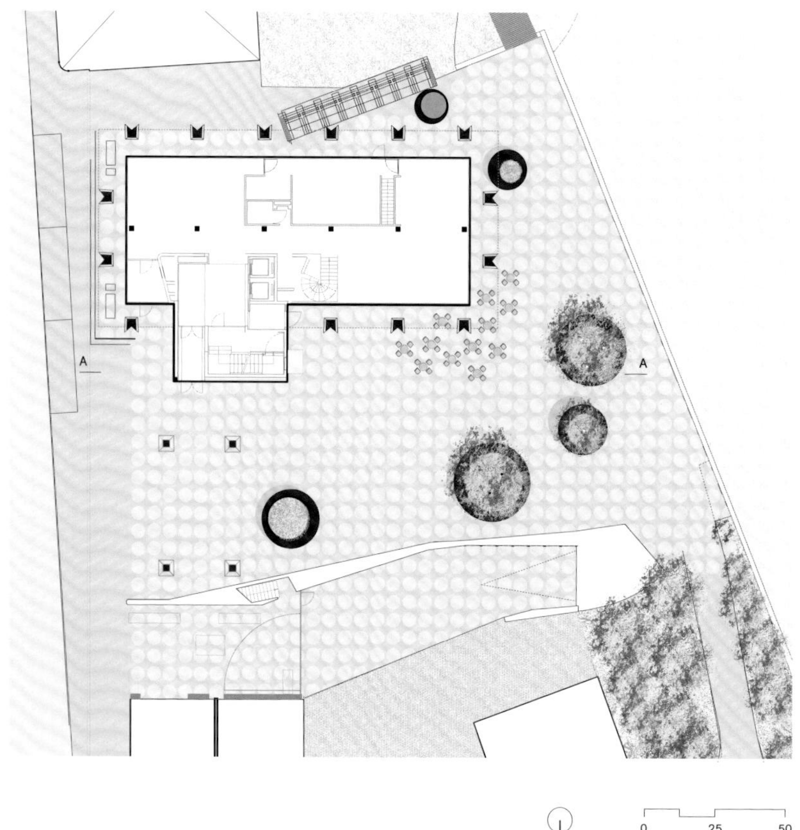
A
A
0
25
50

LE JARDINIER D'ARGENTEUIL

Le jardinier d'argenteuil (The Gardener of Argenteuil) is a French comedy about petty criminals in which Jean Gabin plays the likable pensioner Monsieur Tulipe, who augments his modest income by counterfeiting money. On 1 May, M. Tulipe begins circulating his "blossoms" as change when selling lilies of the valley, from his garden.

The action moves between periphery and centre, garden landscape and economic urbanism. In modern times, the garden was pushed to the edge of the city, where M. Tulipe cares for his garden as well. In the isolation of small villages, there may be endless variations of the same type of garden. Most garden owners searching for a way to express their own personal concept of the ideal get caught up in the fashionable sundries of the garden centre. As a result, gardens as private spaces have turned into anonymous garden landscapes. Today's gardener is far removed from the original function of land use as an existential economic foundation practised by the farmer. The transformation of wild plants into domestic crops was essentially an introduction of a value system into nature, separating crops from weeds. The gardener goes a giant step further. It is no longer the functional value, but the aesthetic value, of plants that matters. The meaning of plants in the structure of the garden is decisive for the self-image of garden culture. *Cultiver son jardin* represents, even in the urban landscape of modern times, a retreat to the private. Yet how can that be possible, if such modern spaces between city and landscape have become a symbol of mass culture?

From the typological series of many gardens, we will choose a current garden form. The collectors' garden focus is the plants that make up the actual substance of the garden. The design principles

GARDEN

edens   islands and oases
mourning melancholy bright happiness

walls clouds stones leaves
flowers   perennials   nurture   shelter
wafting fragrance   paths beds
perfection protected

adornment   prudence variety   order
hedges shrubs
herbs fruit

harmony incursion fences   hedges
inner worlds   bright happiness

are simple and generally respect the specific qualities of the site. What makes the collectors' garden so different is the staging of one or more collections of plants. As in a botanical garden, roses or peonies, irises and hemerocallis are displayed in great diversity. The private garden library reveals a garden owner's individual preferences. The connoisseur invests a great amount of work and time in plant collections, procuring plants, by exchange or sale, that become a part of a personal garden history. And as with any collection, the effort focuses on elements that are still missing. But completion is, of course, unattainable. The principle of continual hybridisation creates an open system that by definition cannot be completed. Let's take a closer look at M. Tulipe's garden.

The characteristics of a plant can be established by looking at a map of its range. Lilies of the valley are found on calcareous rock and in mountain meadows from northern England to the southern Caucasus and northeast Turkey, in the east as far as Japan, and in North America in the Appalachians, Virginia and North and South Carolina. Its botanical name, convallaria, describes its place in the garden. Lily of the valley, lys dans la vallée, or Talkessel, translated into its requirements means: sunny to shady areas under trees or bushes on fresh to moderately moist, nutrient-rich soil. The lily of the valley collector should possess a mature garden. Trees and bushes already supply dappled shade. The garden does already have a history.

What differences do we find between the various lily of the valley cultivars? As with any plant, in its leaves, flowers, fruit and scent. But we will start at the roots. The lily of the valley's root system is very dense. The rhizomes spread out along the ground, form colonies, occupy the territory. It is a form of self-defence, as these plants die down very early, in late summer. It is almost impossible for the seeds of other plants to take hold in ground filled with this dense root system. The lily of the valley's habitat under trees is a timed niche, because until the trees can provide shade with their leaves, the low-lying plants profit from the spring sun. For this reason, leaf, flower and fruit formation are all finished by early summer. The sallow beige colour of the leaves accompanies the fire-red colour of the fruit, the fleshy, round, poisonous berries. The lily of the valley is a liliaceous plant, and for this reason is classified as a monocotyledon plant. The leaf is pedunculate, long-bladed, elliptical or tapered in a lancet-like fashion. Bred differentiations enhance these characteristics: in plant catalogues we find varieties listed with leaves that are moss-green, linden-green, striped with fine linen-white stripes, permeated with fading stripes, edged with narrow white edging or broad, yellow edging, band-like and permeated with yellow, variegated yellow, dappled cream-white or yellow-sprinkled. There is a similar wide range of flowers: waxy-white, pure-white, cream-white, pearl-white, opalescent, cool pink, hot pink, overflowing pink, pale magenta, brimming, half-brimming or simply blooming, with pointed or round flower petals. The pendent, bell-shaped white flowers with connate perigon flowers are almost totally hidden by the leaves. But the real value of the lily of the valley in a garden is its incomparable scent. The plant emits this like a harvested garden fruit, like a cut flower in the home – the highest form of garden culture. Who does not recall this special memory of a scent that evokes things once experienced, which had been thought long forgotten? This insect bait seduces us as well, when it re-enters our homes every year in May.

Carl von Linné ordered and systematised the plant world in his *Systema naturae* (1735). With their endless hybridisation, collector gardeners still follow his example of orderly classification. The series of ever-similar plants with subtle differences in flowers and leaves sharpens our perception. The differences, rules and exceptions function here as a subtext to the design order. A comparative collection along aesthetic lines is very different from a scientific collection. Linné himself accused gardeners of transforming botany into an "Augean stable, because of the most negligible characteristics of exhibited species." His interest lay in reducing the number of species.

Every plant collection is an illustration of the deep private passion of a gardener, who is also a hunter and gatherer. The autobiographical aspect is one of the most important qualities of a collector's garden. The change of garden style, the mixture of styles, is here less a concept than an illustration of the life history of the garden. Its heterogeneity represents time, not space. Poetry emerges where the process of time has restored a credible authenticity to the garden dream. The collector gardener's motivation lies not in the awareness of standing on his own piece of land and being rooted there, but rather in the possession of a unique collection of plants on this soil. In the best of cases, he creates a place of great poetry in an environment marked by laconic normalcy.

"It is the deepest enchantment of the collector to enclose the particular item within a magic circle, where, as a last shudder runs through it (the shudder of being acquired), it turns to stone." (Walter Benjamin, 1931, trans. Howard Eiland and Kevin McLaughlin) *gv*

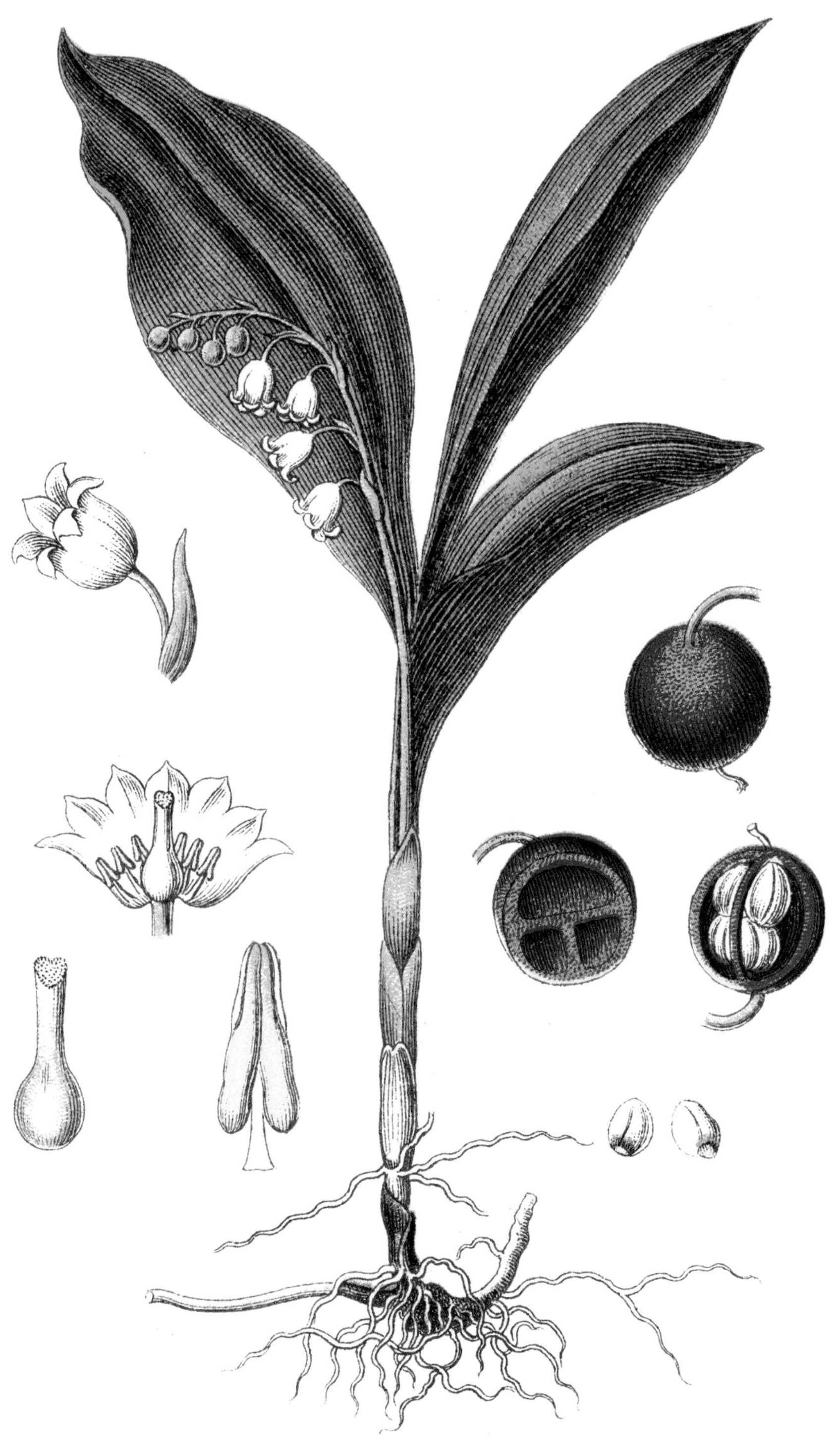

Jacob Sturm and Johann Georg Sturm, “Deutschlands Flora in Abbildungen”. Stuttgart, 1796.

The little Lilies of the Vale,
White ladies delicate & pale;

Colour lithograph after a drawing by Walter Crane. From the series, "Flora's Feast", 1889.

EXPO.02, MURTEN
GARDEN OF VIOLENCE
2001–02 (temporary)

Client: Direction artistique Expo.02, International Committee of the Red Cross, Swiss Red Cross, Stiftung AVINA
Art: Rémy Marlot, Martine Derain – Dalila Mahjoub, Cécile Dupaquier, Tina Keane, Chantal Mélia – Francois Loriot, Jenny Perlin
Area: 5,000 m^2

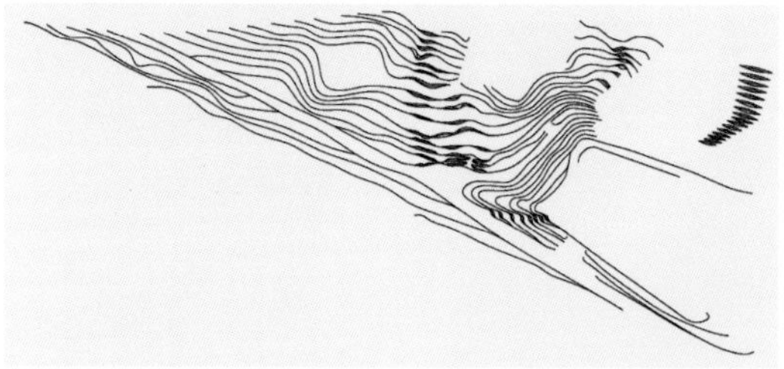

Contours studies.

The Garden of Violence was part of the Expo.02 Swiss national exhibition in Murten, which took place from 15 May to 20 October 2002 at four sites along the Swiss German/French language border: Biel, Neuenburg, Murten and Yverdon. Forty different art and other projects were exhibited, along with theatre, concert and other cultural events. The Garden of Violence project in Murten was conceived to raise awareness of how omnipresent violence is and how you need to look carefully to see it.

In European and Arab/Persian cultural history, the garden acquires an idyllic, paradisiacal character. As an ideal place of peace and beauty it offers a contrast to the world's discord and evils. It is both a presentation and imitation of paradise, as well as an expression of the desire to return to the immediacy of an undivided, unbroken world. The Garden of Violence, located between the dockyard and the central exhibition grounds on Lake Murten, is not a content-related presentation of violence in terms of belittling symbolisation. Instead, it punctuates the idyllic with disruptive factors and illustrates that paradise cannot be kept free from every unpleasant disruption. It suggests that paradise and its separation of the inside from the outside may well have been the original "garden of violence".

The Mediterranean Garden forms the centre of the park grounds. Old knotted olive and fruit trees amidst vegetables and aromatic herbs awaken a sense of familiarity, but also seem foreign in this environment. They are imported from the Mediterranean and recontextualised here. The trees still symbolise a fragment of southern landscape, but gain additional expressive power through contextual displacement.

The remaining sections of the garden also possess subtle disruptions and sharp contrasts within an idyllic context. The steep piece of forest in the east is made more dense with deadwood and, together with the old Hall of Lindens on the sloping edge and the natural terracing, makes up the park's most distinguishing elements. Exotic tree ferns mix with indigenous ground ferns. The tree fern grows freely out of a vegetable carpet that itself grows up to a metre high, covering the entire terrace floor. The combination of large-leaved, deep-green perennials and subtropical tree fern forms an exotic image that contrasts clearly with the adjoining forest. A Nordic grove faces the Mediterranean. The southern grove is designed as a garden-like, domesticated space. The Nordic grove is wilder in comparison, like a found piece of forest characterised by bizarre shapes and forms.

The main disruptive factors and conceptual investigation of violence come from artistic interventions both in the garden and the Town Museum, a former mill. The museum and the garden form a single unit that, because of two pavilions cast in wax, looks both reinforced and alienated.

A garden posing as an intact world is a utopia, a place that does not exist. The Garden of Violence however, which appears as a broken paradise, is a heterotopia, a small world within which many different, even smaller worlds can be at home and intermingle. A place of beauty in the bosom of the horrible.

Contours
The Garden of Violence is permeated by the phenomenon of the border, yet has no external delineating elements, such as hedges or walls. Its structure is formed by accentuating the existing terraced landscape. Black rubber bands line the vertical surfaces between different levels and mark the contour lines. The snaking quality of the terrace functions as an act of resistance against an imposed geometrical structure. In addition to the formal aspect, the material aspect also becomes an arena of conflict. The artificiality of rubber as a material is a strong contrast to the natural environment. The east-west direction of the terracing stands out against the vertical division of four garden zones called Fern Garden, Mediterranean Garden, Grass Steps and Nordic Garden. On the Hall of Lindens the rubber bands flow in waves over the terrace and form benches for sitting.

A, Nordic Garden

B, Mediterranean Garden

C, Subtropical Garden

0 5 10 20

D, Hall of Lindens

E, Forest

SITC, SWISS INSURANCE TRAINING CENTRE, ZURICH

DETAIL IN CONTEXT
1999–2000

Client: Swiss Re
Architecture: Silvio Schmed, Zurich
Area: 1,050 m^2

Belvoir Park originally stretched as far as the lake. The quays that exist today were added later.

The garden of the SITC, Swiss Insurance Training Centre, used to be part of Belvoir Park, one of the oldest landscape gardens in the region, dating from the nineteenth century. On a beautiful site right next to the lake, with a view over the city and mountains, Belvoir Park is still captivating today for its unusual modelling of the terrain, with great variation in height, and its exotic trees. Both qualities can be traced back to the park's original owner and creator.

In the early twentieth century, several villas were built along Seestrasse for the upper middle class. At that time, parts of Belvoir Park were severed and adjoined to the new properties as gardens. When the Schweizerische Rückversicherungs-Gesellschaft (Swiss Reinsurance Company, now Swiss Re) took over these villas and converted them into a training centre, the layout of their gardens was reconsidered and redesigned.

The design for the exterior space is an attempt to use spatial organisation and visual interpenetration to make the different sediments of history – the existing fabric and the interventions, whether historical or new – clearly legible.

An enormous European beech, with its trunk located in the garden area, originally part of Belvoir Park, – clarifies the structural interconnection of the two exterior spaces. A precisely trimmed hedge of beeches provides a point of reference for this striking tree and emphasises its size and volume by tracing in outline the eaves of its crown. This results in a new horizon in the form of an internal structure in the garden area.

One conspicuous element in the garden is the stone pool, which is listed as a historic structure. It has been enclosed within a new steel frame, which is itself filled with water and seems to cause the historical pool to sink. The new construction, with its combination of frame and fill and the material transparency of its water, implies a highly meaningful relation to the historical layers. The dialectic of old and new is made concretely perceptible by means of optic interpenetration.

The extra-wide rows of trimmed box trees are intended as reminiscences of the parterre plantings of the upper-middle-class villas, as a reinterpretation without flowers. As an inner structure for the garden, they connect various built-ins such as the pool, the skylight and the exit from the stairwell, and allude to various spatial and historical layers. The exit from the stairwell at the side entrance to the training rooms in the basement is emphasised with a thick wall of concrete poured in situ, sawn and then ground. The striking mass, surface texture and the particularly strong slope refer to below the earth's surface.

The trimmed strips of hedge along the side borders of the property emphasise the lot structure and reinforce the garden's spatial alignment towards the park. The various flowering trees accentuate the transitions between the neighbouring properties.

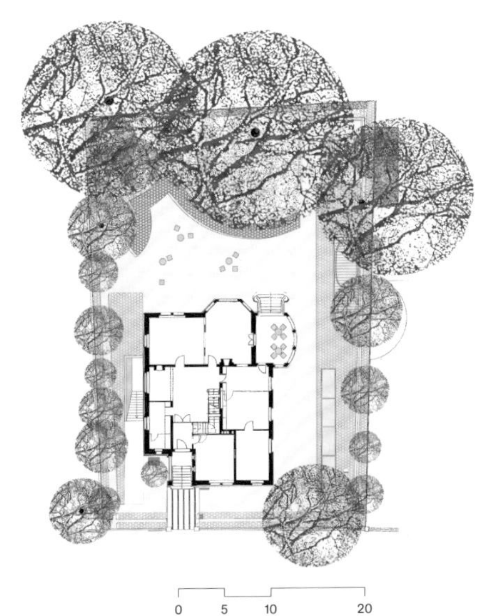

Water basins

R. GARDEN, KÜSNACHT
THE CULTURE OF THE WILDERNESS
1998–2001

Client: Private
Architecture: Meili, Peter Architekten, Zurich
Area: 3,700 m²

Project by Kienast Vogt Partner

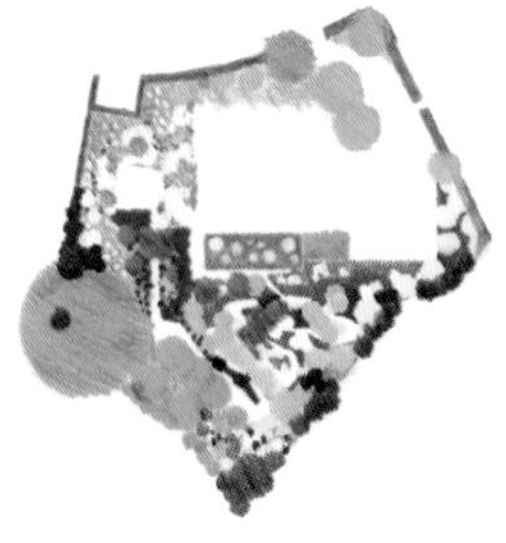

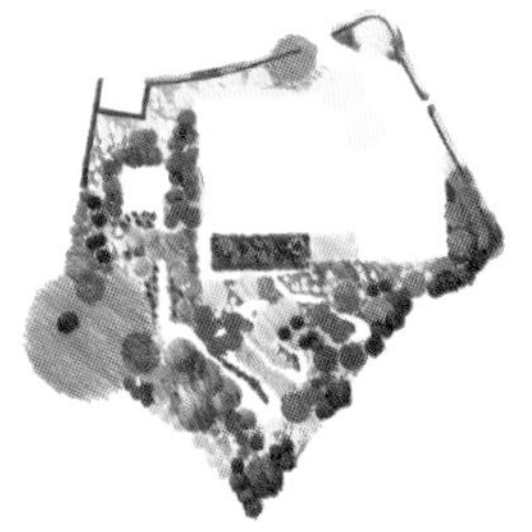

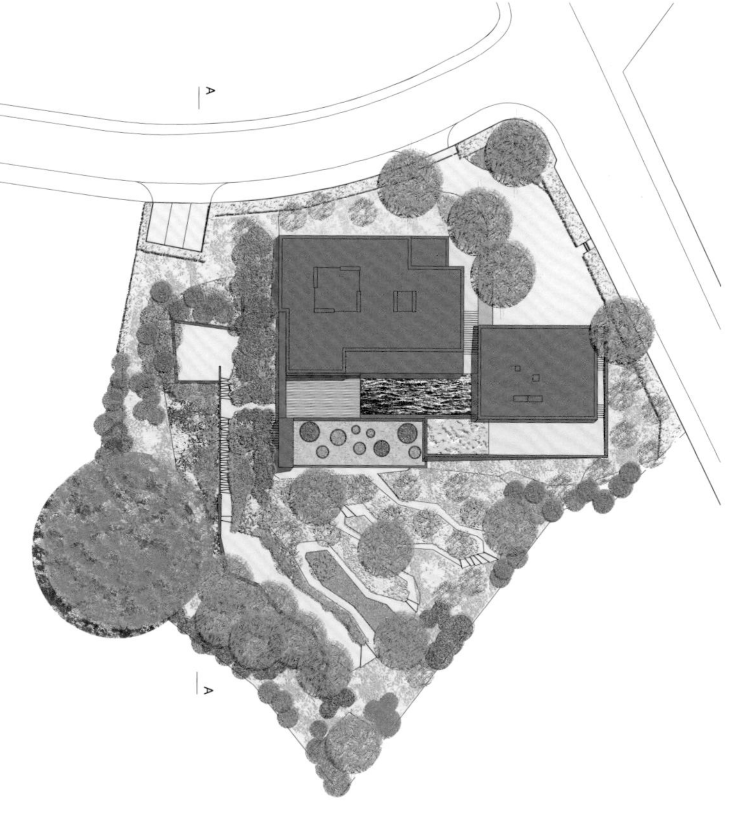

The garden originated in the Arabic cultural world. Drawings in Egyptian tombs demonstrate that gardens were already being planted in prehistory. In its original form, the garden is an excerpt from the landscape that is both enclosed and closed off from the uncultured wilderness that surrounds it. Within this enclosure, the soil is cultivated, designed and tended, which is why this area is clearly demarcated from the raw nature surrounding it.

The point of departure for every garden is the individual yearning for the first garden, for Paradise. It embodies a place of idyll and corresponds, as an "hortus conclusus", to one of the founding myths of our society, which finds support in an ideal that sees nature as fundamentally good. A given garden then emerges from the undistanced relationship to the owner's intimate life history that is being narrated.

The R. Garden has a clearly defined surface with distinct borders. It is not, however, surrounded by the original wilderness but by a hotchpotch of suburban gardens. Against this backdrop, the question of its meaning arises anew.

In the immediate proximity of the villa, the classic elements of the bourgeois garden are subjected to a specific reinterpretation. The constructions and details stand symbolically for taking possession of space, which is why the architecture and the landscape architecture enter into a tension-filled relationship. A densely planted, precisely trimmed cube of lindens serves, on the one hand, a functional purpose by protecting the swimming pool from view. On the other, it marks the living, green volume as a counterpoint to the massive stone house. The juxtaposition of these two bodies makes it clear that both the building and the garden should be regarded as built, and hence artificial.

Also found in immediate proximity to the house are glass rings, which take up the historical flower parterre as their theme. In the R. garden they are reinterpreted and become oversized vases, filled with floral decoration, flowers or fruit, in accordance with the season.

One distinctive feature of this private garden is the spring that surfaces on the property. It is framed and laid bare. In the hollow wooden form of the handrail, the water from the spring accompanies the step stairway leading to the garden, and in this poetic way it can be perceived by all the senses.

Another unusual feature of this garden is that it has no lawns. Its luxuriant growth makes it look almost inaccessible. Its design is like a choreography of cultivated wilderness that increases its internal surface area by means of the density of the planting. It suggests a walk-in landscape, borrowing on the classical motif of the garden labyrinth. The measurement of aesthetic perception is a question of the articulatable cognition of an order recognisable in the supposed wilderness. Botanic knowledge lends weight to the order and makes it legible. To "read" the order, you must first enter the garden.

A

0 5 10 20

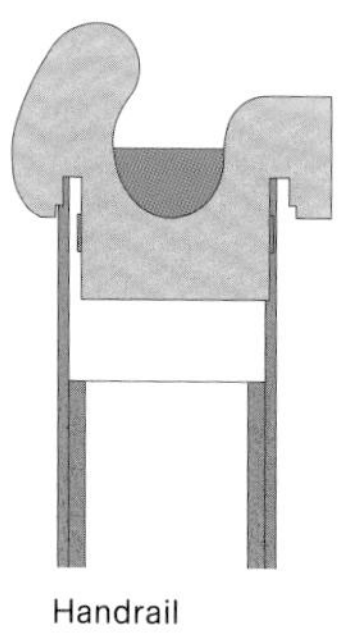

Handrail

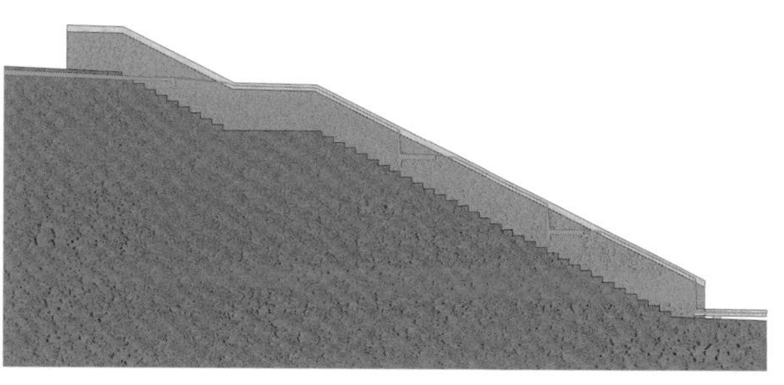

0 1.25 2.5 5

LABAN, LONDON
FOLDED LANDSCAPE
2000–03

Client: Laban, Europe's leading contemporary dance conservatoire, London
Architecture: Herzog & de Meuron, Basel
Area: 7,245 m²

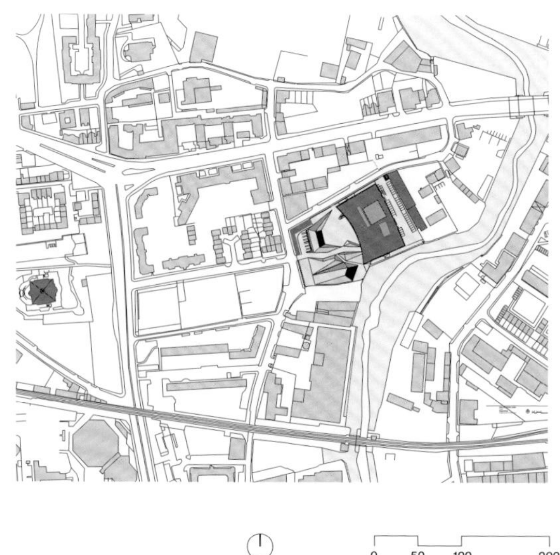

0 50 100 200

The new Laban was established between an urban clash of old warehouses and modern office buildings in the industrial area of Deptford in southeast London. The contemporary dance academy was set up in 1953 at its new base by Austro-Hungarian dancer and choreographer Rudolph Laban (1879–1958). The landscaping here is an integral element of the building project and, along with the architecture, forms an identifiable whole. The complex draws its reference from the Deptford church, which influenced the arrangement of the building and its outdoor grounds.

The garden's design reflects the role that the stage plays in the interior life of the building. A heterogeneous outdoor space was developed to contrast with the neutral and homogeneous spatial configuration of High Modernism. At Laban, various shades of green create a landscape that forms a serene setting for the oscillating building. At night the façade's shimmering colours have a magical effect on the immediate environment, so that only discreet additional lighting is needed.

The path to the main entrance on the west side zigzags slightly on its way through an undulating landscape to the building. Sloping lawns merge into geometric hills and establish the horizontal and vertical structure of the grounds' design. Sweeps and folds create a continuous space with varying qualities and a resemblance to natural landscape, as the small chains of hills and valleys form very different zones. These can be used in a variety of ways, which takes on added importance considering this is an academy of dance and movement. Two main hills form two different seating areas. The one opposite the main façade is introverted and creates a performance space similar to an amphitheatre. The building's façade serves as a backdrop and setting for the open-air stage. The stepped lawns across from this function as an auditorium with space and seating for the public. The second seating area is located near the main entrance of the building. It faces outward toward the entrance path and can be used as a resting or waiting area. It offers a view of Deptford Creek, which is mostly hidden when crossing the artificially created topography of the grounds.

The fact that the design of the dance school's setting is like a garden closed and cut off from the outside world accentuates the feeling that the complex is an intimate interplay between the building and its immediate surroundings. Together, the architecture and landscape create an optical and spatial entity that functions independently of its surroundings. A contributing factor here is the dramatic landscape, which visibly contrasts with the surrounding flat, urban setting. This element of drama was not chosen only for aesthetic design reasons. Modelling the earth also provided a cost-efficient solution to the problem of contaminated soil left over from the construction work. It was an ecological decision, however, not to plant trees. Crows, magpies and other birds of prey would have hunted the rare birds, like the black redstart, that typically inhabit them. Instead, the rooftop was covered with gravel, an ideal habitat for small birds.

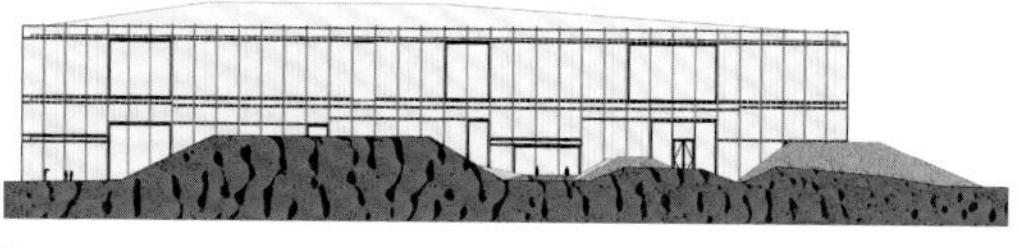
A

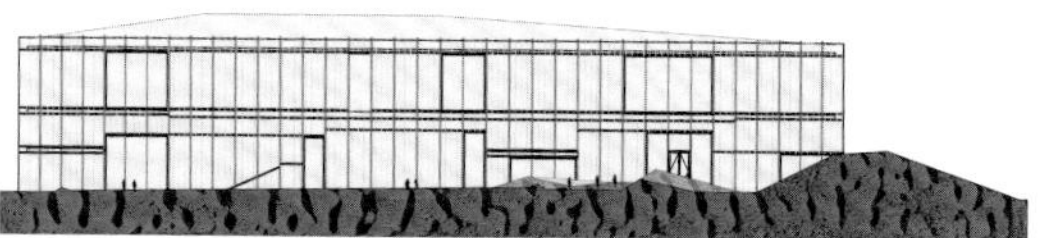
B

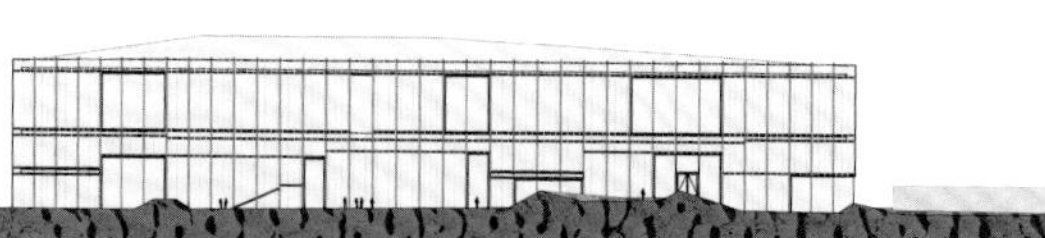
C

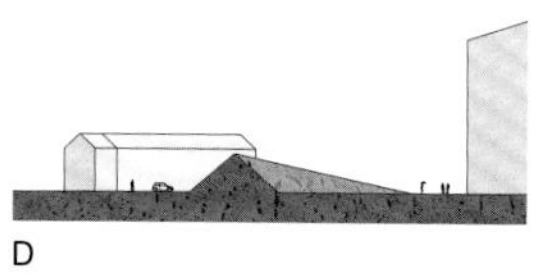
D

Reference Pictures
England's moss and grass landscapes serve as a reference for the Laban's landscaping concept.

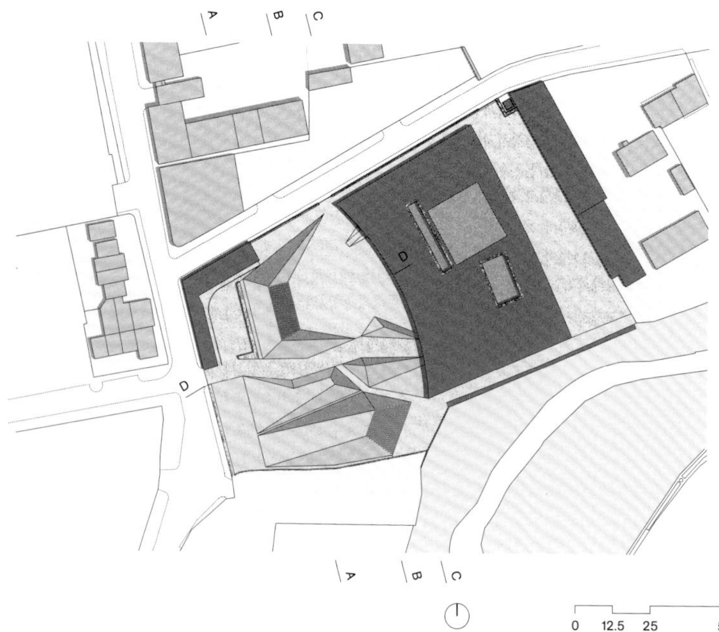

SMELLS & SOUNDS – THE INVISIBLE IN PUBLIC SPACE

MISSING LINK
2006

Intervention as part of the city_space_transitions research project
Research Partners:
Institut für Landschaftsachitektur, ETH Zürich, Prof. Günther Vogt, together with the Institut für Theorie der Gestaltung und Kunst, HGK Zürich, Jürgen Krusche, and the Institute of Art and Design, University of Tsukuba, Prof. Takuro Osaka
Period:
Zurich: 9–14/10/06
Tokyo: 30/10–4/11/06

One fragrance system can be equipped with one to twelve scents. The scents are developed in collaboration with perfumers. A fragrance system consists of containers with fragrance essences equal in number to the scents desired (5 litres for one month). The essences are sprayed by means of hoses and a magnetic valve. A control unit regulates the duration and intervals.

Perfumers mixing essences, 1956.

The research project city_space_transitions deals with current approaches to relativistic conceptions of space. In an interdisciplinary field that includes philosophy, art, architecture and urbanism, as well as sociological and ethnographic urbanology, Western theoretical concepts will be compared with Japanese ones. The study will go beyond observation at the theoretical, philosophical level, using selected theoretical texts from both cultures. Interventions in two selected cities are planned as part of the field research. There will be one week-long investigation on Langstrasse in Zurich and another one in the Yanaka District of Tokyo. Both are planned as interactions with urban street space, which, even apart from the differences in the two cultures, could not be more diverse than in the cities chosen. The long axis of Langstrasse lies within a uniform block-perimeter building plan that dates from the late nineteenth century. By contrast, Yanaka's narrow and winding lanes, often highly private, feed directly into large boulevards.

The centre of the investigation is the perception of the environment and, above all, the invisible boundaries of a space, its transformations and its transitions. People have five senses available to that end, but vision is surely the most pre-eminent of them. The study will investigate what role the other senses play in the perception of urban space. Are they just as influential as sight. How individual is the perception of space.

Two independent interventions of the senses of smell and hearing are planned as part of the research project; they are brought together under the title smells & sounds. The project Missing Link concentrates exclusively on the sense of smell. It will explore the perception of smells and scents in the city. Scents are suggestive, associative, subtle and, above all, more intense than visual impressions. They cannot be perceived from a distance but are immediately present and instantly evoke memories and associations.

In the planned intervention, a scent will be selected and then sprayed at a predetermined location. It defines a new, ephemeral area in the transitory space of the street and can make us aware of familiar, and hence no longer noticed, areas or undefined residual areas. It calls attention to things by way of associations. Even an empty space can be filled with a scent.

The idea for the intervention Missing Link starts out from the idea of a garden and its scents. The garden, as a private space, is found in European cities, but not in public spaces. By contrast, in the Yanaka District small gardens are planted directly in front of homes, thus taking possession of public property, while private gardens along Langstrasse are hidden behind walls and fences on private property. In Zurich, allées of lindens, parks and street-side cafés represent the public green spaces. They are part of European urban culture. With their scent, one can invoke aspects of the urban experience.

But what happens when a new, foreign smell is introduced into a familiar urban space? Or when the scent of one city is exchanged for that of another? With these considerations in mind, a separate synthetic scent is being created to represent each of the two cities. This scent will then be sprayed in the other city.

Zurich

Tokyo

Langstrasse, Zurich
The intervention in Zurich takes place in the Langstrasse neighbourhood. Langstrasse is a long street axis located in a regular block perimeter construction dating from the late nineteenth century. The synthetic fragrance of Tokyo will be sprayed at precisely predefined places in the streetscape. The only visible transformation during this intervention will be to exchange solid manhole covers for perforated ones. The gate to the underworld, the point of intersection between the pleasant and the unappetising, will be exposed. The fragrance system will be installed there. The fragrance of the other city will emanate from it. How will people react? What cultural differences will result between the two cities, Tokyo and Zurich? The results will be recorded in the form of interviews with passers-by.

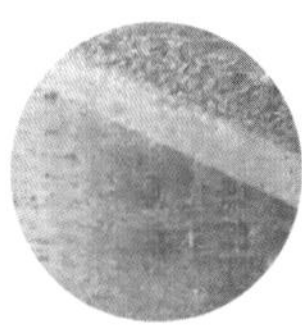

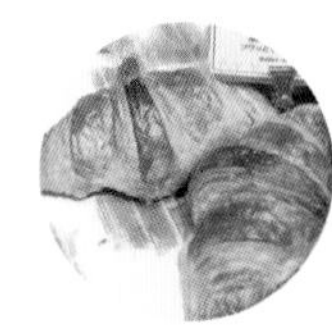

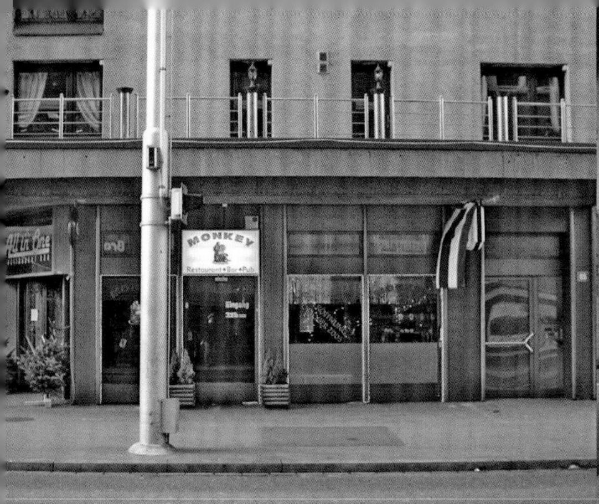

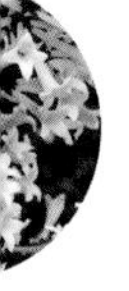

CUBE BAR
GÖFFNET BI
04.00 UHR
St.Pauli Bar
St.Pauli Girls
Non stop ab 20.00 Uhr
St.Pauli Imbis

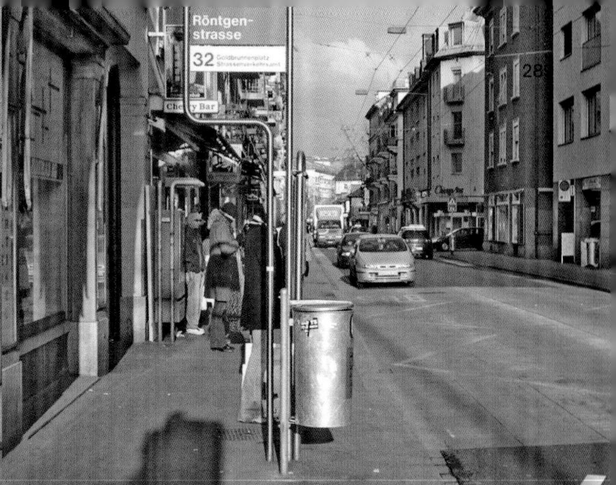

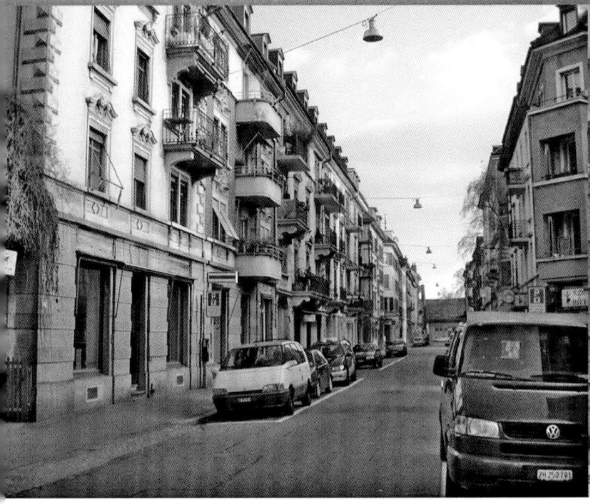

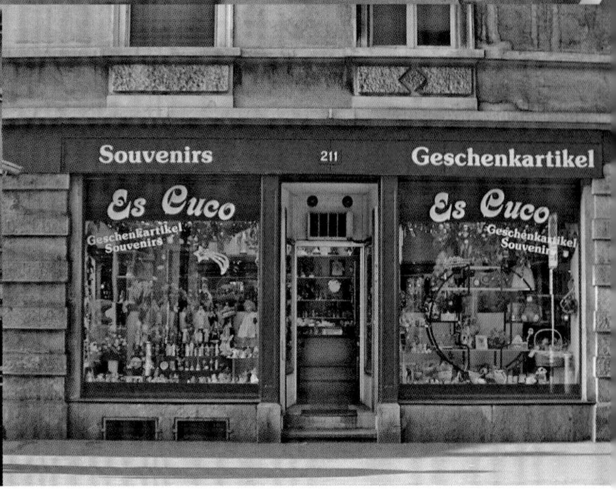

Yanaka, Tokyo
Yanaka, the district of Tokyo selected for the intervention, is distinguished by narrow and winding lanes that seem very private, but feed directly into large boulevards. At selected locations, fragrance systems will spread the scent of Zurich. These systems will be installed under predetermined manhole covers. To that end, the solid manhole covers will have been replaced by perforated ones, so that the fragrance can emanate freely. The reactions of passers-by will be recorded by photographs and interviews and then evaluated.

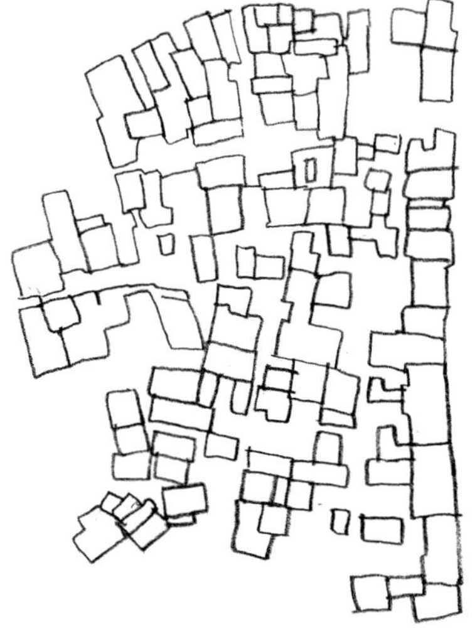

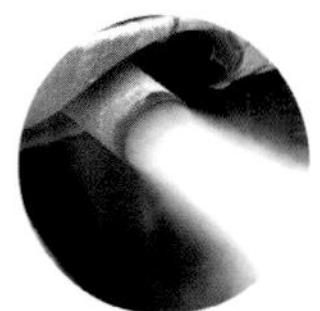

CEMETERY

earth melancholia pilgrimages

ancient stones   time lapse

paths water paths   walls
resting places   city of the dead

graves   quietude   fire   silence
paths walls   far place

THE LIME APHID

The linden tree can be perceived from two perspectives, that of pedestrians and that of the car drivers. The pedestrian will be enraptured by the unrivalled scent of its blossoms, the iridescent green of its leaves in spring, its expressive black trunk after a rain, and its graceful yet stately form. The car driver will complain about the sticky deposits it leaves on any car parked under a linden in summer.

The lime aphid sucks the tree's juice from its leaves, digesting only the protein and excreting the sugar as so-called honeydew. This honeydew gives the leaves of the tree a shiny coating and drips stickily off the leaves onto the ground, or onto cars. When this sticky coating settles on car paint, it is attacked by fungus that, if the process is not interrupted, can leave behind permanent stains. This is similar to what happens to the affected linden tree. Sooty mould spreads along the sugar-coated leaves, staining the leaves black blocking the light needed for photosynthesis, and permanently harming the tree.

A simple example of ecology – the teachings of the ecosystem. We cannot deduce anything from it what is ecologically correct or incorrect. The lime aphid probably could not care less about what we think about its way of life. The simultaneity of diverging social flux can be explained by the falsely understood concept of ecology. The lessons of the ecosystem are basically descriptions of natural processes that contain no value judgements. Exploitation of nature or a respectful protection of it depends on social conditions. The awareness that our relationship to nature must be urgently revised contrasts with the rampant doctrine of exploitation. The term "ecology" or "ecological" is often equated with "paradise" or “paradisiacal”. The so-called ecological balance that suggests there is a harmonious accord in our relationship to nature does not exist, and it is also not the aim of ecology. There is at best an oscillating line of balance. After every intervention in a habitat or biotope, ecology, untouched, describes nothing more than the new life requirements and dependencies. It is the same case with the remaining network or networked system. If a tear appears in the ecological network, the network closes again, and often suffers other tears in the process. Every ecological system we know of originated from another. The stability of a system, as we like to claim for our concept of nature, is not at all a criterion of an ecosystem. Nor is diversity of species a guarantor of a stable habitat. Even the slightest alteration in a parameter can cause the entire system to collapse.

For ecological reasons, the lime aphid should be left in peace. Otherwise, according to the laws of ecology, the postulate of the cycle would be disturbed. Yet we could chop down the lindens, as there would be no measurable change in the ecological parameter for us to record, since their usefulness – that is, their production of oxygen – is equal to their consumption of oxygen. The manufacturers and consumers in a habitat reciprocally convert the available substances. Stones erode, plants thrive on the eroded minerals, herbivores feed on the plants, carnivores feed on the herbivore and the remains of this cycle return to benefit the plants.

Ecology does not describe paradise, nor the path that would lead to it. If the lime aphid and the linden tree were removed, they would not be missed in ecology’s calculative model. We, however, might miss the ability of the aphid to produce sugar from the juice it derives from the linden’s leaves, but it would surely be sad if we could not enjoy the grace of the linden tree. Yet beauty and uniqueness are not ecological parameters. Ecology's networks are so closely linked that we are only able to recognise a fraction of their relationships, dependencies and regenerations. This complexity can be better explained using a pile of sand. When a single grain is removed, the entire form changes. What we learn from the laws of natural balance cannot be used as a guide for our treatment of nature. Ecology helps us understand the processes of nature. Only those who understand nature, who know what goes on behind the scenes, can truly enjoy it. *gv*

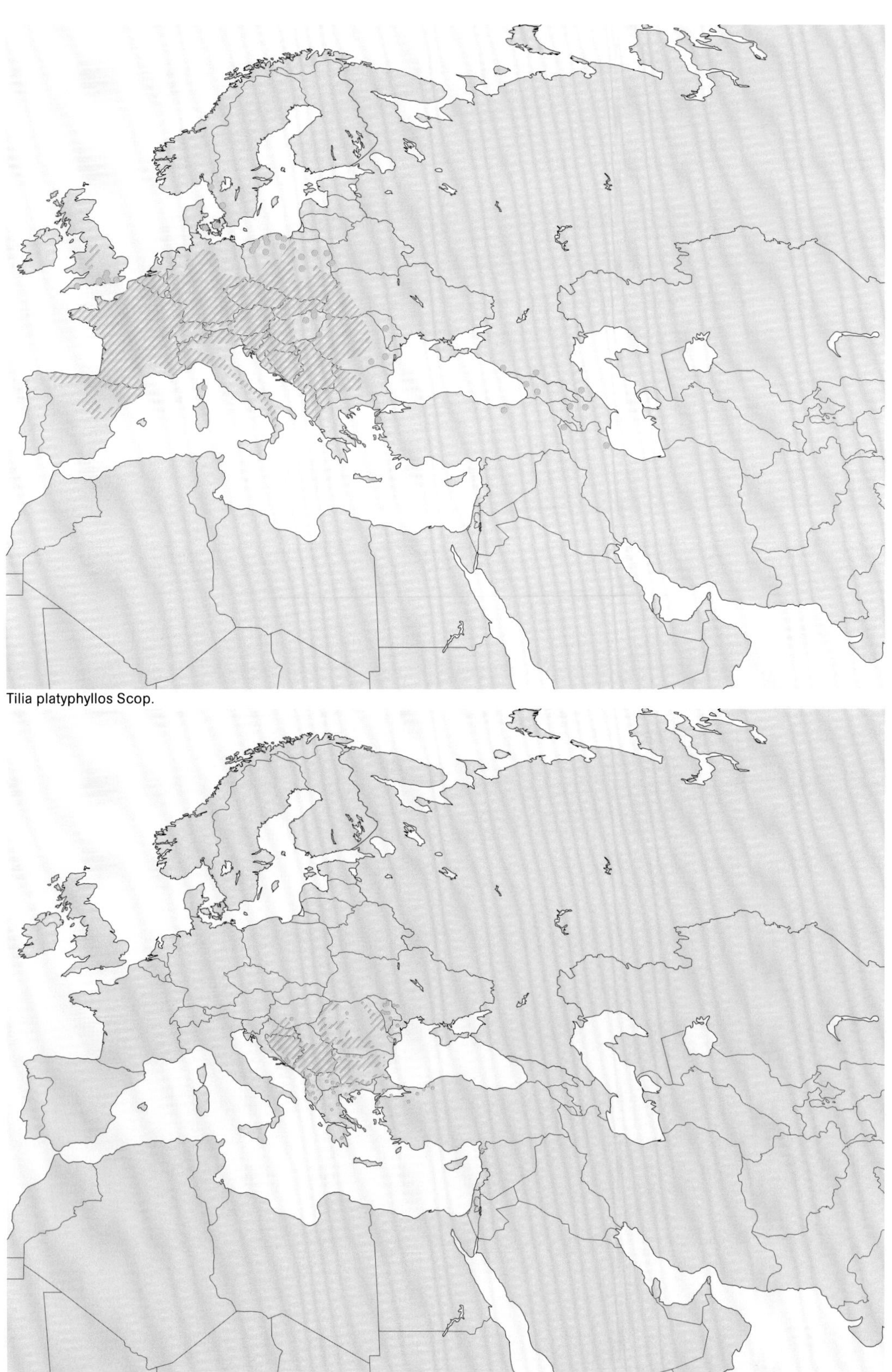

Tilia platyphyllos Scop.

Tilia tomentosa Moench.

Tilia caucasica Rupr.

Tilia cordata P. Mill.

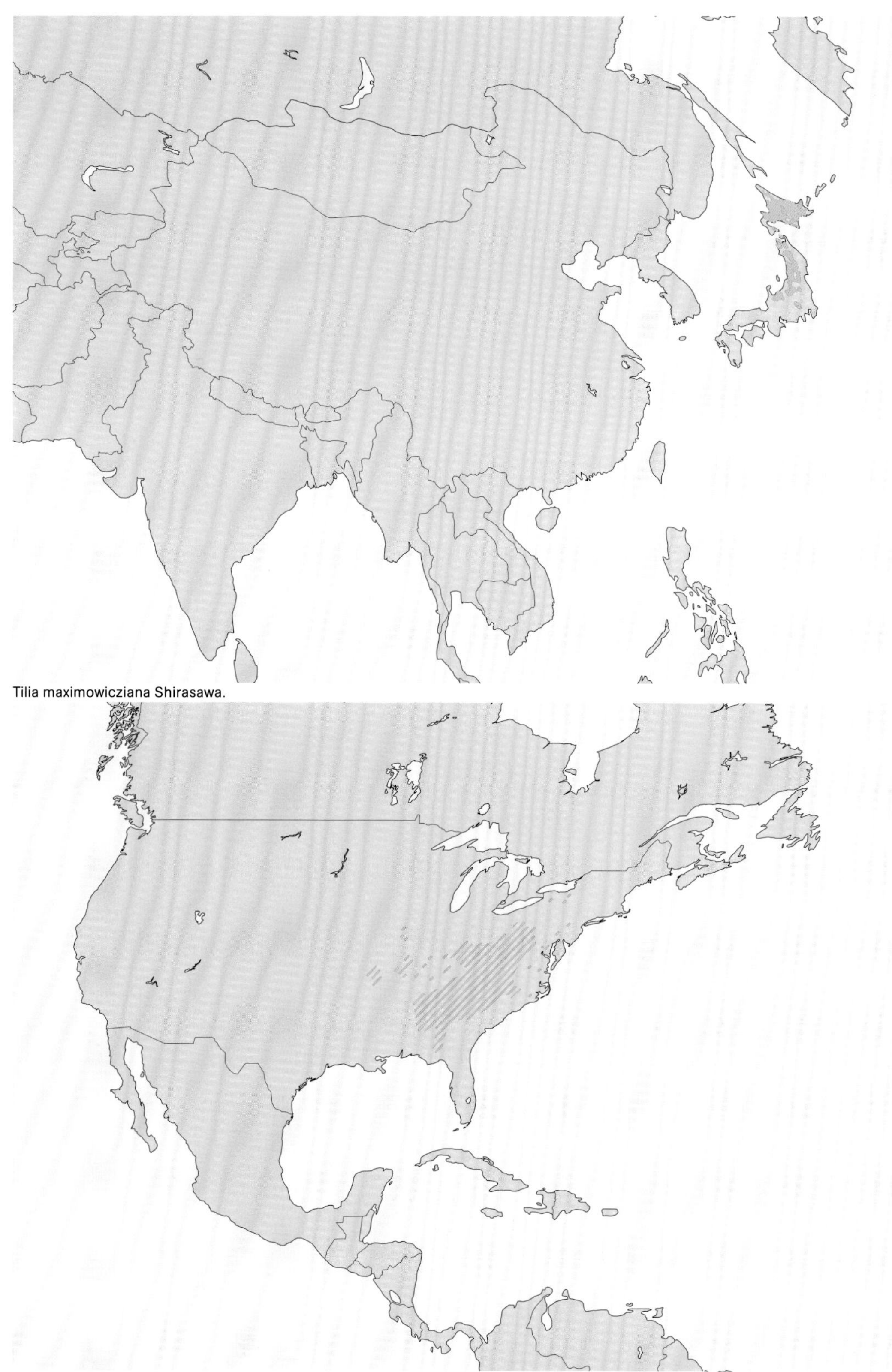

Tilia maximowicziana Shirasawa.

Tilia heterophylla Vent.

Tilia americana L.

Tilia caroliniana P. Mill.

STECKBORN CEMETERY
IN THE LINDENS
2001–09

Client: Stadtverwaltung Steckborn
Architecture: Stoffel Schneider Architekten, Zurich
Area: 3,800 m^2

Linden on town square in Steckborn.

Steckborn is a small town in Switzerland, located directly on the Untersee at the west end of Lake Constance. Reichenau Abbey, situated on an island of the same name, had authority over the village of Steckborn and was responsible for its receiving official status in 1300. Today Steckborn has 3,500 inhabitants.

A competition was announced in 2001 for design proposals to expand the existing cemetery. These were to include architectural elements, such as viewing areas and sanitary facilities, as well as a new arrangement of the graves. The clients wanted an interdisciplinary team of landscape architects and architects to develop a new design solution.

Reconstructing or expanding a cemetery does not allow an autonomous design. The design must refer to the existing structure and react to the specific site. Ultimately, these are small gardens arranged along a perimeter – gardens for the dead. The garden is here a symbol for paradise: the grave as the first and last garden, as the original garden and "hortus conclusus", where the dead can rest in peace.

The design idea is based on the concept of the cemetery as a place of tranquillity and contemplation, a space between the living and the dead. In Steckborn, the cemetery is surrounded by the old cemetery wall, which was expanded in parts. It surrounds the entire grounds and separates this hiatus from the surrounding environment. The buildings are also located along the periphery of the cemetery, and like the wall, function as a border to the outside world.

Within the walls, trimmed linden hedges define the grave areas. They create spaces and recall the hedges that are normally used to delineate gardens. Besides outlining the graves, the linden hedges also line the cemetery wall and lighten up its appearance. The trellises on the wall of urns are also linden. They cover the wall completely, turning it into a foliage element. Linden trees are planted in the gravelled spaces between the graves and buildings. In these meandering long passages, they stand as single trees or in loose groups of twos or threes. The trees interrupt the strict arrangement of space and give it a new rhythm. Finally, the linden hedges serve as a setting and enclosure for all the furnishings – the benches, waste bins, water faucets and the necessary lampposts.

Linden in these different forms is a spatially defining and shade-providing element. These different uses of the linden represent an ornamental choice, but it is also a spatially defining element and offers shade. Focusing on only one type of plant for the cemetery's design marks a strong contrast to the colourful small gardens on the graves themselves. The concentrated use of different varieties of linden refers to the neighbouring town square and its existing mature linden trees. The plant forms a bridge between the introverted cemetery and the city outside.

Forms of Lindens

For the design of the cemetery expansion, lindens were employed in a variety of ways: as extra heavy standard trees, hedges and trellis.

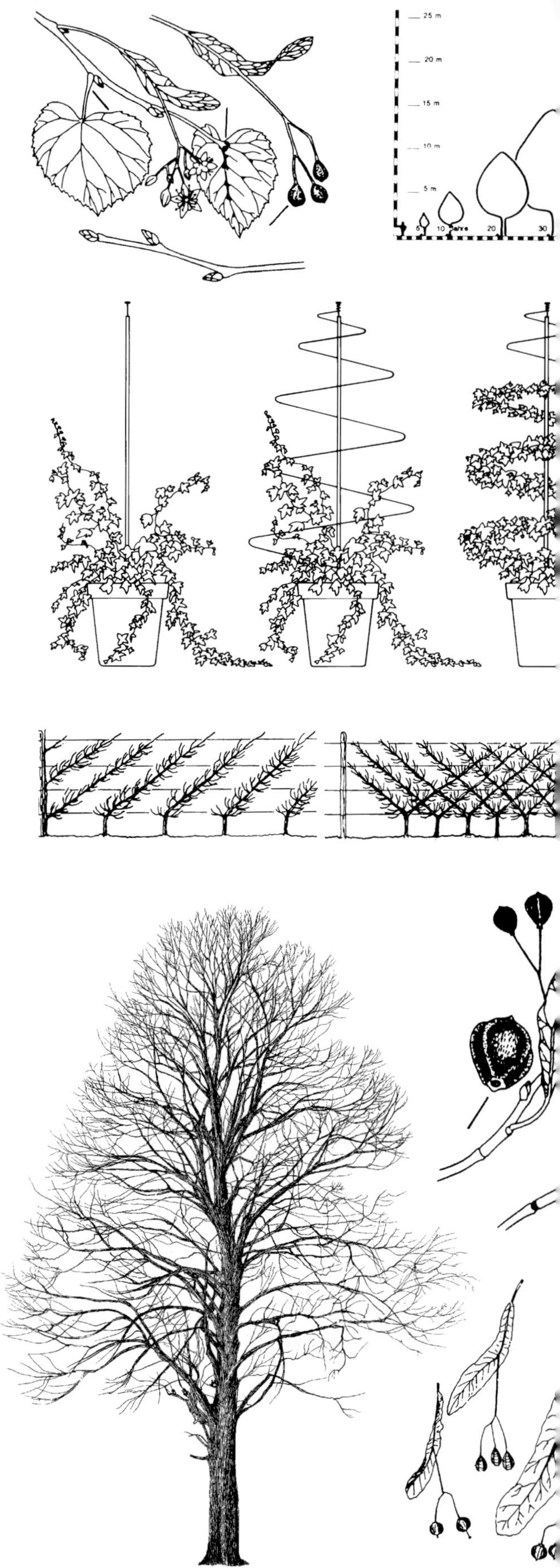

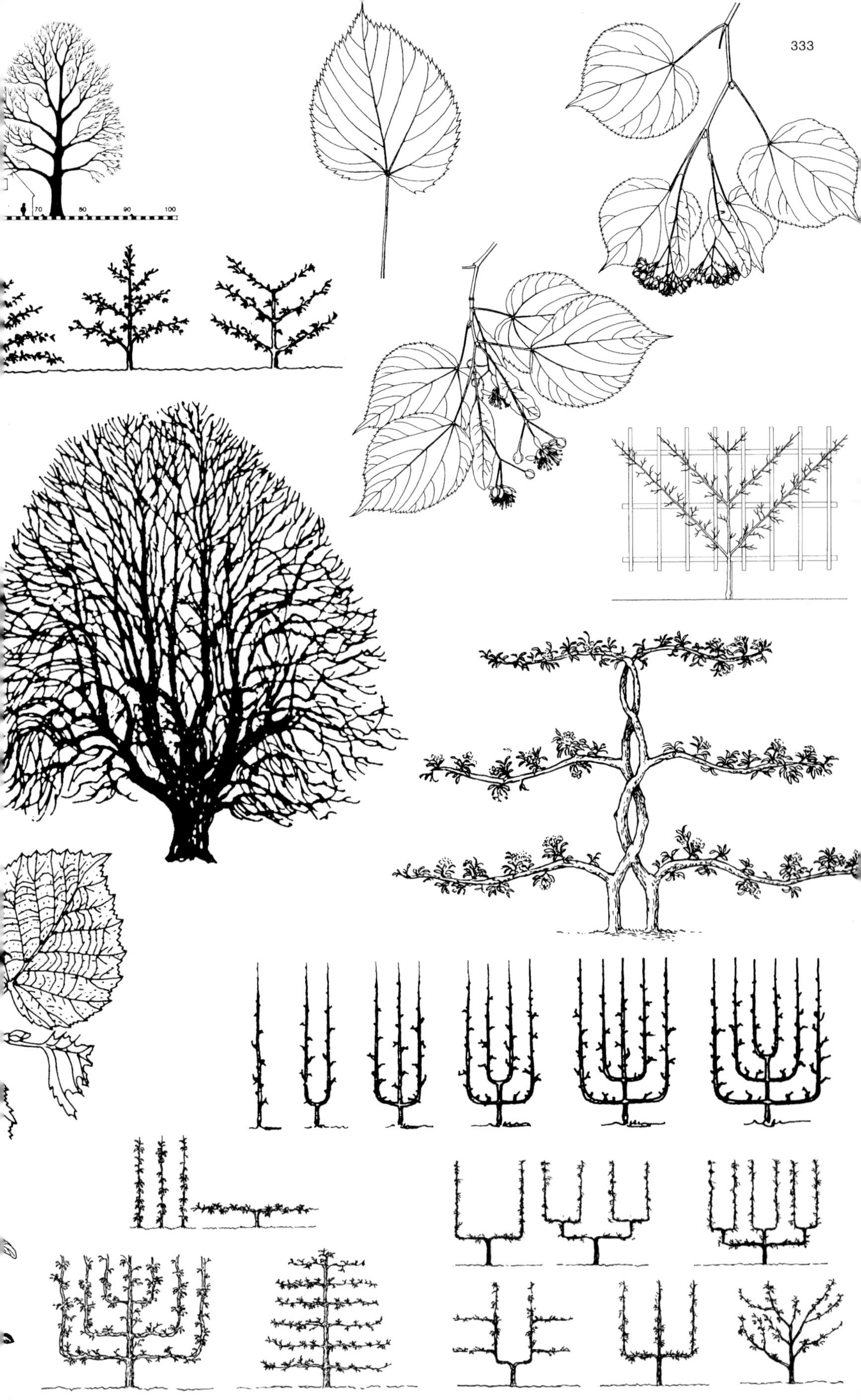
70
80
90
100

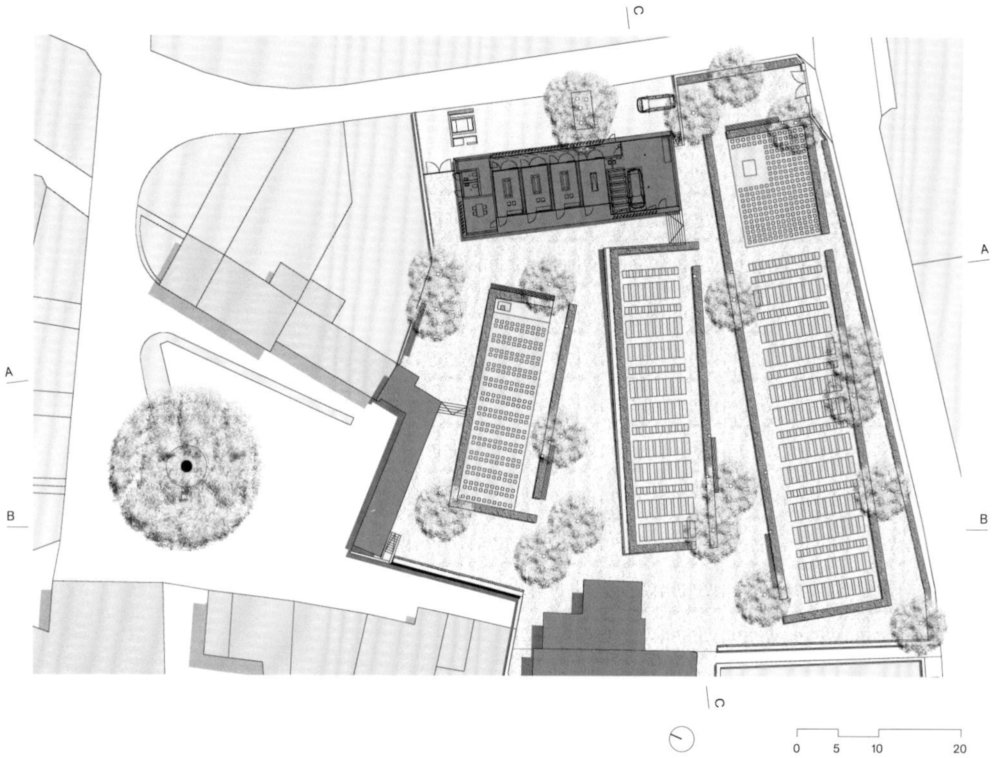

Urn wall

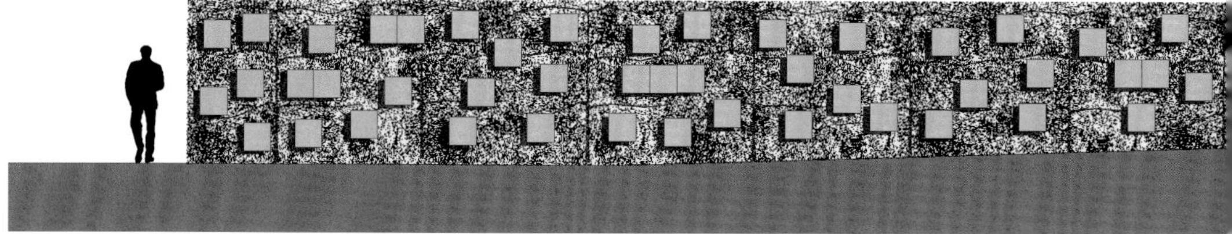

A

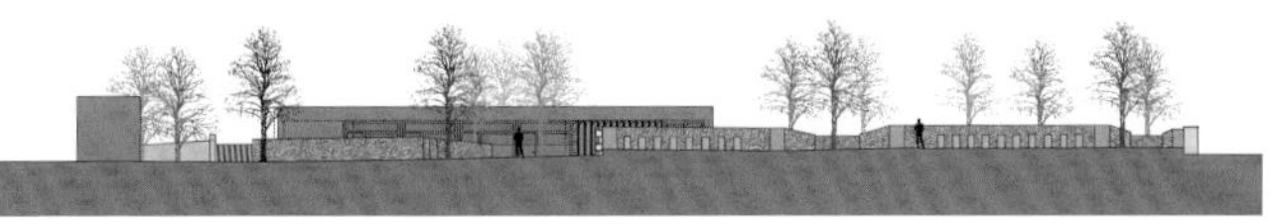

B

C

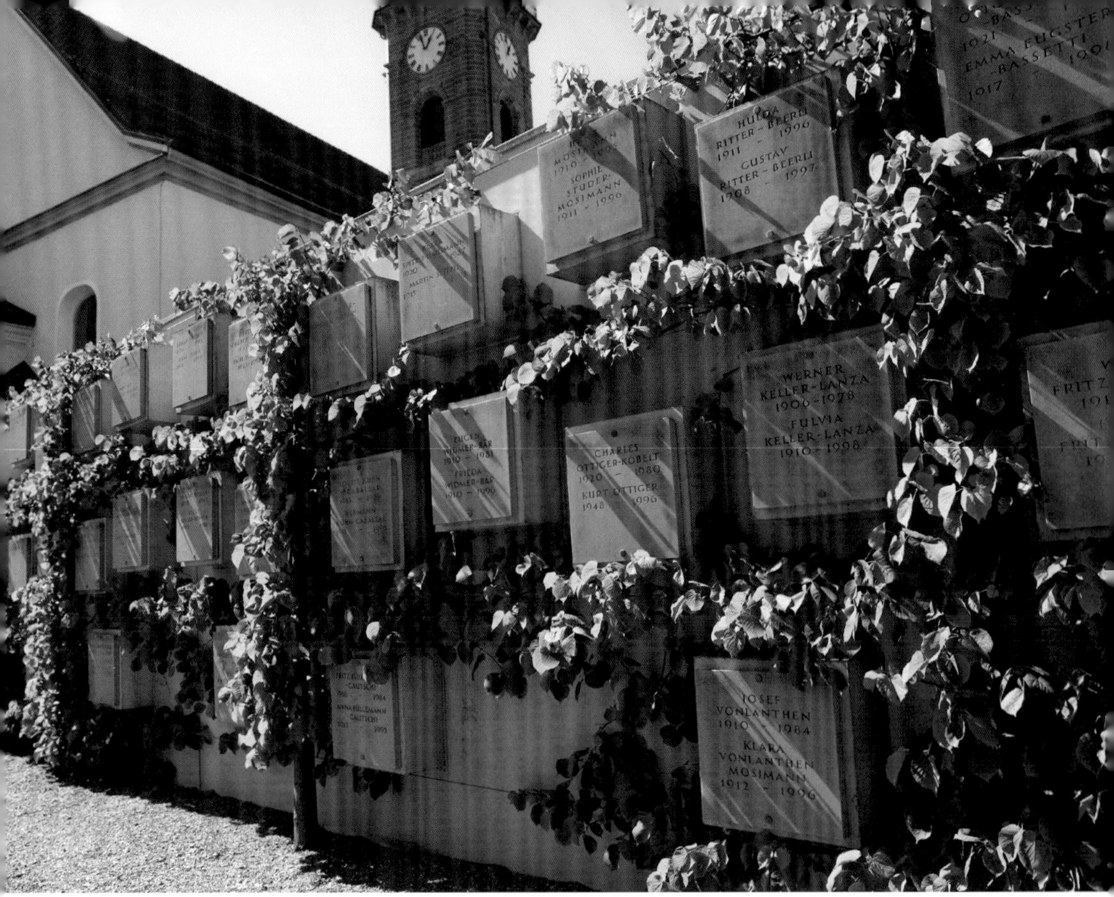
EMMA EUGSTER-BASSETTI
1917
HULDA RITTER-BEERLI
1911 - 1996
GUSTAV RITTER-BEERLI
1908 - 1997
SOPHIE STUDER-MOSIMANN
1911 - 1996
WERNER KELLER-LANZA
1906 - 1978
FULVIA KELLER-LANZA
1910 - 1998
EUGEN WIDMER-BÄR
1910 - 1981
FRIEDA WIDMER-BÄR
1910 - 1996
CHARLES OTTIGER-KOBELT
1920 - 1980
KURT OTTIGER
1948 - 1996
JOSEF VONLANTHEN
1910 - 1984
KLARA VONLANTHEN MOSIMANN
1912 - 1996

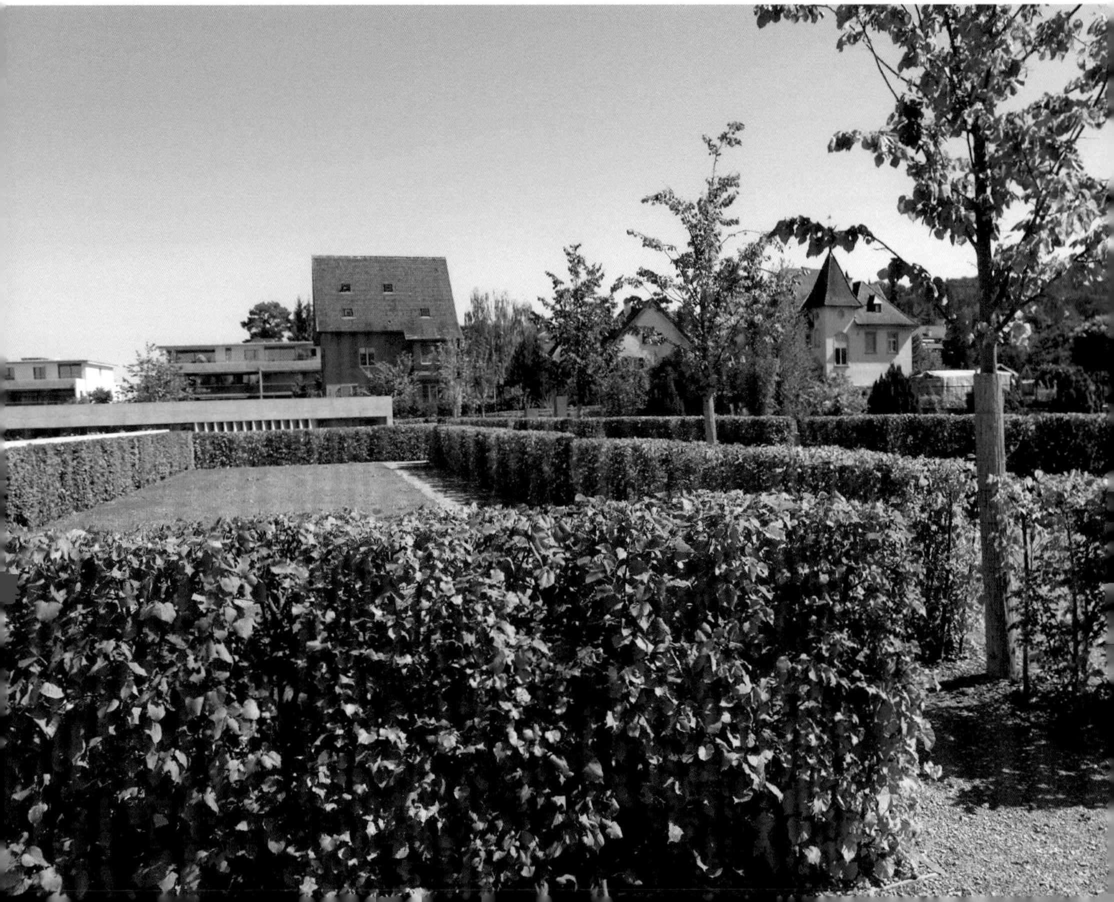

THE MUSLIM BURIAL GROUNDS AT WITIKON CEMETERY, ZURICH

THE CEMETERY WITHIN A CEMETERY
2002–04

Client: Grün Stadt Zürich
Area: 2,400 m^2

Muslim cemetery in Morocco.

Witikon Cemetery is one of approximately twenty cemeteries in Zurich. It was established in 1957 and is situated on the periphery of the city, directly bordering the forest and the agricultural region. In summer 2004, a Muslim burial ground was added to the cemetery to provide the Muslim community with burial alternatives.

The Christian and Muslim sections of the cemetery are visually very different. In the Christian section, the graves are arranged in rows of single plots. Each one is individually accentuated and adorned with cut flowers, plants, sculptures, plaques, crosses and other decorative elements. Even in death, human beings remain individuals in the Christian tradition and receive personal graves with a distinctive, specific, individual character. In contrast, Muslin graveyards are humble and unadorned. The graves themselves are marked only with simple, flat or standing gravestones, or plates. There is no decoration or planting.

Four rules must be adhered to at a traditional Islamic burial. The dead are never cremated. They are merely wrapped in a clean white cloth and buried without a coffin, laid on their right side with their face turned toward Mecca. Islamic burial tradition also prescribes that graves be consolidated in one simple, modestly designed burial ground, and forbids unearthing any human remains. It is possible, however, to reallocate a grave. In Witikon the period of rest is twenty years. The grave can be reallocated when this period expires. It is difficult to follow all of these four conditions everywhere in Zurich, but they can be easily integrated into the local customs and regulations. These guidelines also provide the basis for the design concept of the Muslim gravesite.

The need to have the graves face Mecca was the predominant decisive factor in arranging the burial grounds. This explains why they do not follow the natural topography or the arrangement of the Christian cemetery area. Their location along the edge of the cemetery was chosen so that the two sections allocated for the different denominations would be visually separated from one another.

The two areas completed, of the four originally planned, are surrounded by a wall and form independent, similar sections, joined by a fountain in the graveyard. Each comprises 160 individual graves and a congregation area. Because of Witikon's poor soil conditions, building the walls was initially required to achieve a south-east facing, horizontal level. Yet today they are a distinctive feature of the Muslim burial ground's design and appearance. The walls are made of lime plaster with sandstone plates; their colours, red-brown, beige and yellow, refer to their paragons in the Orient.

The congregation area at the front of the burial grounds establishes the design and the conceptual basis for the cemetery. The courtyard is accentuated by a fountain and group of Persian ironwood trees, or Parrotia persica. These deciduous trees are indigenous to northern Persia and thus a reference to the Islamic landscape. They have extraordinary autumn foliage, ranging from dark burgundy to purple, pink and yellow. The fountain is a reference to the ritual washing of the dead prescribed by Islamic burial traditions. The room allocated for this rite is also located on the cemetery grounds.

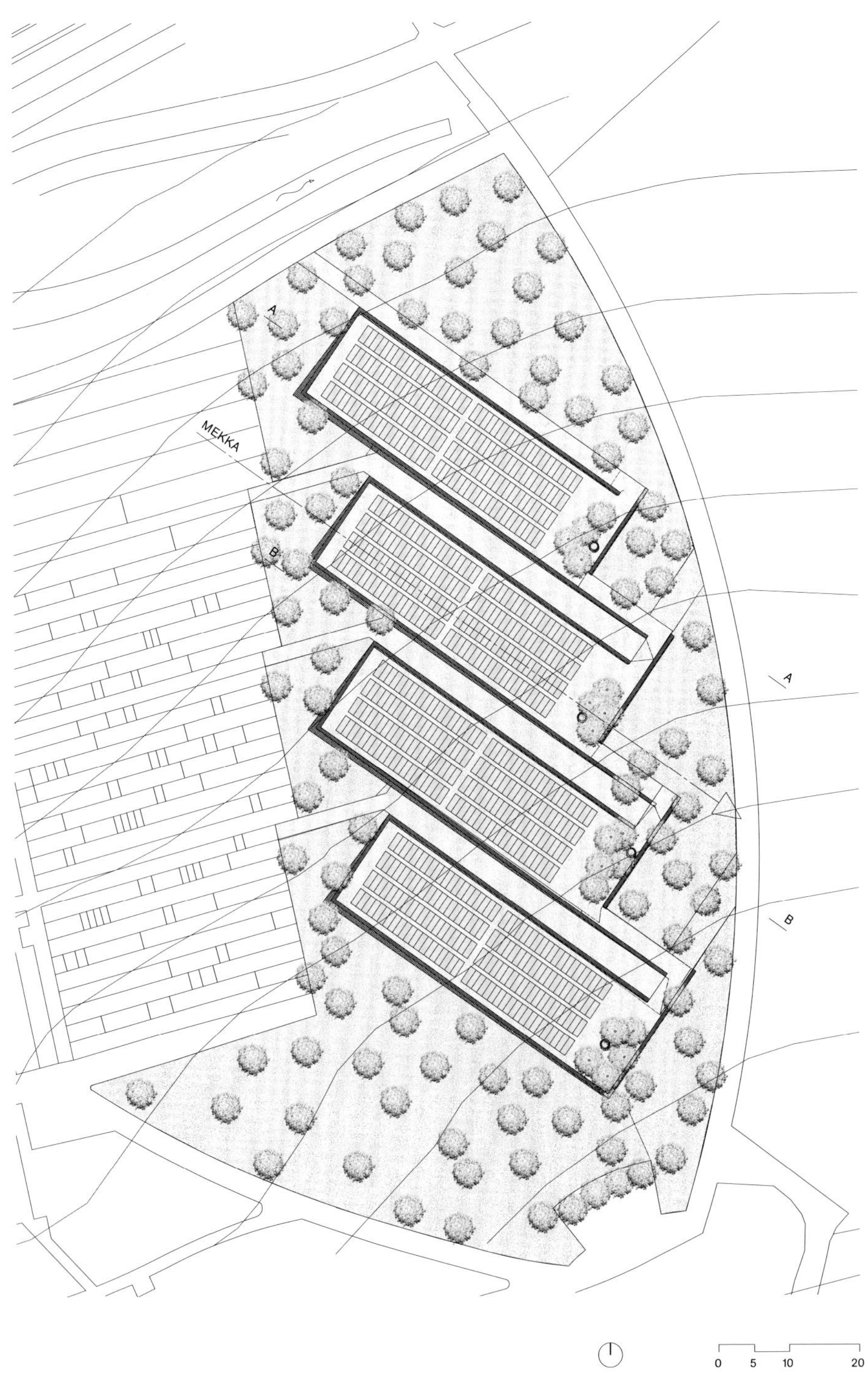

A
MEKKA
B
A
B
0
5
10
20

A

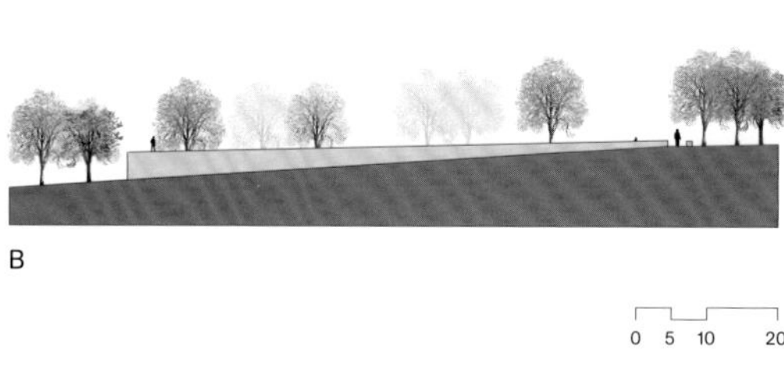

B

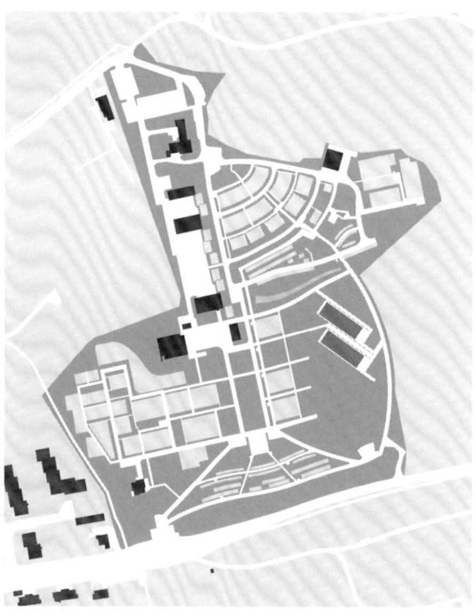

Location of Muslim burial grounds within the Christian cemetery of Witikon.

Brickearth as Building Material
Brickearth is a mixture of clay and fine sand and is produced by the weathering of rock formations. The different characteristics and size of grain of sand and clay minerals allows for a broad spectrum of variations in material. Its composition varies according to where it was unearthed, and can be optimised for construction use by mixing it with aggregates, such as water and plant fibres. Brickearth hardens when dry, but can grow soft whenever it absorbs moisture. Brickearth is an economical building material. It can be found everywhere and is easy to shape when moist. The brickearth technique has a long tradition and is used all over the world. Even today, almost half of the earth's population lives in brickearth houses.

COURTYARD

closed   inside   inner worlds
emptiness calm   enclosed space

solid edges   hard borders
hard ground   walls   silence

backyard buildings   shadowfall
cascades of light   idiosyncrasy

rear façades
secluded   unseen
foreign noise

reverberation   remains
chosen
preordained

SEARCHING IN THE FOG

How does a fisherman on the high seas maintain his orientation and perspective when he is surrounded by fog, when all his charts fail him, when stars and other reference points are invisible?

Michel Serres wrote the story of an old cod fisherman. When his ship is being checked, it is discovered that he had not unpacked his nautical charts. Asked how he found his way on the high seas, he explained: "This is how you get to Saint-Pierre: head toward the setting sun until you see a certain kind of small algae in the water; when the sea turns very, very blue, stay a little to the left, and then you can't go wrong; that is the place the little dolphins like, where there is a strong northern current, where the prevailing wind blows softly, in light gusts, and the swell is always low, then comes the big grey rectangle and then the place when you cross the course of the big icebergs; when you see them, the first reef lies under the wind."

It is much the same with landscape; vegetation and topography are ultimately the orientation aids that show the way. The world of plants is like a seemingly endless library of books. How else to describe the variety of forms, colours, sizes and scents? What cartography could help us maintain perspective? In everyday reality, the manageability of the garden helps; the limitation of dimensions and styles is liberating. It is not the entirety of plants, but the focus on the selection, that demands our attention. A perfect garden can thus affect us more than nature in its unspoilt form. The magic of a garden does not, however, lie entirely in the selection of various plants. The perception of the texture of leaves, the scents of flowers, the shadows of trees is direct and immediate. At the same time, we know that this momentary perception describes only the here and now. Tomorrow the peony will already be showing the fleshy seeds for life the day after tomorrow. This concept presumes knowledge and experience. The knowledge of the continuous transformation to a higher degree of complexity, to a supposed stasis as a result of meteorological influences, and the repetition of the same the following year. And the experience that too much rain and cold could destroy all our efforts.

"He leapt the fence, and found all nature was a garden." Horace Walpole's remark about the landscape architect William Kent describes aptly how the English landscape garden replaced the idea of French absolutism. Dominance of nature was replaced by control of it. Nature as imparted by views and framed like a painting is, however, corrected and dramatised where it seems necessary. The control of nature calls for a plan that decodes the chaos of nature. With the help of maps and plans, the world found just outside our front doors and in faraway lands is not only depicted, but rearranged at the same time. In order to explore and enjoy nature, we give it a form that we can understand.

Inner and outer worlds create a horizon on which every garden is based. Unadulterated nature is no longer to be found, not even in exotic foreign lands. The alternative to the garden in today's world is the wilderness of civilisation. After paradise, gardens emerge everywhere and nowhere, according to individual ideas. Like a palimpsest, the original text is deleted, and every spring a new one is written over the old layers. The horizon, which we call orientation, is to be sought in gardens themselves, and every year they are cultivated, modified and refined. *Cultiver le jardin* also means incorporating social currents. That is why forbidden fruits were first replaced by foreign plants and then by fear of poisonous plants. In Eden, before the expulsion, the plan was for pleasure. Ignorance drove humanity from the Garden.

So today we experience the paradox of having lost control over nature after giving it a place in the garden. At the time we allowed it into the garden, we knew our guest. Now that he has settled in, however, we no longer know his characteristics. Back then we knew that when we found a fly agaric mushroom in the forest, we should not succumb to its beautiful appearance; the more modest-looking porcini could, however, be safely picked not far away.

The nature of the city is mapped. Those who know how may read on the map of the city the biotopes of lake, forest, square, park, promenade, courtyard and garden. No great expectations plague them. They believe they know from experience what to expect. On site, however, this certainty proves deceptive. What names are behind the many trees of the forest? Are the plants in the new city park really all local, as was requested? Exploring the latency of nature demands attention. The library of plants is large. It is open to the willing reader. *gv*

Altocumulus stratiformis
Altocumulus floccus
Cumulus humilis + Altocumulus
Cirrus spissatus
Cumulus humilis + Altocumulus
Cu + Altocumulus stratiformis
Altocumulus lenticularis
Stratocumulus stratiformis
Cirrus undulatus
Altocumulus stratiformis
Cirrus spissatus
Cirrus vertebratus
Cirrus spissatus
Cirrocumulus lacunosus
Cirrus spissatus
Cirrus uncinus
Altocumulus duplicatus
Cirrus spissatus
Cirrus radiatus
Cirrus intortus
Cirrus undulatus
Cu mediocris + Stratocumulus
Cirrostratus nebulosus
Cumulonimbus mamma
Cumulonimbus capillatus
Cumulus congestus
Cumulus mediocris
Cumulonimbus capillatus incus
Cumulonimbus capillatus
Cumulus congestus
Altocumulus lenticularis
Altocumulus stratiformis

Stratocumulus stratiformis
Altocumulus lenticularis
Stratocumulus + Cumulus
Stratocumulus stratiformis
Altocumulus lenticularis
Cirrus fibratus + Stratocumulus
Stratocumulus + Cirrostratus
Cumulus fractus
Cumulus humilis + Cirrostratus
Cu humilis + Cirrus undulatus
Altocumulus lenticularis
Altocumulus lenticularis
Altocumulus undulatus
Altocu stratiformis translucidus
Altocu stratiformis translucidus
Cumulus mediocris
Stratocumulus stratiformis
Cu + Altocumulus lenticularis
Stratus fractus
Altocumulus duplicatus
Altocumulus castellanus
Altocumulus opacus
Altocumulus stratiformis
Altocumulus lenticularis
Cirrus spissatus
Stratocumulus duplicatus
Cirrus fibratus
Altocumulus stratiformis
Altocumulus translucidus
Altocumulus stratiformis
Cirrus fibratus + Altocumulus
Stratus fractus

Mist + Stratocu opacus
Altocumulus stratiformis
Stratus fractus
Cirrus intortus
Stratus fractus
Cumulus humilis
Cumulonimbus praecipitatio
Stratus fractus + Altocumulus
Cumulus fractus + Altocumulus
Stratus fractus
Cumulus + Altocumulus
Cumulonimbus praecipitatio
Altocumulus opacus
Altocumulus virga
Stratus nebulosus
Cirrostratus + Altocumulus
Altocumulus lacunosus
Cumulus fractus
Stratus + Altocumulus
Stratus + Altostratus
Altocumulus + Cirrus fibratus
Cumulonimbus praecipitatio
Cumulus congestus
Stratus nebulosus
Altocumulus lenticularis
Cumulus mediocris
Cumulus humilis
Cumulus fractus
Stratus + Stratocumulus
Stratus + Cu + Stratocumulus
Stratus fractus + Cu mediocris
Stratus nebulosus

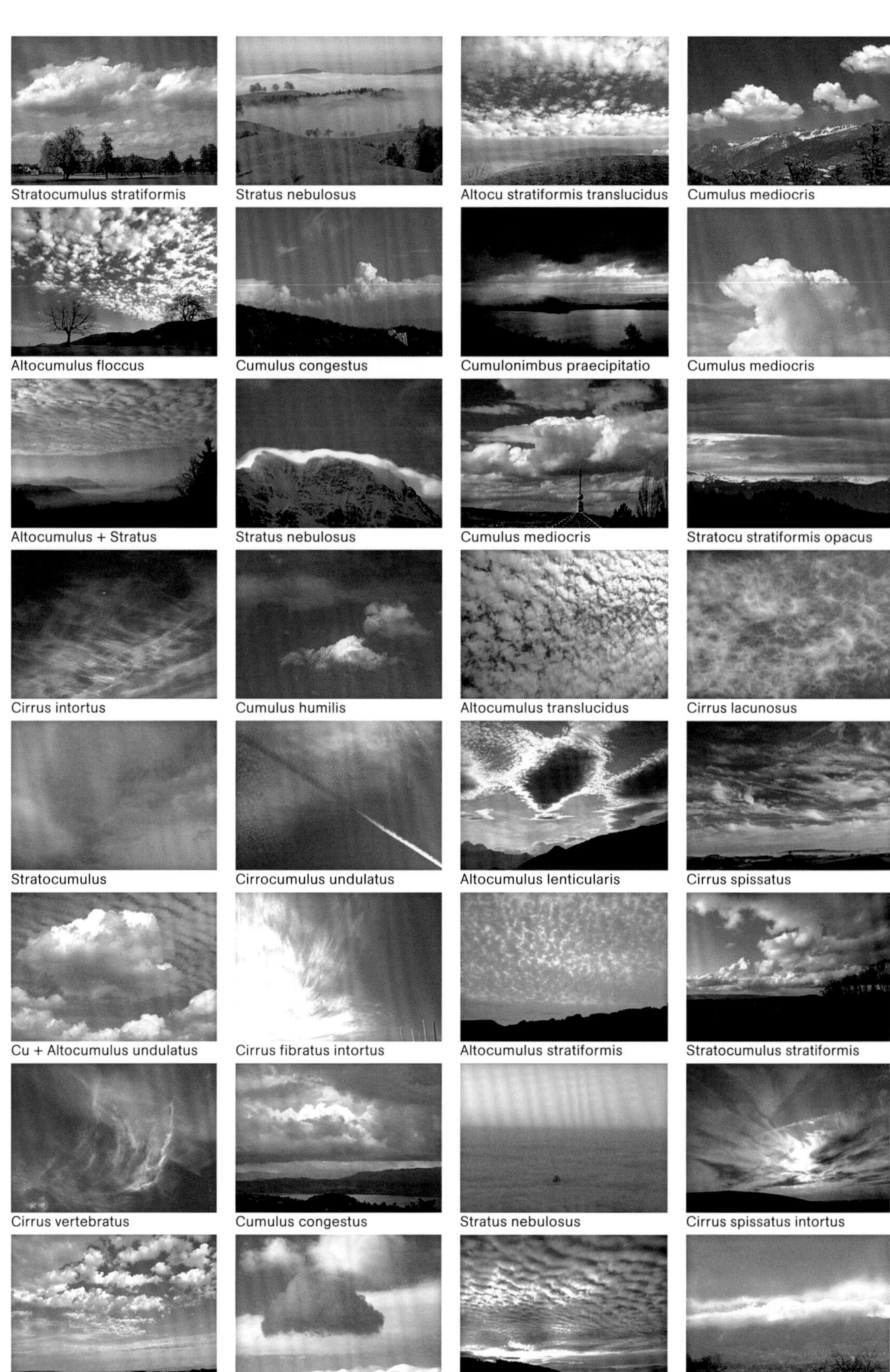

Stratocumulus stratiformis
Stratus nebulosus
Altocu stratiformis translucidus
Cumulus mediocris
Altocumulus floccus
Cumulus congestus
Cumulonimbus praecipitatio
Cumulus mediocris
Altocumulus + Stratus
Stratus nebulosus
Cumulus mediocris
Stratocu stratiformis opacus
Cirrus intortus
Cumulus humilis
Altocumulus translucidus
Cirrus lacunosus
Stratocumulus
Cirrocumulus undulatus
Altocumulus lenticularis
Cirrus spissatus
Cu + Altocumulus undulatus
Cirrus fibratus intortus
Altocumulus stratiformis
Stratocumulus stratiformis
Cirrus vertebratus
Cumulus congestus
Stratus nebulosus
Cirrus spissatus intortus
Altocumulus floccus
Cumulus fractus
Altocu perlucidus undulatus
Stratus fractus

PARK HYATT HOTEL, ZURICH

WEATHER GARDEN
2002–04

Client: Park Hyatt, Zurich,
Hyatt International EAME Ltd.
Architecture: Meili, Peter Architekten, Zurich
Area: 6,565 m^2

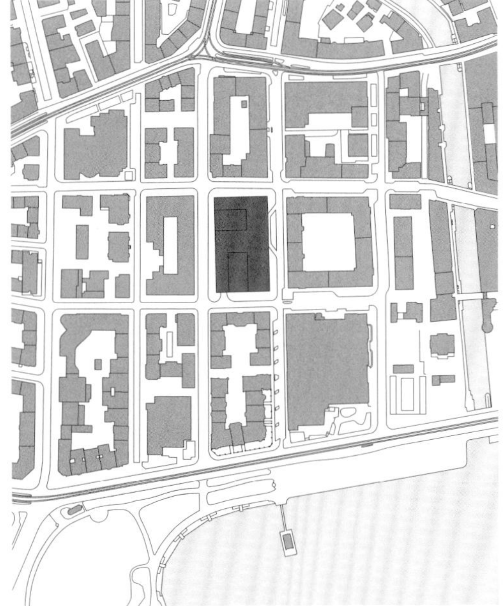

The perimeter block structure of the commercial and office district around the Park Hyatt hotel.

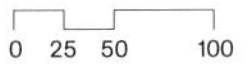

The five-star Park Hyatt hotel stands on the former site of a car park. It is located in an exclusive commercial and office district in the immediate vicinity of the Kongresshaus, the Tonhalle and Lake Zurich. The quarter is distinguished by its perimeter block structure. The new building for the Park Hyatt hotel adopts the scale of these volumes but varies them slightly: at the main entrance, the street area is widened thanks to the considerable overhang of the building. On the third floor, the compact building complex opens up onto the two courtyards, which are in turn open to the street.

The building is slightly recessed from the line of the neighbouring structures. Hedges were planted in the resulting exterior spaces; their placement marks the difference between the accessible public space and the private space belonging to the hotel. Nevertheless, the space is still perceived as a unity. Following the principle of the front garden, the greenery was placed in the sidewalk area like small inserts. The relationship of the various woody shrubs, which are trimmed to form precise hedges, to the semi-basement provides structure to the zone in front of the building. A subtle distinction is made between the areas for passers-by and those for guests; the function and utilisation areas are established, providing a filter between the outside and inside. Existing trees on the street were integrated into the design of the exterior.

Two cuts into the body of the building create courtyards framed on three sides on the roof of the second floor, though no access is provided. The first courtyard has moss growing on tuff ashlar. It is misted by means of nozzles inserted in the joints. This results in a variety of shades of green that adapt to the climatic conditions over time. It presents an image of the interplay of dampness and dryness.

In the second courtyard, the hotel guests look into a stone court with flat, green natural stone slabs. Differences in the rate of drying on the stone slabs, which have been ground in irregular concave and convex shapes, are like traces left behind by the weather. When water forms a thin film on the slabs, they reflect the sky and clouds. As the slabs slowly dry, the images change constantly, because the pattern of the puddles alters as they dry. If there is no rain, this effect can be triggered artificially by nozzles recessed between the stone slabs.

The designs of both courtyards make direct references to the architecture. The monolithic volumes pushing their way into the courtyards react to the strict pattern of the façade and maintain the simple regularity in terms of the number and arrangement of the slabs. At the same time, the roof greenery makes independent volumes that function as autonomous design elements. Hotel guests who remain only a brief time see in the courtyards a changing image of the weather in the place where they are staying – a poetic greeting to the guests.

Karst Landscape
The natural model for the design of the courtyard of the Park Hyatt hotel.

Natural stone slabs.

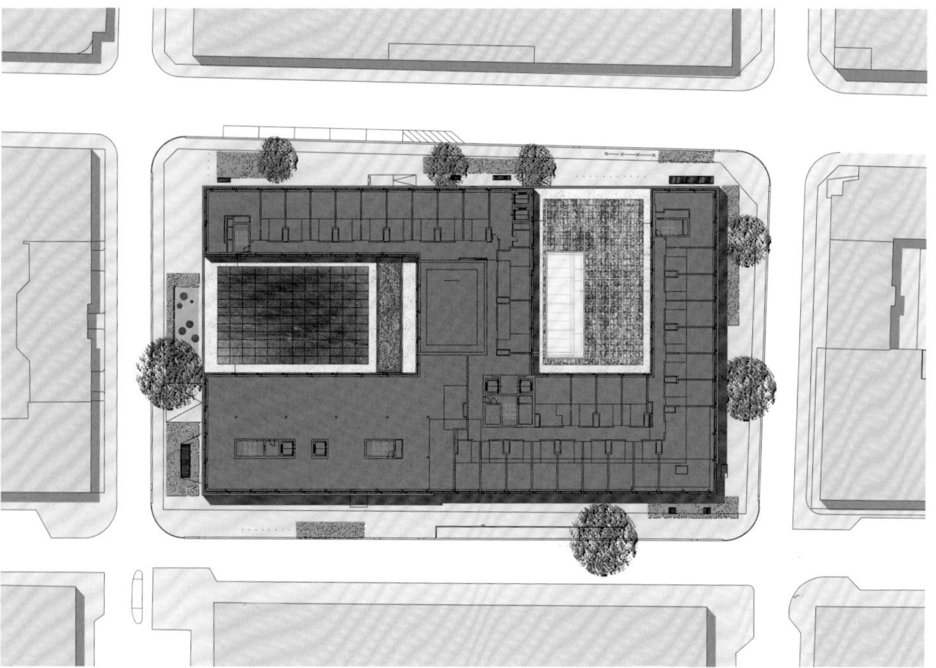

0 5 10 20

Video stills

WSJ-158 SANAA BUILDING, NOVARTIS CAMPUS, BASEL

EXACT LANDSCAPE
2004–06

Client: Novartis Pharma AG, Basel
Master plan: Vittorio Magnago Lampugnani, Studio di Architettura, Milan
Architecture: Kazuyo Sejima + Ryue Nishizawa, Tokyo
Area: 800 m^2

Mock-up of the design of the courtyard.

In the St. Johann industrial zone, located in the border triangle in Basel, modern and attractive workplaces are being built for Novartis on the basis of a master plan. Integrated into urban surroundings, a variety of office buildings are being built by different architects that will transform this production site into a research site.

The Sanaa Building stands at the entrance to the grounds. A slender, six-storey building, it is distinguished by extreme transparency. No more than a transparent shell defines the architectonic volume. Full-height glass windows and recessed pillars are the only recognisable design elements. The architectural program follows a minimalist approach: transparency becomes the concept.

The building encloses an interior courtyard. The offices spaces are located around this narrow space, which extends almost the full length of the building and is open above. Like the architecture, the design of the courtyard is restricted to minimal interventions. Only two elements were used: water and sandstone.

The greenish sandstone slabs were placed in the courtyard according to a strict grid. Because the square natural stone slabs differ in thickness and were stacked in various combinations, there is no uniform plane, but rather an irregular checkerboard pattern. Because they differ in height, certain slabs are above the water level and remain dry, whereas others are barely covered or clearly covered by water. In all, five different levels of slabs make up this artificial, water-covered topography. The different heights also manifest a subtle play of colours, because the stones are darker or lighter when seen through water or not.

The natural stone selected is a sedimentary rock from the Saint Gall region. It formed twenty million years ago, when the entire Lake Constance region was covered by a shallow sea. Sandy beaches formed on the shores of the sea, a result of erosion of what were then the young Alps. During the Miocene epoch, the geological period from 26 to 7 million years ago, this sandstone layer was tilted at an angle by powerful tectonic shifts. The now-exposed layer of rock has been quarried for the last six centuries and more. The choice of this local sandstone gives the design of the courtyard an abstract connection to the geological process of its origins in an interplay of water and stone. The use of Swiss natural stone also anchors the project in local geography.

Apart from rain water that falls into the open court, the water used in the interior courtyard is grey water. It is the product of industrial cooling processes and hence its temperature is slightly raised. As a result of this difference in temperature with respect to the surrounding air in winter, fog forms as the water cools. This phenomenon will obscure the otherwise unimpeded view into the courtyard and the offices opposite and briefly neutralise the transparency of the architecture.

The interior courtyard is accessible. The stone slabs have been placed in such a way that people can cross the courtyard without getting wet. However, the path is not clear. Indeed, in the narrow courtyard space, it disappears for those standing there.

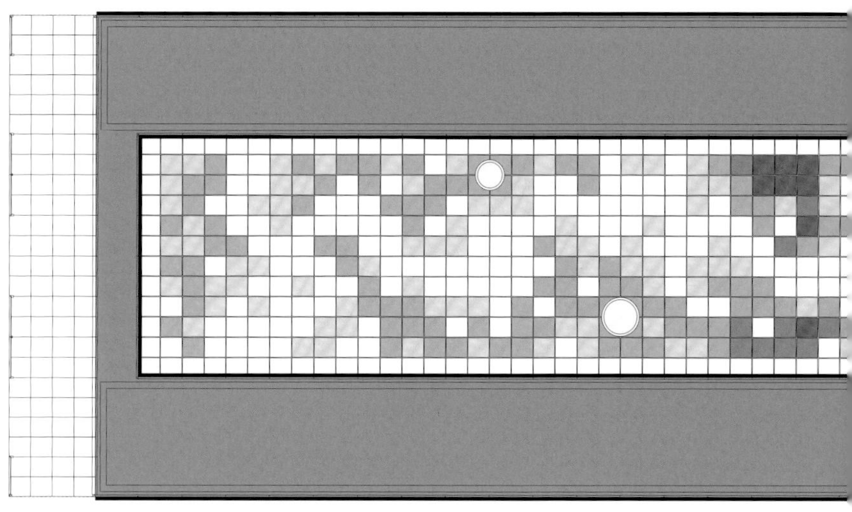

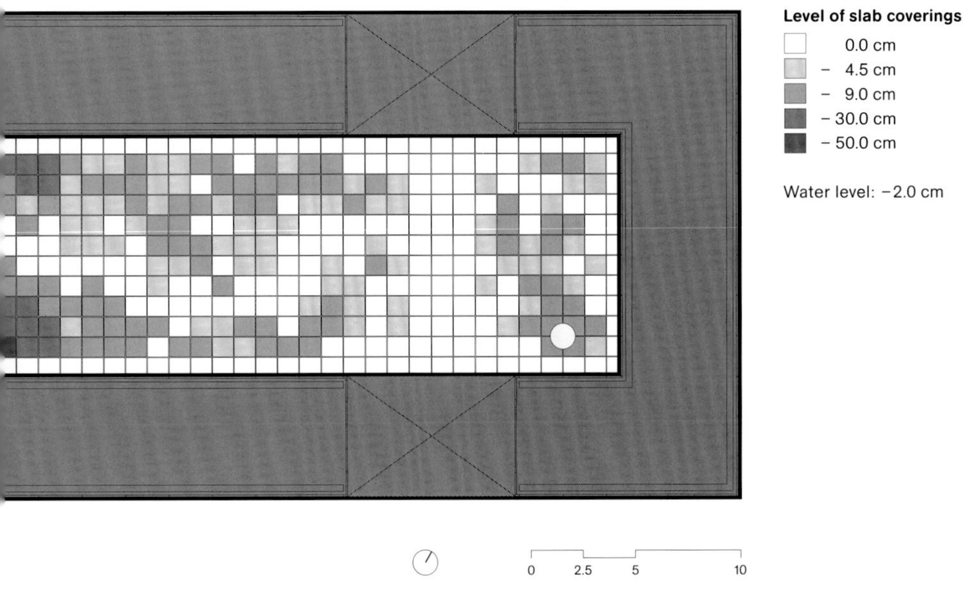
Level of slab coverings
0.0 cm
– 4.5 cm
– 9.0 cm
– 30.0 cm
– 50.0 cm
Water level: –2.0 cm
0
2.5
5
10

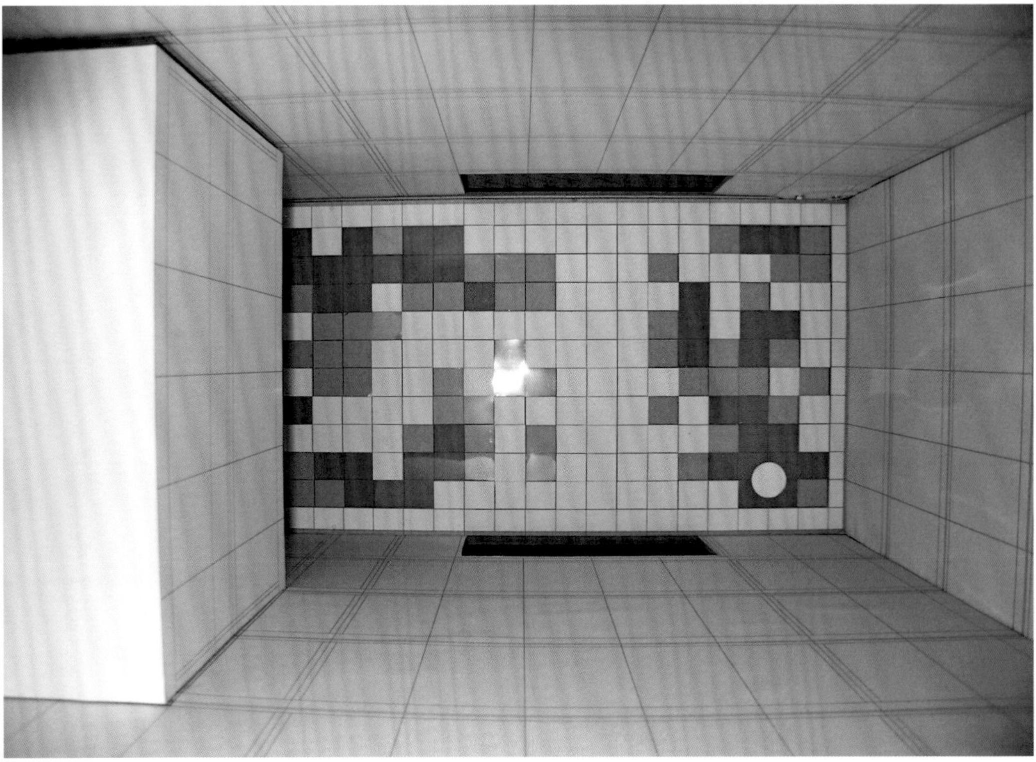

WAREHOUSE AREA, SAINT GALL
MOMENTUM
2002–05

Client: Hochbauamt und Liegenschaftenamt der Stadt St.Gallen
Architecture: New buildings: Baumschlager Eberle Architekten, Vaduz/Senn BPM AG, Saint Gall/Atelier Heinz Tesar, Vienna
Area: 10,000 m^2

Canal du Midi.

Pre-cultivation of the trees in a nursery.

Colour tests for the earth in the courtyard.

Parallel to the railway line and immediately adjacent to the railway station is the warehouse area of the city of Saint Gall. In the middle of a residential neighbourhood, these architectural relics of the former spinning and silk embroidery trade are tangible evidence of the industrial history that was so important to the city and region of Saint Gall. The buildings are no longer used by the textile industry, and new uses demand contemporary solutions for the old building complexes and their exterior spaces.

In the late 1990s, the city of Saint Gall bought the two old warehouses and held a design competition. Subsequently, the warehouses were extended by new structures, which increased both the width and the length of the existing complex. The contrast between the old industrial architecture and the newly added building volumes has created an elongated open space enclosed on three sides: a courtyard. With its elongated shape, it resembles a street. This aspect has determined the designers' choice of plant, with the plane tree as the typical allée tree. However, in contrast to the way the trees are traditionally used, the trees are not planted in a row, or even standing up straight.

There is a striking difference between the plane trees used in the warehouse area and those used in streets, which tend to have an entirely uniform character. As if the wind had ripped through the courtyard, the odd, unmatching trees are crooked and stand leaning in different directions in the courtyard. In this way, they oppose the strict regularity of the façades and create a counterpoint to the regularity of the courtyard walls that define the character of the space and serve as its backdrop. Like individuals, they resist the rigid order and compromise its uniformity with their untamed, lively growth. The trees were cultivated in the nursery according to specifications and developed their peculiar forms without support against the wind. In the cramped environment of the courtyard, they make a powerful impression.

Because the courtyard is only slightly higher than the underground car park beneath it, it is impossible to plant trees there without additional layers to elevate it further. These are supplied by reddish brown soil that shimmers when wet. The courtyard echoes the hilly surrounding landscape of Saint Gall with lightly undulating terrain and naturally shaped "plant islands" of various sizes. These provide the elevation of at least one metre needed by the trees. Each is planted with a different number of the plane trees, which are about ten metres tall. The undulating topography and the soil's play of colours reinforce the lively impression created by the courtyard planting, which closes with a sparse leafy canopy against the sky.

The difference in height between the two halves of the courtyard is accentuated by a compressed concrete wall half a metre thick and about three metres tall. This wall forms part of the exterior design and links the portion of the courtyard given over to deliveries to the portion containing the plane trees, which is higher. The latter can be accessed by a ramp that lines the façade, as well as by a narrow staircase behind the compressed concrete wall.

Design Process
Sketches and collages of the courtyard design.

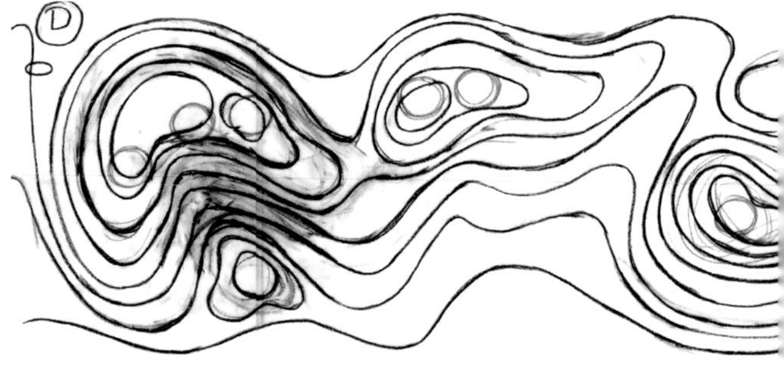

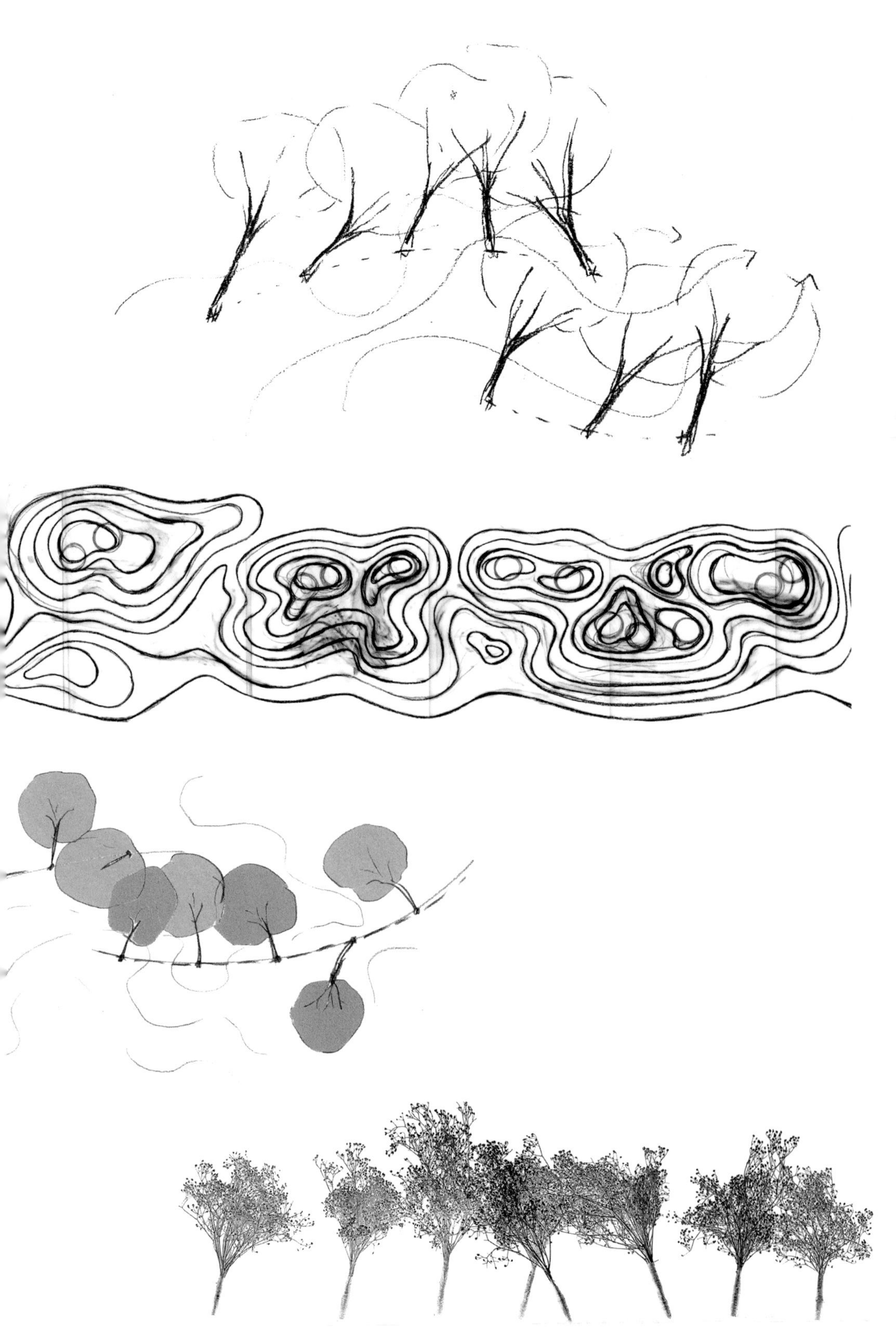

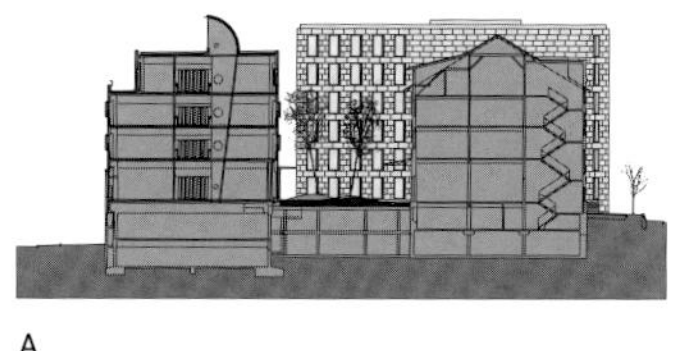

A

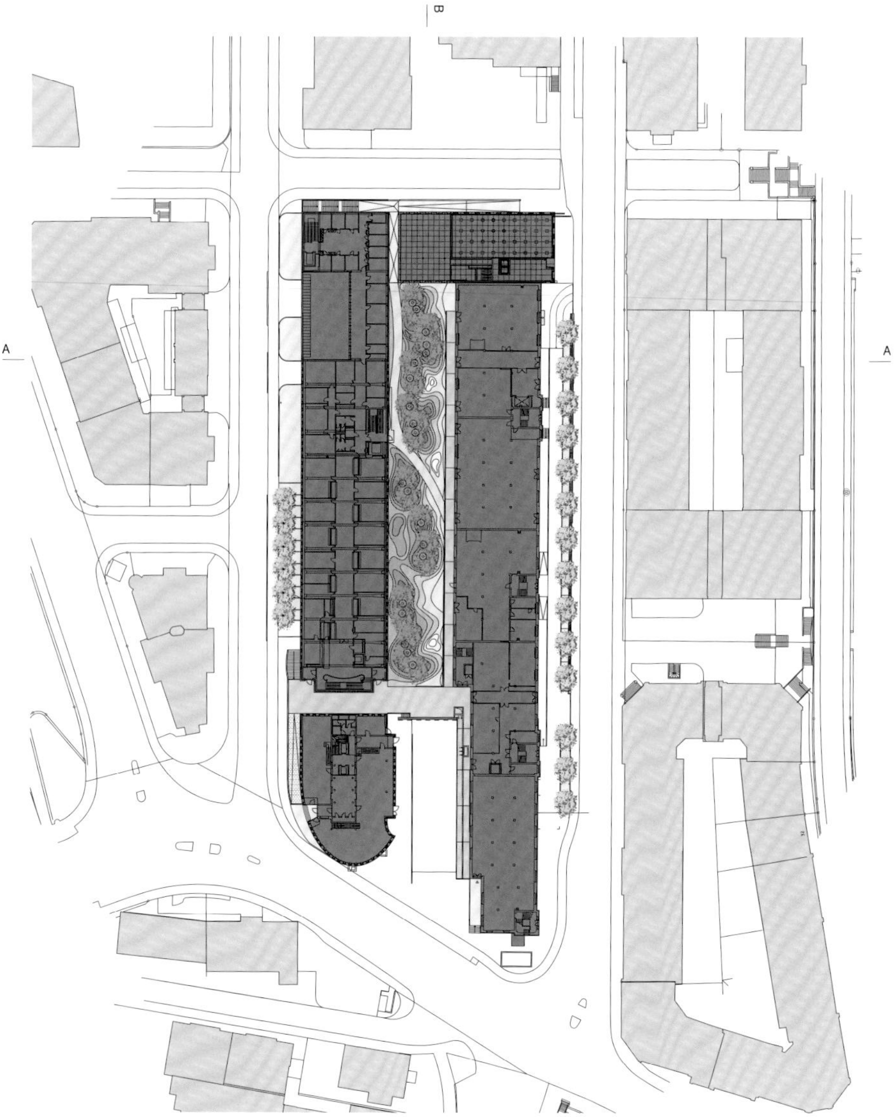

B

A

A

B

0 5 10 20

B

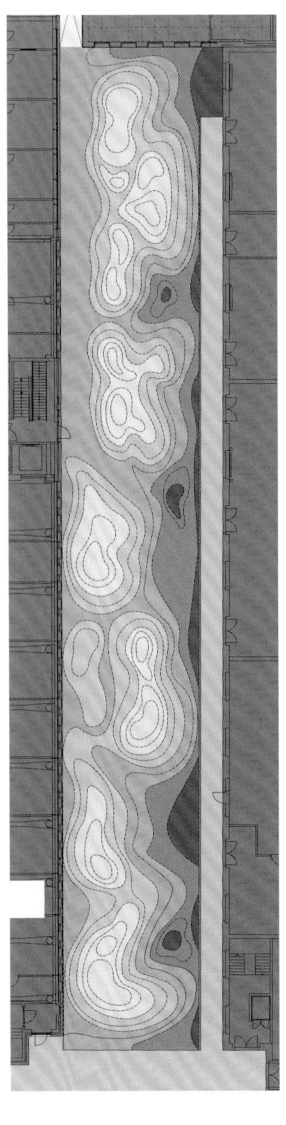

GREULICH HOTEL, ZURICH
DIFFERENT VIEWS
2000–03

Client: Thomas Brunner
Architecture: Romero + Schaefle Architekten, Zurich
Area: 1,100 m^2

Ruderal areas on train station grounds.

Prior to the conversion of this building complex into the Greulich Hotel, the spaces on the ground floor of this corner building of a perimeter block and the building in its courtyard were commercial. The upper floor housed apartments.

The upper floor is still residential. The ground floor and the courtyard buildings have been converted into a design hotel, with the lobby, the hotel restaurant and the bar located on the ground floor of the corner building. The hotel rooms are located in the buildings in the courtyard. The conversion resulted in two focuses for the exterior design: a courtyard facing the restaurant and one facing hotel. The latter is accessible only to hotel guests.

The courtyard facing the restaurant provides space for outdoor seating in summer. Enclosed by buildings on two sides, it becomes an atmospheric, protected space – an outdoor room. The courtyard area is distinguished by clinker flooring, which recalls brick and hence its history as a factory courtyard and its commercial use. The stone trough, the only element in the courtyard, is also made of clinker. Inspired by southern models, it is conceived as a permanent piece of furniture to provide a stage for warm summer nights – as a pool of water with rose petals or, covered, as a stone buffet table for banquets. The courtyard is separated from the car park and delivery area on a lower level by a wall that provides privacy and blocks out noise. The fourth side of the courtyard is a wooden grille through which guests in the restaurant can view the adjacent birch courtyard. Thus guests of the restaurant can see into the courtyard, though they cannot enter it. The wooden grille overlaps visually with the birch trunks, offering a perplexing view that does not reveal everything.

One central element of the exterior design of the Greulich Hotel is the birch courtyard, with a design distinctly different from that of the restaurant courtyard, creating an exciting contrast. Growing in the gravel-covered soil are a number of densely planted birches. They were taken from the Garden of Violence exhibited at Expo.02, the Swiss national exhibition. The serial and yet arbitrary arrangement of the trees dominates the image. The visual power of the courtyard is, unlike the adjacent restaurant courtyard, not derived from emptiness and the accentuation of its demarcation, but rather from its content. The sides of the courtyard recede into the background and become projection screens for the shadow theatre of leaves, caused dappled lighting of the trees along the walls of the building. The delicate leaves and the rustling leafy canopy of the birches separate the courtyard from the sky. This lively volume constitutes the courtyard space and allows viewers to experience it, seeing different aspects depending on their point of view. Whether standing in the garden or watching from a hotel room or the restaurant courtyard, the picture presented is always different. The trunks, crowns and grove-like canopy of leaves can only be viewed in excerpts.

The lower level, where the car park and delivery area are situated, is also planted with birches, which serve to delineate the parking places. Their white trunks contrast with the black asphalt. Lily of the valley is planted under them, exuding an intense fragrance in the spring.

Wild Birches
Birches growing in nature as the inspiration for the courtyard design.

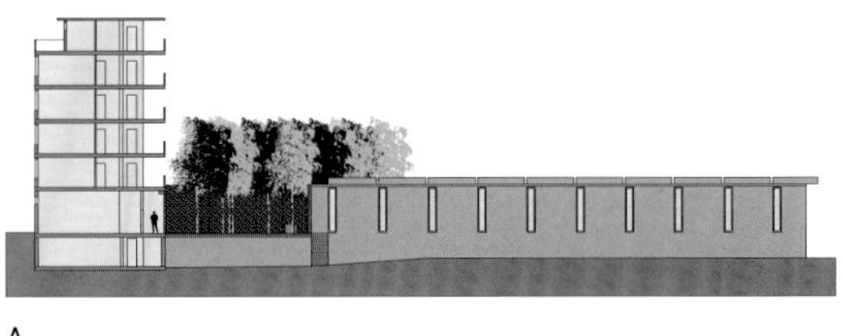

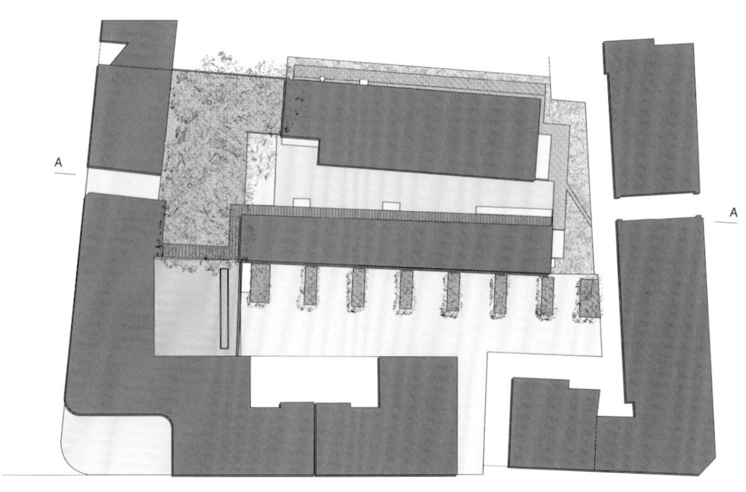

GREENCITY MANEGG, SPINNEREIPLATZ

"A MAGICAL FOREST"
2011–16

Client: Losinger Marrazzi
Master plan: Diener & Diener Architects, Basel
Area: 600 m^2

Hornbeam 'Carpinus betulus'

The historical usage of water power in the area between Sihl and Entlisberg reflects the fact that the place was once heavily industrialised. Water taken from the Sihl via a canal drives turbines inside the base of the historically preserved spinning mill, transforming the water into electricity. The process of subtly revealing the energy gained this way, in combination with the witnesses to history – water tower, canal and spinning mill – form the starting point for the intervention in the central square of this new residential and commercial quarter in the south of Zurich.

Fifty-six hornbeams (Carpinus betulus) laid out in a geometrical pattern fill the square. The trunk of the hornbeam is distinctive; one can see and feel the bulges and recesses of the trunk's surface, the waves in the wood. This kind of twisting appearance, grown into the tree trunks over the course of the years, is the starting point for the artistic creation: as if on a stage, one of the trees in the middle of the woods starts to revolve around its own axis for a moment. The energy created thus becomes visible for a brief second. This tree then continues to twist, following a certain kind of choreography, and thus stands out from the many other trees, as if it were dancing or trying to look in all directions. At the same time this helps it to define its own space in the vicinity of its neighbours.

The hornbeams are planted at regular intervals of 7.5 meters, marking the intersections of the grid. Since the tree has multiple trunks, each tree develops its own individual appearance, disturbing the predefined grid pattern. Their individual shapes and their silvery grey colour are captivating. They do not grow to great heights and one can get the impression that their roots continue all the way up to their crowns. Throughout the year, the tree's serrated, dentated leaves look as if they are just about to really unfold.

The colour of the ground covering echoes the silvery grey of the tree trunks and creates a uniform texture on the ground, which serves as a background for the hornbeams. The greyish macadam, which is stabilized in some areas of the development, can be driven upon or is suited to a long game of bocce. In other areas it permits rainwater to be absorbed, which is essential for the growth of the trees.

To employees who spend their lunch hours there, as well as to visitors, the small hornbeam woods offers protection and a pleasant place to while away the time. The pattern of trees creates small avenues that are inviting pathways for strolling. Tree trunks form visual axes, like an intersection, while also offering visual cover. From the windows in the upper storeys of the building, the gaze falls upon thick crowns of trees, which look like a green carpet, whose texture and colour is always changing as the seasons go by, and depending on the weather. In the rectangle of the wind-protected treetops, the momentary motion occasionally interrupts the monochromatic, still image. With a simple twist of the tree, a light, poetic rustle is heard. The dancing tree emerges from its state of stillness and refers to the collective system of the group or the forest; it draws the attention of all, while, at the same time, it remains mysterious.

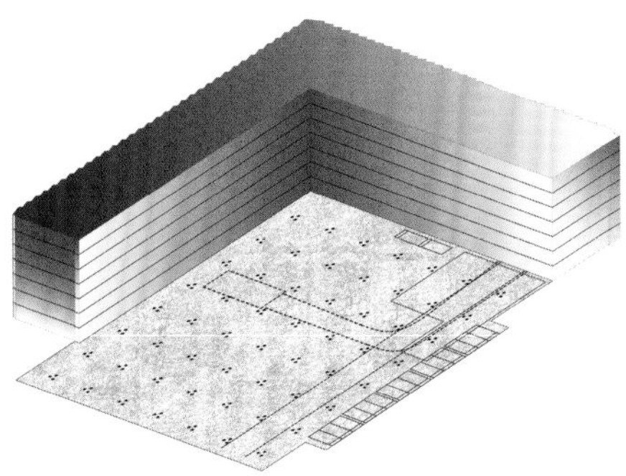
Accessible common area

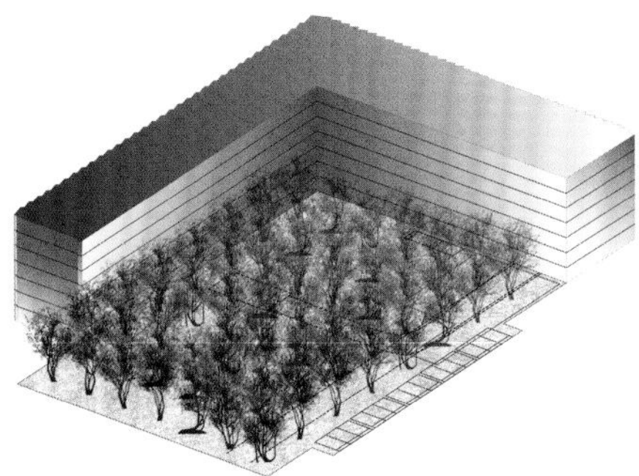
Wood geometry

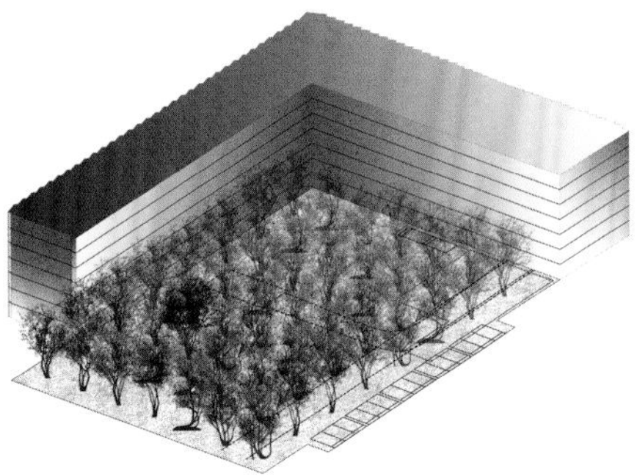
Twisted tree

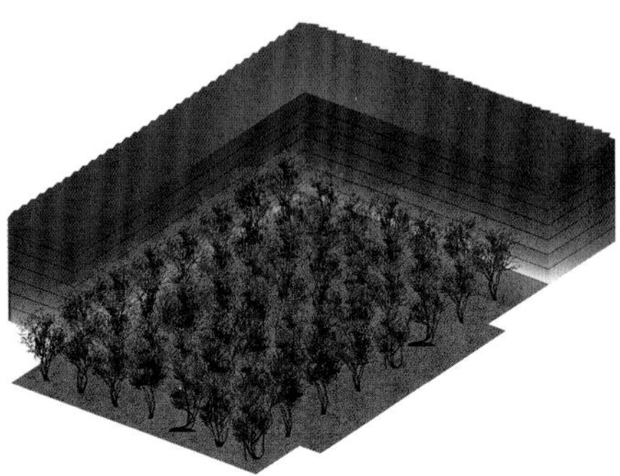
Forest shadows

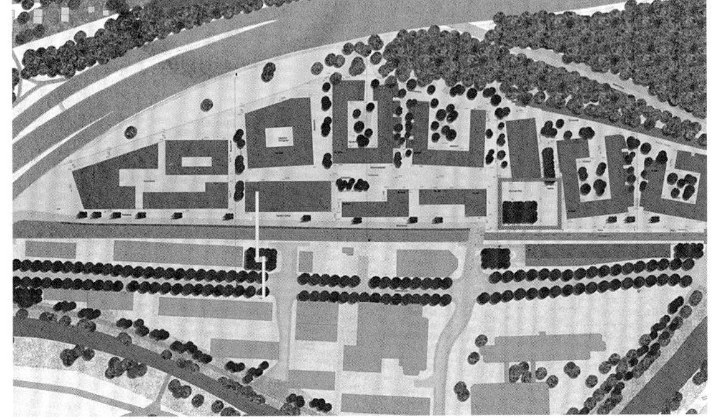
Green City Area with Spinnereiplatz.

http://www.vogt-la.com/en/panopticon/rotating-tree

KOLKATA MUSEUM OF MODERN ART (KMOMA), INDIA
OVERLAPPING NARRATIVES
2008–14

Client: The KMoMA Trust, Kolkata, India
Architecture: Herzog & de Meuron, Basel
Area: 27,000 m^2

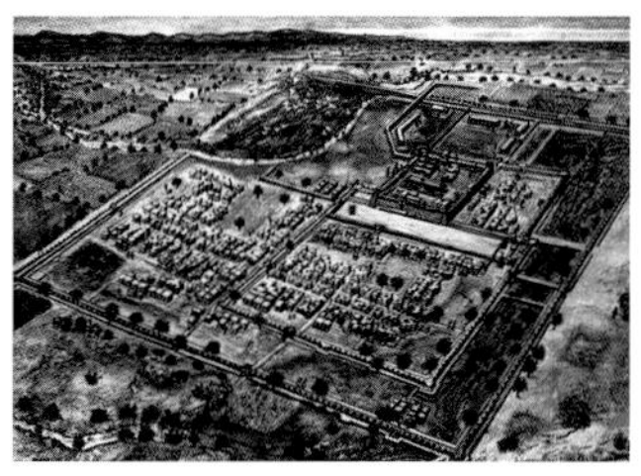

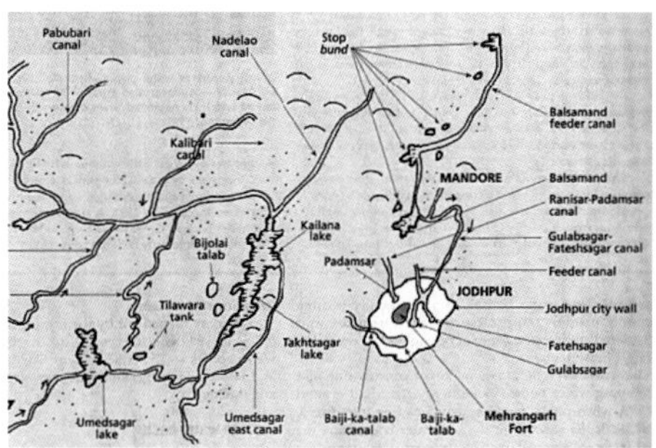

Jodhpur City.

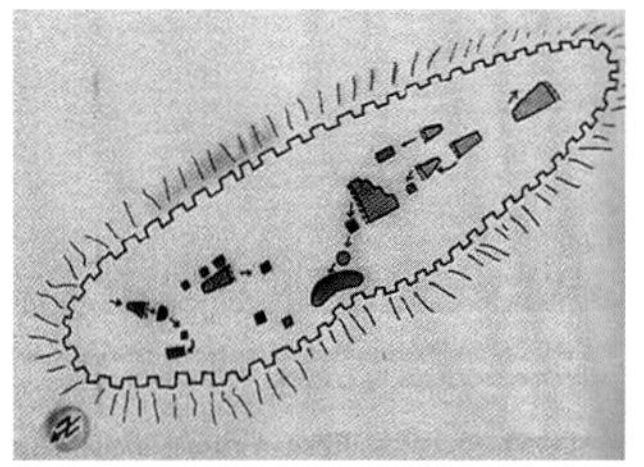
Chittorgarh Fort.

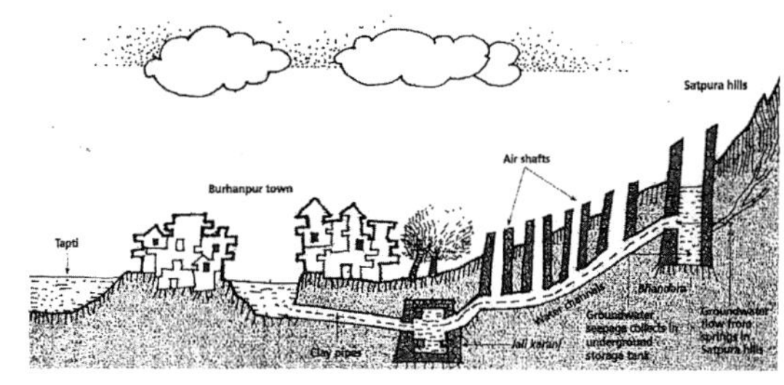

Burhanpur City.

The weather and the phenomena of the monsoon, the issue of technical irrigation and working with scale were the three main themes for the concept for the Kolkata Museum of Modern Art (KMoMA), West Bengal, India.

Looking at India, the techniques and methods of water harvesting vary from region to region depending on their specific problems, nature of terrain, climate and hydrogeological conditions. Mainly water harvesting is used for irrigation but is also used for replenishing drinking wells and hand pumps. Even today many afforestation and land improvement projects are combined with water harvesting. In semi-arid regions water is only harvested for drinking purposes. The water runs through a system of pipes and channels and is stored in a tank above or below ground. Sophisticated irrigation systems and hydraulic structures have been found dating back to 1500 BC.

Unique structures of various shapes and sizes to collect rainwater have been made using locally available material. They are placed in courtyards, in front of houses and temples, villages squares and in open agricultural fields.

One will always find a linkage between water tanks and vegetation. When building ponds and tanks villagers would plant trees at the embankment to avoid erosion and the tank being silted. The second reason was so that these groves could provide meeting places with an ideal setting for various occasions such as social gatherings, festivals, picnics, marriages and religious rituals. One can find rare and endemic species in a Sacred Grove, and these can be regarded as a remnant of the primary forest left untouched by the local inhabitants due to the belief that deities reside in these forests. The age of a tank relates to the age of the plants, which are usually rather distinct from the adjoining grove. They are like small botanical gardens. A total of 14,000 Sacred Groves have been found throughout India, and the number could be even higher.

The idea for the museum site is to capture rainwater throughout the site and from the roof of the cultural complex of the museum and to use the water for irrigation, groundwater replenishment and as water features in the landscape.

The landscaped spaces created by the building footprint are divided into a series of open-space typologies, ranging in scale and degree of openness and enclosure. The streets lead into the museum complex and open out on the largest and most prominent landscape space, the Central Square. As you move towards the interior of the building complex, the landscape will become more refined, organised and distinctive. The alleys leading to the courtyards refer to the alleys found in forts in India and act as a threshold that will ultimately reveal the "sacred" space of the square beyond. The interior and private landscape spaces are small courtyards adjacent to the art studios that will function like display boxes in the sense that each one will feature one type of landscape element, such as water, hedge, tree or stone.

The concept for the Central Square is to create a water element with a tank that acts as a drainage basin for the entirety of the square and is connected to a larger, underground network of water storage. During monsoon season, the tank will swell, allowing a sheet of water to cover a larger portion of the square. During dry months, the water from the square will recede and the tank water level will fluctuate depending upon the irrigation needs of the vegetation on site. Adjoining the water element is the so-called Sacred Grove with a wide variety of different flowering tree species.

Gujarat

Arunachal Pradesh

Kerala, Karnataka

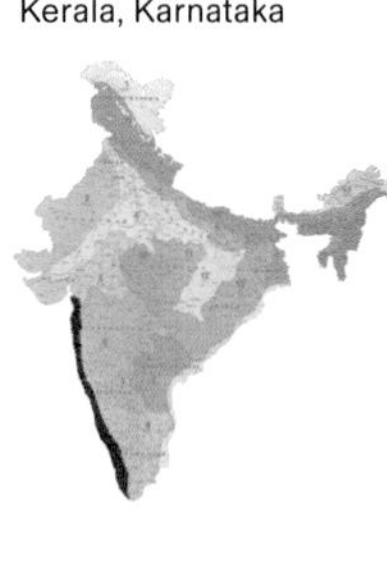

Rajasthan

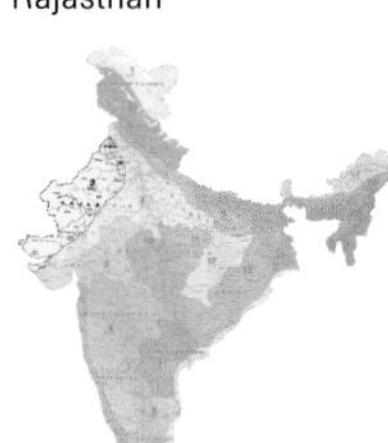

Tamil Nadu

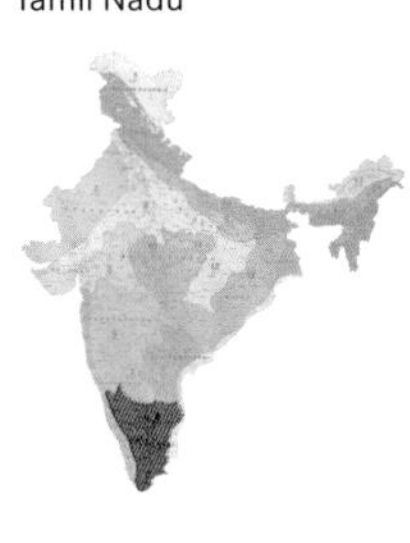

Assam

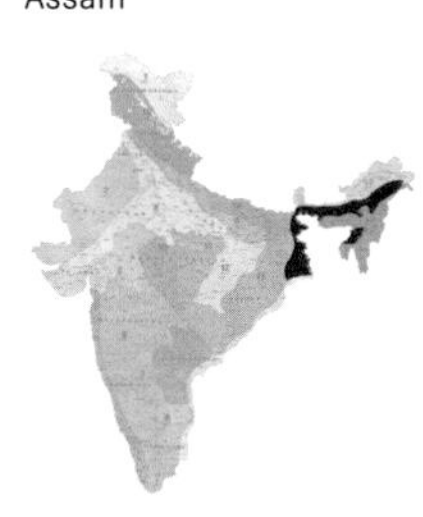

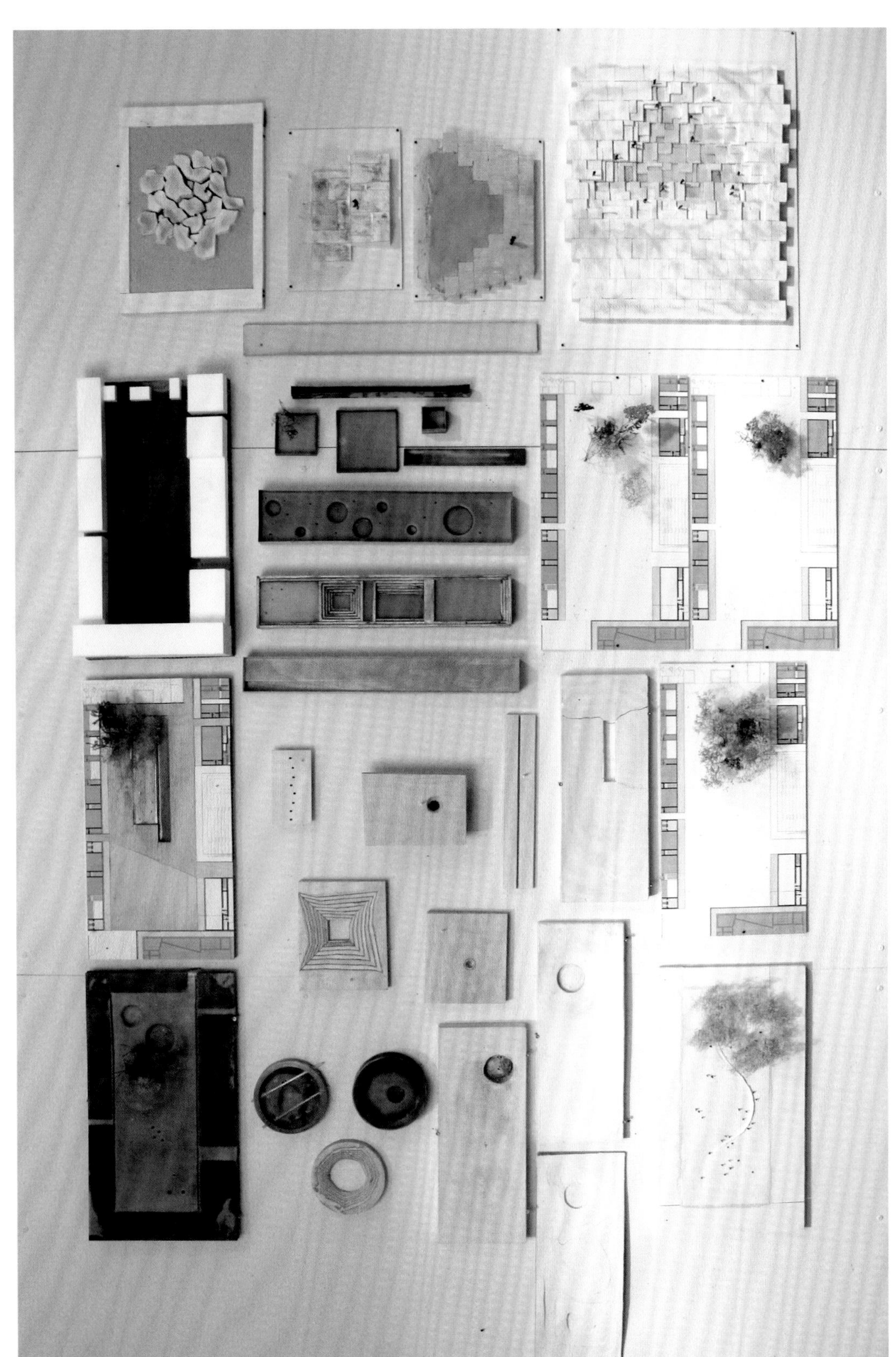

THE PRODUCTION OF PLANTS

Olaf Unverzart

Plants, the raw material of gardens, are mass-produced today, like all other consumer goods. Olaf Unverzart's photographic research is about the places where they are produced. Amsterdam, Hamburg, Bremen, Düsseldorf and Florence are the stops on his journey. The production, trade and transport of plants make up the subject matter of his photographs. His photojournalism always raises the question of the future context of these plants. What will the imaginary gardens look like where the individual plants from this mass production will later find a place?

14

A1
A2
AALSMEER
SELINK TWELLO
8 TOUCH ME GM
11873 03850
VAN DUN BOOMKWEKERIJ
PRUN LA ROTUNDIFOLIA
902
00
POTGEDRUKT
8738 04180
POTROZEN KOOS N
RO KORDANA GEME

PROMENADE

for anyone
  at any time

  aligned extending

idlers benches chairs
  trees banks borders grasses

walking strolling ambling paths
  dogs pensioners shadow light

looking seeing walking waiting

  unbounded and enclosed

MIMICRY OF THE PEPPERED MOTH

The peppered moth, Biston betularia, is frequently found along riverbanks, in fens and in mixed deciduous forests. It has also been found on cultivated and formerly cultivated land and even in densely settled areas. Between May and June, the caterpillar of the peppered moth feeds on poplar, birch, willow and oak leaves. The nocturnal insect has a wing span of 55 millimetres. The species typically has brightly coloured wings that provide ideal camouflage from its predators against the bright trunks of the birch. In the middle of the nineteenth century, peppered moths with darker and darker colours were found near the British industrial cities of Manchester and Liverpool. By the beginning of the twentieth century, nearly all the moths had dark colours. Since the decline of heavy industry in that area in the mid-twentieth century, half of the moths found are lighter in colour again. Scientists call this phenomenon industrial melanism.

Melanism, deposits of dark pigments in skin, is a phenomenon frequently observed in nature. An obvious explanation, of course, was that the moths were adapting to their environmental conditions. On birch trunks darkened by industrial pollution, only wings with dark markings were effective as camouflage. Because global warming occurred at the same time as industrialisation, the colour adaptation is increasingly attributed to changes in weather and climate. What ever the reasons may have been, the massive change to the landscape of central England in the wake of industrialisation was the basis for this phenomenon. The construction of industrial buildings resulted in enormous fallow lands that provided a larger habitat for pioneer trees like willows, poplars and birches. These changes gave the birch a chance to establish itself over a wide area, offering the peppered moth a habitat. Birch forests are typical of the northern hemisphere, and within that the east, of the rising sun. Approximately forty species grow in the modern northern and arctic zones stretching from Canada, the United States and Europe by way of Siberia to China and Japan. The birch needs light; it cannot survive in the shade of the forest, in competition with other species. It finds opportunities to grow along the wet peripheries of riverbanks or in dry, sandy soils. This wide range of habitat from wet to dry reflects a process of displacement. Where conditions are more desirable, the birch functions only as a pioneer, a first settler. Under the protection of sparse birch forests, beeches and oaks grow; they displace the birches in a climax, the final stage of the European forest. Between the ice ages the birch, along with the hazel and alder, were the characteristic trees of the landscape – living conditions that are still found in the climates of Canada and Siberia. There the birch does not grow as it does in a garden, as a picturesque isolated tree, but in a dense arrangement of trunks in a grove or even small forest. The survival strategy of a birch is simple: rapid growth and abundant seed production. Every seed develops. The growing trunks do not compete. The foliage of many trunks together forms a filigree veil, not shade. The shade of such a forest is the depth of the space, the density of the trunks. As with any forest, the protection, the immovability is absolute. A forest can be felled, but not moved. Entering a forest with many trunks, visitors become observers of the nearby, not the distant. The familiar strangeness comes from the reference of the picturesque individual trunks familiar to us from gardens and the strange density of the same trees on vacant lots of cityscapes.

On the periphery of the city, in the neighbourhoods of single-family homes near vacant areas, birches are encountered again. In the endlessly escalating attempts to escape the hotchpotch gardens of the masses in the private garden, the birch is found as a singular phenomenon. The imaginary forest behind the individual tree is no longer found in these modern gardens. The miniaturisation of nature is a misguided effort to make an individual represent a whole. Dwarf trees and flowering meadows, united in a cramped space, reveal the problem of scale today's gardeners face. Like the peppered moth, we too need time to adapt to the changes in the environment. In the tumultuous modern age, increasing alienation from nature has shaken our self-assurance in dealing with gardens. The meaning of the garden has until now been sustained by the tension between inside and outside, present and past, with connotations of happiness or idyll. The garden today is one ideal of nature among others. The garden as a model for the city is no longer a hidden nature where we move about like noble savages in real nature, searching for a meaning it should be possible to find there. Today we enter a garden and hope to find utopia and idyll simultaneously. *gv*

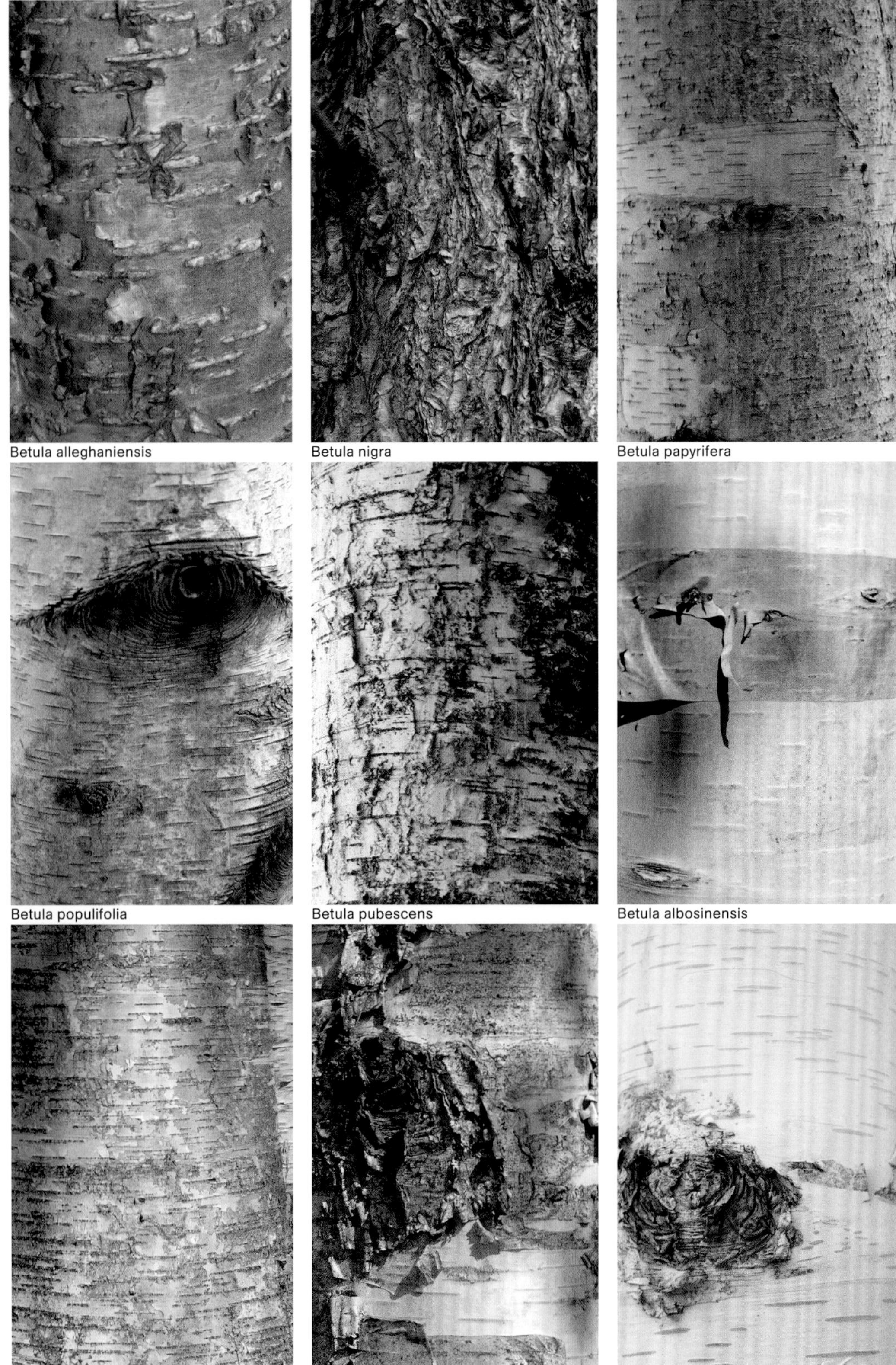

Betula alleghaniensis

Betula nigra

Betula papyrifera

Betula populifolia

Betula pubescens

Betula albosinensis

Betula x koehnei

Betula utilis var. jaquemontii

Betula utilis

Betula pendula

Betula pendula

Betula pendula

Betula pendula

Betula pendula

Betula pendula

ELSÄSSERTOR OFFICE BUILDING, BASEL

REPRISE AND CONTINUUM

2003–05

Client: ARGE Generalplaner Elsässertor, Basel
Architecture: Herzog & de Meuron, Basel
Area: 2,700 m²

System of green spaces in the centre of the city of Basel.

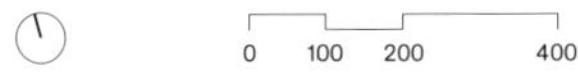

The concept for planting 160 trees in front of the Elsässertor office building is based on two design elements. One is the specific site of the project, the abandoned railway tracks adjacent to the French train station in Basel. The second design element is typological. Planting the trees along Elsässertor has nothing to do with the allée concept. It refers rather to park-like green corridors and thus to the English landscape park concept of plants and nature.

The Elsässertor office building is situated on abandoned railway tracks. There is a long metropolitan forecourt on Viaduktstrasse, in front of the building, which is little more than a large pavement – a promenade. It follows the Aeschengraben park-like green corridor along the Elisabethenanlage, passes Centralbahnplatz and continues to the zoo. The forecourt is directly integrated in the city and is part of the metropolitan green areas program.

Developing the obsolete railway track facilities near the train station closed a gap in the urban structure. Tram tracks pervade four-lane Viaduktstrasse, which once adjoined the French train station's holding track facilities. These were situated four metres below street level. Filling in these grounds, along with the building development and the striking landscaping, gives Viaduktstrasse lateral closure.

The landscaping concept accommodates this site-specific situation. Pioneer trees like birch and locust would normally settle here under natural conditions, incorporating the fallow grounds as a part of a process of succession. Planting the same species of trees is an adaptation of this natural process, without remaining a static snapshot. Instead, the trees will change with time, according to natural, dynamic processes, and distinguish a prominent location in the city. Specific maintenance steps like clearing and replanting will support this development. The maintenance program is not intended to care for individual plants, but is directed more at sustaining the plant system as a whole.

The design of the grounds does not refer to the classic allée-like trees along the street. Its rhythmic and loose arrangement resembles rather an English landscape park, without idealising it. The idea of the abandoned industrial wasteland is ubiquitous, and is referenced by the plant bed surrounded by railroad tracks and covered with gravel.

Two almost identical, closed courtyards are detached from the forecourt and located on the second floor. The landscaping here also takes up the idea of the special or border locations of trees, and implements the plants' ability to settle in places such as these. Flat plant areas with meagre substrates are embedded in a geometric architectural topography of glass and chrome. Twenty thousand beech trees, equivalent to a two-hectare forest, compete here for slim resources on a surface area of about 100 square metres. The beech tree's natural growth problems, as found in exposed areas with immature, fossil-rich soil in neighbouring Jura, are induced here in a restricted, controlled space – a concept similar to the culture of Japanese bonsai trees.

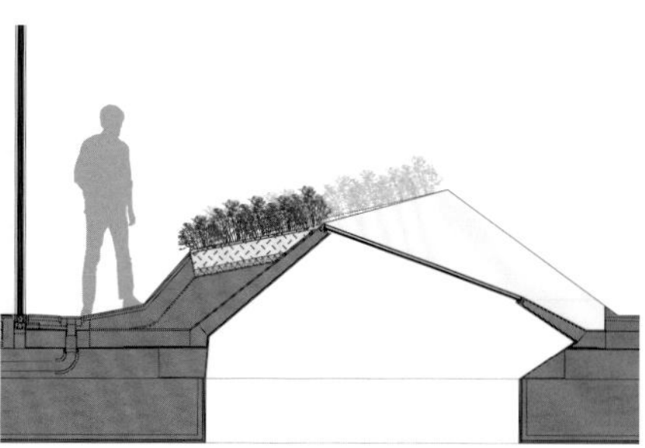

Detail of the beech forest.

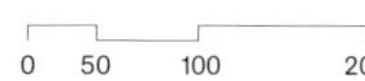

Process of Succession
Birch and locust trees are typical pioneer trees that settle on unused terrain and occupy fallow grounds as part of a process of succession.

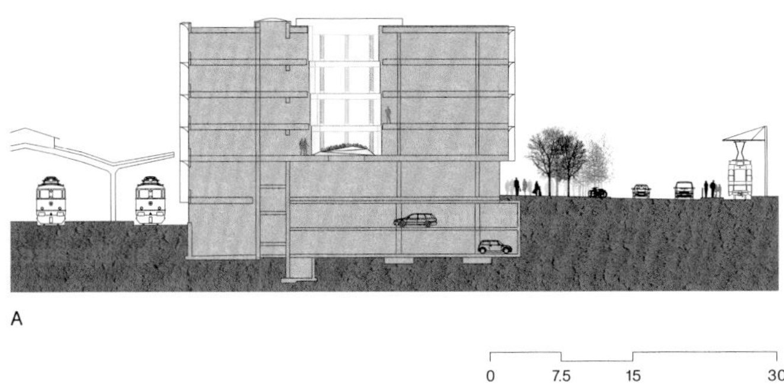

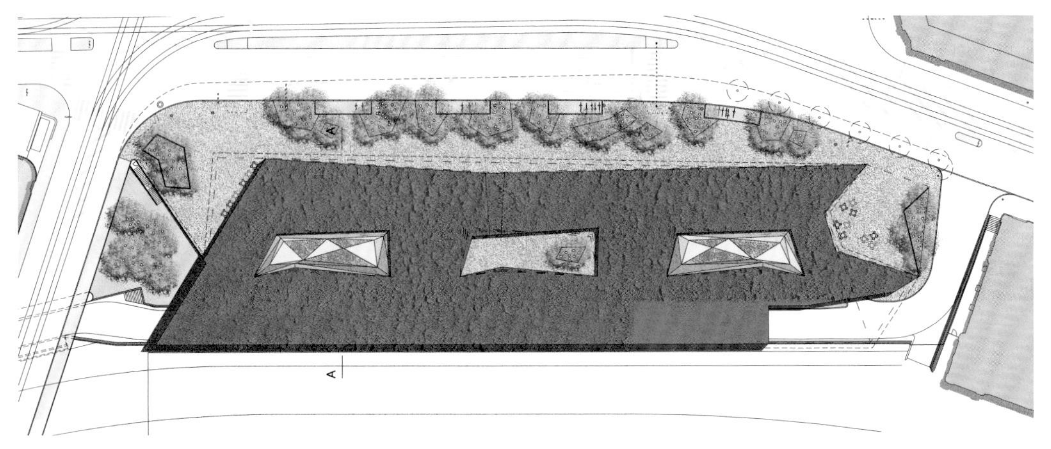

AIRPORT CITY, DÜSSELDORF
GENIUS LOCI
2004–08

Client: Düsseldorf International, Flughafen Düsseldorf GmbH
Area: 200,000 m²

Aerial view of the Airport City development site.

The Airport City development site spans part of a former barracks compound and directly borders the sprawling grounds of Düsseldorf airport, Germany's third largest airport in terms of passenger volume. The military buildings dating from 1939 are now abandoned and most are in need of repair. Small residential areas adjoin the area on the southern side, beyond the landscape bridge over the highway. The area is to be developed, according to a master plan, into an exclusive office and service site that, in terms of town planning and transport, will be well connected to existing structures. Development plans, environmental reports and noise ordinances have to be considered at the planning phase.

The project is based on a planning competition for an open space held in June 2003. It defined the sprawling site as an intermediary element in this contrasting neighbourhood of public and private, which integrates the numerous open spaces into one unified concept. The planning concept develops existing qualities and uses basic elements and materials that can be employed on a large scale. Because building zoning is the only planning applied to the high-rises thus far, the concept has to provide an independent skeletal structure for the external grounds, as well as an appropriate amount of flexibility. The master plan creates a total concept for parks, squares and streets, which touches upon classical elements of landscape design. This includes the existing solitaire trees and tree groups, which will remain dominant features in the space for the next fifty years, combined with lawns and forest-like areas, water surfaces and terrain modelling using retrieved soil from excavations.

The prevailing linear elements of the greening concept are the green strips running in an east-west direction, whereas the north–south streets and pathways are subsidiary. The two squares, the city square and the hotel forecourt, as well as the interior and intermediate courtyards, function as green areas.

The most important street is pan street B, a large park lane lined with loosely arranged, varying species of stock trees and new plants. The green strip that follows the street will be modelled with grassy hills and depressions. The grass areas will be planted with stock trees and new plants in loose single and group arrangements. Pathways and parking spaces have been integrated but are subsidiary in regard to design and function.

Flughafenstrasse C has a very different character. Here there are tree groupings of a single tree species, which divide the street into sections. The concept does not emphasise the lateral, but creates spaces via rhythmic articulation. Only one row of trees is continuous.

Plan street G and H are subsidiary. In design they refer to plan street B, as do many of the crossways that lead from park lane to the landscape bridge, and are characterised by their park-like quality with a loose arrangement of trees.

Additional, important open areas are the city square, the hotel forecourt and the city garden. Here, the central themes of Airport City's landscaping are introduced: grass-covered hills and water surfaces as retention volumes or reservoirs for the periodic accumulation of rainwater, organisation of the areas surrounding important stock trees, and compact grid-like formations of new plants, as well as simple pavements and installations.

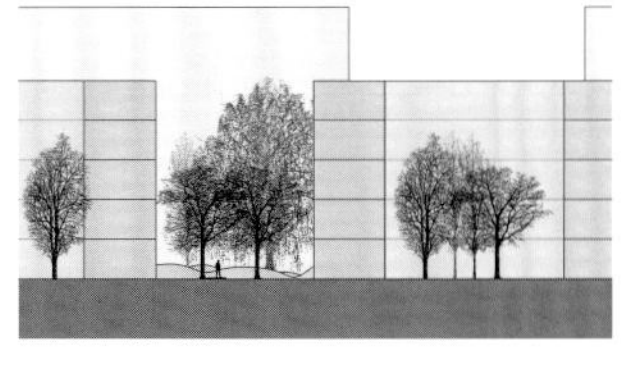

A

B, Park lane

E, City square

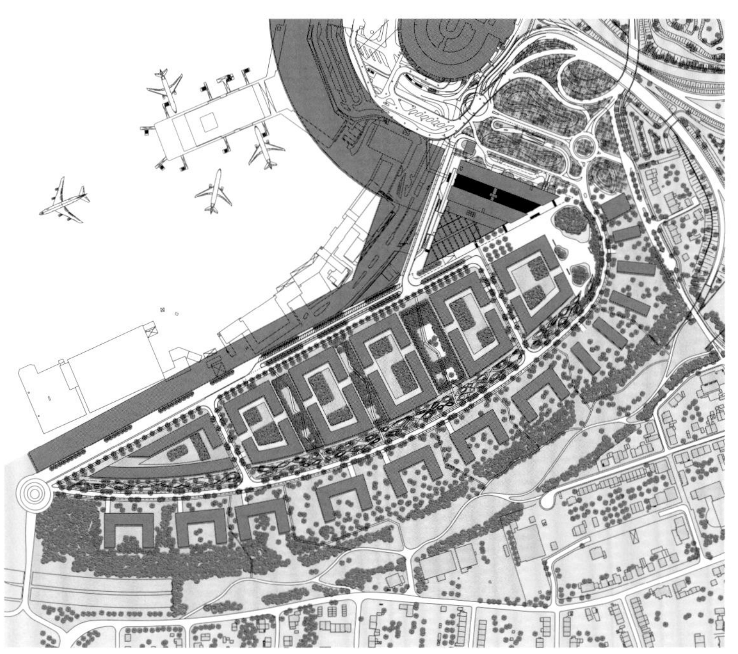

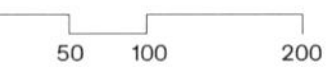

C, Airport street

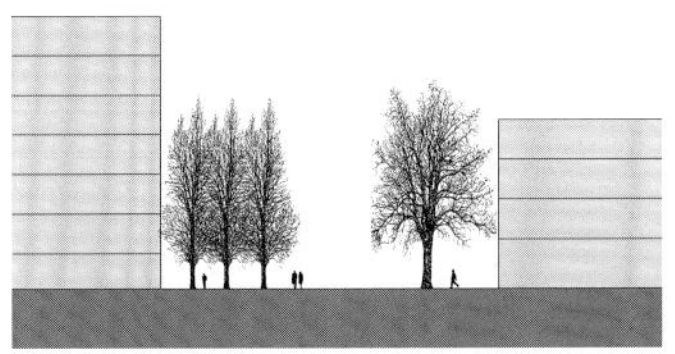

D

F, City garden

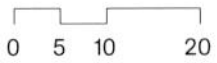

0 5 10 20

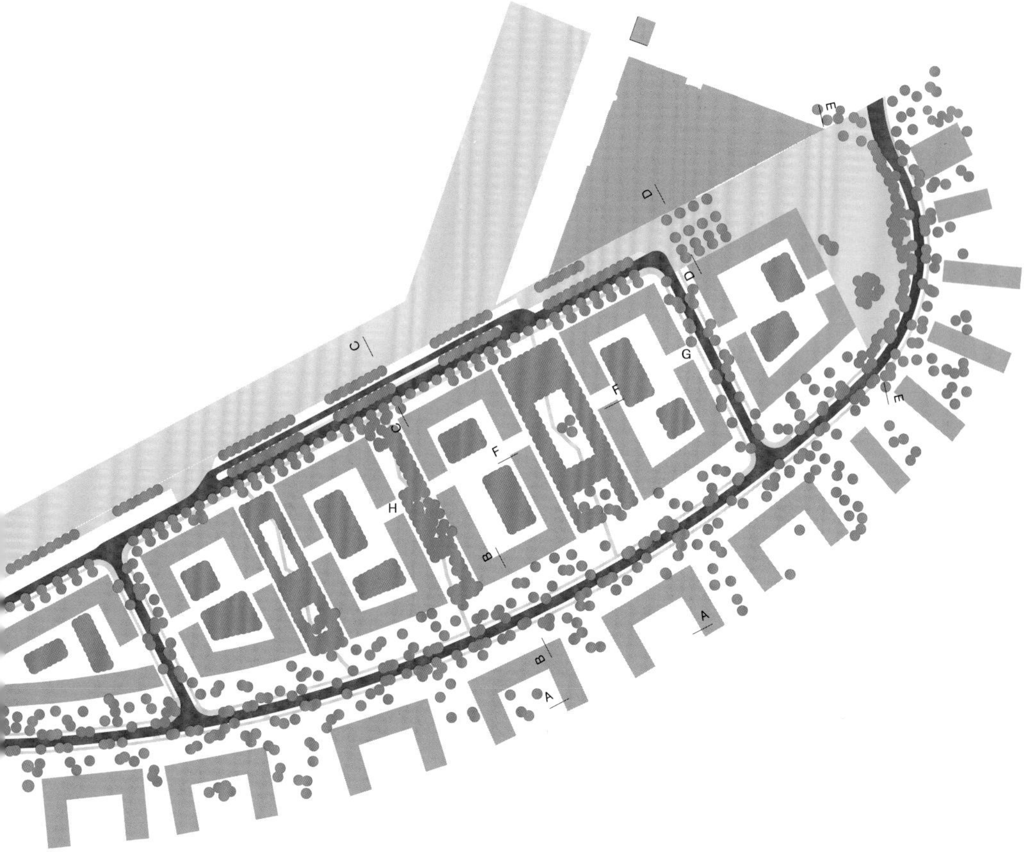

System of green spaces

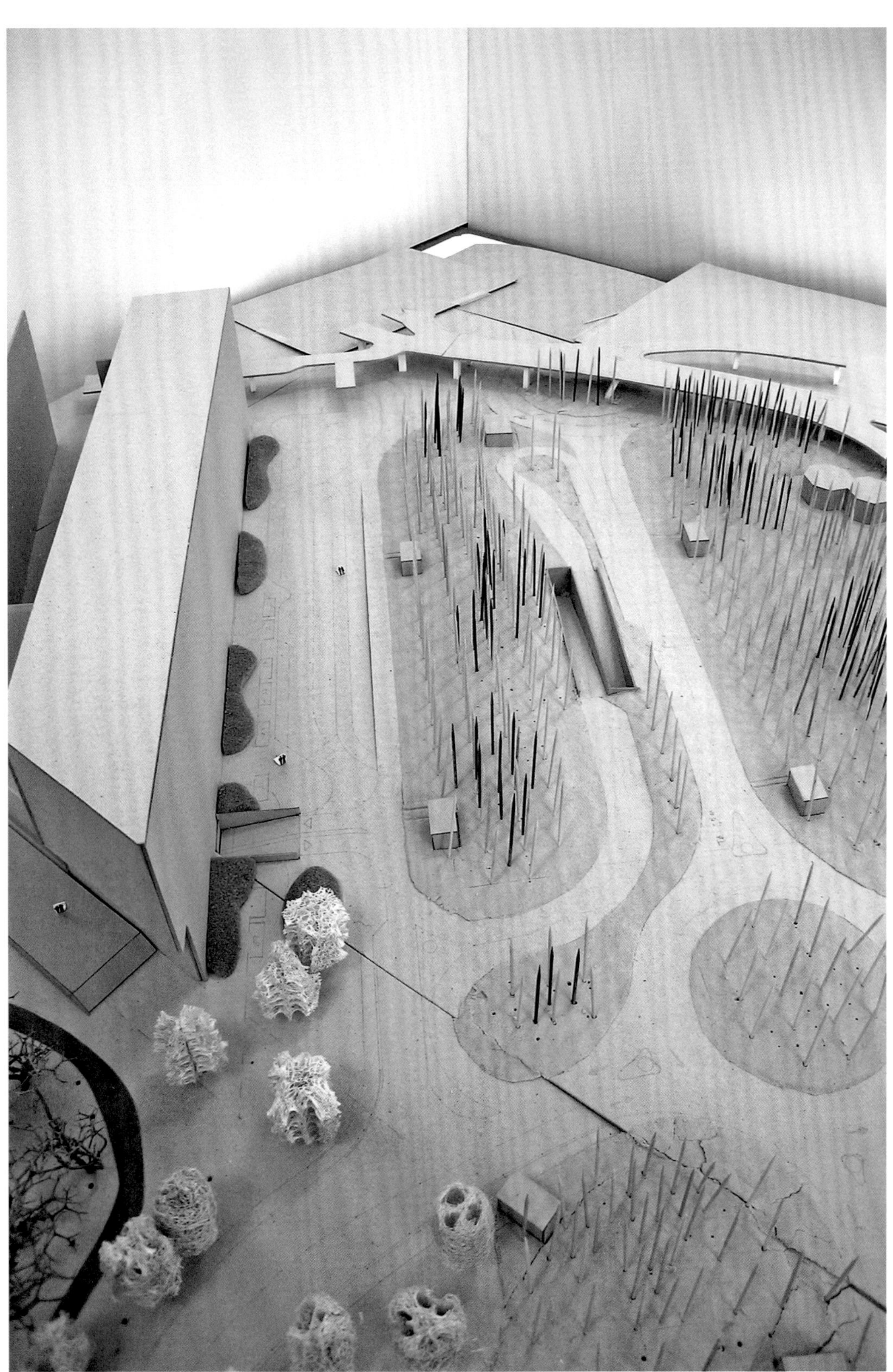

Hotel forecourt

City square

City square

City square

THE END OF THE HUNT

The physician Nathaniel Bagshaw Ward (1791–1868) invented the Wardian case, which is named after him: it is a kind of portable miniature greenhouse he developed in the early days of the industrial revolution. The newly planted ferns in his London garden were suffering from the increasing air pollution. In order that his ferns might thrive, he thought up various devices to prevent air pollutants from reaching them – twenty years before the ingenious glass palaces like the Crystal Palace of Sir Joseph Paxton. After initial attempts with small glass houses made of wood – today we would call them terrariums – in 1833 he sent one such greenhouse planted with ferns to Australia, and the plants survived the ordeal of the six-month journey on deck with no appreciable damage. Ward called his invention a fern case or fern vitrine. He published his findings in an article "The Growth of Plants without Open Exposure to the Earth". The contemporary penchant for living plants and opulent ornamentation triggered such frenzied demand for these miniature greenhouses planted with ferns that the ferns in London's forests were nearly eradicated. The interest of professional plant hunters was awakened as well. Joseph Hooker was one of the first to send plants to England using the new Wardian cases. Robert Fortune transported 20,000 tea plants from Shanghai to Assam and established the still thriving production of tea there. Rubber trees from Brazil were brought to Kew Gardens in England. From there the plants travelled in glass cases to Malaysia and Sri Lanka, where the British rubber industry established its principal growing area.

The chronology of important plant discoveries reads like a history of globalisation. In ancient Egypt, the plants used for incense came from neighbouring African countries to the south. The Romans

INTERIOR

horizonless artificial wondrous
within

unearthbound and encapsulated
encircled   enclosed and foreign

self-imposed self-centred beholden
inserted

artificialities growth profusion
enclave ingrowth

foreign place

brought grapevines, walnuts, cherries, damson plums and other classical cultivated plants to northern Europe during their military campaigns. Monasteries and royal houses cultivated and exchanged medicinal plants, spices and fruits even prior to the Middle Ages. The voyages of discovery of the sixteenth century enriched European gardens with American and African plant species.
In the eighteenth century, England became the home base of plant hunters, in keeping with its position as a world power. Thousands of species from all continents were brought to England; cultivated plants were exchanged among the new colonies; tropical plants for the new greenhouses were shipped across the world's seas. Captain Cook, Joseph Hooker, John Veitch and Ernest Henry Wilson were hired by wealthy park owners or by Kew Gardens. Their rich spoils promised prestige to those who hired them, but sometimes they brought ruin as well, as the tulip speculation did to Dutch merchants in the seventeenth century. Scientific research experienced a heyday in the eighteenth and nineteenth centuries in parallel with this history of a worldwide hunt for plants. Carl von Linné systematised the plant kingdom; Charles Darwin developed his theory of the evolution of species.

The discovery of the world was at the same time the discovery and domestication of the plant world. The production of plants is still subject to globalisation. Like every mass product, plants are reproduced and marketed worldwide using industrial processes. Just as Nathaniel Ward originally sought to protect his plants from external influences, we too have reasons to build ideal landscapes indoors. The glass-and-steel constructions of the late nineteenth century have since been replaced by synthetic materials that permit even larger constructions. In contrast to the old orangeries, palm houses, window gardens and botanical museums, today we are more interested in the holistic qualities of natural spaces than in specific plant themes. Unspoilt vegetation on the level of image and perception contrasts sharply with the necessity to control an artificial biotope. Photographs of great naturalness are controlled by technologically ambitious devices and machines. Artificial paradises follow a secret architectural plan like machines. Elementary properties perceived by the senses, such as climate, scents and varied vegetation, turn the artificial landscape into a *locus amoenus*. This beautiful place, where everything is familiar and ultimately consumable without scruple, calls for an alternative world where the wild, unpredictable, immeasurable lurks. Whereas every garden is based on a horizon between the interior and exterior worlds, in artificial paradises no horizon of orientation can help us. Rather, they recall the urban covered arcades built at the end of the nineteenth century. For a brief time, we enter a different climate, and the façades become backdrops against which real trees and vines seem like architectural ornaments. The domination of nature, expressed in the French garden in formal elements like the lines of sight between the trimmed hedges, is replaced by control of nature. It is a considerably subtler operation, because the invisibly controlled biotopes are at once exhibit and exhibition. Along with the knowledge that the rain forests are being destroyed, we assimilate the other, the thing destroyed.

By the middle of the twentieth century, the borders of the world had been staked out once and for all. Plants from all over the world stow away in our baggage, uninvited guests that drive out native vegetation. They include such garden escapes as the butterfly bush, which broke out of the idyll of gardens and is now found on every construction site. On *terrains vagues*, the indefinite places and vacant lots of the city, the dynamics of urban vegetation are obvious. The living conditions change, mosaic-like, at every step. Gravelly, dry soil, puddles on compacted surfaces, sealed asphalt and concrete areas, stone or brick remnants of buildings – the contemporary urban botanical garden is found in such places. And the cartography of plants is expanding. Acacia and goldenrod from North America, butterfly bush and tree of heaven from China, knotweed from Japan, garden balsam from Mongolia, giant hogweed from the Caucasus, chamomile and Cornelian cherry from southern Europe, coltsfoot and birch from central Europe. These invading species have subversively crept in below the radar of the natural garden movement that aims to use native plants. In view of the rather modest knowledge that most in our society have of plants, in practise this concern is reduced to the question of whether the plants used are poisonous. What people do not know frightens them.

Ecology, the study of nature's household, teaches us that the prey controls the hunter. The end of the hunt is the end of the control we thought we had. *gv*

Straw cover and glass funnel, 1631.

Glass bells. Elsholz, 1684.

Straw and glass bells. Engraving, late 18th cen

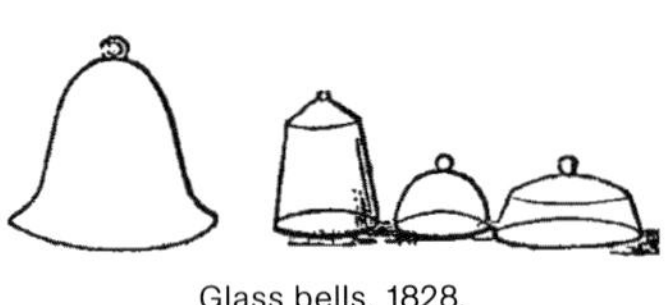

Glass bells, 1828.

Composite glass bells. Elsholz, 1684.

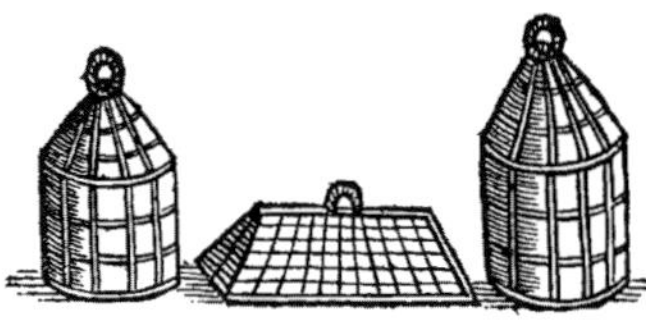

Glass bells. Van der Groen, 1669.

Glass cover.

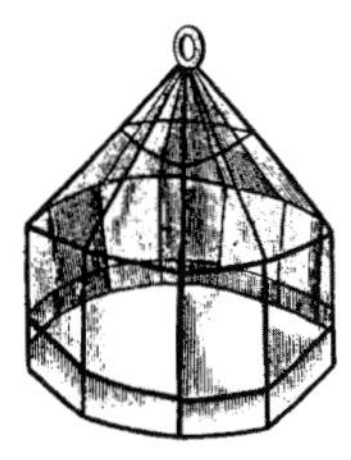

Glass globe, 1819.

Copper and cast-iron hand glasses, 1828.

Cast-iron hand glasses, 1828.

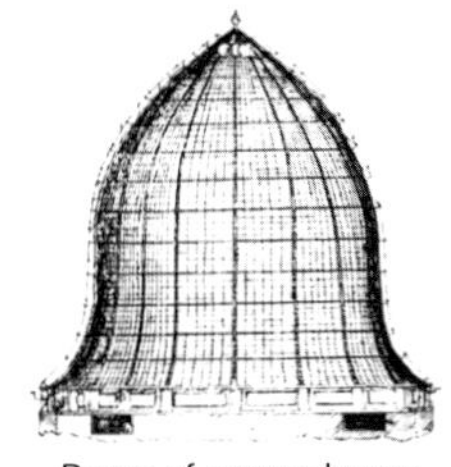

Dome of a greenhouse.
J. C. Loudon, 1817.

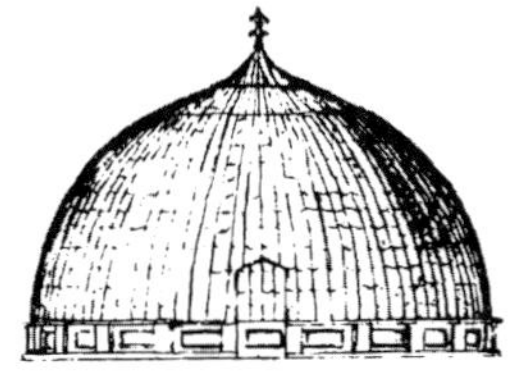

Dome of a greenhouse.
J. C. Loudon, 1817.

Hothouse Regent's Park London, 1837.

Royal Botanic Garden
Berlin-Schöneberg, 1896.

Greenhouse in hut form.

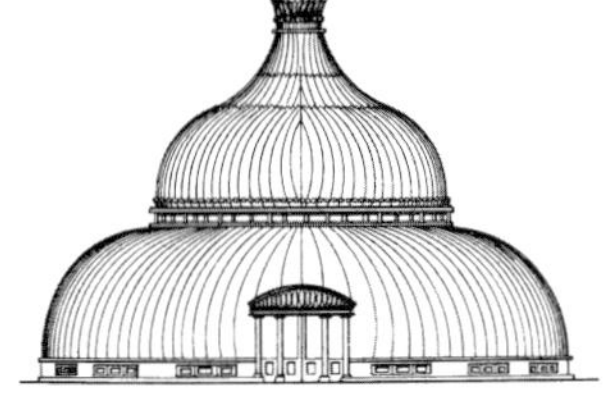

Palm house, Yorkshire. J.C. Loudon, 1833.

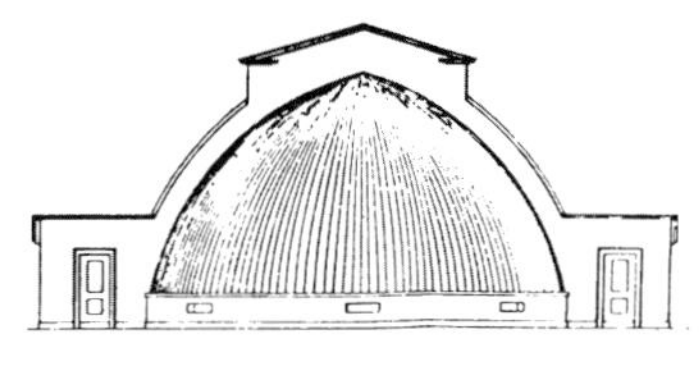

Glasshouse with hemisphere, circa 1830.

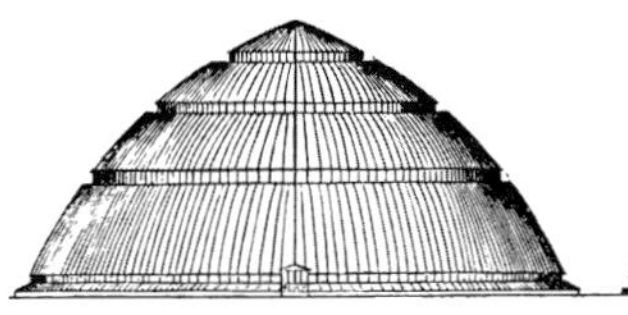

Winter garden, botanical garden
Birmingham, 1831.

Container for transporting tulips, 17th cent.

Case for transporting plants.

Ornamental vitrine for plants.

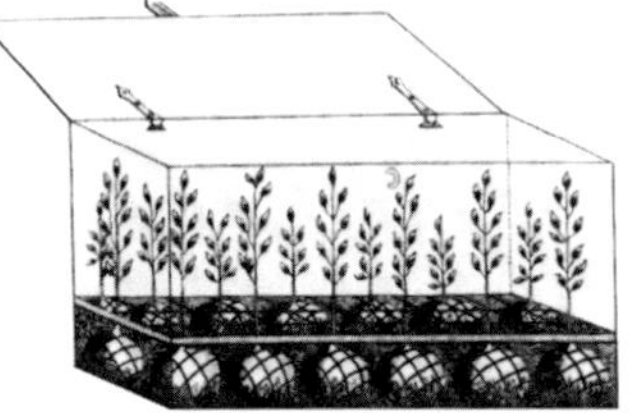

Container for sending plants.

Case for transporting plants.

Salon aquarium by Nathaniel Ward.

Wardian case.

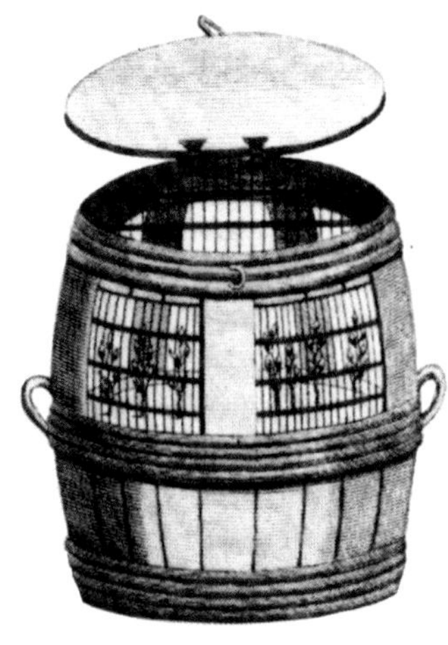

Transportable container for sprouting seeds.

Glass bell with iron frame, 19th cent.

Glass bells, 20th cent.

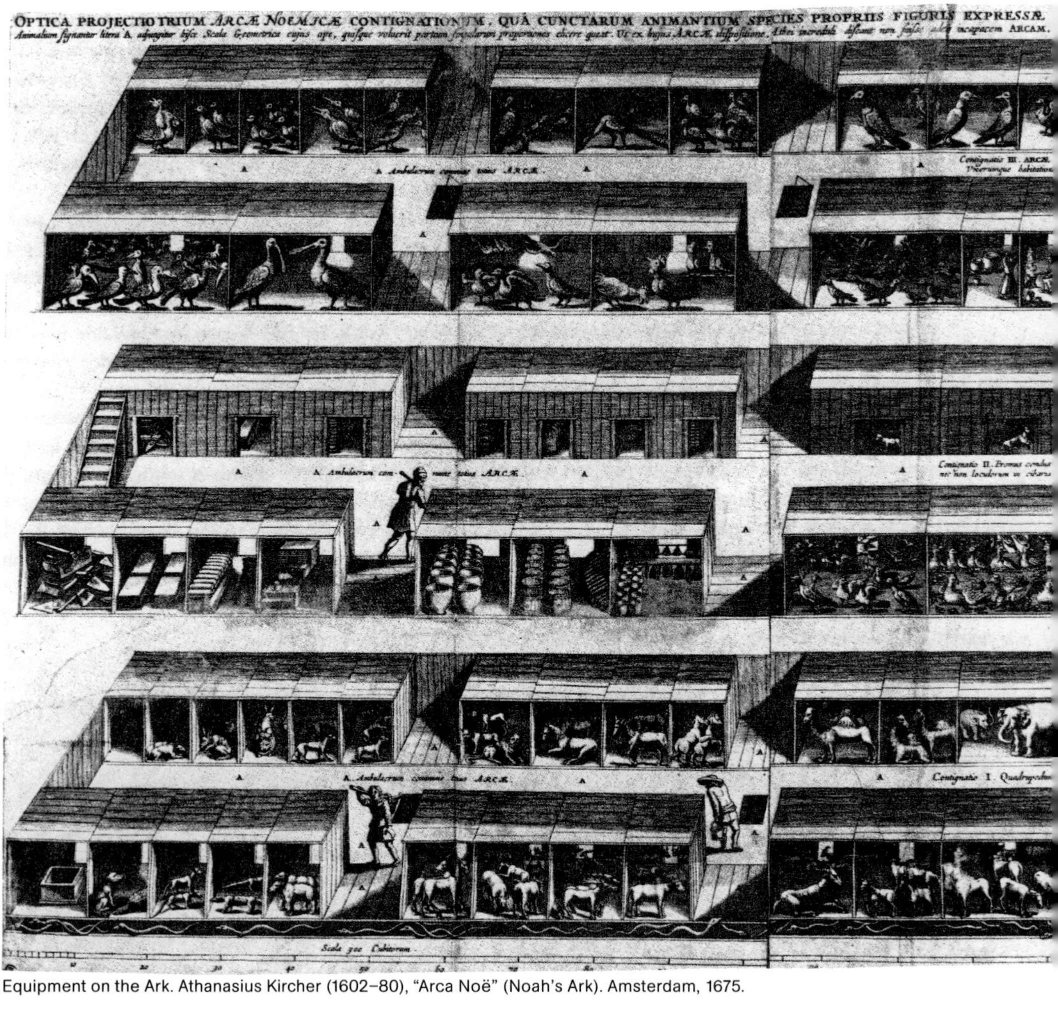

Equipment on the Ark. Athanasius Kircher (1602–80), "Arca Noë" (Noah's Ark). Amsterdam, 1675.

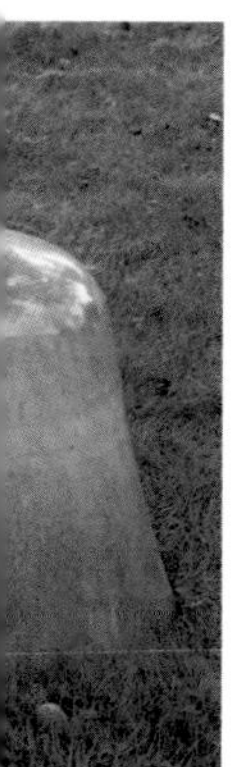

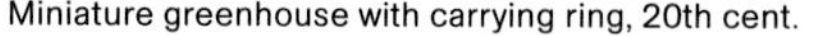

Miniature greenhouse with carrying ring, 20th cent.

Terracotta rhubarb forcing pot, 19th or 20th cent.

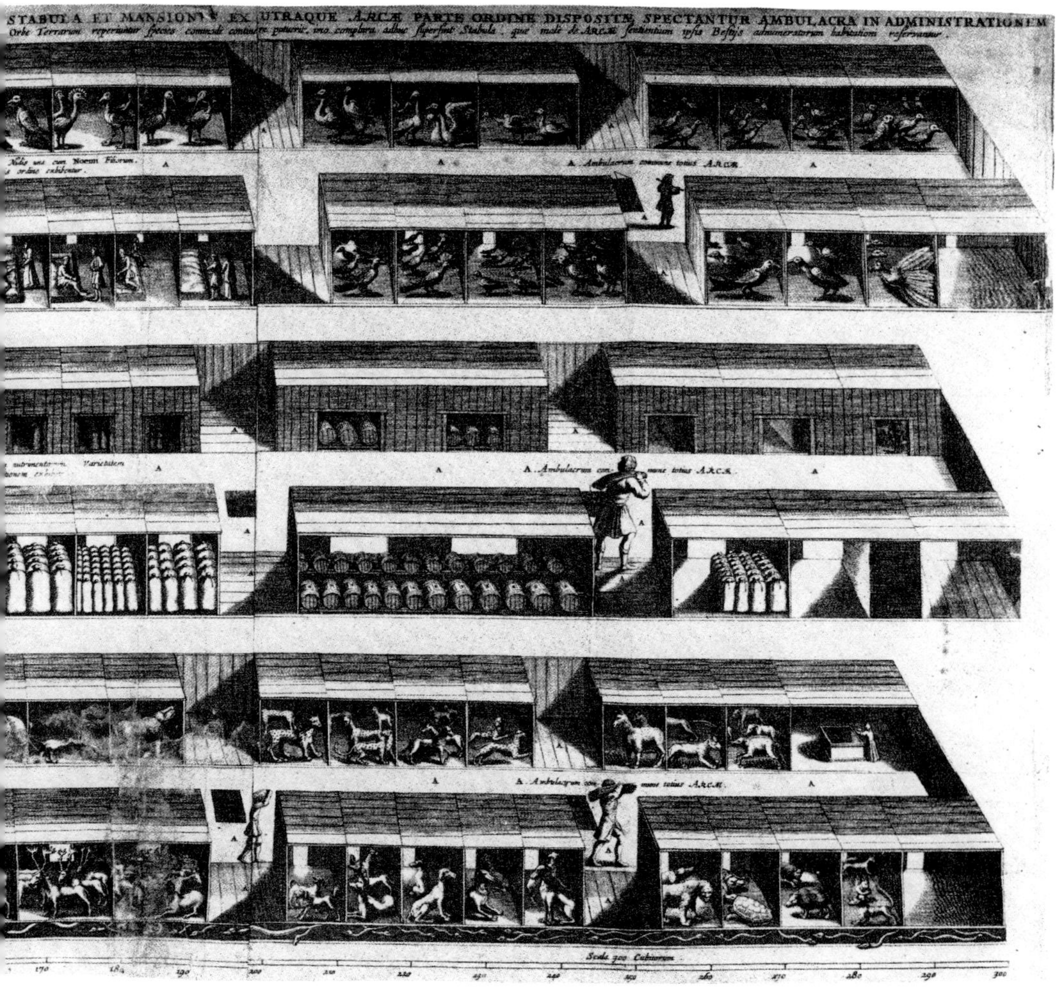

STABULA ET MANSIONES EX UTRAQUE ARCÆ PARTE ORDINE DISPOSITÆ, SPECTANTUR AMBULACRA IN ADMINISTRATIONEM

A. Ambulacrum commune totius ARCÆ.

Scala 300 Cubitorum

Conservatory, London, 1860–1861.

Conservatory and Birdhouse, Tollcross Park, Glasgow, 1880/1905.

Palm house, Schönbrunn Castle, Wien, 1882.

National Botanic Gardens in Glasnevin, Dublin, 1843–1849.

Greenhouse, Ramsgate, Kent, ca. 1822.

Jardin d'Hiver, Les Serres Royale, Brüssel-Laeken, 1875–1892.

Palm house, Royal Botanic Gardens in Kew, London, 1844–1848.

Jardin des Plantes, Serres Trianon, Rouen, ca. 1840.

Crystal Palace during the opening of the World's Fair, 1851, in Sydenham, London.

MASOALA RAIN FOREST HALL, ZURICH ZOO

CONSTRUCTED NATURE
1994–2003

Client: Zurich Zoo
Architecture: Gautschi Storrer, Zurich
Area: 10,800 m^2

Project by Kienast Vogt Partner

Madagascar.

It is the enormous size of the Masoala Rain Forest Hall at the Zurich Zoo (the exhibit is 120 metres long and 90 metres wide, and reaches 30 metres in height) that enables it to reproduce the lowland rain forest, a type of primeval forest, so convincingly. The architectural envelope fades from view behind the exhibits, behind nature.

Situated at Africa's front door and less than four hundred kilometres from the coast of Mozambique, in floristic and geobotanical terms Madagascar shows similarities not only to Africa but also to India and the Indomalaysian archipelago. As a result of Madagascar's early isolation from the vast southern supercontinent of Gondwanaland, the flora of what is today the earth's fourth largest island developed along its own individual lines. A unique type of vegetation came into being. Eighty per cent of the animals and plants in Madagascar do not exist anywhere else, and Madagascar's primeval forest is also highly unusual in its structure and composition. Its most characteristic feature is the way the treetops meet and come together to form a characteristic, homogeneous, wavy canopy of leaves. As in a natural site, in this exhibit hall there are three storeys. The plants are divided into a tree layer, a shrub layer and a ground layer. The first consists of trees 25 to 30 metres tall; the second of smaller trees and shrubs 8 to 18 metres tall; and the third of a patchy herb layer of low plants, broad-leaved grasses, dwarf palms and shrubs up to 3 metres tall. The Madagascan flora is distinguished by woody plant species. Except for orchids, which grow primarily on trees in an incredible array of roughly a thousand different species, there are virtually no herbaceous plants. Trees are the basic structure on which most of the island's animal species live. There are 490 known indigenous genera of plants, 161 of which are found nowhere else in the world. In the vegetation-rich rain forests, nutrients and minerals are rarely stored in the soil but are bound in plants and animals instead, in the living biomass. When a living organism dies, ground-dwelling fungi decompose the organic matter with lightning speed and provide it to the roots of living plants. Thus, despite their luxuriant vegetation, the soils of Madagascar are practically infertile.

The most defining experience of visiting the exhibit is the unfamiliar weather. With humidity as high as one hundred per cent, temperatures reaching 32 degrees Celsius, and rainfall twice as high as in Zurich, visitors are aware that they are entering a humid world. Plants that are familiar at first, such as rubber plants and dracaena palms, are planted more densely than usual and have unaccustomed dimensions. In them, birds, reptiles and lemurs live without the usual bars or cages. The "peep show principle", in common use at zoos and botanical gardens, is replaced by the direct participation of the observers. The path through the highly mobile landscape leads past swamp zones – the habitat of numerous colourful frogs – to the six-metre-high waterfall, where little kingfishers hunt for fish and ibis take showers. Hunting and climbing trails lead deeper into the forest and invite the visitor to explore individual biotopes more closely. But, as is only proper for guests, human beings are not to leave the forest's paths and trails. The process of change is part of the concept here. Lava rocks rather than soil are the foundation for the plants, as is always the case at the beginning of a vegetal development cycle. In the course of time, leaves and branches will form a tropical forest floor. The variety of developmental stages allows the visitor to participate in a natural process, which only becomes understandable after multiple visits. Neither the plants nor the animals are named or described on panels.

Tree Nursery
It is impossible to create an identical replica of a rain forest – the best one can do is come as close to the reality as possible. Even that, however, requires detailed knowledge of the structure of the forest and the course and appearance of streams and waterways.

One of the most demanding aspects of the project was the process of obtaining the plants. Project representatives looked for more than five hundred plant species in large-scale nurseries in Malaysia, Thailand and Florida and transported them to Zurich. At the same time, a nursery was constructed at the edge of the rain forest in Madagascar specifically for the Masoala Rain Forest Hall Project. There seedlings are raised which are then brought to Zurich and planted underneath the large trees. There they grow and flourish beneath the sheltering canopy of leaves, until little by little they replace the initial planting. This nursery is part of the Masoala Rain Forest Hall Project, which the Zurich Zoo created in 1992 on the basis of the conservation strategy of the International World Conservation Union (IUCN). This project seeks not only to provide an appealing experience of nature, but also to inform and enlighten visitors about disappearance of the rain forests, as well as to provide a third of the long-term maintenance costs for the National Park in Madagascar.

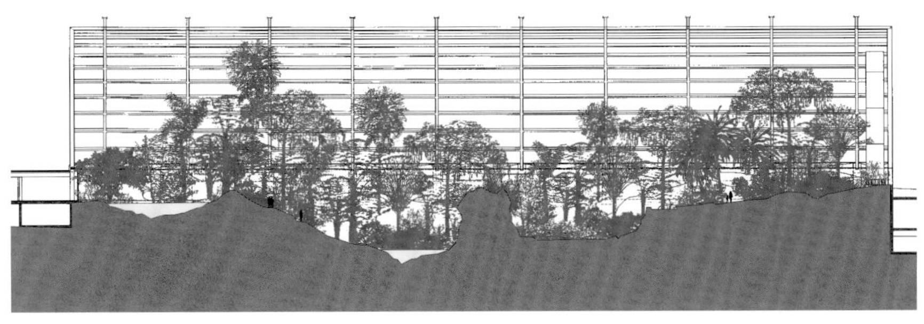

A

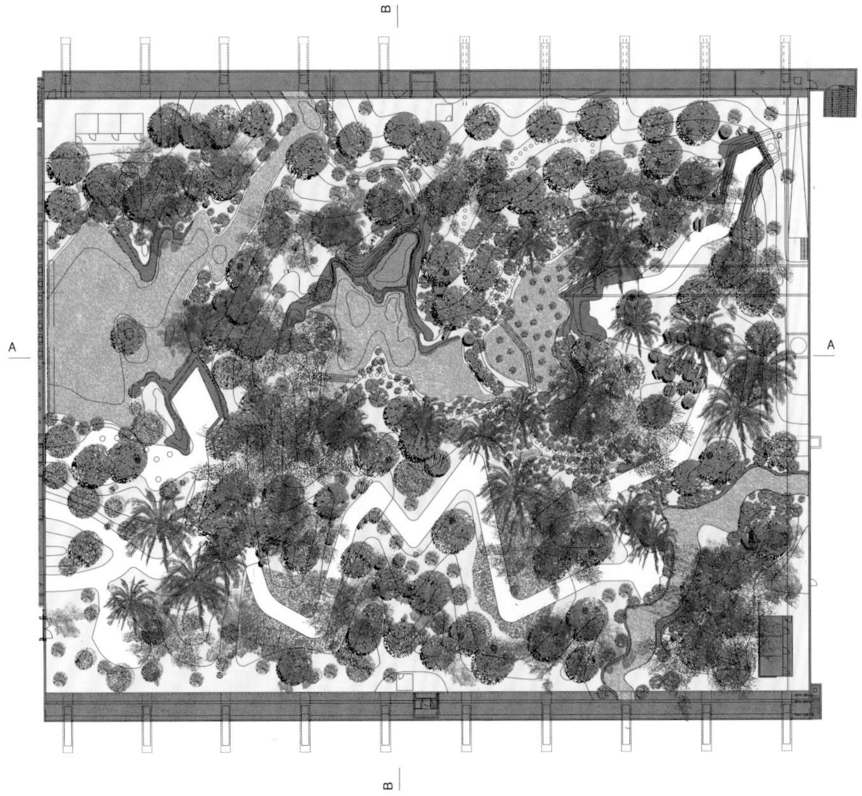

B

Gondwanaland, super-continent on the southern hemisphere (until 250 million years ago).

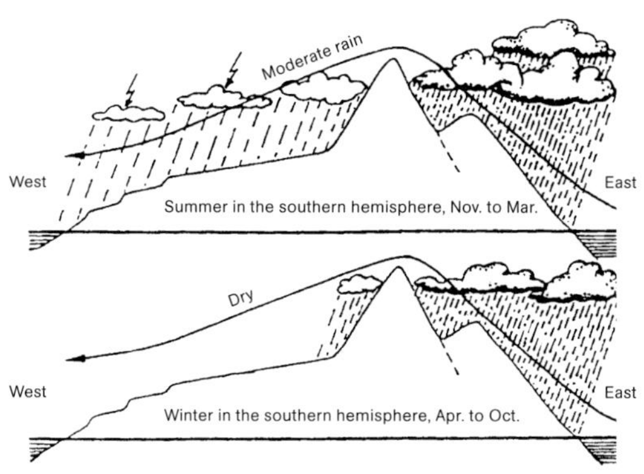

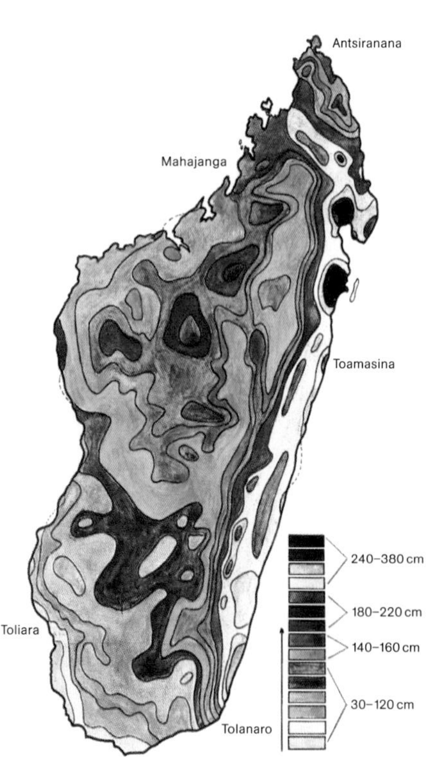

Precipitation levels and distribution on Madagascar.

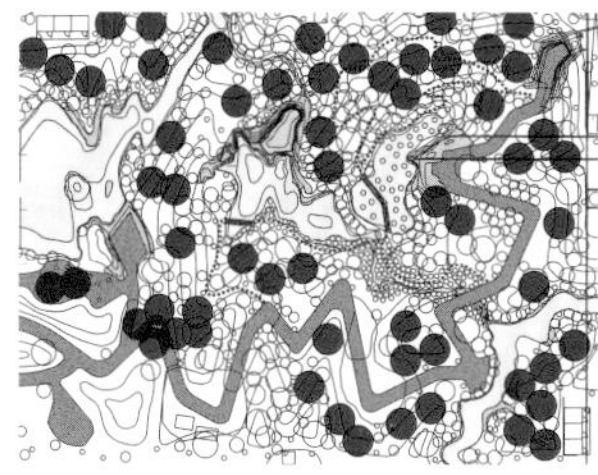

Dominant trees, 20–30 m

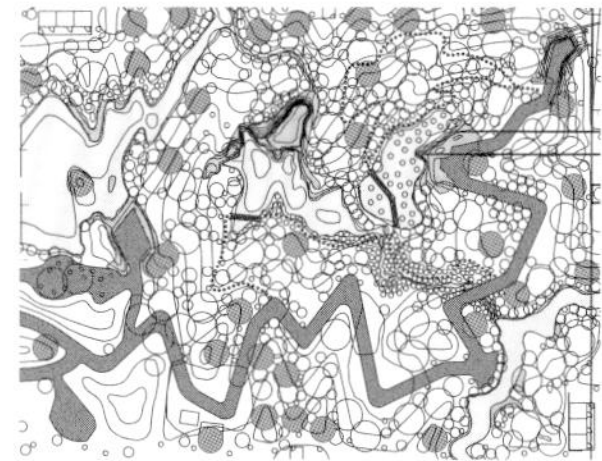

Subdominant trees, 15–20 m

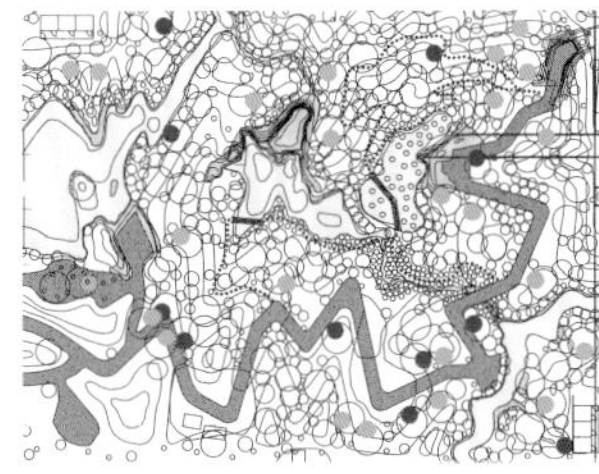

Epiphytes

Orchids

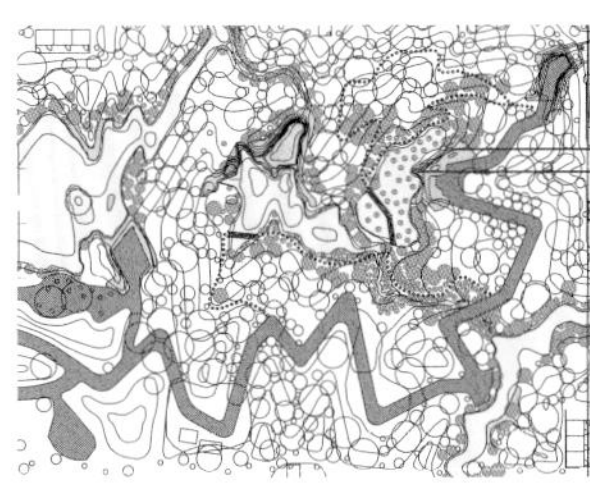

Swamp plants

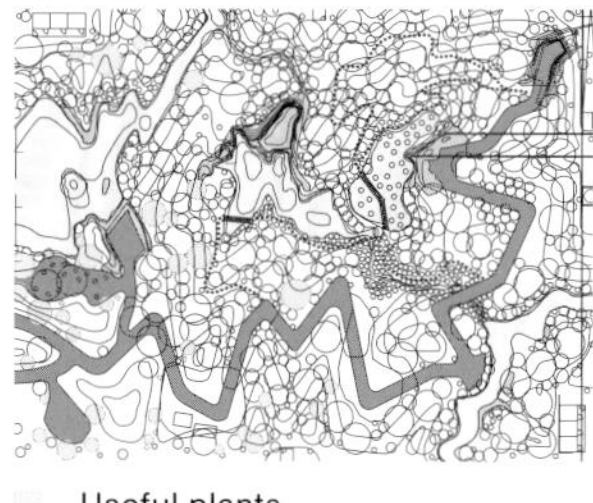

Useful plants

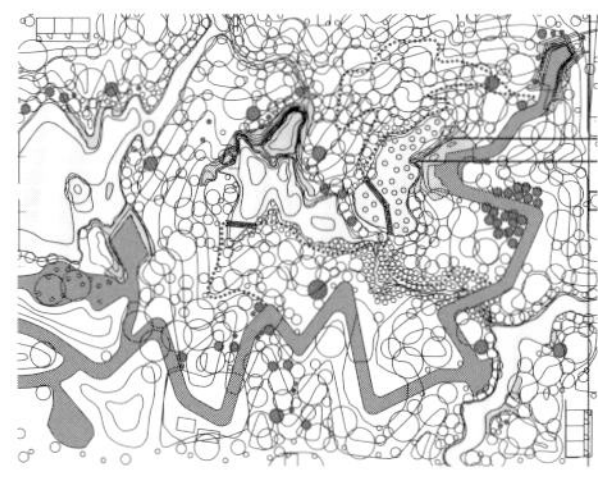

Palms

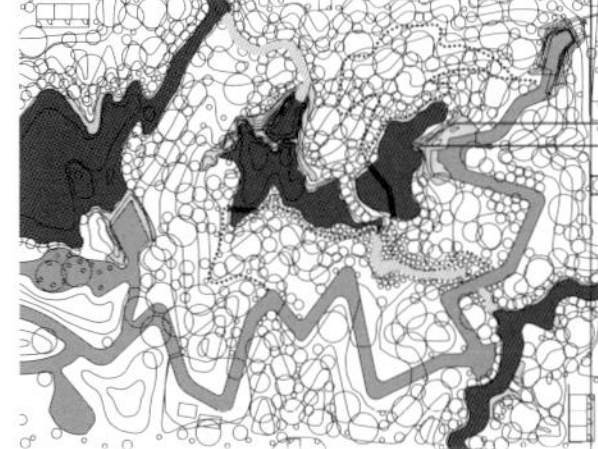

Lake
Stream

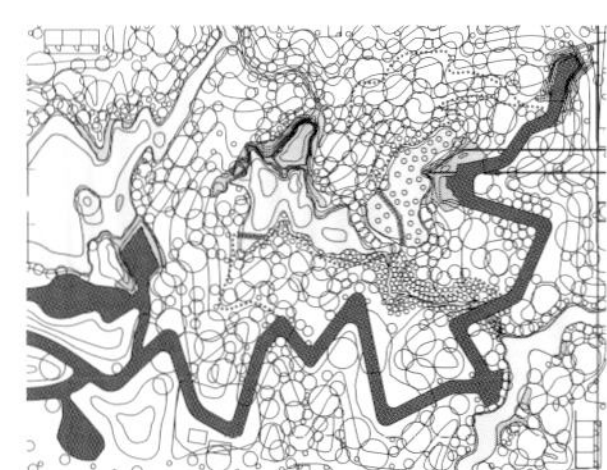

Major path
Beaten paths

FORUM 3, NOVARTIS CAMPUS, BASEL
ROOM OF PLANTS
2003–05

Client: Novartis Pharma AG, Basel
Master plan: Vittorio Magnago Lampugnani, Studio di Architettura, Milan
Architecture: Diener & Diener Architekten, Basel, with Helmut Federle and Gerold Wiederin
Area: 180 m^2

Empire apothecary, Pharmazie-Historisches Museum Basel.

The Novartis St. Johann factory site in Basel's Dreiländereck (border triangle) – Novartis's corporate headquarters – is being converted from a production site into a centre for research and administration. The concept calls for several office buildings by different architects, which are planned or already under construction. The first to be completed is the office building Forum 3.

The Room of Plants in the Forum 3 office building on the Novartis campus is located at the western end of the structure. The climate-controlled space rises from the first floor through the building's four upper storeys and ends beneath the roof. Galleries on the third, fourth and fifth floors enable the visitor to observe the luxuriant, multilayered spectacle of large trees, orchids and climbing plants from various heights.

The selection of plants points to their various useful aspects, from their suitability as potential medicines to their ornamental value. Many of the medicinal plants come from the tropical rain forests. The active agents extracted from them are still the basis of medicines today, in the age of gene therapy. With its selection of plants, the plant room of Novartis's office building points to these useful properties. As in nature, medicinal, nutritional and fibre plants live side by side and create a little jungle. It takes the wisdom of shamans and medicine men as well as the detailed and technical knowledge of contemporary science, with its research into and analysis of the specific active agents involved, to make these plants useable for us.

In the intense and stressful daily work world, the room of plants is also a welcome diversion from the office routine. Entering the plant room directly and sensuously conveys a sense of overabundance, with constantly shifting configurations of plants and the scent of growth and decay. The most powerful sensory impression is the unfamiliar climate, characterised by its warmth and by the heavy, humid tropical air. As with an urban shopping arcade, the visitor is briefly immersed in a microcosm, where longings are artificially staged, free from the influence of seasons and shifts in temperature.

Just as in an actual rain forest, every storey displays a different picture of nature. On the first floor, the observer's gaze lights upon the gigantic tree trunks. Reddish brown tiles lead to the plant area, out of which grow the mighty trees, some of which are twelve metres tall and weigh more than ten tonnes. Thick branches and ferns can be seen from the second storey. From the third and fourth storeys, the visitor sees orchids, the leafy chaos of the treetops and the lianas.

This exotic botanical world, with its tropical sultriness, beguiling scents and colourful splendour beneath a glass sky that abolishes spatial boundaries, stands in sharp contrast to the surrounding Basel cityscape. This makes it all the more fascinating that, thanks to the building's glass façade, the surroundings can be seen from inside the room and the room can be seen from the outside. In this way, the exotic and artificially cultivated vegetation and the native flora are interwoven, separated only by a thin glass pane. The result is a fascinating interplay of nature and artifice.

The Journey of the Trees
A total of fourteen hundred plants were planted in the Room of Plants, including eleven giant trees, some of which are up to twelve metres tall and weigh more than ten tonnes. All of these come from large-scale nurseries in Malaysia, Thailand and Florida. In August 2004, they were transported by sea in shipping containers at great expense to greenhouses in Holland, where they were acclimatised. Some months later, in March 2005, they journeyed on to Basel, Switzerland in climate-controlled lorries. In the Room of Plants, they are thriving in a humid microclimate with a stable room temperature of twenty degrees Celsius, which is regulated by an automatic temperature control system.

SK

A

Distribution of base plates.

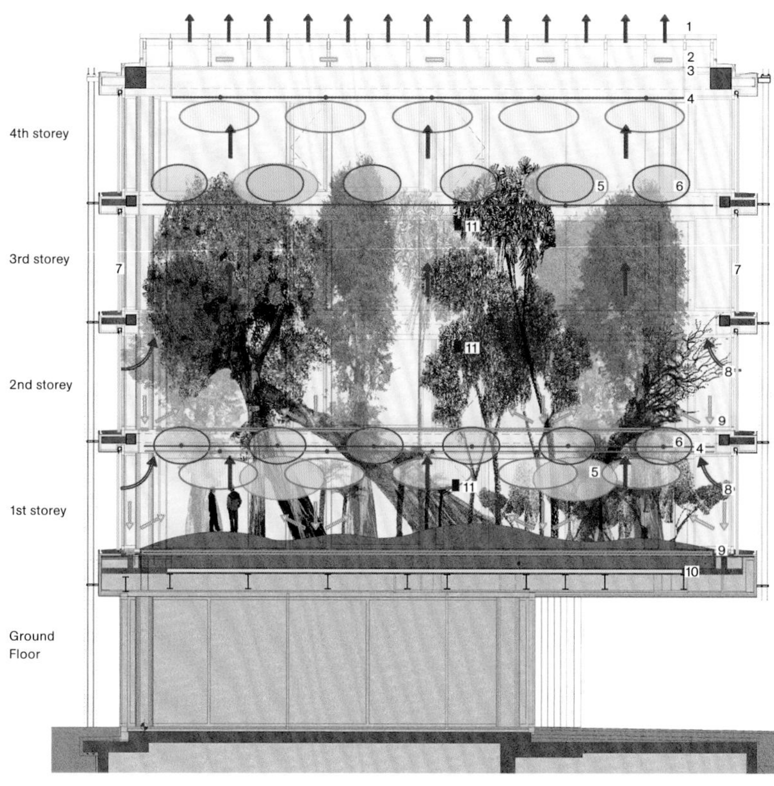

B

1 Vitiated air, 15.8 m²
2 Assimilation
3 Awning
4 Rain
5 Dampening and cooling with ventilator
6 Dampening and cooling with jets
7 Sun blinds
8 Air intake
9 Heating
10 Drip irrigation
11 Measuring box

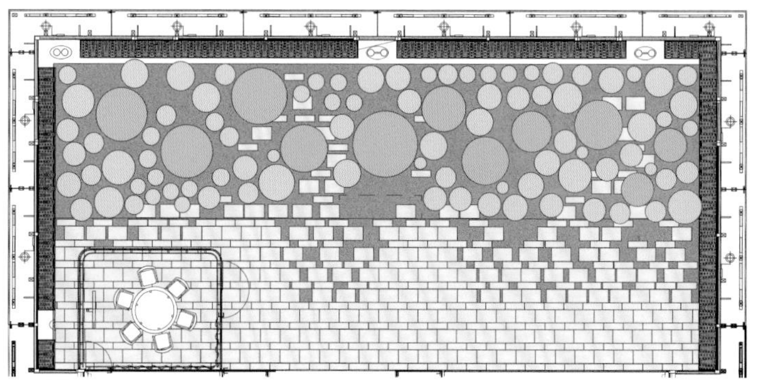

Distribution of large trees.

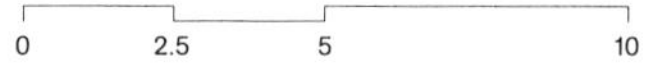

The Floors of a Rain Forest
Characteristic of a rain forest is the way the treetops meet and come together to form a typical homogeneous, wavy canopy of leaves. As in nature, the forest in the Room of Plants is divided into four different storeys: a ground layer, consisting of a patchy herbaceous layer of low plants, broad-leaved grasses, dwarf palms and shrubs up to three metres tall; a shrub layer of smaller trees and shrubs three to forty metres tall; and a tree layer sixty to seventy metres tall. In addition, there are also climbing plants and epiphytes and orchids, which grow on other plants.

4th storey
Climbing plants.

3rd storey
Epiphytic orchids.

Structure of a rain forest.

2nd storey
Epiphytic ferns.

1st storey
Root grasses.

30 ST MARY AXE, LONDON
WILDERNESS
2002–04

Client: Swiss Reinsurance Company
Architecture: Foster and Partners, London
Area: 1,000 m^2

The London skyline showing 30 St Mary Axe.

In English and Scottish landscape parks, "wilderness" indicates a part of the garden that remains un-designed and left to nature.

The building at 30 St Mary Axe was opened in London's financial district in April 2004. At 180 metres with forty floors, it is one of the tallest buildings in London. Its scaled pinecone-like shape makes it one of the London skyline's most eye-catching and famous structures.

Despite the importance of its design, the building's owners, Swiss Re, were equally concerned with observing the company's philosophy by building a structure that meets contemporary ecological standards. Natural light floods the building, reducing the need for artificial lighting, while individual work places can be individually shaded. The multi-layered glass façade has individual windows that can be opened – uncommon in most tall buildings. The building has its own weather station, which assesses the present weather conditions to determine if natural ventilation will suffice without the added use of the climate control unit. Outside temperature and wind conditions allowing, the climate in the building can be largely regulated by fresh air supply alone – saving up to 50 per cent of the heating and cooling costs typical of comparable conventional tall buildings.

The building's innovative climate control system maintains a constant interior temperature. Room humidity is also adjusted according to the outside climate. As a result of these two conditions, tropical flora that thrive in this climate were chosen for the interior of the building.

Just as the high-tech building controls the climate by traditional means via fresh air supply, the interior landscaping also fuses the traditional and the innovative. It is based on the concept of the English garden, which is in contrast to the strict, formal layout typical of the French garden. The English tradition is rooted in the notion of naturalness and transcendence in nature as an expression of an enlightened and liberal philosophy. In the seventeenth and early eighteenth centuries, an additional characteristic, called "wilderness", became common in English and Scottish gardens. This concept allowed part of the garden to remain un-designed and left to nature. Scattered groups of bushes and shrubbery arranged in a labyrinth manner were left to grow freely and imbrute – without artificial cultivation. These areas could also be fenced in, separating the wilderness from cultivated nature. Of course, crossovers happen in this struggle between the tame and the wild. The border between inside and outside is blurred, and it is left undecided which side should be fenced in and ultimately become the object of our desire.

The enclosed potted plants inside 30 St Mary Axe reflect this idea of the English landscape park. The pots are not fixed to the floor, but can be "moved" by visitors or employees due to the concave aspect of the torispherical head type floor. The garden tips as soon as an onlooker leans on the railings. It is a disruptive element and a reference to the fragility of nature in a high-tech world.

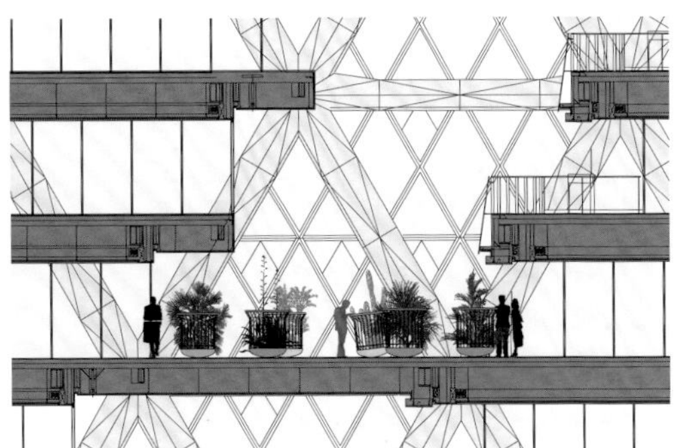

Position in the room.

0 2.5 5

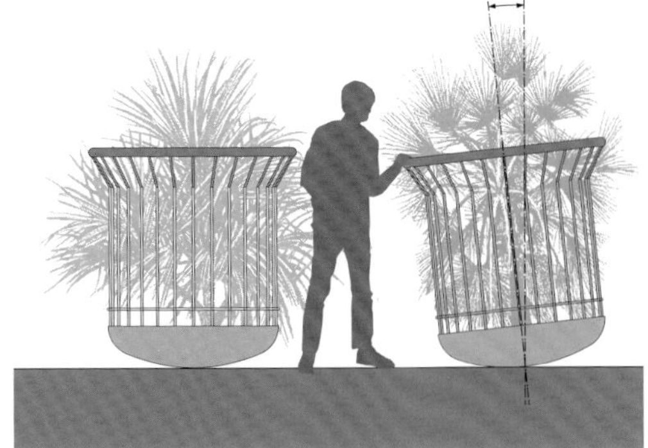

Plant containers.

EXHIBITION AT THE KUNSTHAUS BREGENZ
"THE MEDIATED MOTION"
31/03–13/05/01

Client: Kunsthaus Bregenz
Exhibition: In collaboration with Olafur Eliasson
Area: All floors

Invitation card to the exhibition opening.
Flood of the century in Bregenz, May 1999.

Kunsthaus Bregenz's austere, orthogonal concrete-and-glass architecture is transformed during the exhibition "The mediated motion". All four levels are altered by smell, fog, water, plants and earth in a path that takes one through the question of the artificiality of nature and the influence of culture on human perception.

The idea for the installation at the Kunsthaus Bregenz is based on the building itself. It is integrated as a central element in the exhibition, in that its spiral path leading to each floor is emphasised and enhanced as a basic principle. In his search for a possible form of manifesting the time-based process of movement and orientation, Olafur Eliasson discovered landscape architecture, which had already cultivated this process. This led to collaborating with Vogt Landscape Architects. "That's why I turned to Günther Vogt, whose sensitivity for the process of cultivation was the most important source for the development of this project."[1]

"The mediated motion" is not an exhibition about gardens, their history or culture. The focus is on presenting the simplest natural phenomena, which the public can then experience in the museum in a more intense and fresh way. These simple, everyday natural phenomena, overlooked in their real surroundings, are given new significance in the exhibition and so sharpen the observations and sensations of the viewer.

The prelude to the exhibition is provided by tree trunks covered with mushrooms, which lean against the wall in the reception area. They are Lentinus edodes, or shiitake mushrooms, which grow on the dead wood of deciduous trees, generally oak, chestnut and hornbeam. They are among the most popular edible mushrooms, which is why the knowing museum visitor secretly picks them. The mushrooms continue to grow overnight for the entire run of the exhibition.

The first floor is entirely under water. A boardwalk is installed over the five-centimetre-deep body of water, and provides the only way of crossing the space. The water is covered with Lemna minor, or floating duckweed. Yet the plants only truly flourish on the first floor at the Kunsthaus Bregenz because the natural light here supplements the space's artificial lighting. The plants reproduce.

A rough-timbered, wooden staircase installed over the concrete steps leads to the next floor. This makes the staircase appear longer, steeper and narrower. It leads to the light, whereas descending the stairs takes you back into the darkness.

The smell of earth dominates the third floor. It forms a sloping surface over the entire space. With an incline of 1.5 metres from the entrance to the exit, a completely different spatial sensation is created, in addition to the scent of soil. It causes many visitors to hesitate to leave the security of the boardwalk and enter the space and, thus, walk across the rammed earth. For the exhibition "The mediated motion", the 470-square-metre space on the second floor is filled with 23 cubic metres of brickearth, weighing a total of 50 tonnes.

Spatial borders dissipate on the top floor of the exhibition. The space is filled with dense fog. You cannot see the end of the bridge suspended in the room. An air conditioner, which usually provides fresh air, supplies a fine mist to the third floor for 60 seconds every 40 minutes. Thermal lift causes the mist to rise – influenced by the body heat and movement of the visitors in the space. Half an hour later, the fog dissipates and the show starts again from the beginning.

1 Olafur Eliasson in the exhibition catalogue, "The mediated motion", Cologne, 2001, p. 7

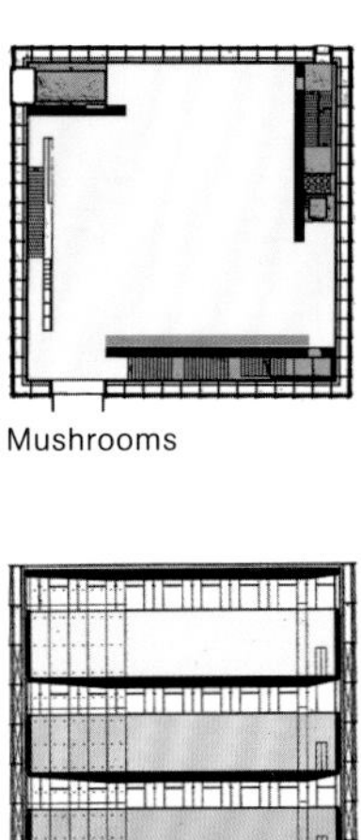

Mushrooms

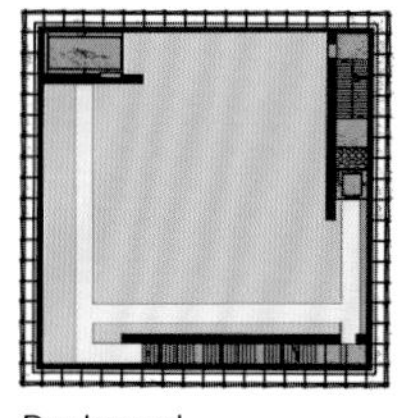

Duckweed

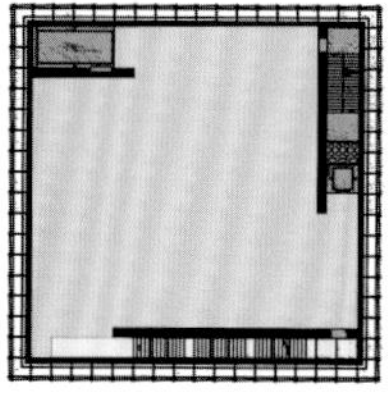

Rammed earth

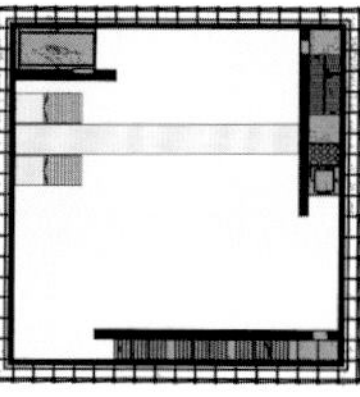

Fog

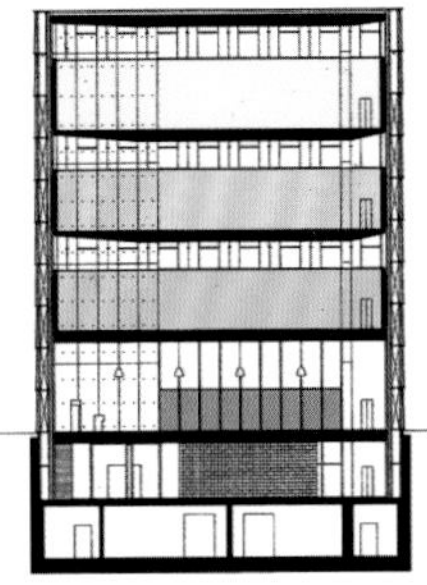

Exhibition spaces

THE MADAGASCAR HALL SERIES, 2005

Olafur Eliasson

Olafur Eliasson's photographs of the Masoala Rain Forest Hall in the Zurich zoo are the result of a journey together. Just as Eliasson explored the natural spaces of Iceland and compiled a photographic encyclopaedia of the nature in his country, here too he has captured in detail a Madagascar habitat transplanted to Switzerland, in hundreds of photographs with a very direct grasp of what is found there. He chose from all these photographs a series in which the horizon, the boundary of this artificial paradise, becomes tangible.

THE WORKSHOP

Cultivating an apple from its wild form to what we think of as an apple takes a great deal of time. The appearance, scent and taste of its fruit, the tree's ability to grow, and its resistance to disease and pests were continuously improved by cultivation. The method begins with selection, the choice of individual plants with specific qualities. Then they are deliberately hybridised to combine certain characteristics of two individual plants. Today we manipulate specific qualities by genetic methods. The yellow apple mutates into a red one, and both taste the same.

Our approach to inorganic matter is similar, extending from clay bricks by way of willow-reinforced rammed-earth walls to today's high-performance concrete, which is mixed with chemicals. What moves us to push these developments, refining them over generations and constantly improving them? What is ultimately behind the speculative research is an intention to find order in our environment and also to give it order. Order can have a natural or cultural origin.

Designing a garden or a landscape means having a dialogue with a locally determined manifestation of nature. Scientific disciplines, geology, plant sociology, soil science and meteorology are the bases, and the history of the garden, sociology, politics and the economy are the cultural partners in this dialogue. When the substratum of the place is determined with the help of various approaches, the only question remaining is how to maintain an overview in this Babel-like confusion of languages. The best description of the problem is surely the following passage in the novel *Great Expectations* by Charles Dickens:

[Walworth] appeared to be a collection of back lanes, ditches, and little gardens, and to present the aspect of a rather dull retirement. Wemmick's house was a little wooden cottage in the midst of plots of garden, and the top of it was cut out and painted like a battery mounted with guns.
"My own doing," said Wemmick. "Looks pretty; don't it?"
I highly commended it. I think it was the smallest house I ever saw; with the queerest gothic windows (by far the greater part of them sham), and a gothic door, almost too small to get in at.
"That's a real flagstaff, you see," said Wemmick, "and on Sundays I run up a real flag. Then look here. After I have crossed this bridge, I hoist it up – so – and cut off the communication."
The bridge was a plank, and it crossed a chasm about four feet wide and two deep. But it was very pleasant to see the pride with which he hoisted it up and made it fast; smiling as he did so, with a relish and not merely mechanically.
"At nine o'clock every night, Greenwich time," said Wemmick, "the gun fires. There he is, you see! And when you hear him go, I think you'll say he's a Stinger."
The piece of ordnance referred to, was mounted in a separate fortress, constructed of lattice-work. It was protected from the weather by an ingenious little tarpaulin contrivance in the nature of an umbrella.
"Then, at the back," said Wemmick, "out of sight, so as not to impede the idea of fortifications – for it's a principle with me, if you have an idea, carry it out and keep it up – I don't know whether that's your opinion –"
I said, decidedly.
"– At the back, there's a pig, and there are fowls and rabbits; then, I knock together my own little frame, you see, and grow cucumbers; and you'll judge at supper what sort of a salad I can raise. So, sir," said Wemmick, smiling again, but seriously too, as he shook his head, "if you can suppose the little place besieged, it would hold out a devil of a time in point of provisions."
Then, he conducted me to a bower about a dozen yards off, but which was approached by such ingenious twists of path that it took quite a long time to get at; and in this retreat our glasses were already set forth. Our punch was cooling in an ornamental lake on whose margin the bower was raised. This piece of water (with an island in the middle which might have been the salad for supper) was of a circular form, and he had constructed a fountain in it, which, when you set a little mill going and took a cork out of a pipe, played to that powerful extent that it made the back of your hand quite wet.
"I am my own engineer, and my own carpenter, and my own plumber, and my own gardener, and my own Jack of all Trades," said Wemmick, in acknowledging my compliments.
Charles Dickens, *Great Expectations*

The description of Wemmick's garden from the perspective of its designer reveals the idea of the garden in terms of its qualities that communicate directly via the senses. Moreover the story sounds more like a description of a model than of a real garden. The spatial dimensions and the choice of means and tools are limited for

Wemmick. He uses the possibilities available to him, respects the existing conditions and supplements them with things he has at hand. We are confronted with similar problems today when we design a landscape. Landscape begins where the natural sciences and the humanities fall silent.

Working with a model, anticipating reality, is the obvious method for implementing design strategies. Models provide more than a scaled-down overview of the whole. Perception focuses first on the whole and only then are the individual parts perceived. Although we are familiar with such excerpts from nature in our daily lives at home, the scale is reversed. The familiar typologies are enlarged or reduced to an almost monstrous extent. As with ships in a bottle or an aquarium, however, we lose sense impressions like smells and noises; things cannot be picked up or touched. So we find ourselves in a world where something is always missing, the temporal or spatial dimension, the volume or tangible impressions. The challenge of replacing the missing parts with the imagination is the poetic power inherent in models.

Both the design process and the depiction of projects moves within the tension between what can really be perceived and the imagination. The plan and the model as preliminary steps of the new reality can only fulfil the role of mediators if they are translatable alternative images of projected reality. Because our gaze is no longer directed at the horizon, and because the tangible reality before us is unbalanced as a whole, we are forced to interpret and regulate that which already exists using the meanings it posits itself. The continuous feedback between reality and project, between strangely familiar outside world and an inner world shaped by the imagination, becomes evident in the models as a montage. The montage of images is the basis technical procedure in film.

It presumes a fragmentary reality and describes the manner of construction in the process. The materials used in the models break the connection to reality. Their link to what they usually say changes, though their form does not. The crucial thing is no longer the individual elements in their specific character, but the constructional principle upon which the elements are based.

Other examples of alternative images of reality are exhibitions in museums or galleries that are not representations of works but projects in themselves. They do more than just narrate the story of how a piece of nature was constructed. In their interpretive order, in which the specimens of fauna and flora are exhibited as if in a science museum, various soil samples stand around in glasses; photographs with details of the landscape and certain plants appear in a model of paths on the wall; reading material in a library is spread out and films run behind the horizon of a rammed-earth floor; they become new constructions whose theme is nature and its design in landscape architecture.

"Anyone who knows how to design a park properly," Marc-Antoine Laugier wrote in 1753 in *Observations*, his theory of urban design, "will have no difficulty designing the plan by which a city will be built in terms of its area and location. Squares, intersections and streets are needed. Regularity and strangeness are needed, correspondences and antitheses, accidents that vary the picture, great order to the details, but confusion, clashing and tumult in the whole." *gv*

BUTTERFLY GARDEN
SPIRAL OF FOG
2000–11

Client: Private
Material: Glass, steel
Size: Approx. 4.5 × 3.7 m

Displays tell a story, and if living tropical butterflies are to become actors on a kinetic, theatrical stage, it is necessary to construct a framework that functions as part of the presentation. Humidity, warmth and a climate in motion are combined with butterflies and plants to fill a space that is technically controlled to the highest degree, but nevertheless, on the visual level, has an extremely natural appearance.

In order to maintain the proper humidity, fog is sprayed through the glass house several times a day. This process is staged like a theatrical event, since the fog is driven by air jets so that it rotates, resulting in a spiral of fog. The damp air, which has a temperature of 25 degrees centigrade and contains 70 to 90 percent humidity, is whirled around inside the glass house, thus creating the living conditions for the butterflies and the tropical plants that are cultivated here during the winter.

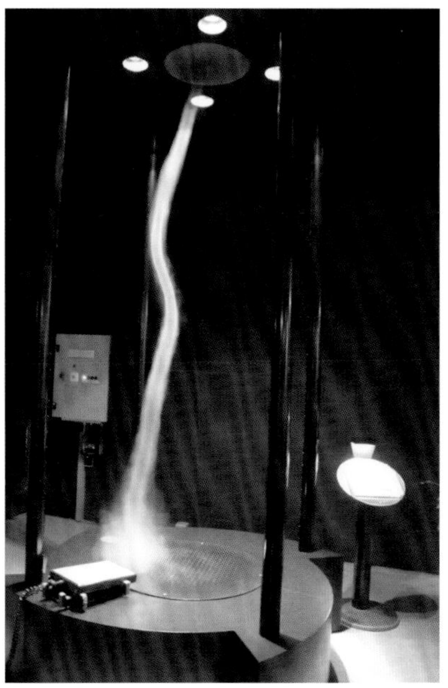

Technorama, existing tornado installation, Winterthur, Switzerland.

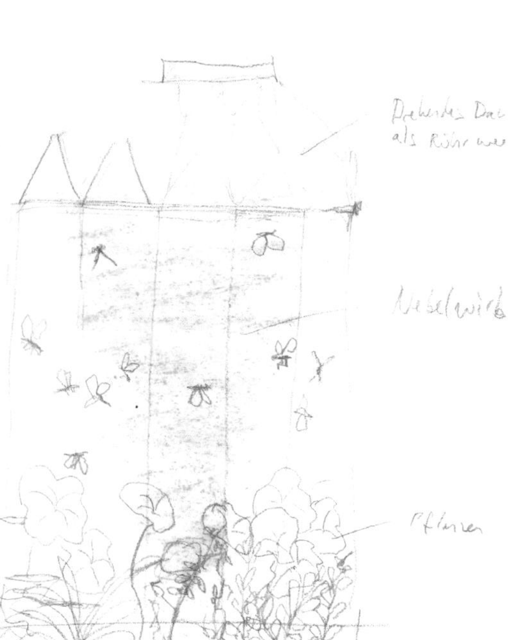

Model studies, 1:10.

DIORAMA FOR THE LOBBY AT MÜHLEBACHSTRASSE 20
WINDOW ON ASIA
2006–08

Client: Diethelm Keller Holding, Zurich
Architecture: Romero & Schaefle Architekten, Zurich
Size: Indoor: 160 × 240 × 60 cm (H × L × W)

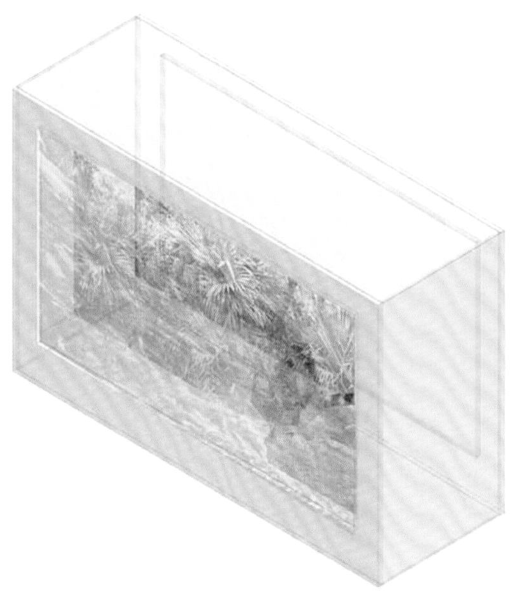

The diorama in the small lobby of the global concern features a view of a rainforest. This view – from the company headquarters in Zurich straight into the South-east Asian rainforest – reflects the commercial exchange between Zurich and Asia. Selected details from the picture of the jungle are linked to the history of the company, turning the rainforest into a DKSH-specific rainforest garden. The fan tree – the motif from the company logo – can be seen, as can the trunk of a rubber tree, along with various birds and beetles. The diorama is a three-dimensional, staggered installation with details of varying precision in the fore- and background. Creating a three-dimensional illusion, it seems as if one could reach out and touch the vista.The background photograph was taken in Masoala Hall at the Zurich Zoo, and the plants in the foreground were prepared by a scientific taxidermist.

LONG BENCH
SITTING DOWN TOGETHER
2007–08

Client: Baudepartement des Kantons Basel-Stadt
Material: Stainless steel, high-pressure laminate
Size: From 5 m, one element: 57 cm

This classical bench winds through the terrain like a caterpillar on many slender feet made of chrome steel. Originally developed for the Elisabethenanlage project, a little historic park in Basel, the design is ideal for sites with declining ground and meandering paths. The bank's bearing surface consists of single seats overlapping and compensates in this way height differences. Length and form are individually adapted to the spatial situation and the course of the paths. Seats and backrests are made of a specific laminate robust enough for use in public spaces and yet made of wood. The subtle pattern embossed in the laminate is based on the patterns bark beetles gnaw into wood.

Silicon cast.

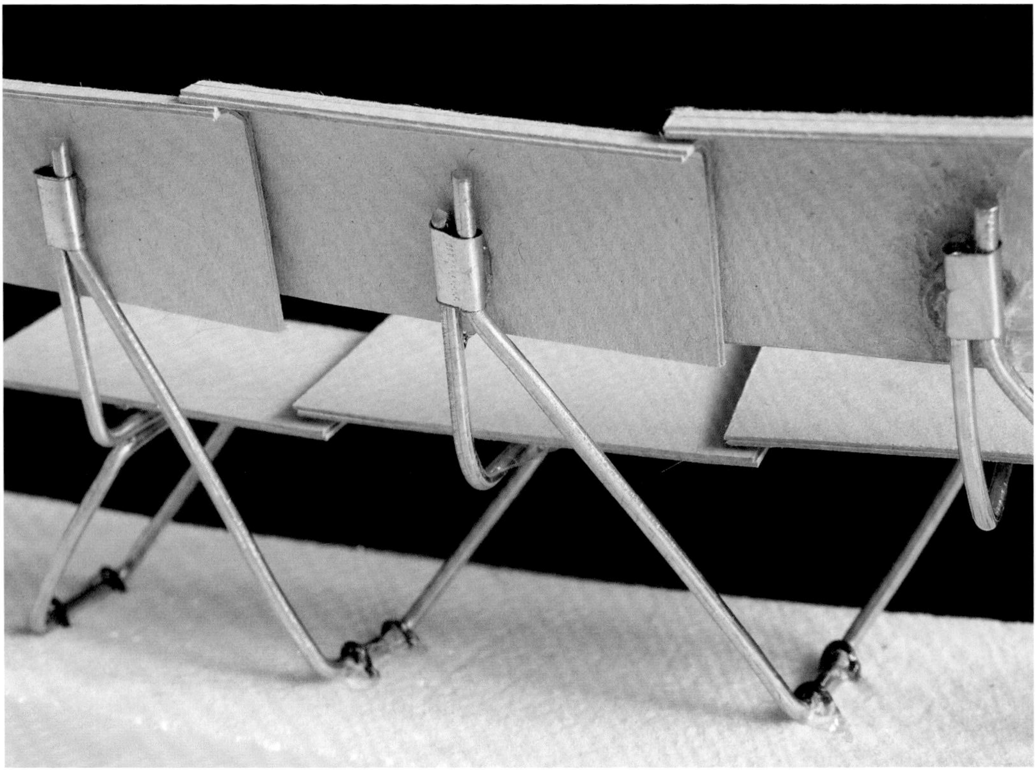

OCTAEDER
NOVARTIS CAMPUS
2009

Client: Novartis Pharma AG
Material: Oak, cedar, sequoia, robinia
Size: 59 × 54 cm (W × H), 60 to 120 cm (L)

Octaeder is a piece of outdoor furniture designed specifically for use on uneven terrain, such as gravel, but can, of course, be used on all kinds of surfaces.

What seems to be an amorphous piece of rock when seen from afar, reveals its characteristic, artificial form and its functionality upon closer inspection. Designed as a contorted octahedron with rounded edges, the stool is cut out of one piece of solid wood and ground to create a smooth surface.

This design, half way between naturalness and artificiality, is the distinctive feature of Octaeder. The stool can be placed on each of its eight sides.

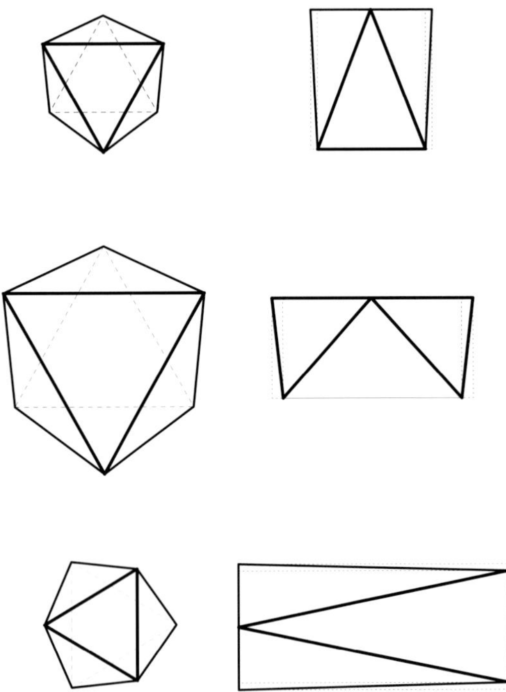

Octahedron: Triangle, Stool, Bench

BRICKCOMB
BRICK WALL FOR THE LOHSEPARK
2009–11

Client: HafenCity Hamburg GmbH
Material: Brick
Size: Brick: 20 × 21 × 16 cm

The mineral composition and colour of the wall structures for the Lohsepark are derived from the construction material traditionally used in the city of Hamburg, the clinker brick. The brick and stone structures of the city and its harbour areas are contrasted with a living construct of intervals. The colour scheme is taken from the variety of burnt clay. Depending on the combination of the different sides of the bricks, the geometry of the bricks forms a variety of large polygonal and hexagonal openings. Like a reversible figure, the structure of the wall or the individual openings in it seem to alter, depending on the focus of the viewer.

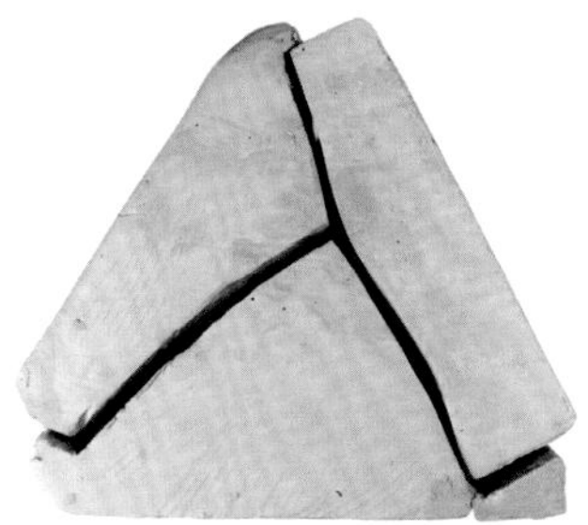

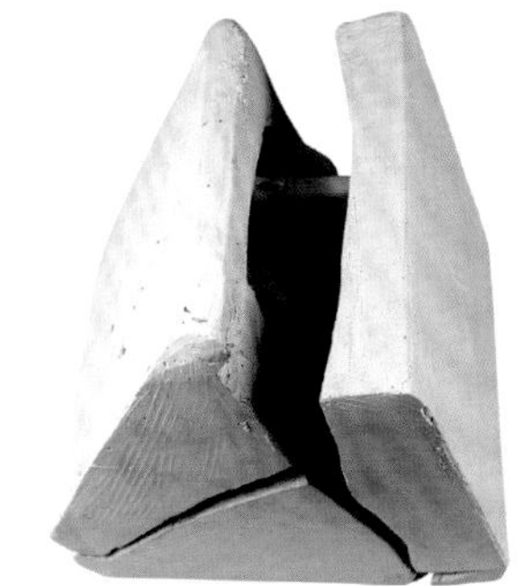

Scale model: plaster casts and wall (installation, VOGT window).

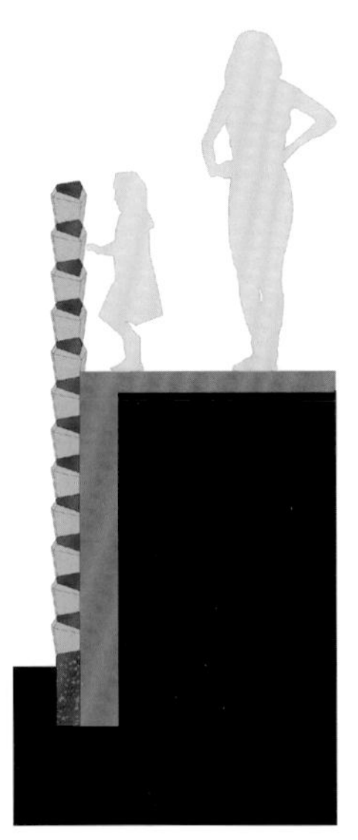

Hardened lava rock: basalt quarry near Hegau Singen, Germany.

CROSS-LEGGED CHAIR
STOOL WITH ANGULAR SHAPES
2008–09

Material: Rice husks and lignin
Size: 44 × 36 × 22 cm (H × W × D)

Chairs in public outdoor areas are as rare as they are coveted; whereas park managers tend to replace chairs with unmovable benches for fear of theft and disarrangement, users enjoy portable seating opportunities and being able to participate in the design of the exterior space. VOGT solves this dilemma with the cross-legged chair, a stool that not only fulfils the requirements of all parties but also those of the zeitgeist. A stool that combines practical aspects, high-quality design and sustainable production.

The chair is 100 per cent recyclable, lightweight and easily transportable, but sufficiently bulky as not to be an easy target for thieves. With its unique form and colouring, and the possibility of individual imprints, the stool can also be used as a stylish image and advertising medium. The seat is designed for temporary use outdoors and can be composted with the garden rubbish in autumn.

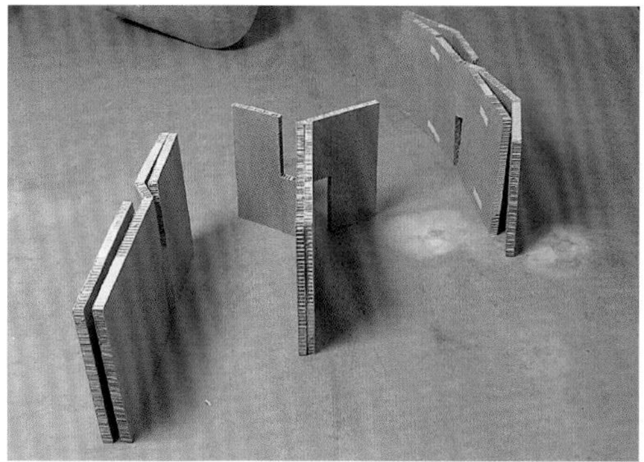

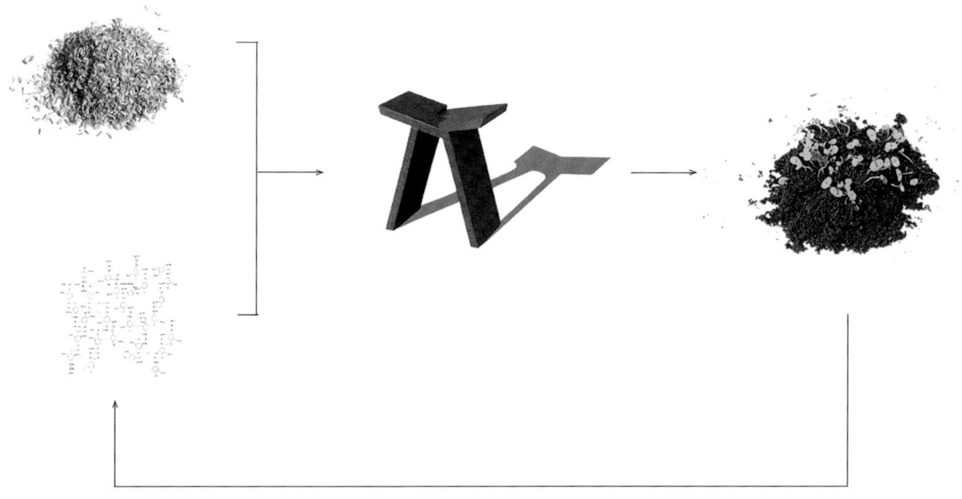

Material cycle: both types of material (rice husks and lignin) are vegetable matter and compostable waste products from paper manufacturing and rice production.

WORKING TABLE
WORKING IN A PARK
2008–09

Client: Novartis Pharma AG
Material: Stainless steel, high-pressure laminate
Size: 44 × 36 × 22, 62 × 45 × 38 cm (H × W × D)

Flexibility has been the key aspect in the design and construction of this folding table. Due to its low weight and elaborate folding system, it can easily be placed wherever wished. The little yet robust laminate table offers space for a laptop and notepaper or an outdoor lunch. The slender chrome steel feet make it stand firm even on grass. When folded, it requires minimal storage space.

Carl Müller Wien
OPTIKER
401

faserverstärktes Polyurethan Verbundmaterial aus der Autoindustrie
12.11.06
Höhenausgleich
Kurve?
Torsion
Höhenausgleich
Mitte
Vorne
Kreuzung fest verbinden
ZIRKUS
VERKAUFEN
MUSIZIEREN
GERÄUSETURM
RUTSCHEN
WOHNUNG
BRUNNEN
WASSERMÜHLE
BACH
GARTEN
SITZEN
AUSSTELLEN
KLETTERN
VERSTECKEN
ZOLL
MARKT-
PLATZ
WASSER-
BECKEN
SANDGRUBE
ANMALEN
SCHAUKELN/
KRAN

ca. 50 cm
ca. 90 cm
60 cm

2.2.2 TATE WEST END
2.2.3 TATE ROOF

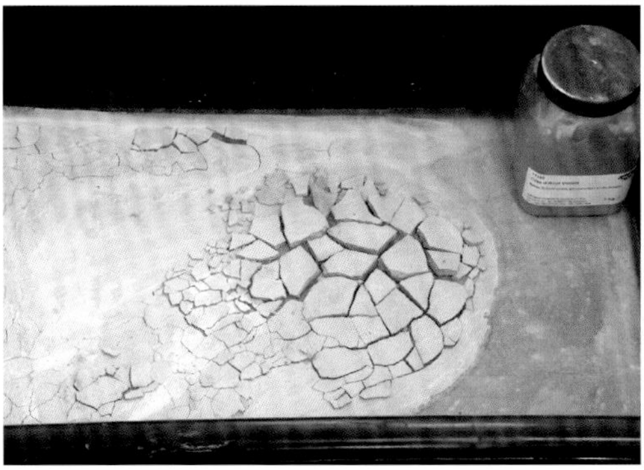

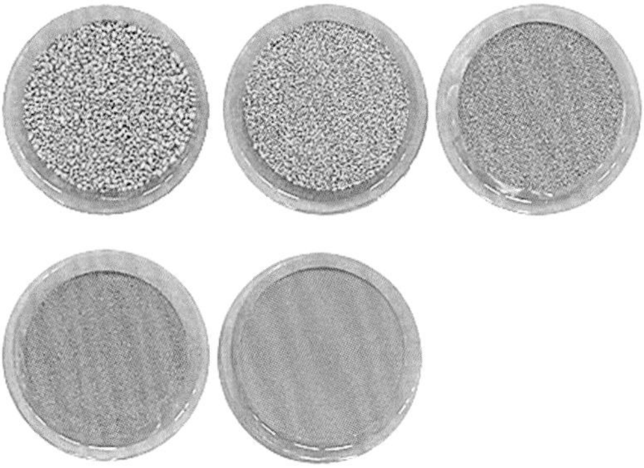

KREMER-PIGMENTE
KREMER-PIGMENTE

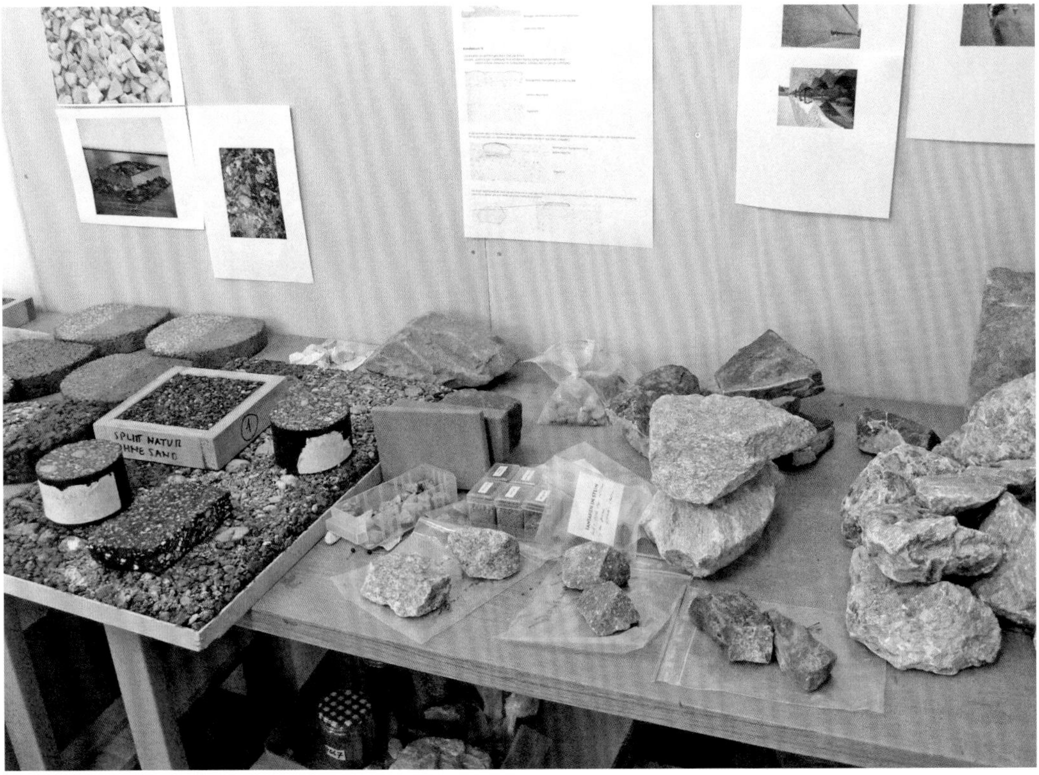
SPLIT NATUR
OHNE SAND

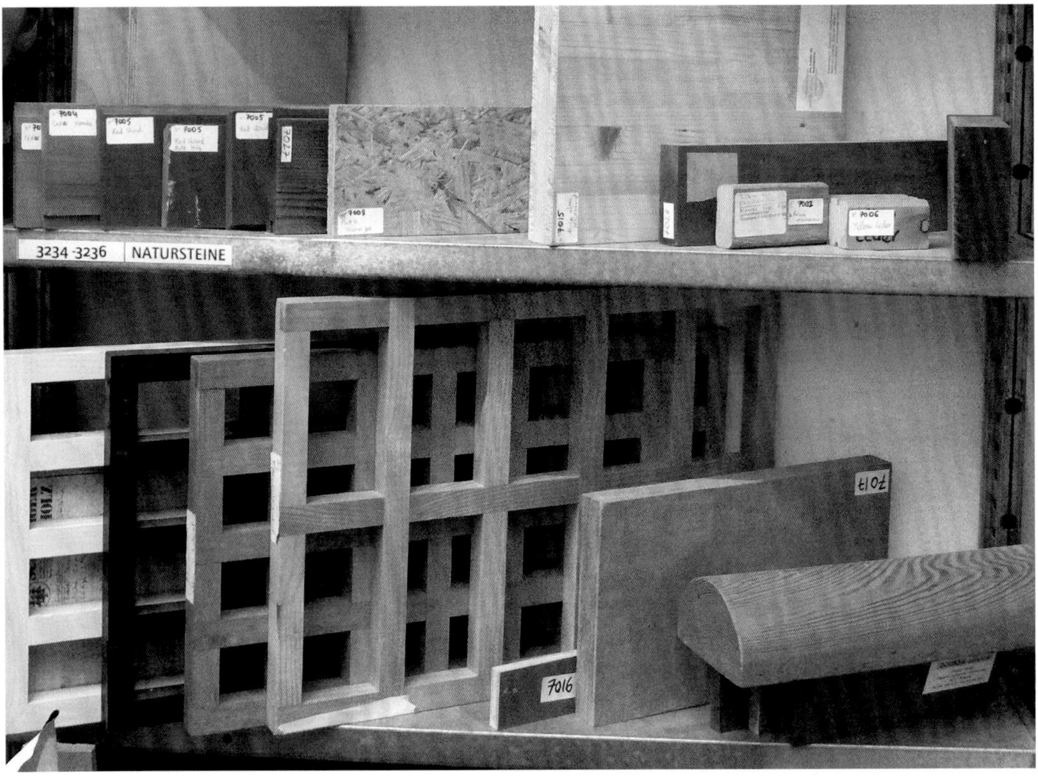
3234-3236
NATURSTEINE
7016
7017

Swiss Architecture Museum, Basel, 2004–05.

Architekturgalerie München, Munich, 2005.

Architekturgalerie Aedes, Berlin, 2007.

Museum für Gestaltung Zürich, 2007.

Foundation's Rochelle School, London, 2010.

Museum Bellerive, Zurich, 2011.

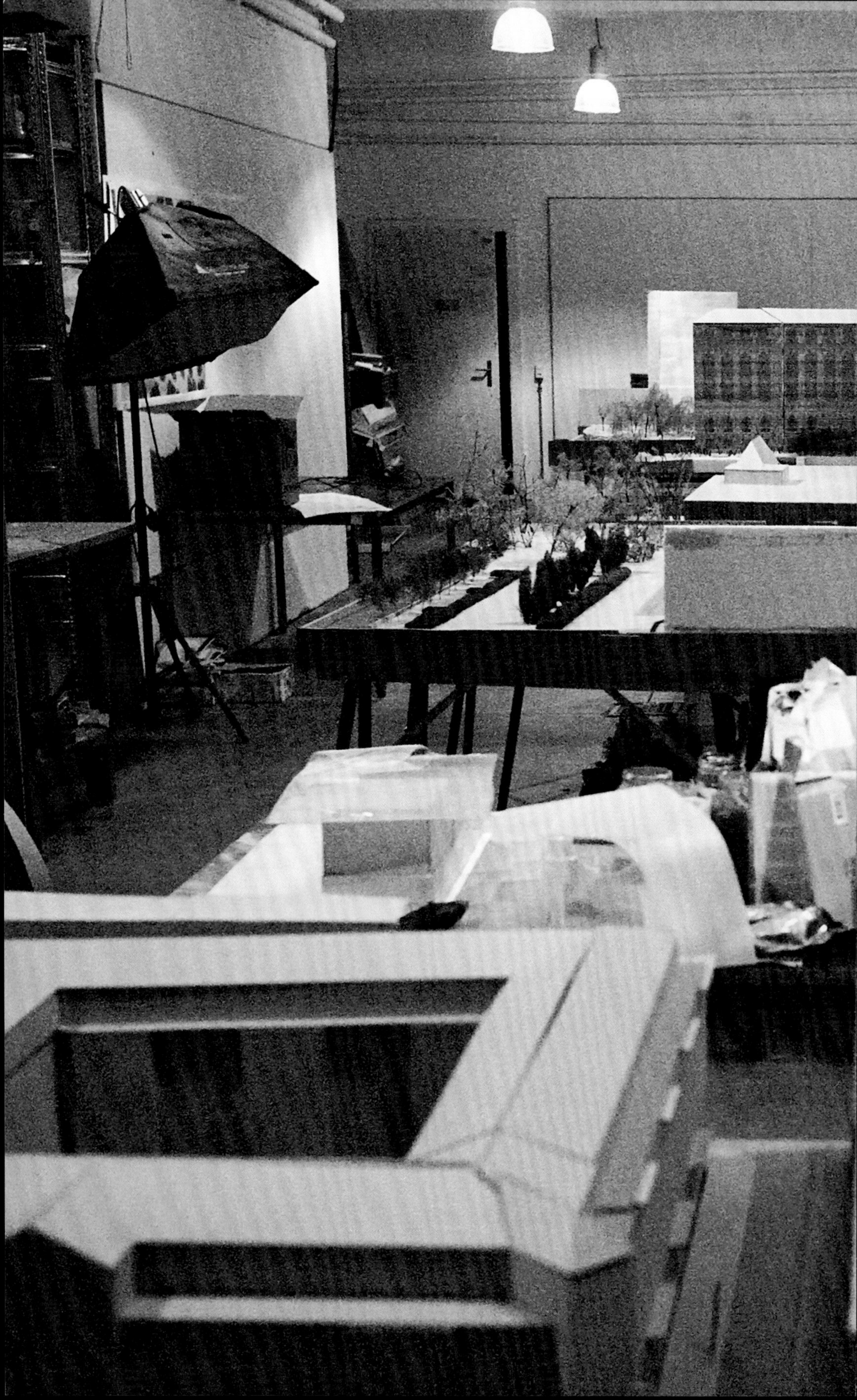

1845-1 SRN
Arch. Aufbauten

URBAN COMPONENTS

Case Studio

London

Zurich

Berlin

Glarus, Switzerland, 2006.

Maggia Valley, Switzerland, 2007.

Gotthard Pass, Switzerland, 2008.

Lake District, England, 2009.

Aletsch Glacier, Switzerland, 2010.

Jura, Switzerland, 2011.

Catalogue of Projects
Selection

PROJECT NAME
Working Title
Address, Location
Competition
Client
Architect
[Planning period] Implementation period
Area
Brief description

MASOALA RAIN FOREST HALL
Constructed Nature
Zurich Zoo
Project by Kienast Vogt Partner
Research competition
Zurich Zoo
Gautschi Storrer, Zurich
[1994–2000] 2001–03
10,800 m²
Reproduction of the Madagascan rain forest's ecosystem in Masoala in a hall, based on the basic principles of multilayered vegetation. (→ p. 466)

MOABITER WERDER
Collection and Exhibition
Berlin
Project by Kienast Vogt Partner
Two-phase competition 1991: First prize
Deutsche Stadt- und Grundstücks-entwicklungsgesellschaft
[1990–1998] 1999–2002
45,000 m²
Two-section park along the Spree near the former Hamburg-Lerther depot and west of Paulusstrasse.

TATE MODERN
An English Square
London
Project by Kienast Vogt Partner
Tate Modern, London
Herzog & de Meuron, Basel
[1995–97/2005–] 1998–2001
25,000 m²
A hybrid of square and park developed as an English square.

SITC, SWISS INSURANCE TRAINING CENTRE
Detail in Context
Zurich
Swiss Re
Silvio Schmed, Zurich
[1999] 2000
1,050 m²
Redesign of a bourgeois villa garden, emphasising its historical stratifications.
(→ p. 290)

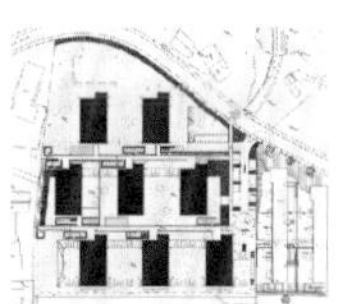

ACHSLEN PARK
Saint Gall
Senn BPM AG
Baumschlager Eberle Architekten, Vaduz
[1999–2002] 2001–02
15,000 m²
Design of grounds around a residential development.

Central Park
Berlin
Project by Kienast Vogt Partner
Re-use proposal concept
Senatsverwaltung für Stadtentwicklung, Umweltschutz und Technologie
Prof. Bernd Albers, Berlin
[1998/2006–]
3,000,000 m²
Concept for the re-use of the decommissioned Tempelhof Airport, with the aim of opening Tempelhof field to the city as a twenty-first-century park.

R. GARDEN
The Culture of the Wilderness
Küsnacht
Project by Kienast Vogt Partner
Private
Meili, Peter Architekten, Zurich
[1998] 1999–2001
3,700 m²
A dense, lushly planted garden.
(→ p. 296)

RICOLA MARKETING
Synthesis
Laufen
Project by Kienast Vogt Partner
Ricola AG
Herzog & de Meuron, Basel
[1998] 2000
Roof: 565 m²; Garden: 950 m²
A garden and roof greening concept in collaboration with the architects. Twining plants and vines on the long, projecting roof canopies serve as protection from the sun.

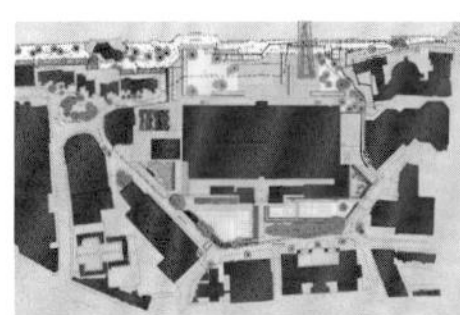

TATE ENVIRONMENT
London
Project by Kienast Vogt Partner
London Borough of Southwark
London Borough of Southwark
[1999–2000]
26,863 m²
Design of the grounds surrounding Tate Modern.

PSYCHIATRISCHE KLINIK BEVERIN
Forest Clearing
Cazis
Project by Kienast Vogt Partner
Hochbauamt des Kantons Graubünden
New building: Max Kasper, Zurich
Redevelopment of existing buildings: Gross und Rüegg, Trin
Art in public space: Hans Danuser, Zurich
[1996–99] 2000–04
24,000 m^2
A park embedded in a forest.

SWISS RE CLUBHAUS
Artificial Natural World
Zurich
Project by Kienast Vogt Partner
Swiss Re
Redevelopment: sam Architekten und Partner, Zurich
[1998–99] 1999–2000
2,700 m^2
Birch garden and cafeteria courtyard design with rammed-earth walls.

MÜNCHENER RÜCK
Image and Context – Seeing and Remembering
Munich
Project by Kienast Vogt Partner
Invited competition 1998: First prize
Münchener Rückversicherungs-Gesellschaft
Baumschlager Eberle Architekten, Vaduz
[1998–99] 2000–01
11,000 m^2
Courtyard with oak grove and moss garden on the first floor.

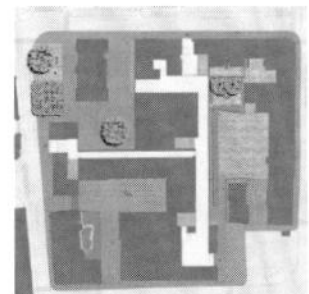

FREE UNIVERSITY OF BOZEN-BOLZANO
Bolzano
Autonomous Province of Bolzano
Bischoff Azzola Architekten, Zurich
[2001–03]
6,800 m^2
Concept for the grounds of the university complex.

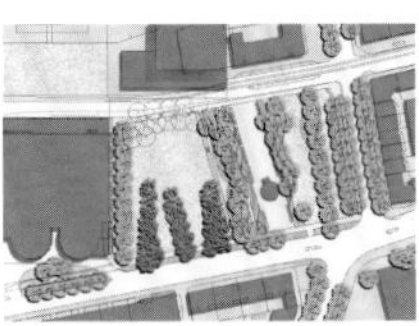

ROSENTALANLAGE
Landscape in the Park
Basel
Competition 1999: Second prize
Baudepartement des Kantons Basel-Stadt
Fair tower: Morger Degelo Marques, Basel
[1999, 2002–2008]
12,000 m^2
An urban park near Messeplatz.

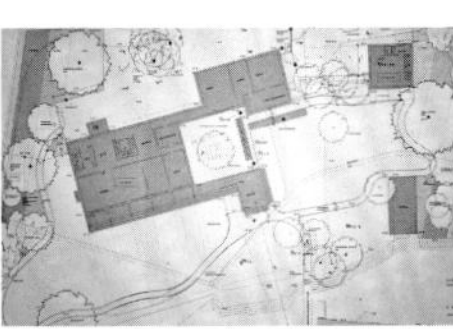

S. VILLA
Stäfa
Private
sam Architekten und Partner, Zurich
[1999–2000] 2001–03
5,000 m^2
Design for a private garden.

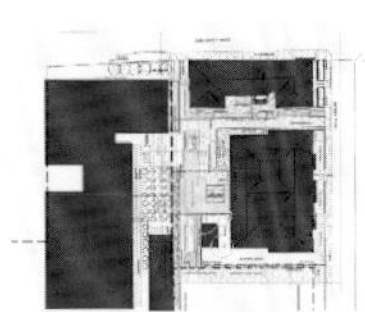

ALLIANZ GISELASTRASSE 27/29/31 AND KÖNIGINSTRASSE 101
Munich
Allianz AG, represented by Allianz Immobilien GmbH
[1999–2001] 2001–03
1,080 m^2
Design of the grounds of the office building.

EXPO.02
Garden of Violence
Murten
Direction artistique Expo.02, International Committee of the Red Cross, Swiss Red Cross, Stiftung AVINA
Art: Rémy Marlot, Martine Derain – Dalila Mahjoub, Cécile Dupaquier, Tina Keane, Chantal Mélia – Francois Loriot, Jenny Perlin
[2001–02] 2002 (temporary)
5,000 m^2
The Garden of Violence was part of the Swiss National Exhibition, Expo.02 in Murten. (→ p. 274)

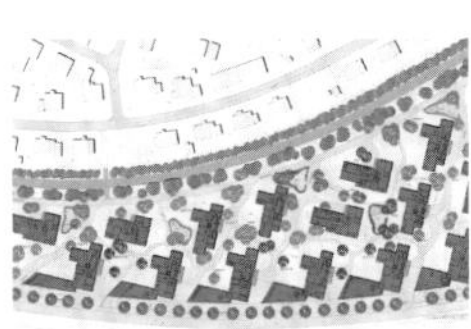

TALWIES WINTERTHUR
Hedged Space
Hegistrasse 35c–41, Oberwinterthur
Winterthur Versicherungen
Hopf & Wirth Architekten, Winterthur
[2003–05]
18,000 m^2
Between open areas of green with a sparse population of trees, hedges create spaces with varying possibilities where children from the future residential development Talwies can play and interact with the space.

OFFICE BUILDING MÜHLEBACHSTRASSE 9
City – Nature
Zurich
Ernst Basler & Partner
Romero & Schaefle Architekten, Zurich
2000–01
298 m^2
Second phase of the design of the grounds along Mühlebachstrasse.

TRAFOPLATZ
Rediscovering the Landscape
Baden
Invited research competition 1999: First prize
Stadt Baden, Planung und Bau
Urbanistic master plan: Diener & Diener Architekten, Basel
Burkard, Meyer., Baden and Ken Architekten, Baden
[1999–2002] 2002–06, 2011–14
7,402 m²
On the square, vegetation examples from the surrounding cultural landscape are presented on plinths as spatial, three-dimensional exhibition pieces. (→ p. 212)

LABAN
Folded Landscape
London
Laban, Europe's leading contemporary dance conservatoire, London
Herzog & de Meuron, Basel
[2000–02] 2002–03
7,245 m²
A geometric hill landscape creates external spaces for the dance school in the industrial area of southwest London. (→ p. 304)

UNIVERSITÄTSSPITAL ZURICH
USZ Park, Zurich
Hochbauamt Kanton Zurich
Eberli Weber Braun Architekten, Zurich
[2001–02] 2002–04
5,000 m²
Park maintenance work.
Vegetation concept for the existing park at Universitätsspital Zurich (university hospital).

LINDEN PRIMARY SCHOOL
Lindenstrasse, Niederhasli
Primarschulgemeinde Niederhasli
Bünzli & Courvoisier Architekten, Zurich
[2000–03] 2002–03
10,300 m²
Design for grounds of a primary school, including the playground and sports field.

PARK HYATT HOTEL
Weather Garden
Zurich
Park Hyatt, Zurich, Hyatt International EAME Ltd.
Meili, Peter Architekten, Zurich
[2000–02] 2002–04
6,565 m²
A stone and moss courtyard on the roof of the second floor as a view of green space for the hotel guests. (→ p. 358)

VERWALTUNGSZENTRUM WERD
Werdstrasse 75–79, Zurich
Stadt Zürich, Amt für Hochbauten
Burkhalter Sumi Architekten, Zurich
[2001–06] 2005–07
3,300 m²
Redesign of the existing grounds of a former bank office tower into the new administration centre of the City of Zurich.

BALZERS PRIMARY SCHOOL
Balzers
Competition 2000: First prize
Gemeinde Balzers
Bishop Hubert, Wolfhalden
[2000] 2001
10,000 m²
Design of the grounds of the school complex.

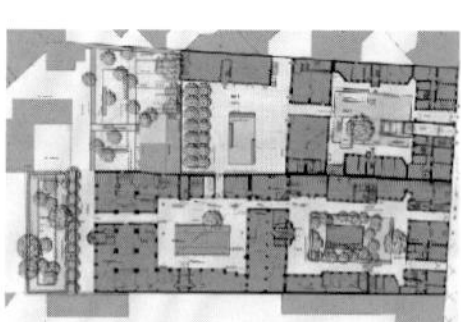

FEHRBELLINER HÖFE
Berlin
Treuhandliegenschaftsgesellschaft mbH
Thomas Müller Ivan Reimann Architekten, Berlin
[2001–02]
5,500 m²
Design of the office building's grounds.

GREULICH HOTEL
Different Views
Zurich
Dr Thomas Brunner
Romero & Schaefle Architekten, Zurich
[2000–03] 2003
1,100 m²
The striking element of the grounds design is a birch courtyard that is only accessible to hotel guests. (→ p. 386)

S. VILLA
The Alluvial Garden
Bäch
Private
Antonio + Luca Antorini Architekten, Lugano
[2001–02] 2002
2,800 m²
Design of a private garden.

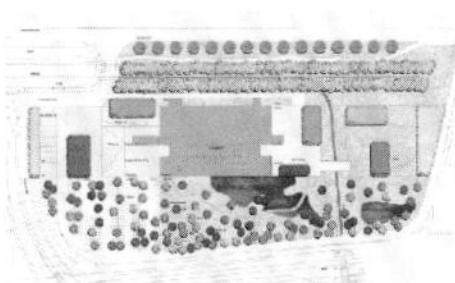

TECHNORAMA WINTERTHUR
Winterthur
Stiftung Technorama
Dürig & Rämi Architekten, Zurich
[2001–03]
18,000 m²
Feasibility analysis for an open space design.

HEADQUARTERS OF HELVETIA PATRIA VERSICHERUNGEN
Mountains of Flowers
Saint Gall
Helvetia Patria Versicherungen
Herzog & de Meuron, Basel
[2001–04] 2004
23,000 m²
Densely planted, lush perennials as the greening design for the grounds of the insurance company headquarters.
(→ p. 118)

PENSIONERS RESIDENCE ALBULA
Forum of Larches
Alvaneu
Competition 2001: First prize
Gemeinde Alvaneu, Dorf Zweckverband Alters- und Pflegeheim
Philipp Esch, Detlef Schulz Architekten, Zurich
[2001–03] 2003
4,490 m²
Park-like design for the grounds around the nursing home.

MESSESTADT RIEM 1. BA WA1
Munich
Gemeinnützige Wohnungsfürsorge AG
Ateliergemeinschaft Müller-Naegelin, Basel; Herzog und Partner, Munich
[2001–02] 2003–05
9,550 m²
Design of open spaces surrounding the residential community, with pruned larch hedges and spaces for different trees.

RIGISTRASSE
Zug
Private
Diener & Diener Architekten, Basel
[2001–06] 2006–08
4,325 m²
In the courtyard, amid the complex of old and new buildings, the focus is directed upward, to a raised garden or the sky.

OFFICE BUILDING MK4
Munich
Bayerische Versorgungskammer
Beyer und Schubert Architekten, Berlin
[2001–03] 2003–04
2,500 m²
Design of the grounds of an office building, using Japanese maple trees with different coloured foliage planted on narrow roof terraces.

AFG ARENA
Saint Gall
HRS Hauser Rutishauser Suter AG
Clerici Müller Architekten, Saint Gall
[2001–06] 2007–08
17,590 m²
New design of the stadium's forecourt and the surrounding open spaces.

APARTMENT BUILDING HEUGATTERSTRASSE
Kirschenhain
Dübendorf
Swiss Re Investors
Romero & Schaefle Architekten, Zurich
[2001–04] 2003–04
3,285 m²
White cherry blossom trees, meandering asphalt pathways and gently modulated lawns define the spaces between the two buildings.

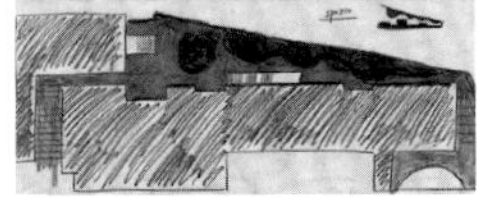

GALLERIA NAZIONALE 'ARTE MODERNA
Onde
Rome
Galleria Nazionale d'Arte Moderna
Diener & Diener Architekten, Basel
[2001–06] 2007–08
3,970 m²
A planted interior courtyard bounded by the complex of old and new buildings and an old wall.

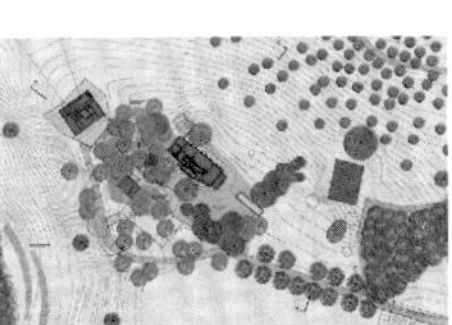

HAUS AM SEE
Ermatingen
Private
Herzog & de Meuron, Basel
[2001–04] 2004–05
20,000 m²
Design of a private garden.

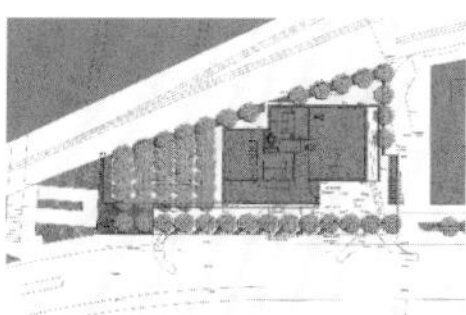

OFFICE BUILDING HOHLSTRASSE 614–24
Altstetten
Senn BPM AG
Baumschlager Eberle Architekten, Vaduz
[2001–04]
3,970 m²
Design for grounds of an office building.

ELISABETHENANLAGE
Chronicle of the Trees
Basel
Realisation competition 2001: First prize
Baudepartement des Kantons Basel-Stadt Architeten
Christ & Gantenbein, Basel
Art: Erik Steinbrecher, Berlin
[2001–06] 2006–07
20,000 m²
New design of a park dating from the early twentieth century. Because of the heavy traffic through the entrance to the inner city, the main focus was the development of a system of pathways, improving the possibility of leisure, care and protection of the valuable existing tree population and the development of a new generation of trees. (→ p. 150)

STECKBORN CEMETERY
In the Lindens
Steckborn
Competition 2001: First prize
Stadtverwaltung Steckborn
Stoffel Schneider Architekten, Zurich
[2001–06/2007, 2009] 2006–09
3,800 m²
The design of the cemetery is characterised by the differentiated use of the linden.
(→ p. 330)

EMPA
Dübendorf
Amt für Bundesbauten Zurich
Burkhalter Sumi Architekten, Zurich
[1996–99] 2001–03
100,735 m²
Master plan for open spaces.

SCHWEIZER VIERTEL
Berlin
Gagfah P GmbH
Thomas Müller Ivan Reimann Architekten, Berlin
[2001–02]
600,000 m²
Urban planning concept.

THE MUSLIM BURIAL GROUNDS AT WITIKON CEMETERY
The Cemetery within a Cemetery
Zurich-Witikon
Grün Stadt Zürich
[2002–04] 2003–04
2,400 m²
Design and integration of four Muslim graveyards into the Witikon cemetery.
(→ p. 338)

LEIPZIGER PLATZ
Berlin
Württembergische Lebensversicherung/Sony
Thomas Müller Ivan Reimann Architekten, Berlin
[2001–05]
1,300 m²
Design of the grounds of the courtyard building.

WAREHOUSE AREA
Momentum
Saint Gall
Hochbauamt und Liegenschaftenamt der Stadt St. Gallen
New buildings: Baumschlager Eberle Architekten, Vaduz, Atelier Heinz Tesar, Vienna
[2002–05] 2005
10,000 m²
The courtyard's distinctively long, extended shape is defined by gently modulation of the grounds and the plane trees planted at various angles to the perpendicular. (→ p. 376)

JUSTIZZENTRUM AACHEN
Established Expanse – Accessible Restriction
Aachen
Competition 2001: Third prize
Bau- und Liegenschaftsbetrieb NRW
Weinmiller Architekten, Berlin
[2001–07] 2004–07
33,500 m²
The design for the judicial centre in Aachen comprises a new park and the design of a covered courtyard. (→ p. 162)

30 SAINT MARY AXE
Wilderness
London
Swiss Reinsurance Company
Foster and Partners, London
[2002–03] 2003–04
1,000 m²
Design of the interior space using tipping plant pots. (→ p. 488)

ALLIANZ ARENA
Mimesis
Munich
Two-phase negotiated procedure 2002: First prize
Allianz Arena München Stadion GmbH, Alpine Bau Deutschland GmbH, FC Bayern München, TSV München 1860
Herzog & de Meuron, Basel
[2001–04] 2004–05
160,000 m²
The visitor approaches the new football stadium via the esplanade, a designed open space extending over the roof of the multistorey car park, which was conceived as a landscape, using plants and vegetation elements typical of the local countryside. (→ p.52)

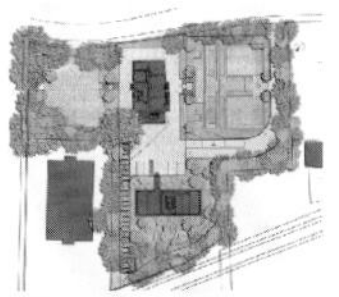

HEADQUARTERS OF THE INTERNATIONAL ICE HOCKEY FEDERATION
Clubhaus Villa Landolt
Zurich
HRS Hauser Rutishauser Suter AG
Tilla Theus und Partner, Zurich
[2002–03] 2002–03
2,700 m²
Design of the villa grounds.

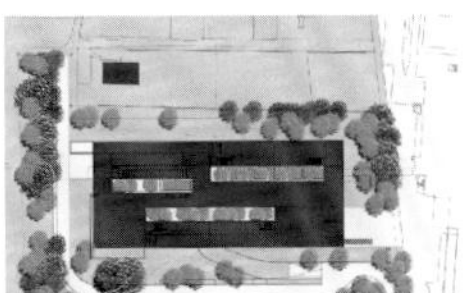

ONUSIDA/UNAIDS
Geneva
FIPOI Fondation immobilière pour les organisations internationales
Baumschlager Eberle Architekten, Vaduz
[2002–05] 2005–06
9,300 m²
Design of the grounds of different courtyards with water, land, stone as the unifying theme.

ÉCOLE PRIMAIRE DE LA MALADIÈRE
Topographie en tant que Spectateur
Neuchâtel
Competition 1999–2000: First prize
Ville de Neuchâtel Direction de l'Instruction Publique Andrea Bassi Architecte, Geneva
[2002–05] highrise
2003–06, surroundings 2005–06
6,835 m²
New building for Ecole Primaire de la Maladière (primary phase) with school courtyard and new design of the bordering park.

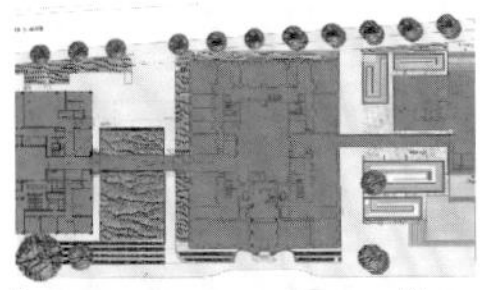

SWISS RE MYTHENQUAI 50/60
Zurich
Swiss Re Investors
[2002] 2002
930 m²
Design of the office building's grounds.

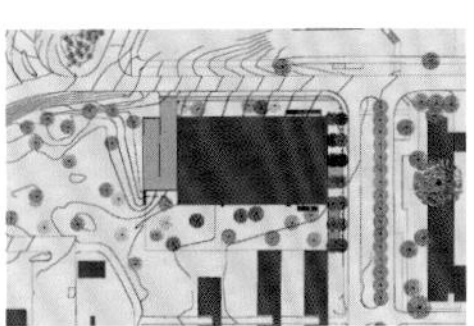

E-SCIENCE LAB ETH/ NEW BUILDING HIT
Zurich
ETH Zürich Hönggerberg
Baumschlager Eberle Architekten, Vaduz
[2002–04] 2006
4,700 m²
The grounds of the Hönggerberg campus of the technical university.

CAMPUS AND PARK AT JUNGFERNSEE/TERRACES AT JUNGFERNSEE
Waiting for a Park/Is It – Is It Not – Will It Be a Likeness?
Potsdam
Two-phase realisation competition Campus 2002: First prize
PHF Projectmanagement und Baubetreuungsgesellschaft GmbH, Objektgesellschaft Campus am Jungfernsee GmbH
Ortner & Ortner, Berlin
[2002–04]
Promenade: 2,100 m²;
Square: 17,500 m²; Park: 22,700 m²
The new campus of a technology park, situated on former barracks grounds, consists of two squares and a promenade as high terraces above a lake. A park stretches along the slope of the lakefront to the lake.

THEATERPLATZ BADEN
Baden
Competition 2002: First prize
Stadt Baden, Planung und Bau
Diethelm & Mumprecht Architektur, Zurich
[2002–06] 2006–07
3,950 m²
Redesign of a former park square into an urban square.

WEIDSTRASSE 8
Rüschlikon
Bauherrengemeinschaft Weidstrasse 8
Gigon / Guyer Architekten, Zurich
[2002–04] 2004–06
2,000 m²
Design of the grounds of a residential community.

FORUM 3, NOVARTIS CAMPUS
Room of Plants
Basel
Research competition 2002: First prize
Novartis Pharma AG, Basel
Master plan: Vittorio Magnago Lampugnani, Studio di Architettura, Milano
Diener & Diener Architekten, Basel, with Helmut Federle and Gerold Wiederin
[2003–04] 2005
180 m²
Air-conditioned four-storey space for plants at the west end of the office building. (→ p. 478)

RESIDENTIAL BUILDINGS IN BROËLBERG
Secret Gardens
Kilchberg
Baukonsortium Broëlberg
e2a, eckert eckert architekten, Zurich
[2003] 2004
25,400 m²
Design of park-like garden grounds surrounding residential units.

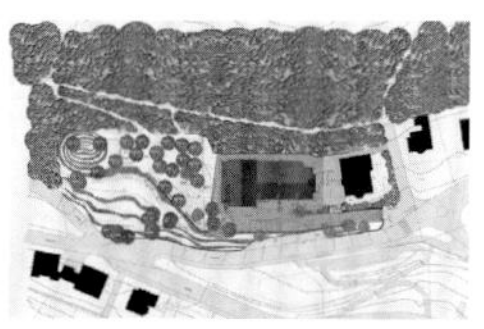

RIGIBLICK HOTEL/RESTAURANT AND THEATRE
Zurich
Stadt Zürich, Amt für Hochbauten
Burkhalter Sumi Architekten, Zurich
[2002–04] 2004–05
6,000 m²
Design of grounds for a hotel and restaurant.

ELSÄSSERTOR OFFICE BUILDING
Reprise and Continuum
Basel
ARGE Generalplaner Elsässertor
Herzog & de Meuron, Basel
[2003] 2004–05
2,700 m²
Design of the grounds for an office building on former train tracks near the train station. Courtyard design referencing the cultivation of Bonsai trees. (→ p. 436)

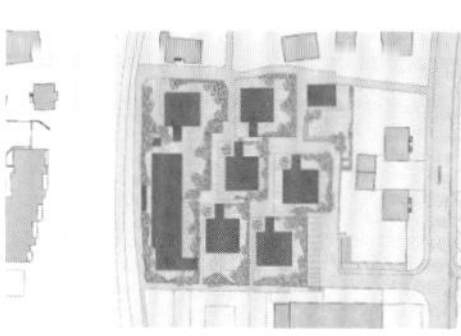

VILLAGO
Männedorf
Staub Holding AG
sam Architekten und Partner, Zurich
[2004–06] 2007–08
5,000 m²
The grounds of the terraced residential development include a partial roof greening. A continuous line of hedges of one species articulates the area and emphasises the differences in height.

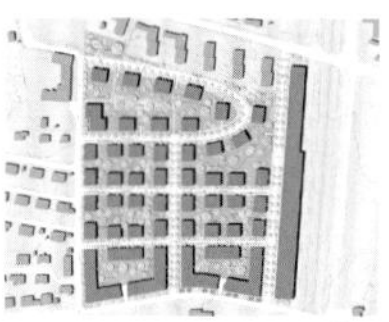

LEITPLANUNG SCHÖNBERG-OST
Bern
Stadtplanungsamt Bern
Atelier Prof. Hans Kollhof, Zug
[2003]
90,430 m²
The urban planning concept for the district is characterised by the development of clear typologies for the front garden, courtyard, and park spaces.

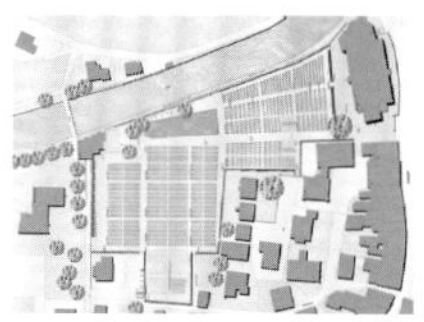

APPENZELL CEMETERY
Au-delà
Appenzell
Realisation competition 2003: First prize; Feasibility analysis
Katholishe Kirchenverwaltung St. Mauritius Appenzell, Kirchenpflegeamt
Bünzli & Courvoisier Architekten, Zurich
Art: Eva Afuhs
[2003]
9,700 m²
New design of the cemetery in close connection with the parish church and the characteristic grounds of the river Sitter.

SÜDPARK BASEL-BAUFELD D
Petit Déjeuner en Fourrure
Basel
SBB AG Immobilien
ARGE Generalplaner Süd Park Basel, Herzog & de Meuron, Basel, Proplaning AG
[2004–07] 2007–12
4,590 m² (Roof: 2,300 m²)
Surroundings and interior courtyard of an apartment house with commercial spaces and restaurants on the ground floor.

MÜNSTERPLATZ
Return to the City
Constance
Two-phase open realisation competition 2003: First prize
Stadt Konstanz
[2003–04] 2005–06
6,000 m²
A square in the old town of Constance provides the setting for the great Unserer Lieben Frau cathedral with a small garden at the cloister.
(→ p. 250)

ST. ANDREAS
Historical Park
Cham
Private
Herzog & de Meuron Architekten, Basel, Diener & Diener, Basel
[2003–10] 2006–12
Ca. 75,000 m²
New design of the grounds surrounding three new buildings as a continuation of the English park. Maintenance work on the park and careful restoration of the tree population were part of redesigning the old park section.

HOME OF FIFA
The Game of Continents
Zurich
International Football Association Fifa, Zurich
Tilla Theus und Partner, Zurich
[2003–05] 2005–06
40,000 m²
A private park with diverse plants that refer to the respective character of the vegetation culture of the six Fifa confederation members. There are artificial tree sculptures in the interior courtyard. (→ p. 134)

AIRPORT CITY
Genius Loci
Düsseldorf
Invited open-space planning competition 2003: First prize
Düsseldorf International, Flughafen Düsseldorf GmbH
[2004–06] 2006–08
200,000 m²
Master plan for the former barracks grounds, including the implementation of three sub-projects. (→ p. 442)

RAPID-AREAL
Dietikon
Design plan
Halter Generalunternehmung AG, Caretta Weidmann AG, Atelier Prof. Hans Kollhoff, Zug
[2003–09] 2010–14
103,860 m²
Residential courtyards, gardens, residential street and urban square in a new residential area on Limmatufer in Dietikon.

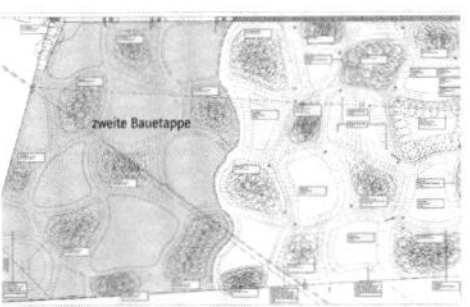

LAKESIDE SCIENCE & TECHNOLOGY PARK
Klagenfurt
Lakeside Science & Technology Park GmbH
ARGE Egger Fercher Güldner, Klagenfurt
[2004–05] 2004–06
55,000 m²
The grounds of a new research and technology centre.

SMELLS & SOUNDS
The Invisible in Public Space
Missing Link
Zurich and Tokyo
Institut für Landschaftsarchitektur, ETH Zurich Prof. Günther Vogt, in collaboration with the Institut für Theorie der Gestaltung und Kunst, HGK Zurich, Jürgen Krusche, and the Institute of Art and Design, University of Tsukuba, Prof. Takuro Osaka
[2005–06] Zurich: October 9–14, 2006 / Tokyo: October 30–November 4, 2006
Air fresheners are used to help examine how the scent of another city affects association and imagination in passers-by. (→ p. 314)

TRAMMUSEUM ZÜRICH
Zurich
Stadt Zürich, Amt für Hochbauten
Schmed Architekten, Zurich
[2004–05] 2005–06
2,000 m²
Redesign of an old tram depot into a museum with offices and shops.

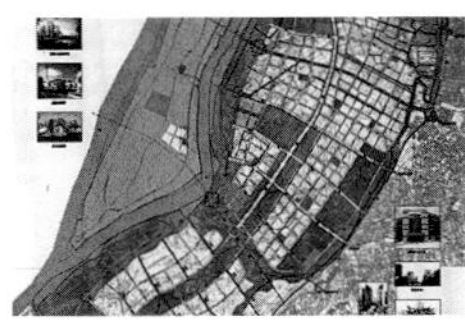

NANJING RESIDENCE, CHINA
Nanjing
Baumschlager Eberle Architekten, Vaduz
[2004–04]
130,490 m²
Design of the grounds for a large-scale residential development.

WSJ-158 SANAA BUILDING, NOVARTIS CAMPUS
Exact Landscape
Basel
Novartis Pharma AG
Master plan: Vittorio Magnago Lampugnani, Studio di Architettura, Milan
Kazuyo Sejima & Ryue Nishizawa/ Sanaa Architects, Tokyo
[2004–06] 2006
800 m²
Design of the interior courtyard without plants. A topography made from large stone plates partially covered by water. The results are an image of landscape that is an adaptation of the Japanese garden tradition. (→ p. 366)

KLINIK HIRSLANDEN ZÜRICH
HL 07
Zurich
Hirslanden Head Office
sam Architekten und Partner AG, Zurich
[2004–05] 2006–07
10,000 m²
The design of the grounds comprises a roof garden and an interior courtyard covering various levels of new buildings, sunken, reclusive courtyards, and a small private park.

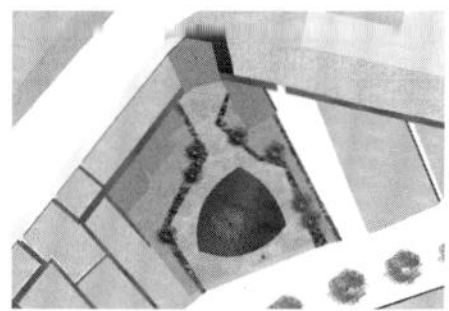

BERNTORGASSE 8/10
Thun
Stadt Thun
[2004–06] 2007
950 m²
Design of the square with a strong reference to the urban context, especially to the existing city wall and gate.

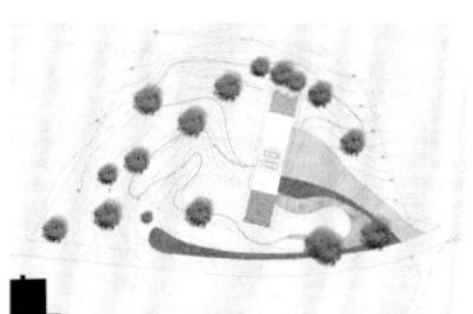

SINGLE-FAMILY HOUSE S.
Schönenberg
Private
Meinrad Morger, Basel
[2004–06] 2006
34,002 m²
Design of the private garden.

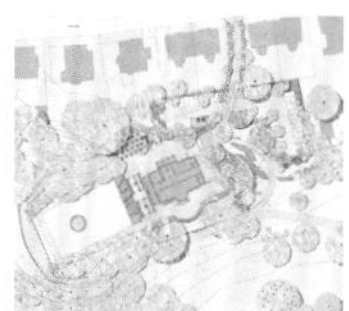

MASTER PLAN BELVOIRPARK
Zurich
Research competition 2005: First prize
Liegenschaftsverwaltung der Stadt Zürich
[2005–08] 2008–12
6,100 m²
Gentle new design of the historic, listed park surrounding Villa Belvoir located west of Lake Zurich.

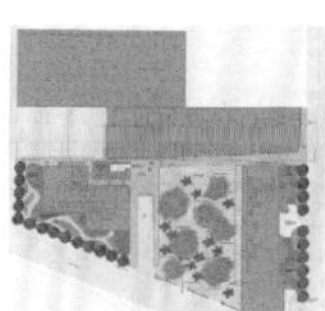

CENTRO HELVETIA
Milan
Competition 2005: First prize
Helvetia Patria Versicherungen, Milan
Meili, Peter Architekten, Zurich
[2005–06] 2007–09
5,000 m²
The grounds design for the office building comprises the entrance area, roof terrace, and façade greening.

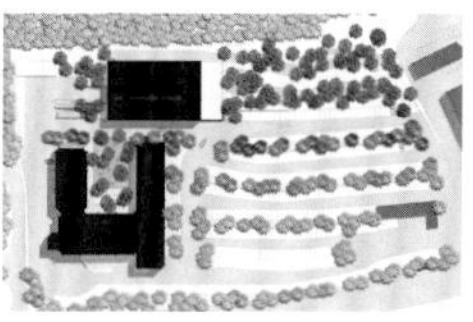

HILTI TRAININGSZENTRUM
Terra Cognitiva
Schaan
Concept and realisation competition 2003: First prize
Hilti AG
Baumschlager Eberle Architekten, Vaduz
[2003–06] 2006–07
7,000 m²
Overall concept for the grounds design, including the training centre driveway and car park areas.

SIA HOCHHAUS
Around the House
Zurich
Research competition 2004: First prize
SIA Haus AG
Romero & Schaefle Architekten, Zurich
[2004–06] 2006
1,380 m²
The existing interior courtyard is transformed into a transparent urban space. The pavement is asphalt with a repetitive circular pattern etched into the surface by sandblasting. (→ p. 258)

BAHNHOFSPLATZ LANDQUART
Red Earth
Igis-Landquart
Research competition 2005: First prize
Gemeinde Igis, Gemeindeverwaltung Igis-Landquart
[2005–06] 2006
3,000 m²
A square of red, rammed-earth pavement receives travellers arriving in Landquart. The space is divided into an urban area and a small city garden surrounded by hedges. (→ p. 224)

DORFZENTRUM DOMAT/EMS
Sequenzas da spazis
Domat/Ems
Realisation competition 2005: First prize
Gemeinde Domat/Ems
[2005–08] 2005, 2008
10,000 m²
The village centre of Domat/Ems will be renovated in several phases.

WASSERSCHÖPFI
City Country Village
Zurich-Heuried
Helvetia Patria Versicherungen
Althammer Hochuli Architekten, Zurich
[2005–06] 2006, 2008
16,500 m^2
The entire surface of Wasserschöpfi, the planned residential development, will be defined by organically shaped terraces and a foliage concept of large and small trees.

BREGENZ FESTSPIELHAUS FORECOURT
Platz der Wiener Symphoniker
Bregenz
Project competition 2005: First prize
Amt der Landeshauptstadt Bregenz, Hochbau
Dietrich Untertrifaller Architekten, Bregenz
[2005–06] 2005–06
21,000 m^2
On the grounds between the festival hall and the shores of Lake Constance, a large square surrounded by indigenous alluvial woody plants bridges the gap between urbanism and nature. (→ p. 234)

GÄSSLISTRASSE RESIDENTIAL COMPLEX, TUGGEN
Research competition 2006: First prize
Vetimag AG, Zurich
Meili, Peter Architekten, Zurich
[2006] 2007
2,400 m^2
Exterior design for residential complex.

CHAM HIGH-TECH PARK
Cham
Pavatex Immobilien AG
Steinmann & Rey Architekten/ Starenhof AG, Basel
[2005] 2008–09
100,000 m^2
Exterior and courtyard design.

DESIGN FOR THE VILLAGE OF BALZERS
Sequence of Spaces
Balzers
Concept competition: First prize
Gemeinde Balzers
[2005] 2006
206,000 m^2
Green space plan for all open areas in the village of Balzers.

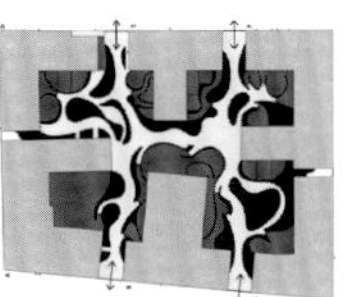

VILLE DE BOULOGNE-BILLANCOURT
Iles de Lierre
Paris
Competition 2005: First prize
SAEM Val de Seine
Urban planning proposal:
Diener & Diener Architekten, Basel
Architecture: Agence Dominique Perrault, Paris; Brochet lajus Pueyo, Bordeaux; Colomer + Dumont Architects, Paris; Diener & Diener Architekten, Basel; Meili, Peter Architekten, Zurich; Reichen et Robert et associés, Paris
[2005–06] 2007–08
12,000 m^2
On a site formerly belonging to Renault, an ensemble of buildings is being created based on six different styles of architecture. The interior courtyard framed by the buildings is completely covered with ivy, in the form of hedges, groundcover and climbing plants, and with Gleditsia.

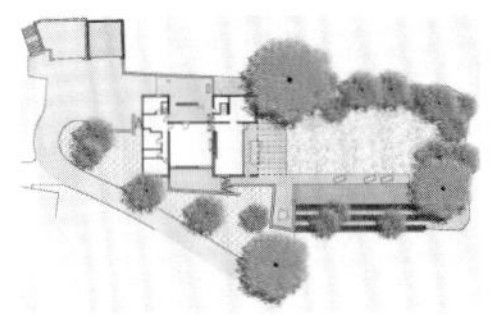

G. GARDEN
Herrliberg
Private
[2005–06] 2006–07
1,500 m^2
Redesign of the garden of a private home.

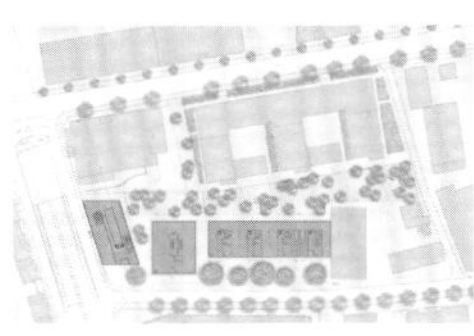

BOURQUIN-AREAL
Zurich-Altstetten
Credit Suisse
Baumschlager Eberle Architekten, Vaduz
[2005–07]
5,400 m^2
Urban forecourt and residential park and green space for a new residential and commercial development.

SCHOOL ACADEMY LOOP THE LOOP
Southwark 4 London
Future Systems
Future Systems, London
[2005–07] 2007–10
28,000 m^2
Redesign of a school on a site with archaeological findings. Kindergarten to high school.

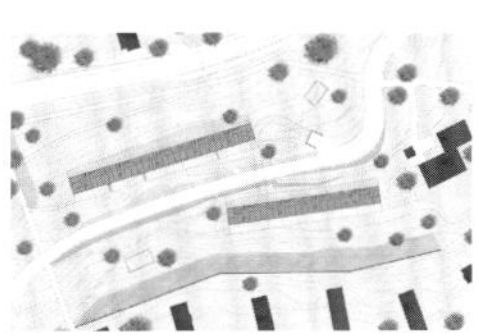

BIRNBÄUMEN
Saint Gall
Helvetia Patria Versicherungen, Saint Gall
Christian Kerez Architekt, Zurich
[2005]
18,300 m^2
Minimal interventions with a few elements to preserve the character of the present meadow landscape.

SUNNIGE HOF
6 Houses, 2 Gardens, 1 Park
Zurich-Albisrieden
Following a competition
Siedlungsgenossenschaft Sunnige Hof,
Burkhalter Sumi Architekten, Zurich
[2005–10] 2011–12
11,750 m²
New park-like design for the surroundings of six new buildings in an existing housing complex, with most existing trees preserved. New buildings included a kindergarten and a garden for the elderly in care.

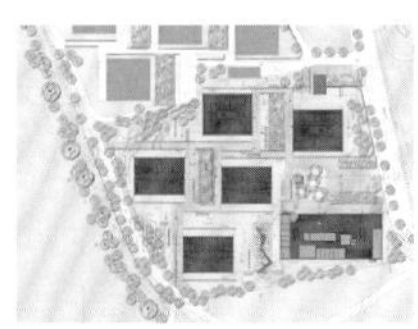

RESIDENCES AT THE LOHBACH II
Innsbruck
Research competition
Neue Heimat Tirol Gemeinnützige Wohnungs- und Siedlungsgesellschaft GmbH
Baumschlager Eberle Architekten, Vaduz
[2005–06] 2007–08
6,638 m²
Topographically influenced exterior design for a residential complex.

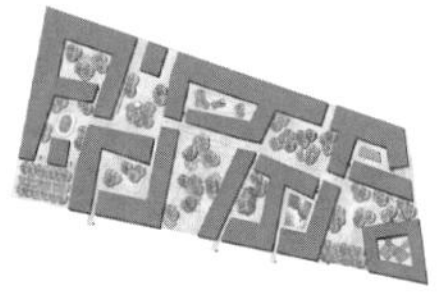

ØRESTAD SYD
Footprints of Landscape
Copenhagen
Kuben Byg, Areea Ørestadt ApS Entasis, Copenhagen; Jensen og Skodvin Arkitektkontor, Oslo; Windgårdhs, Gothenburg
[2006–10]
20,500 m²
Design of a variety of interior courtyards and a spacious roof landscape in a neighbourhood of new buildings.

SCHAFFHAUSERSTRASSE
Zurich-Seebach
Research competition 2006: First prize
ASIG Genossenschaft
Bünzli & Courvoisier Architekten, Zurich
[2006–10] 2011–13
17,133 m²
Park-like design for the exterior of a planned residential complex on Schaffhauserstrasse.

FACHHOCHSCHULE AACHEN, JÜLICH DEPARTMENT
Jülich
Realisation competition 2005: First prize
Bau- und Liegenschaftsbetrieb NRW
[2006] 2007–08
73,000 m²
Surroundings of the new building with park, sport, drainage and parking areas. The landscape design combines functional waste areas with lounge areas. Uniform bands of various species of trees structure the area into various defined spaces.

NOVARTIS CAMPUS PARK
To the Rhine
Basel
Novartis Pharma AG, Basel
[2006] 2007–08, [2010–13] 2013–16
63,000 m²
The design of the park corresponds to a composition of geomorphological and vegetative phenomena of the Rhine Valley, reconstructed by means of design. The focus of the design is the terracing and the dynamics of flowing water from the mountain stream to the meandering river. (→ p. 174)

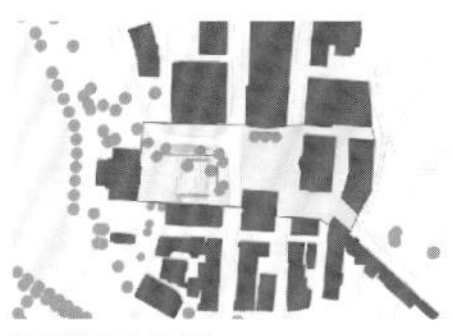

POSTPLATZ
Zug
Baudepartement Stadt Zug
[2006]
6,000 m²
Conceptual study for the design of the square.

NOVARTIS CAMPUS “THE GREEN”
Basel
Novartis Pharma AG
Frank O. Gehry Architects, Los Angeles
[2006–07] 2007–08
6,000 m²
A green centre of the Novartis Campus intended for intensive use.

SCHLOSSBERGBEBAUUNG
Böblingen
Stadt Böblingen
Barkow Leibinger Architekten, Berlin
[2003]
8,000 m²
Design of historic castle mountain with adjacent park.

BAHNHOFSPLATZ MUNICH-GIESING
Space-Time
Munich
Realisation competition 2003:
First prize
Landeshauptstadt München
Brigitte Kochta, Berlin
[2003–07] 2007–10
Square: 9,235 m²; Green belt: 5,625 m²
The designing of the public square of a train station as a place for trees in the city. The determining elements of this open space are the ten high-trimmed, mostly pinnate trees, which unite to form a transparent canopy that changes with the seasons. (→ p. 242)

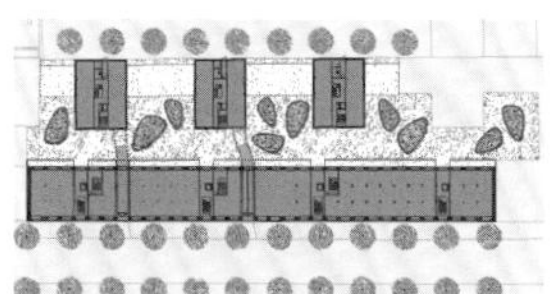

CORNLOFT SALDOVA
Prague
Realisation competition 2002: First prize
Real Estate Karlin Group
Baumschlager Eberle Architekten, Vaduz
[2004–06] presumably 2007–08
2,000 m²
Design of interior courtyards of an industrial building converted to loft apartments as a common area with a continuous covered path, connecting to water and dense groups of pillar-like trees.

DRÄGER MEDICAL
Lübeck
Invited realisation competition 2005:
First prize
Drägerwerk AG, CommerzLeasing
Goetz & Hootz Architekten, Munich
[2005–07] 2007
55,000 m²
This park-like area dramatises its borders, the routes of the paths as harmonised with the existing trees, and the groupings of trees.

MESSESTADT RIEM 2. BA WA 1
Munich
Gemeinnützige Wohnungsfürsorge AG
Ateliergemeinschaft Müller-Naegelin, Basel
[2004–07] 2007–08
7,300 m²
Design of the residential surroundings with strong spatial articulation by means of freely formed hedges and dense groups of trees.

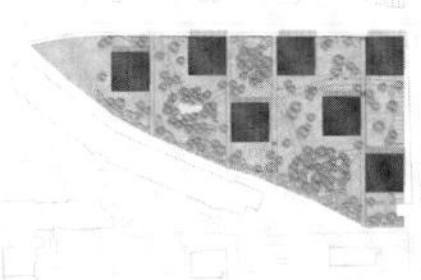

CERVENY VRCH
Prague
Červený vrch spol, s.r.o.
Baumschlager Eberle Architekten, Vaduz
[2005–06 (first construction phase)]
Presumably 2006–08
30,000 m² (all construction phases)
The residential buildings are given park-like surroundings in which orthogonal access routes have superimposed on them a plane of free-form park paths, and squares with dense groups of varied trees.

NEW ECB PREMISES
Frankfurt am Main
Competition 2005–06
European Central Bank
Coop Himmelb(l)au, Vienna
[2006–09] 2011–14
120,000 m²
The exterior areas of the new headquarters of the European Central Bank have to conform to complex requirements in terms of operation procedures and security. Relationships to the urban surroundings and the potential natural space were developed by means of topography, vegetation, and surfaces, to create an open space that is a hybrid of landscape and park.

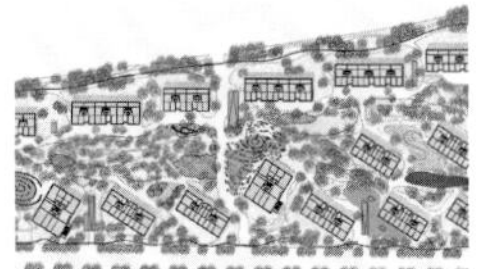

AN NING ZHUANG
Beijing
Beijing Modern Real Estate Development Co. Ltd.
Baumschlager Eberle Architekten, Vaduz
[2005–07]
70,000 m²
The open space of this residential neighbourhood picks up the formal language of the adjacent river.

GAOLIYING HOUSING DEVELOPMENT
Under the Sign of Water
Beijing
Beijing Dong Jun, Real Estate Development Co. Ltd., Beijing
Baumschlager Eberle Architekten, Vaduz
[2005–10]
1,275,000 m²
Design of open spaces in a new district of the city with varied residential types and free spaces, while returning the existing course of the river to its natural state.

SIEMENSAREAL OBERSENDLING, ISAR SÜD
Munich
Siemens Real Estate GmbH & Co. OHG, Munich
Diener & Diener Architekten, Basel
2005–10
142,000 m²
Development of private and public free spaces for a new residential area that are intended to be perceived as a continuous park.

TRANSFORMING TATE MODERN
Local Horizons
Bankside, London
Tate Modern
Herzog & de Meuron, Basel
[2004–12] 2013–15
26,863 m²
The landscape of Tate Modern will be redeveloped to improve connections to the wider public realm, creating a public green space at the heart of Bankside.

NOVARTIS TRAINING CENTRE
Risch
Novartis Pharma AG
Peter Zumthor Architekten, Haldenstein
[2004–12] 2013–16
93,000 m²
In the chequered landscape around Lake Zug, the Novartis training centre is being constructed on an old estate and its neighbouring fields. The main features of the project are the restoration of the historical English landscape garden and the surrounding moraine landscape, as well as the creation of a meadow landscape. Anyone walking through this park landscape will sense a playful interaction of nature and culture – a prefigured image.
(→ p. 80)

ALFRRED ESCHER STRASSE 86/88
Zurich
Schweizer Rückversicherungen
Romero & Schaefle Architekten, Zurich
[2004] 2006
375 m²
Landscape design.

ROTHPLETZ / LIENHARD
Aarau
Rotpletz, Lienhard + Cie AG
[2006] 2006–08
2,000 m²
Due to the renovation of the headquarters of Rothpletz/Lienhard a revision of the surroundings took place. The building and its forecourt became more crucial by changing the traffic routing of the old town of Aarau.
A "curtain" of aspens defines an easy changeover between private and public space.

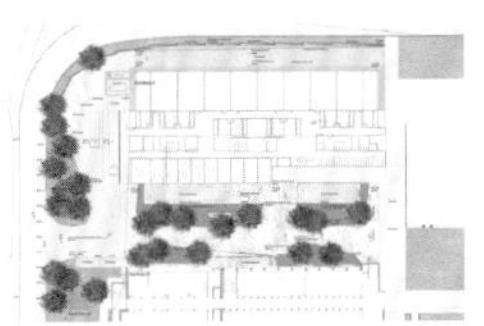

HPL, ETH ZURICH
Forest Edge
Zurich
ETH Zürich Hönggerberg
Burckhardt & Partner Architekten, Zurich
[2007–10] 2011–12
2,700 m²
The special site on the upper cliff of the ETH Areal in Hönggerberg, directly on the eastern edge of the Käferberg forest, creates a close relationship between the building and the surrounding landscape, which is the essence of the design for the HPL building and its environment. The concept clearly differentiates among the square, the delivery area and atria.

HOTEL BAUR AU LAC
Zurich
Baur Au Lac
[2006–10]
3,400 m²
Master plan and maintenance concept. The park landscape of the hotel was built in the second half of the nineteenth century. Therefore a conscious orchestration between natural and artificial visual links is an eminent attribute of the concept.

SCHULHAUS EICHMATT
Cham
Competition 2006: First prize
Einwohnergemeinde Cham / Hüneberg
Bünzli Courvoisier Architekten, Zurich
[2006–09] 2009–10
15,000 m²
Landscape design.
The overall design theme is a meadow with fruit trees which refers to the pastoral, formed structures of the surroundings adjoining the new school building.

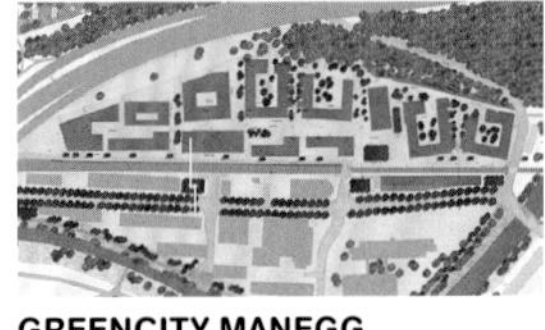

GREENCITY MANEGG
Concept study, Design plan
Zurich
Losinger Marrazzi
Diener & Diener Architekten, Basel
[2006–13] 2013–16
67,400 m²
The area of the former Sihl paper manufacture is supported to be transformed into "GREENCITY". The area is embedded in the river-bed of the Sihl and the foothill of the Entlisberg. (→ p. 396)

KOLUMBA
Between old walls and new architecture
Cologne
Erzdiözese Köln
Peter Zumthor Architekten, Haldenstein
[2007] 2007
315 m²
The gentle site modelling contrasts the clear architectural shapes with more organic stylistic elements, simultaneously creating the height required for the tree planting. A single sculpture on a stone bench by Hans Josephson can be found.

ALBERT-SCHWEITZER-STRASSE / FRÖBELSTRASSE LAHR
Living at the Park
Lahr
Competition 2006: First prize
Stadt Lahr / Städtischen Wohnungsbau GmbH Lahr
Baumschlager Eberle Architekten, Vaduz
[2007–08] 2009
20,000 m²
The small city park mediates between the new residential quarter and the older, mature urban areas. Groves of trees, rich in species; open lawns and meadows; and curving paths form the basic structure for the simple, robust design. Hedges and trees with small crowns frame the new residential district and underscore its location on the edge of the park.

KAPLANKAYA
Akbuk, Bodrum
Baumschlager Eberle Architekten, Vaduz, Forster + Partner, London
[2006–08]
110,000 m²
Creation of a Turkish Mediterranean townscape.
The project is envisioned to become the first international destination resort town on the Turkish coast that would consist of residential communities and tourism facilities.

HAMOIR/LATERAL UKKEL
Brussels
Diener & Diener Architekten, Basel
[2007–09] 2010–11
15,000 m²
The design area is located at the former BASF Headquarters at Avenue d'Harmoir.
This redesign aims to upgrade the quality of the park and shows various possible aspects of improvement.
The concept proposes to change the vegetation in species and quality, the materials of the road, equipment such as water, light or the entrance gate, as well as possibilities of hiding or integrating functional elements within the design.

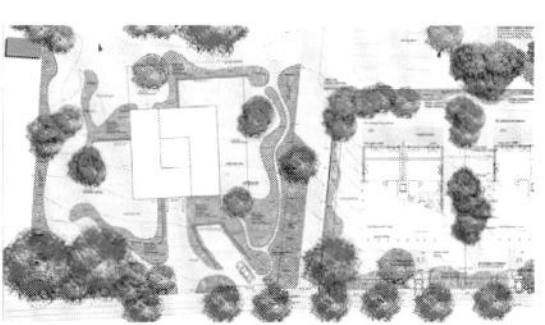

DEUX ALICE UKKEL
Waiting for a Park
Ukkel
Diener & Diener Architekten, Basel; awg Architekten, Antwerp
[2007–12] 2013–18
6,800 m²
In nineteenth-century Ukkel (Uccle in French), a bourgeois landscaped park might have been built on the property, but instead there is now a retirement home with some remaining agricultural areas. In the wake of building the urban periphery, the role model is not the small, individual garden, but this imaginary park, with large trees, views and borders.

COLLECTION OSKAR REINHART
Winterthur
[1998–2001, 2007–10]
150 m²
The Merten brothers' well-preserved historical garden consists of two areas, one symmetrical, the other agricultural. Unobtrusive additions, new and replacement plantings, and maintenance interventions do justice to the age of the garden, the architectural changes to the museum and the transformation of the surrounding urban environment.

POSTPLATZ/EMMA HERWEGH PLATZ
Liestal
Competition 2002: First prize
Stadt Liestal
Christ & Gantenbein, Basel
[2006–08] 2009–10
2,400 m²
The design derives from the landscape context and a strong typological potential of the place. Based on the overall concept of the competition, both public open spaces – Emma Herwegh Platz and Postplatz – are connected in one design through the adjacent bus station area.

EUROPEAN HARBOUR BREMEN
Terra Recognita
Bremen
Realisation competition 2007: First prize
Big Bremen
[2007–08] 2009–12
40,000 m²
The old dockyards close to the urban centre are converted into residential areas, retail space and office development, thus reintegrating the area into the public and social life of the city. The design concept is based on three typologies of open spaces: the promenade, the square and the park.

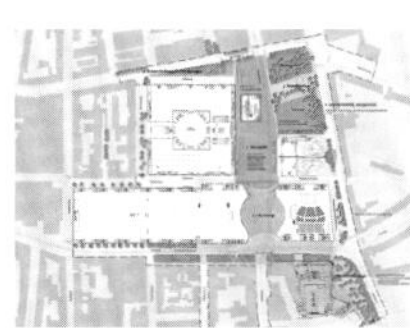

MESSE BASEL
Basel
Messe Basel MCH Group
Herzog & de Meuron, Basel
[2005–07] 2007–14
800 m²
The development of Messe Basel changes the arrangement of public open spaces. Surrounding greenery and public open spaces are joined in one overall concept to strengthen weak elements, to connect isolated areas and to enhance the whole area in its functions and qualities.

MATHILDE ESCHER HEIM
Zurich
Mathilda Escher Heim Stiftung
Darlington Meier Architekten, Zurich
[2005–08] 2010–11
8,400 m²
The character of the design area is mainly affected by a strong topography. The new terrain modelling addresses the special demands of the physically disabled patients in order to make the area barrier-free and accessible. Areas with a difference in quality and level are clearly defined.

EFH SCHIEDHALDESTRASSE
Küsnacht
Private
Gret Löwensberg Architekten, Zurich
[2007–09] 2010
900 m²
Design for a private garden.

DORFPLATZ BONADUZ
Bonaduz
Competition 2007: First prize
Gemeinde Bonaduz
Walter Bieler AG Engineering, Bonaduz
[2007] 2007–08
2,050 m²
With a few design elements on the surface, some precisely placed trees, a thirty-metre-long bench and a fountain, what was a former rest area grew into a simple, lively village square.

SCHULPLATZ BALZERS
Balzers
Gemeinde Balzers
[2007] 2008
2,000 m²
The new play areas find inspiration in the movement of the adjacent Schlossbach creek. Densely planted groves of birch and poplars create introverted and extroverted play areas.

SWISS NATIONAL MUSEUM
Zurich
Bundesamt für Bauten und Logistik, Schweizerisches Landesmuseum
Christ & Gantenbein Architekten, Basel
[2007–11] 2012
19,000 m²
Rediscovery of a central urban square and the redesign of the entry to Zurich's oldest public park.

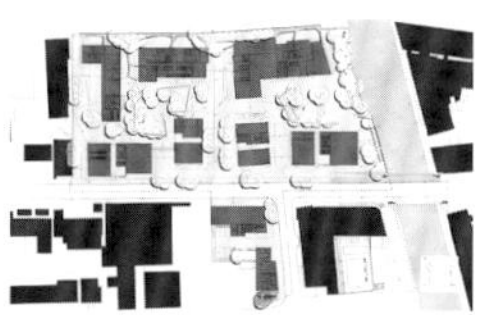

CASPIAN WHARF
London
Hawkins Brown Limited, London
[2007]
12,000 m²
From the Limehouse Cut up to Devons Road the whole area can be regarded as a development and regeneration area. The inner part of the urban scheme will be dedicated to slower forms of movement. A sequence of open spaces will lead pedestrians from the Devons Road Station to the Limehouse Cut canal. Each space will have its own specific character though sharing the same generosity and quality.

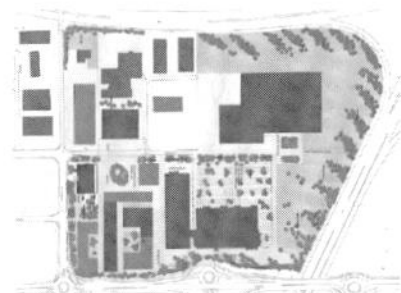

FORRENAREAL – ROCHE DIAGNOSTICS
Rotkreuz
Roche AG
Leutwyler Partner Architekten, Zug
[2007–09] 2010–11
11,000 m²
The future development is tending to connect and densify the separated building structure. While strengthening the urbanistic image a development and transformation to an identifiable and accurate public urban structure is crucial.

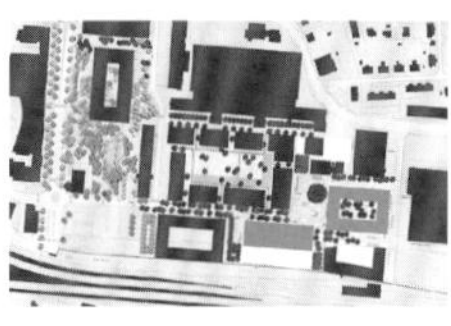

THEILERPLATZ ZUG
New design for city square
Zug
Stadt Zug
Diener & Diener Architekten, Basel
[2008]
90,000 m²
The new city square has the characteristics of a society and reception room. It combines the headquarters and the casino with the adjacent buildings, the promenade and the arboretum.

HOHENEGG PRIVATE HOSPITAL
Landscape Inlay
Meilen
Privatklinik Hohenegg
Romero & Schaefle Architekten, Zurich
[2009–10] 2010–13
13,000 m²
Landscape master plan and implementation of design. With the renovation of the Hohenegg private clinic, constructed by the architects Rittmeister and Furrer in the early twentieth century, the surrounding free spaces will be redesigned. The close connection between the inside and the outside agricultural landscape is a key element of the design.

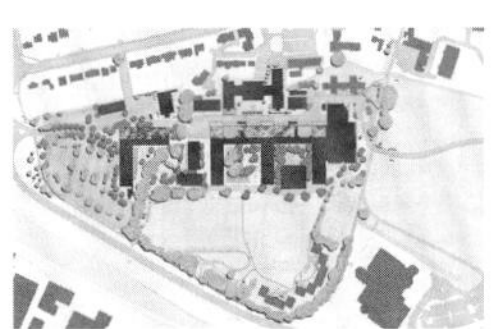

CHICHESTER & BRINSBURY COLLEGE
Structure, Function, Ornament
Chichester College
Hawkins Brown Limited, London
[2007–10]
2,306,700 m²
Landscape master plan.
The master plan aims at implementing designed structural elements within the campus, which are inspired by the outside landscape. It provides a sense of enclosure while still allowing the overarching framework of openness to be apparent.

LA ROCHELLE
La Rochelle
Ville de la Rochelle
Dan Graham, New York
[2007–08]
5,400 m²
In-between the harbour promenade and cultural buildings, a hard urban square is transformed into a tree-filled environment for a mirrored sculpture by Dan Graham.

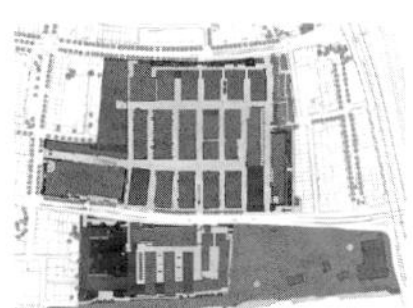

GREENERY CONCEPT ROCHE AREAL
Basel
Roche AG
Herzog & de Meuron, Basel
[2007–12]
274,500 m²
The dense structure of the urban neighbourhood is not defined by fences but by public open spaces and visual openings, the transition between industrial and residential use. The roads are activated as public open spaces.

UMM LAFINA
Abu Dhabi
Herzog & de Meuron, Basel
[2007–08]
9,800,000 m²
Two islands in Abu Dhabi will be developed; they will contain a variety of individual and multi-family residences. Accompanying this are examples of diverse outdoor areas, ranging from the garden to the park, and defining the context of the landscape.

PARLIAMENT SQUARE
The shape of a walk
Westminster, London
City of London
Hawkins/Brown & DSDHA, London
Conceptual study
[2007–08]
12,000 m²
The geological and historical background as well as the British tradition of walking inspired the design concept for Parliament Square: a radical reinterpretation of the London garden square type that refers to the walker's perspective in its topography and design.

WINDOW ON ASIA
MÜHLEBACHSTRASSE 20
Zurich
Diethelm Keller Holding
Romero & Schaefle Architekten, Zurich
[2006–07] 2008
2 m³
Indoor greening.
The glass case gives an image of the rainforest. Thus forming the principle of a symbolic gateway of the client's business relationships to South-east Asia. (→ p. 530)

CARLSBERG MASTER PLAN
The story of the hill
Copenhagen
Calrsberg
Entasis Architects, Copenhagen
[2005] 2007–11
330,000 m²
On the basis of the general urban master plan, the landscape master plan provides a palette of materials, plants and general design parameters for use by the landscape architects to develop the Carlsberg open-space area.

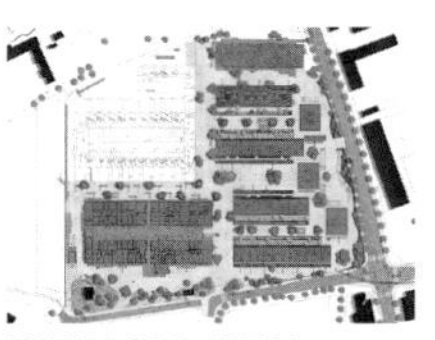

FREILAGER AREAL
Zurich
AXA Winterthur
Meili Peter Architekten, Zurich
2008–13
70,000 m²
The new public open space and its path system provide a soft transition between a dense urban area and the green garden city. The site is structured by pre-zones, inner promenades, district squares and courtyard living areas.

KVADRAT
Around form
Ebeltoft
Kvadrat
Olafur Eliasson, Berlin and Copenhagen
2008–12
57,000 m²
The design is based around the concept of form, contrast and sightlines with emphasis on the landscape.
The park-like landscape surrounding the Kvadrat headquarters will hold in total three copses of different sizes and directions. Each of these tree copses is planted with one species to create a uniform appearance.

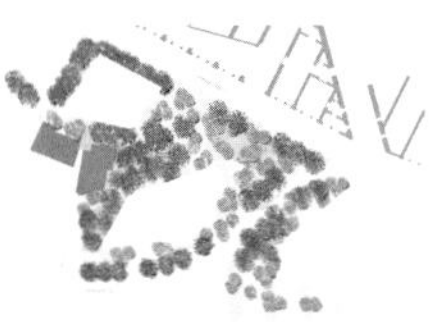

3 HOUSES, ST THOMAS STREET
London
Herzog & de Meuron, Basel
[2008]
9,500 m²
Three first-class residential high-rises in London's Bankside help redefine the outdoor space, bringing a sense of openness and drawing attention to an almost forgotten quarter.

EAST VILLAGE LONDON
Waiting for a city
London
Fletcher Priest (Urbanist), London
[2008–10] 2010–12
151,000 m²
Landscape master plan.
The Stratford City development is a new residential community located to the north of Stratford Town Centre in East London. The site will be used as the Athletes Village in 2012. It will be transformed afterwards into a legacy community containing residential, retail, office and educational facilities.
(→ p. 68)

SCHLOSSPLATZ AARAU
Aarau
Stadtbauamt Aarau
Diener & Diener Architekten, Basel
[2006] 2008–14
3,600 m²
An upgrade and redevelopment of the city square awards the distinctive character and consequently strengthens the identity. History is to be preserved: the city square occurs as a contemporary witness of the development of urban planning.

LINDENPARK
Frauenfeld
LB Architecture, Altishofen
[2009] 2010
22,100 m²
With the transformation of a railway environment into a residential location, an existing urban area with trees is turned into a neighbourhood park.

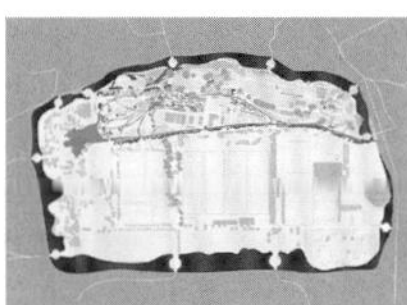

MERIANPARK MASTER PLAN
Concept study
Basel
Merianstiftung
[2008]
230,800 m²
The design guidelines are based on the idea of the first garden: the Garden of Eden. Six basic topics define the garden design: border, entrance, water, vegetation, choreography and metaphor.

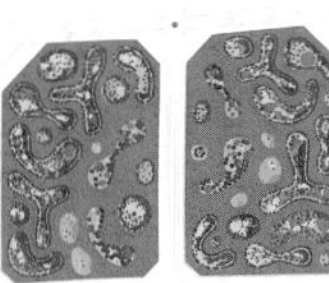

AL GHURAIR – BAWADI DEVELOPMENT
Inverse oasis
Dubai
Kazuyo Sejima & Ryue Nishizawa/ Sanaa Architects, Tokyo
[2008–10]
50,000 m²
The design for the luxurious building complex is inspired by the surrounding desert landscapes. The design concept proposes sand and stone materials as well as typical vegetation. In addition, the deficit and importance of water as a essential element to life treats the design in a particular way.

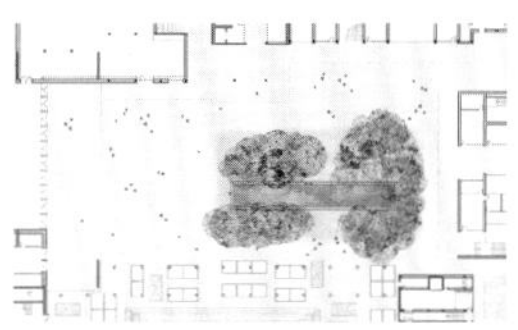

KOLKATA MOMA (KMOMA)
Overlapping Narratives
Kolkata
KMOMA
Herzog & de Meuron, Basel
2008
40,500 m²
An elaborate water harvesting network is distributed throughout the site, surfacing in unique ways. The building complex is looked at as a fort condition: as one crosses the threshold of the gates and travels deeper into the complex, the landscape shifts from urban and unrefined to sacred and lush.
(→ p. 400)

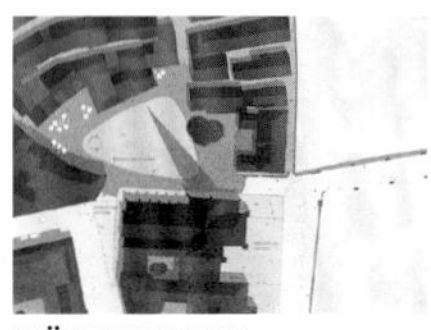

MÜNSTERHOF
Study assignment
Zurich
Tiefbauamt Stadt Zürich
Romero & Schaefele Architekten, Zurich
[2008–12] 2013–15
4,000 m²
The extraordinary shape of the square is combined and solved by a basic geometric shape which interacts with the nearby fountain. Another compositional element is established through a group of lime trees developing a traditional social public meeting point.

LJUBLJANA MASTER PLAN
Smartinksâ
Ljubljana
Hosoya Schaefer Architekten, Zurich
[2008–09]
65,000 m²
Urbanistic master plan.
Landscape design for Kolinska Park, Kolinska Square, Kavciceva ulica – Boulevard, Smartinska Cesta, Zito Park and Zito Square, Esplanada, Park and BTC Plaza.

BBVA MADRID
La nueva sede
Madrid
Competition 2007: First prize
BBVA
Herzog & de Meuron, Basel
[2008–10]
16,600 m²
A private square, long inner courtyards and streets, and a small park are created for the new bank headquarters. Various methods of irrigation are formal and technical motifs of the garden design.

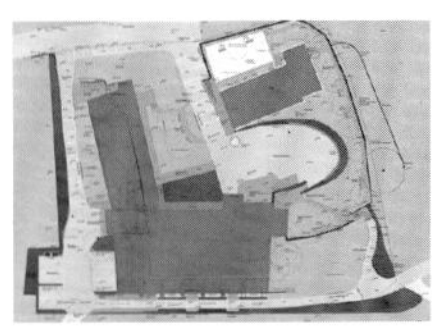

ECCLESIASTIC CENTRE
Altstetten
Evangelische Kirchgemeinde Altstetten
Silvio Schmed Architects with Arthur Rüegg, Zurich
[2009–11] 2011–12
3,000 m²
Renovation and transformation of the open space system surrounding the church.

ROCHE AREAL ROTKREUZ
Reclining Monoliths
Rotkreuz
Roche AG
Leutwyler Partner Architekten AG, Zurich
[2008–09] 2010–11
8,800 m²
The design concept relates to the geology, morphology, topography and vegetation of the site, which was linked in former times to Lake Zug. The new planting correlates to wetlands, which also includes trees many thousands of years old. Seeds and traces of these plants of the Late Tertiary can still be found in the soil.

VILLA ROSAU
Onlookers & silent gates
Zurich
Gigon / Guyer Architects, Zurich
[2009–12] 2013–14
5,500 m²
Private garden.
The garden encloses the villa and the new building, therefore the main design theme is based on the fusion between architectural and organic shapes which divide the garden in different areas of utilisation.

ABBEY OF EINSIEDELN
A square within the square
Einsiedeln
Competition 2008: First prize
Kloster Einsiedeln, Stadt Einsiedeln
Romero & Schaefle Architects, Zurich
[2009–10 / 2011–13] 2010 / 2014–16
40,000 m²
The master plan design emphasises the importance of the square in front of the abbey as a representative, central meeting point with a simple but effective intervention: a step underneath the Lady Fountain optically completes the oval which is implied by the arcades in front of the abbey. This way the step and the arcades create a "square within the square". Like an inlay it is set into the major paving of the entire space connecting the abbey with the town of Einsiedeln.

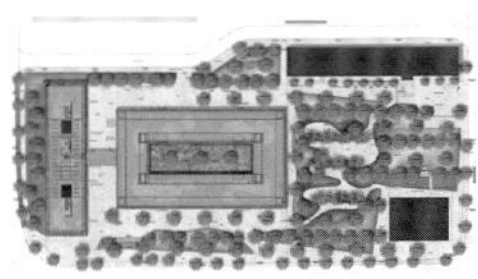

FOYER ZUG
The Arboretum
Zug
Competition 2004: First prize
Siemens AG
Axess Architects AG, Zug
[2009–11] 2011–13
26,000 m²
Landscape design.
A square covered by an open-plan pavement occurs while concurrently intensive vegetation and lawns break through. The dense vegetation and the assortment of tree species suggest a park landscape.

DAGENHAM DOCK LONDON
Sustainable Industries Park
London
Sergison Bates, London
[2009–10] 2012–18
295,000 m²
The development concept embeds the industrial park in a comprehensive exterior design which is sustainable on multiple levels. The core area enables flexible industrial use while allowing spatial and technical synergies. The linkage with the surrounding residential areas and the existing secondary ecosystems allows the area to keep its own urban identity rooted in a local context.

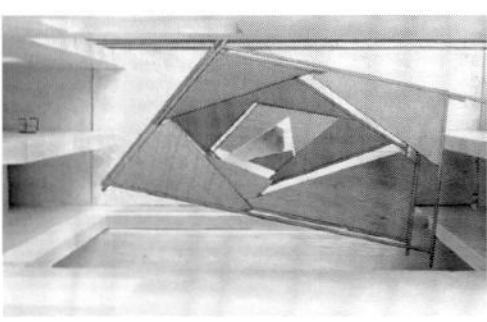

NING GUO FU
Capturing the picturesque
Shanghai
David Chipperfield Architects, London
[2009–12] 2012–13
1,200 m²
Ten spacious, luxurious houses are organised around a protected yet shared street/courtyard. Each house is built around a courtyard, in an allusion to the courtyards in Chinese houses; the diverse designs cover several levels and are based on common themes.

SWISS RE ZÜRICH HEADQUARTERS
Zurich
Competition 2009: First prize
Swiss Re
Diener & Diener Architects, Basel
[2010–12] 2013–15
3,700 m²
The sequence of several magnificent buildings of the late nineteenth and twentieth century at the Zurich Mythenquai is enmeshed in a dense network of historical parks, promenades and the landscape. The restructuring and the construction of new buildings requires new solutions in the field of tension between representation, public relations and desired distance.

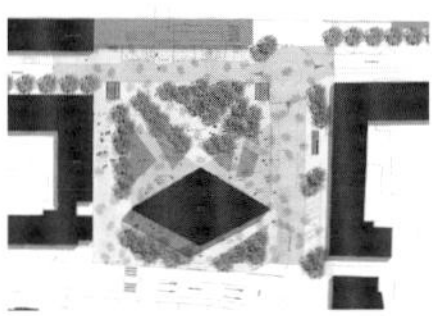

BAHNHOFSPLATZ PRATTELN
Pratteln
Competition 2007: First prize
Christ & Gantenbein, Basel
[2009–12] 2013–16
5,500 m²
As part of a high-rise construction at the Pratteln station, a new space which is surrounded by two walls is being created. The surface coating makes space for tree planting and water basins appear. The "hidden landscape" opens up and becomes a space-defining element.

LEGACY MASTER PLAN FRAMEWORK
Legacy Communities Scheme
London
Allies and Morrison, Kees Christiaanse, Witherford Watson Mann, Maccreanor-Lavington, Caruso St John, Panter Hudspith et al.
[2009]
655,000 m²
The master plan concept is based on five principles: connectivity, water-scape, program, variety of atmospheres and waterfront.

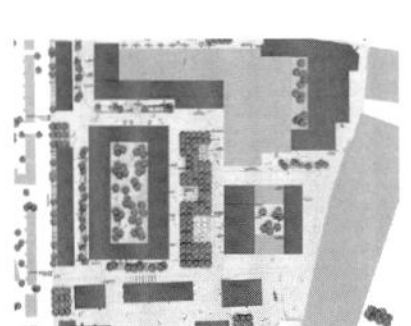

FREIRAUMKONZEPT SULZER
Sequences of garden
Winterthur
Sulzer Immobilien
Gigon / Guyer Architekten, Zürich
[2009–10]
35,000 m²
With the transformation of the industrial area into a residential and business area, a centrally located city district opens to the public. Different types of gardens offer a basic element for varying uses.

DEN FRIE UDSTILLINGSBYGNING
Copenhagen
Bente Lange, Copenhagen
[2010–12] 2013–14
4,700 m²
The early twentieth-century exhibition pavilion is brought back to life, and its surroundings are once again functional. Precisely planted groups of trees set up the context in the urban space.

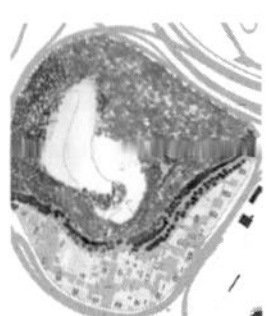

THE CIRCLE
Mapping Memories: From Forest to Panorama
Zurich Airport
Riken Yamamoto & Field Shop, Yokohama
[2010]
124,000 m²
The landscape proposal reshapes and reforests the Butzenbüel hill, transforming an ambiguous forest landscape into four distinct forest types. The traveller passes from a "no-place" landscape into a recognizable set of landscapes or memories and discovers the "real place" by cresting the Butzenbüel.

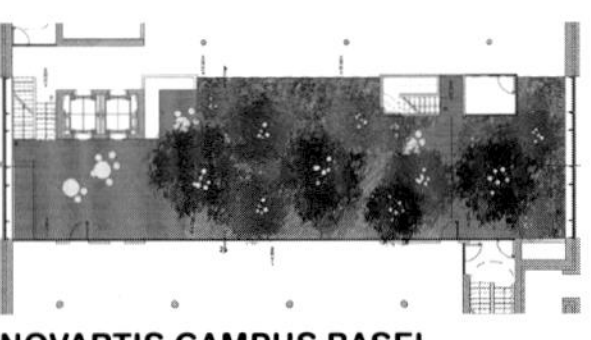

NOVARTIS CAMPUS BASEL
Virchow 16
Basel
Novartis Pharma AG
RMA Architects, Mumbai / Boston
[2010–12] 2013–16
1,200 m²
Virchow 16 plans a pioneering "lap of the future". One of the major design ideas is to establish a green and comfortable working environment. This is on the one hand a transparent green façade which allows the experiencing of the changing seasons from both the outside and inside of the building; on the other it is a three-storey-high atrium with exotic tropical plants of all different heights.

ROYAL INSTITUTE OF HUMAN DEVELOPMENT
Court of the Crown Prince of Bahrain
Bahrain
ACME, London
[2011–13]
6,500 m²
A landscape framework has been developed for the expansion of the court linking future developments back into the existing campus. A detailed design has also been undertaken for the areas around the building creating plaza, garden and courtyard spaces that relate directly to the international building program.

FRONT DE LYS A HALLUIN
An Industrial Urban Centre
Lille
AAM – Atelier Aurélien Masurel, MAGEO MOREL Associés, ALPHAVILLE
[2012] 2013–14
110,000 m²
The project aims to generate an active urban centre integrated in the industrial area, in contrast to most industrial areas today that tend to be isolated from the city. This is a project that is both rooted in the local area and open to the world.

LOHSEPARK HAMBURG
From water to water
Hamburg
Competition 2009: First prize
HafenCity Hamburg
[2009–13] 2014–19
46,800 m²
The design idea is based on the view axis between river and canal and the scale by drawing at historical, park and urban levels. Terraces build a connecting element. (→ p. 194)

KINGSGATE HOUSE
London
Lynch Architects, London
[2010–12] 2013–14
6,800 m²
The landscape design includes the introduction of a series of public spaces on street level increasing permeability and the reconnecting of Victoria Street with its immediate surroundings, a proposal to turn an exciting, unused land lying over the tube line into a new public park, and a succession of roof gardens on the higher floors of the office building.

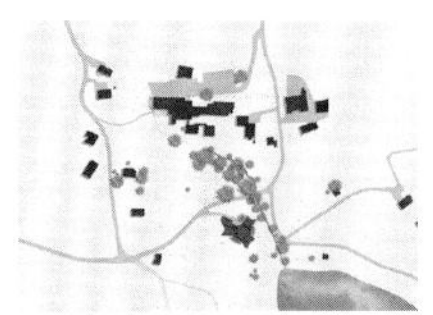

KLANGHAUS TOGGENBURG
Toggenburg
Competition 2010: First prize
Kantonale Bauverwaltung St. Gallen
Meili Peter Architekten, Zurich
[2011–13] 2013–16
7,000 m²
The architecture of the "tonehouse" with its parabolic forms corresponds with the surrounding landscape. View axis support the connection compositional to the qualities and typical elements of the landscape.

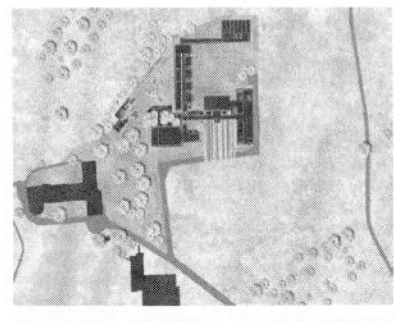

SCHULHAUS MENZINGEN
Menzingen
Competition 2010: First prize
Bünzli & Courvoisier Architekten, Zurich
[2011–12]
3,100 m²
The site-surrounding landscape is fairly affected in its design language by the Swiss landscape architect Ernst Kramer. Interventions are largely restricted to renovation in regard of keeping space typologies and vegetation. Additionally an outdoor classroom has been added as a new function.

RECTORY FARM
London
Carmody Groarke
[2011– ongoing]
400,000 m²
Rectory Farm is a forty-hectare park located in Hounslow within the London Green Belt. The project seeks to develop a large urban park that connects the surrounding communities and green-belt landscapes.

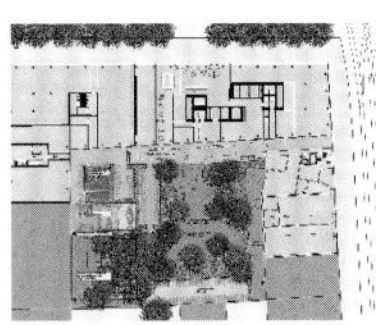

CLARATURM / CLARA TOWER
Basel
Competition 2007: First prize
UBS AG
Morger & Dettli Architekten, Basel
[20011–12] 2013–14
1,900 m²
The many functional elements of the high-rise are circumscribed and zoned by hedges in the courtyard. They conceal these elements and flowing, flexible, functional open space bridges the gaps. Stands of mighty trees make the inner courtyard a special place.

DROOGDOKKENPARK
Antwerp
Competition 2011: First prize
Stadt Antwerpen
Van Belle & Medina Architects, Antwerp
[2012–13] 2014–16
154,000 m²
The project forms a key part of Antwerp's development plan to transform a former industrial harbour site into a vibrant new park on the northern edge of the city of Antwerp, on the banks of the Scheldt River. The project aims to link the park with the former industrial docks whilst preserving their distinct characters.

SLAUGHTERHOUSE AREA
Zurich
Diener & Diener Architekten, Basel
[2011]
55,000 m²
When the Zurich City Council decided to maintain the slaughterhouse in the Letzi Quarter, the planning team was commissioned to come up with a strategy to partially open up the site and turn it into a functional spot for the lively district.

LE LOCLE
Funiculaire
Diener & Diener Architekten, Basel
[2011–14]
500 m²
An incline lift will connect the train station and the downtown area. It runs through old gardens and open spaces, and will become part of the vegetation and the topographical experience.

SUURSTOFFI
Between city and park
Rotkreuz
MZ-Immobilien AG, Zug
Diener & Diener Architekten, Basel
[2011]
Master plan.
The Suurstoffi development combines various uses, requiring different typologies of open space regarding size, use and degree of privacy. The central open space, inspired by the classical English square, is the heart of the area, created by a central open lawn and clumps of trees which define the space and form a park landscape. City gardens around the central lawn provide more intimate spaces for local residents to gather and for children to play in-between hedges and flowering trees.

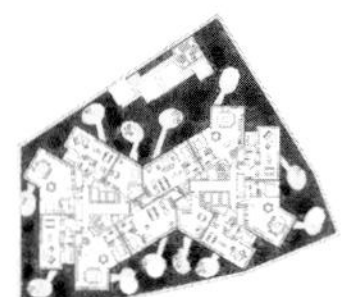

HAUS ZUR ENGE
Buchengarten
Zurich
Swiss Life AG
SAM Architekten und Partner, Zurich
[2011–12] 2013–15
1,100 m²
A modification of a former office building.
The creation of a large beech woodland garden provides the residents of the second floor a view to a miniaturised landscape within an urban space.

HIRSGARTEN
Volkspark
Cham
Competition 2009: First prize
Gemeinde Cham
Dr Lüchinger + Meyer Bauingenieure, Zurich; Romero & Schaefle Architekten, Zurich
[2011–14] 2014–
22,000 m²
As Cham was industrialised, the Hirsgarten was created for the public amid the stately private homes on the bank of Lake Zug. A study has been commissioned to show how significant landmarks in the Volkspark in the Hirsgarten could be brought back to life and reinforced.

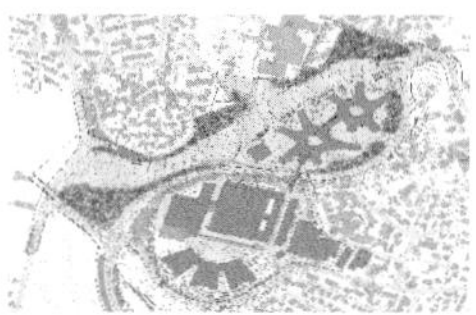

FESTO ESSLINGEN
Esslingen
Festo
Architekturbüro Jaschek, Stuttgart
[2008–12] 2013–16
155,000 m²
An important cold-air corridor, it guides cool air from neighbouring heights down into the Neckar Valley. In order to optimise the flow of cool air in the valley, the elevated "edges" of the park are planted with trees which encircle the entire space, creating a clear entrance / exit to the valley area.
The new park will harmonise with the surrounding landscape, while at the same time serve as a "sign" for the Festo Company.

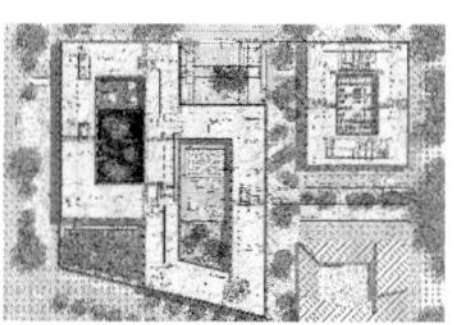

UNI CAMPUS WESTEND
Frankfurt
Competition 2007: First prize
Stadt Frankfurt
Thomas Müller Ivan Reimann Architekten, Berlin
[2008–12]
12,000 m²
The courtyards surrounding the campus buildings are planted intensively, so that the contrast between the artificiality of the place and the luxuriant vegetation of shrubs and trees will be brought forth. As the detail of an image that is not accessible, the courtyard functions as an inlay within the building.

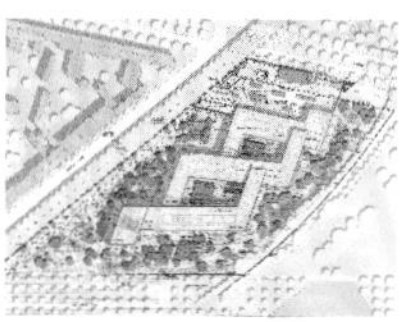

BMI MOABITER WERDER
Berlin
Competition 2007: First prize
Bundesamt für Bauten, BBR
Müller Reimann Architekten, Berlin
[2007–12] 2013–14
37,000 m²
Outdoor area for the Federal Ministry, with various functions such as city square, protocol courtyard and service courtyard are embedded in a park-like setting. The park landscape itself is considered an abstract fragment of natural vegetation, where only a variety of different hornbeams are planted.

SUMC
Shantou
Herzog & de Meuron, Basel
[2012] 2013–14
42,000 m²
A park landscape with lush meadows, dense groves and a bouquet of flowering trees for the new medical campus of the Shantou University, China

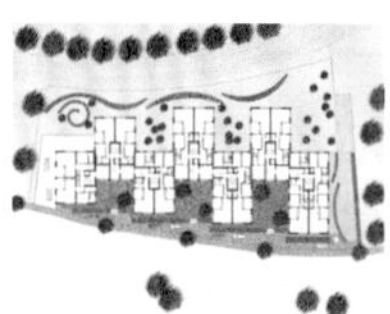

LANDOLT AREAL
Zurich
Competition 2011: First prize
Bünzli Courvoisier Architekten, Zurich
[2012–13] 2014–15
3,300 m²
On the grounds of the former Landolt winery a new housing residence is planned. The courtyards on one side of the building are open to the green space of the river Sihl; the other side is open to the street and is designed as fixed courtyards.

ROCKET 1978

Roman Signer

The ambiguity of Roman Signer's interventions can hardly be exceeded. Although he works in nature by means that are often violent – explosions, blasts and rockets – nature is not destroyed by his actions. Usually he is visible in the work as its author. He does not hide behind his almost brutish-seeming concepts. Time is an essential factor in his work. The idea and concepts develop over months; the action itself lasts a few fractions of a second, and everything is embedded in a landscape that carries within it the temporal dimensions of the history of the earth.

p. 598 Roman Signer, Rocket 1978

BIOGRAPHIES

Günther Vogt, 1957
Born in Liechtenstein.
Trained and studied in Switzerland.
Since 2000 owner of Vogt Landscape Architects, Zurich London and Berlin.
Since 2005 Professor for Landscape Architecture at the Swiss Federal Institute of Technology (ETH) Zurich, Department of Architecture
2012 guest lecturer at Harvard's Graduate School of Design.

Olafur Eliasson, 1967
Born in Denmark.
Studied at the Danish Royal Art Academy, Copenhagen.
Lives and works in Berlin and Copenhagen.

Hamish Fulton, 1946
Born in London.
1964–9 Hammersmith College of Art, London; St Martin's School of Art, London; Royal College of Art, London.
Since 1969 he has wandered in Great Britain, Ireland, France, Italy, Switzerland, Austria, Germany, the Netherlands, Norway, Lapland, Iceland, Spain, Portugal, USA, Canada, Mexico, Peru, Bolivia, Argentina, Nepal, India, Australia, Japan and Tibet.
Lives and works in Canterbury, United Kingdom.

Roman Signer, 1938
Born in Appenzell, Switzerland.
Taught and worked as architectural draughtsman.
Arts and crafts schools in Zurich and Lucerne.
Art academy in Warsaw.
Lives and works in St. Gallen.

Olaf Unverzart, 1972
Born in Waldmünchen, Germany.
Secondary school in Cham.
Internships in photography.
Studied photography at the Hochschule für Grafik und Buchkunst, Leipzig, receiving his degree in art photography under Joachim Brohm in 2000.
Lives and works in Munich.

Christian Vogt, 1946
Born in Basel, Switzerland.
Since 1970 photographic and visual concepts for himself and commissioned by others. Books, monographs, catalogues and exhibitions.

LIST OF EMPLOYEES FROM 2000 UP TO AND INCLUDING FEBRUARY 2011
INTERNS AND WORK-STUDY STUDENTS

Abegg Reto
Agnese Saggia
Albrecht Sonja
Alvaker Karolina
Ammann Ulrich
Amstutz Erika
Armonat Thomas
Assargard Hanna
Aufermann Katja
Balliana Sandro
Bark Franziska
Bauer Christian
Bäuerle Kristina
Baumann Hans
Baumgart Andreas
Bender Eva
Beyeler Fabian
Blaczejewski Martin
Bock Georg
Boden Andreas
Boegly Marie
Brakebusch Maren
Breer Rolf
Brenner Barbara
Bruder Tobias
Brunier Laurent
Buchwald Anna
Bueckers Dominik
Bundt Maike
Butt Verena
Büttner Susanne
Carstensen Sophia
Cebrian Hildegard
Cebulsky Jennifer
Cerlini Luisa
Cha Yong Wook
Choy Amy
Christinaz Fanny
Clade Linus
Current Jennifer
Daan Berte
De Buhr Christian
Delpy Annette
De Molfetta Federico
Di Carmine Aline
Dinauer Ulrike
Djao-Rakitine Irène
Dohrn Olaf
Downes Ryan
Dreyer Nadine
Duckart Christoph
Eiffler Nicola
Ermer Martin
Fabre Jerome
Faiss Jürgen
Fank Martina
Fehr Diana
Feinle Frank
Feldhusen Sebastian
Feldschmid Philipp
Fernandez Garcia Isabel
Fichtl Rina
Filler Simon
Förster Jan
Foxley Alice
Frank Feinle
Frochaux Marc
Gallus Miriam
Ganic Anesa
Geller Andrea
Gerhardt Uta
Geser Andreas
Ghiggi Dominique
Giesbert Charlotte
Gillet Emeline
Golz Ingo
Graf Christian
Granetzny Tobias
Griffiths Tom
Gutierrez Maria Angelica
Gutzen Aaron
Haney Marc
Hartert Jan Hendrik
Häusler Thomas
Heine Johannes
Heinrich Benjamin
Helmke Frank
Hjerl Martin
Hinnenthal Michel
Hirschler Natalie
Hitz Manuel
Holsmölle Klaus
Holzer Sebastian
Horber Alexander
Hortig Hans
Hughes Nick
Hügle Johannes
Hugtenburg Jasper
Ihling Moritz
Illien Rita
Izhar Rani
Jakuposstovu Malan
James Claire
Jeffrey Colin
Kalicinska Monika
Karg Philipp
Kicherer Andreas
Kienast Nicole
Kienitz Henriette Theresa
King Daniel
Klahm Andreas
Klussmann Karin
Knödler Luc Walter
König Martin
Kolendowicz Tanja
Konnovsky Reimo
Krieger Mark
Kroll Simon
Krüger Franziska
Kühne Florian
Künzler Martina
Kuo I-Chun
Labitzke Sylvia
Lara Jonas
Le Marie Thibault
Lechner Korbinian
Lee I Hsiang
Leinich Anja
Lerch Gabriele
Le Thi-lu
Loock Jakob
Lösing Julia
Lu Yan
Lueg Sophie
Lund Signe
Madricardo Costanza
Matter Elise
Mayr Dennis
Mebes Johannes
Mehr Ursula
Meincke Anika
Meneguz Adrian
Meneses Ana
Meyer Kerstin
Mezher Ramzi
Michel Denise
Miltner Udo
Möser Maria
Muldoon Rupert
Müller Klaus
Naebers Alexander
Nel Jaco
Neumeister Claudia
Nieder Piet
Nobiling Friederike
Odermatt Severin
Olden Ruth
Ozod Seradj Tamim
Peisl Julius
Peter Meret
Pinet Maude
Podlewski Katarzyna
Pogoda Lars
Poon Lyn
Pourhashemi Hosna
Probst Rita
Pytlik Dennis
Quarz Evelyn
Rabe Luise
Rademacher David
Redlich Clara
Reinstädtler Sandra
Riede Carolin
Ries Katja
Riggenbach Diego
Roser Mattias
Roth Lea Johanna
Rothert Alexander
Ruge Lars
Saadan Madina
Sack Matanya Tanja
Saggia Agnese
Salewski Maria Johanna
Schaffer Lilith
Schaffner Sabina
Schalk Günter
Schmeing Silke
Schmeiser Franziska
Schmidt Birger
Schmidtke Sönke
Schneemann Christina
Schneider Jörg
Schneider Winfried
Schnidrig Beat
Schrämmli Stefan
Schübl Andreas
Schulze Bodo
Schuster Martina
Schwarz Holger
Scopinich J. Federico
Seghers Harold
Seifriedsberger Stephanie
Senn Corinne
Severin Lone
Sijssens Vincent
Sima Christine
Siress Cary
Slob Martijn
Sobeck Simone
Soller Nicole
Sowa Sebastian
Spring Patricia
Stein Thomas
Steiner Marco
Steinmann Thomas
Stilz Markus
Stockmann Martin
Strauss Florian

Streithoff Daniel
Strotzer Stefan
Stutz Daia
Suzuki Hanako
Teller Katrin
Thiel Viola
Thomas Emma
Tietz Martin
Trevisan Smykalova Jitka
Trzebitzky Jakob
Tsolakis Emmanuel
Turquin Remy
Ullmann Emanuel
van Haaften Michel
Vogel Raymond
Vogt Günther
Vogt Joachim
Vollmer Hans
Von Gunten Violanta
Voss Ralf Günter
Walker Sabine
Wallner Regina
Walter Renate
Wanner Teresa
Weinig Markus
Weissflog Enrico
Wengemuth Steffen
Wespe Rahel
Westendorf Andreas
Wiesner Sarah
Wilhelm John
Wille Stefanie
Winkler Andreas
Witt Anette
Wuhrmann Chantal
Wussling Uta
Yamato Céline
Zevnik Barbara
Zheng Nenshi
Zingler Bernhard

EXHIBITIONS
Selection

The mediated motion. Olafur Eliasson. Kunsthaus Bregenz, 31 March – 13 May 2001.

Metropolis Exhibition. International Biennial of Architecture and Design, São Paulo, September – November 2003.

Berlin in Madrid. Stiftung der Architektenkammer/Goethe Institute, Madrid, October – December 2003.

Von Büchern und Bäumen. Architekturmuseum Basel, November 2004 – January 2005.

Stadt, Platz, Landschaft. Vogt Landschaftsarchitekten. Architekturgalerie Munich, May – July 2005.

Smells & Sounds – The Invisible In Public Space. Intervention, exhibition within the project "city_space_transitions", Zurich, October 2006; Tokyo, October – November 2006.

"Spiegel Nebel Wind". Contribution to Nature Design. Von Inspiration zu Innovation, Museum für Gestaltung Zurich, August – December 2007.

"Four Tor Panorama". Exhibition at A Foundation's Rochelle School, London; part of the exhibition Switzerland – Design for Life, produced by the Embassy of Switzerland in the UK, June – July 2010.

"Laubvulkane", Contribution to Perfume, Bottling Seduction, Exhibition at Museum Bellerive, Zurich, December 2011 – April 2012.

AWARDS

Special Award for Outstanding Work in Design Development for the redesign of Parliament Square, London, The Westminster Society.

Schulthess Garden Prize 2010 from the Swiss Heritage Society (SHS).

LECTURES

"Landscape as an Attitude", TU Berlin, Fachbereich Landschaftsarchitektur / Freiraumplanung, Berlin, 2012

"After the Party's Over: Large Events and Local Residents". Lecture at the Swiss-Brazilian symposium "Challenges for Metropolitan Cities in the 21st Century", Rio de Janeiro, 2010.

"Felsengärten, Gartengrotten, Kunstberge". U. Hassler and G. Vogt, chairs, conference at the ETH, Zurich, 2010.

"Designing Models: Conditions and Principles, Presence and Representation". Lecture presented at the "World in Denmark" conference, Copenhagen, 2010.

"Naturmodelle – Modelle der Natur. Die Menagerie der Pflanzen". Panel discussion, Novartis Lectures, Basel, 2009.

"Urbild, Abbild, Trugbild. Vorlesung innerhalb der Vorlesungsreihe 'Die Assymmetrie des Gelingens. Vision und Wirklichkeit in der Kunst'". Muthesius Hochschule, Kiel, Prof. Jürgen Partenheimer, 2009.

"Von der Kartoffel zur Solarzelle". Lecture on the theme of sustainability at the SIA (Swiss Association of Engineers and Architects), Zurich, 2009.

"This Is not Landart". Academie van Bouwkunst, Amsterdamse Hogeschool voor de Kunste, 2008.

"Modernism in European Landscape Architecture". Lecture, Chandigarh, India, 2008.

"City Planning as Branding". Lecture, part of the MAS Lecture Series, Department of Landscape Architecture, ETH, Zurich, 2008.

BIBLIOGRAPHY
Selection

Spilt – Rocker: A Tipping Figure, Essay By Günther Vogt in Jeff Koons, Fondation Beyeler, 199-201

MMMP, VOGT "5 Orte in der Schweiz", August 2012

"Wir müssen das Programmantische nicht vergessen", Garten + Landschaft, July 2011, 8–9

Swiss Landscape Architecture: The political, social, and geographical context, Article by Gunther Vogt published in Harvard Design Magazine Spring/summer 2010

Von der Kartoffel zur Solarsiedlung, Essay by Günther Vogt on sustainability in TEC21, issue 24, 26–9

Franziska Bark Hagen, Paradise: The Search for Happiness in the Garden, Günther Vogt Chair, Department of Architecture, ETH, Zurich. Baden: Lars Müller Publishers, January 2011.

VOGT ed. Urbild, Abbild, Trugbild. Archetype, Representation, Illusion, January 2011.

"Horizont in Schräglage". disP – The Planning Review 182, no. 3 (2010): 6–7.

Dominique Ghiggi, Tree Nurseries – Cultivating the Urban Jungle. Günther Vogt Chair, Department of Architecture, ETH, Zurich. Baden: Lars Müller Publishers, October 2010.

Jürgen Krusche, Frank Roost, Tokyo. The Street as an enlived space. Günther Vogt Chair, Department of Architecture, ETH, Zurich. Baden: Lars Müller Publishers, January 2010.

Alice Foxley, Vogt Landscape Architects. Distance and Engagement – Walking, Thinking and Making Landscape. Baden: Lars Müller Publishers, January 2010.

Jürgen Krusche, Streetscapes Berlin Shanghai Tokyo Zurich, Günther Vogt Chair, Department of Architecture, ETH, Zurich. Baden: Lars Müller Publishers, January 2009.

"Missing Link – Eine Intervention von Vogt Landschaftsarchitekten im öffentlichen Raum von Zürich und Tokyo". In Jürgen Krusche, ed. Der Raum der Stadt, Raumtheorien zwischen Architektur, Soziologie, Kunst und Philosophie in Japan und im Westen. Merlag: Jonas Verlag, 2008. 98–104.

Günther Vogt, ed. Miniature and Panorama. Baden: Lars Müller Publishers, 2006.

"Nature in the Picture". In Architekturmuseum Basel, ed. Photographic Essays on Space: Works by Christian Vogt. Exh. cat. Architekturmuseum Basel, 8 April – 28 May, 2006. Basel: Christoph Merian, 2006. 49–56.

"Design bestimmt unser Sein, auch auf dem Friedhof". In Edition Museum Bellerive, ed. Friedhof: Design. Zurich 2005. 22–31.

"Das Seelchen unter den Giftpflanzen". du – Zeitschrift für Kultur, nos. 6 / 7 (July – August 2005): 41.

Architekturmuseum Basel and Ulrike Jehle-Schulte Strathaus, eds. Novartis Campus – Forum 3: Diener, Federle Wiederin. Exh. cat. Architekturmuseum Basel, 11 June – 14 August 2005. Basel: Christoph Merian, 2005.

Vogt Landscape Architects, ed. City Square Landscape. Vogt Landscape Architects. Exh. cat. Architekturgalerie Munich, 20 May – 2 July 2005.

"Die Geschichte des Gartens". In e2a – Eckert and Eckert Architekten, eds. Wohnbauten in Broëlberg. Sulgen: Niggli, 2005. 60–63.

Architekturmuseum Basel, ed. About Books and Trees: Vogt Landscape Architects. Exh. cat. Architekturmuseum Basel, 27 November 2004 – 30 January 2005. Includes DVD with exhibition films. Basel, 2005.

"Landschaftgarten – Parklandschaften". In Landschaftsverband Westfalen-Lippe, ed. Parks + Gärten: Links und rechts der Ems. Münster-Hiltrup: Landwirtschaftsverlag, 2004. 10–11.

"Das fremd Vertraute". Schweizer Monatshefte 83, no. 5 (2003): 23–4.

"Leidenschaftliche Landschaften". Hochparterre, no. 4 (2003): 20–27.

"Der Garten der Gewalt". In Schweizerisches Rotes Kreuz, ed. Der Garten der Gewalt. Bern: Stämpfli, 2002. 28–41.

Kunsthaus Bregenz, ed. Swiss Re Rüschlikon: Centre for Global Dialogue. Werkdokumente 20. Ostfildern: Hatje Cantz, 2001.

Eckhard Schneider and Kunsthaus Bregenz, eds. The mediated motion. Exh. cat. Kunsthaus Bregenz, in collaboration with Olafur Eliasson, 31 March – 13 May 2001. Cologne: Verlag der Buchhandlung Walther König, 2001.

"Die Gärten der Tate Modern". In Edition Architekturgalerie Luzern, ed. Suggestions: Architektur im Spannungsfeld der Disziplinen. Exh. cat. Architekturgalerie Luzern, 2–3 March 2001. Basel: Birkhäuser, 2001. 72–75.

"Die Form, der Inhalt und die Zeit". Topos 2 (1993): 30–41.

"Die Gleichzeitigkeit des Anderen: Friedhoferweiterung Baden-Rütihof". In Dieter Kienast with Günther Vogt. Zwischen Arkadien und Restflächen. Lucerne: Edition Architekturgalerie Luzern, 1992. 18–26.

"Die Unterwelt der Aussenwelt". Anthos 31, no. 1 (1992): 8–10.

"Friedhofserweiterung Baden-Rütihof". Anthos 29, no. 4 (1990): 18–22.

"Das Paradies und die Geometrie". Anthos 28, no. 3 (1989): 34–9.

ILLUSTRATION CREDITS

Unless otherwise indicated, the copyright for the illustrations, plans and photographs is held by Vogt Landschaftsarchitekten AG.

(l) = left
(r) = right
(t) = top
(b) = bottom
(m) = middle

1–15, 18–33, 52, 58–65, 67, 82–3, 126–33, 144–9, 156–159, 168–73, 190–93, 218–22, 230–31, 239–41, 252–253, 256–57, 262–65, 280–9, 292–5, 298–303, 308–11, 344–7, 364–5, 372, 374–5, 382 (b), 384–5, 389–95, 437, 440–41, 448–53, 472–7, 485–7, 488 (tl), 490–1, 533 (b), 556–7 Illustration material based on photographs by Christian Vogt
16–17, 54–5 Manfred Jarisch and Ulrike Myrzik
19–22, 148–9 Fifa
40–49 Xaver Imfeld, Mountain panorama from Belvedere toward the Zürichberg. Zurich, Caesar Schmidt
50 Fotoarchiv Schweizerisches Alpines Museum, Bern (tl, ml)
ETH-Bibliothek, Kartensammlung, Zurich (bl, tr, br)
51 ETH-Bibliothek, Kartensammlung, Zurich
68 Survey Maps, London Sheet 42, The Godfrey Edition (tl); Royal Swedish Academy of Fine Arts, Stockholm (tr); British Geological Survey, 1/50 000 series, England and Wales, assembled sheets (b)
76–9 Mike Odwyer
80 "Geological Investigation of the Alluvial Valley of the Lower Mississippi River" H. Fisk, 1944 (b)
80 Eiola AG
96–107 Hamish Fulton
114–7 Fritz Schweingruber
120–21 Illustration pages based on photographs by Rita Illien, Mark Krieger, Vogt Landschaftsarchitekten AG
134 © Bibliographisches Institut & F.A. Brockhaus AG
136–7 Illustration pages based on photographs by Sophia Carstensen, Mark Krieger, Claudia Neumeister, Meret Peter, PixelQuelle.de, Joachim Vogt
150 Staatsarchiv Basel, Planarchiv C6 84 (tl); Original in the Grundbuch- und Vermessungsamt Basel Stadt (tr); Kunstmuseum Basel, Kupferstichkabinett (br)
174 Alice Foxley
176 Peter Rey (ml)
The Jesse Earl Hyde Collection, Case Western Reserve University (CWRU) Department of Geological Sciences (tl)
178 Lehrmittelverlag des Kantons Basel-Stadt, Max Moor (b)
179 Deutsche Verlags-Anstalt Stuttgart, Hermann von Pückler-Muskau (mr)
Lehrmittelverlag des Kantons Basel-Stadt, Max Moor (ml)
184 Schule für Gestaltung Basel, S. Käser, © S. Käser
194 HafenCity Hamburg GmbH
206–207 L. Walthert, S. Zimmermann, P. Blaser, J. Luster, P. Lüscher, Waldböden der Schweiz, vol. 1: Grundlagen und Region Jura: Birmensdorf, Eidgenössische Forschungsanstalt WSL. Bern, Hep Verlag, 2004. 768 pp.
208 S. Zimmermann, J. Luster, P. Blaser, L. Walthert, P. Lüscher, Waldböden der Schweiz, vol. 3: Regionen Mittelland: Birmensdorf, Eidgenössische Forschungsanstalt WSL. Bern, Hep Verlag, forthcoming.
209 S. Zimmermann, J. Luster, P. Blaser, L. Walthert, and P. Lüscher, Waldböden der Schweiz, vol. 3: Regionen Voralpen: Birmensdorf, Eidgenössische Forschungsanstalt WSL. Bern, Hep Verlag, forthcoming.
210 P. Blaser, S. Zimmermann, J. Luster, L. Walthert, and P. Lüscher, Waldböden der Schweiz, vol. 2: Regionen Alpen: Birmensdorf, Eidgenössische Forschungsanstalt WSL. Bern, Hep Verlag, 2005. 918 pp.
211 P. Blaser, S. Zimmermann, J. Luster, L. Walthert, and P. Lüscher, Waldböden der Schweiz, vol. 2: Regionen Alpensüdseite: Birmensdorf, Eidgenössische Forschungsanstalt WSL. Bern: Hep Verlag, 2005. 918 pp.
212 Stadt Baden, Entwicklungsplanung/ Luftbild Schweiz (tr)
Acer buergerianum, Ronny Vannuten (ml)
Photo CNAC/MNAM Dist.RMN – © Adam Rzepka (br)
214 MCK Environnement – Bryotec
215 Illustration pages based on photographs by MCK Environnement – Bryotec, Mark Krieger, Meret Peter
222 Olaf Unverzart
223 Esther Schütz
224 Gemeinde Igis-Landquart (tl)
234 Heidegger Fotografie KEG, Bregenz (tr); Bregenzer Festspiele (ml, mr); andereart (bl)
242 PixelQuelle.de
250 Stadt Konstanz, Tiefbau- und Vermessungsamt
272 www.biolib.de
273 akg-images
290 Geomatik und Vermessung Stadt Zürich, date of flight 8 April 2003
307 Illustration pages based on photographs by Mark Krieger and Vogt Landschaftsarchitekten AG
312 Tim Crocker (t); Laban archive (b)
313 Tim Crocker (t); Laban archive (b)
278 Sensarama Consulting GmbH (tr); akg-images (bl)
315 Google Earth
316–17 Anette Witt
318–19 Jürgen Krusche
326–9 Data from the Institut für Geobotanik und Botanischer Garten, Universität Halle/Saale
330 Egon Eggmann
332–3 Illustration pages based on illustrations from Berterams Planungshilfe, 1994; Heinz Bogner; Ernst Halwass after models by Sylvia Metzner and Gerd Grossmann; Rosmarie Hinzel; A. Kelle, H. Sturm and H. Theiss; Gerd Krüssmann; Cesare Leonardi and Franca Stagi; Eva Melady; Jane Porteous; Zeitschrift Deutscher Gärten
342–3 Illustration pages based on photographs by Martin Rauch, Lehm Ton Erde, and Vogt Landschaftsarchitekten AG
354–7 MeteoSchweiz/Käslin
362 Video stills, Hugofilm Productions GmbH
366, 370–1 Arcoplan Generalplaner AG
382 Vogt Landschaftsarchitekten AG (t)
386, 389 Nicola Eiffler
392–3 Hans-Peter Siffert
402 Jeff Amrhein (tl); Rajendra Kumar (ml)
403 Mallikarjuna Hosapalya (tl, tr); Shree Padre (ml, mr)
410–27 Olaf Unverzart
434–5 Illustration pages based on photographs by Pflanzenhandel Lorenz von Ehren GmbH & Co. KG and Vogt Landschaftsarchitekten AG
439 Illustration pages based on photographs by Sophia Carstensen, Nicola Eiffler, Alexander Kochan
442 Stadt Düsseldorf, Vermessungsamt und Katasteramt
460 Illustration page based on illustrations from Allgemeine Deutsche Bauzeitung 49 (1837): pl. CLXXV, figs. 1–5; W. and D. Bailey, 1830; Elsholz, 1684; The Gardener's Magazine 8 (August 1832): 420–22; J. J. Journey; G. Kohlmaier and B. von Sartory after Neumann 1862, fig. 136; pl. XXXIII; G. Kohlmaier and B. von Sartory after Architektenverein zu Berlin, ed., 1896, vol. II, pp. 254–5; J. C. Loudon, 1817, pls. IV, V; Neumann 1862, figs. 76–8, pl. XIX; Van der Groen, 1669; Zandera 2003, no. 18.
461 Illustration page based on illustrations from The Bridgeman Art Library/Stapleton Collection/Private Collection; Caisse Nationale des Monuments Historiques et des Sites, Archives phot/Spadem; Chinecastle from The Window Garden and Rustic Adornments for Homes of Taste;Anthony Huxley; David Bateman Publishers; M. Montespan; Royal Horticultural Society, Lindley Library
462 Alistar Morris, 1996. (t)
from Athanasius Kircher, Arca Noë. Amsterdam 1675. © The British Library Board, HMNTS 460.c.9. (b)
463 Alistar Morris, 1996. (tr)
464 Ruth-Maria and Walter Ullrich
465 Guildhall Library, City of London/ The Bridgeman Art Library
468–9 Illustration pages based on photographs by Jürg Waldmeier (t) and Vogt Landschaftsarchitekten AG (b)
478 akg-images
480–81 Illustration pages based on photographs by Ki Plant International

and Vogt Landschaftsarchitekten AG
483 Based on Diener & Diener, Gysi Gebr. (t)
484 From Strasburger Lehrbuch der Botanik, 1991 © Elsevier GmbH, Spektrum Akademischer Verlag Heidelberg (l)
Mark Krieger (r)
488 (tr) Humphry Repton, Designs for the Pavilion at Brighton. London [1808]
492 Rudolf Sagmeister
494–9, 501 2001 by Kunsthaus Bregenz, Olafur Eliasson and Verlag der Buchhandlung Walther König, Cologne; photograph: Markus Tretter
500 2001 by Kunsthaus Bregenz, Olafur Eliasson and Verlag der Buchhandlung Walther König, Cologne; photograph: Olafur Eliasson
504–21 Olafur Eliasson
526–7, 531, 542–3, 554–5, 562–3, 565–7 Florian Holzherr
528 Joachim Vogt
598–9 Photograph: Emil Grubenmann © Roman Signer.

Idea and concept: Lars Müller, Günther Vogt
Design: Lars Müller, Esther Butterworth,
Integral Lars Müller
Authors: Günther Vogt, Meret Peter (project texts)
Word fields: Peter Erni and Lars Müller
Pictorial essays: Olafur Eliasson (pp. 503–21),
Hamish Fulton (pp. 95–107), Roman Signer
(pp. 598–9), Olaf Unverzart (pp. 409–27),
Christian Vogt (pp. 1–33).

Project management: Meret Peter,
Maren Brakebusch
Translation: Laura Bruce, Steven Lindberg and
Allison Moseley
Copyediting of texts by gv: Angeli Sachs
Proofreading: Susan James, Daniel Morgenthaler
and Jonathan Fox
Picture research: Meret Peter, Carolin Riede
Typographic work: Esther Butterworth,
Integral Lars Müller
Lithography: Ast & Fischer AG, Wabern
Printing and binding: Kösel, Altusried-Krugzell
Paper: 150g/m², BVS, 0.9

Vogt Landschaftsarchitekten AG, Zurich
www.vogt-la.ch

Vogt Landscape Ltd, London
www.vogt-la.com

Vogt Landschaft GmbH, Berlin
www.vogt-la.de

Lars Müller Publishers
Zürich, Switzerland
www.lars-mueller-publishers.com

ISBN 978-3-03778-233-0

Printed in Germany